RUSSIA

TELECOM INDUSTRY BUSINESS OPPORTUNITIES HANDBOOK

VOLUME 1
STRATEGIC INFORMATION, REGULATIONS, OPPORTUNTIES, CONTACTS

International Business Publications, USA
Washington DC, USA- Russia

RUSSIA
TELECOM INDUSTRY BUSINESS OPPORTUNITIES HANDBOOK
VOLUME 1 STRATEGIC INFORMATION, REGULATIONS, OPPORTUNTIES, CONTACTS

UPDATED ANNUALLY

We express our sincere appreciation to all government agencies and international organizations which provided information and other materials for this handbook

\
Cover Design: International Business Publications, USA

International Business Publications, USA. *has used its best efforts in collecting, analyzing and preparing data, information and materials for this unique handbook. Due to the dynamic nature and fast development of the economy and business environment, we cannot warrant that all information herein is complete and accurate. IBP does not assume and hereby disclaim any liability to any person for any loss or damage caused by possible errors or omissions in the handbook.*
This handbook is for individual use only. Use this handbook for any other purpose, included but not limited to reproducing and storing in a retrieval system by any means, electronic, photocopying or using the addresses or other information contained in this handbook for any commercial purposes requires a special written permission from the publisher.

2018 Edition Updated Reprint International Business Publications, USA
ISBN 1-4330-4213-4

For additional analytical, business and investment opportunities information,
please contact Global Investment & Business Center, USA
at (703) 370-8082. Fax: (703) 370-8083. E-mail: ibpusa3@gmail.com
Global Business and Investment Info Databank - www.ibpus.com

Printed in the USA

For additional analytical, business and investment opportunities information,
please contact Global Investment & Business Center, USA
at (202) 546-2103. Fax: (202) 546-3275. E-mail: rusric@erols.com

RUSSIAN
TELECOM INDUSTRY BUSINESS OPPORTUNITIES HANDBOOK
VOLUME 1
STRATEGIC INFORMATION, REGULATIONS, OPPORTUNTIES, CONTACTS

TABLE OF CONTENTS

**For additional analytical, business and investment opportunities information,
please contact Global Investment & Business Center, USA
at (202) 546-2103. Fax: (202) 546-3275. E-mail: rusric@erols.com**

For additional analytical, business and investment opportunities information,
please contact Global Investment & Business Center, USA
at (202) 546-2103. Fax: (202) 546-3275. E-mail: rusric@erols.com

**For additional analytical, business and investment opportunities information,
please contact Global Investment & Business Center, USA
at (202) 546-2103. Fax: (202) 546-3275. E-mail: rusric@erols.com**

**For additional analytical, business and investment opportunities information,
please contact Global Investment & Business Center, USA
at (202) 546-2103. Fax: (202) 546-3275. E-mail: rusric@erols.com**

STRATEGIC AND DEVELOPMENT PROFILES

IMPORTANT FACTS

IMPORTANT FACTS

Capital (and largest city)	Moscow 55°45′N 37°37′E55.75°N 37.617°E
Official language(s)	Russian official throughout the country; 27 others co-official in various regions
Ethnic groups	81% Russians 3.7% Tatars 1.4% Ukrainians 1.1% Bashkirs 1% Chuvashes 11.8% others and unspecified
Demonym	Russian
Government	Federal semi-presidential constitutional republic
- President	Vladimir Putin
- Prime Minister	Dmitry Medvedev
Legislature	Federal Assembly
- Upper house	Federation Council
- Lower house	State Duma
Formation	
- Rurik Dynasty	862
- Kievan Rus'	882
- Vladimir-Suzdal Rus'	1169
- Grand Duchy of Moscow	1283
- Tsardom of Russia	16 January 1547
- Russian Empire	22 October 1721
- Russian Soviet Federative Socialist Republic	7 November 1917
- Union of Soviet Socialist Republics	10 December 1922
- Russian Federation	25 December 1991
Area	
- Total	17,075,400 km^2 (1st) 6,592,800 sq mi
- Water (%)	13 (including swamps)
Population	
- 2012 estimate	143,100,000 (9th)
- Density	8.3/km^2 (217th) 21.5/sq mi
GDP (PPP)	2011 estimate
- Total	$2.383 trillion
- Per capita	$16,736
GDP (nominal)	2011 estimate
- Total	$1.850 trillion

For additional analytical, business and investment opportunities information, please contact Global Investment & Business Center, USA at (202) 546-2103. Fax: (202) 546-3275. E-mail: rusric@erols.com

- Per capita	$12,993
Gini (2008)	42.3 (83rd)

Currency	Ruble (RUB)
Time zone	(UTC+3 to +12 (exc. +5))
Date formats	dd.mm.yyyy
Drives on the	right
ISO 3166 code	RU
Internet TLD	.ru, .su, .рф
Calling code	+7

Russia also officially known as the **Russian Federation** (Russian: is a country in northern Eurasia. It is a federal semi-presidential republic, comprising 83 federal subjects.

From northwest to southeast, Russia shares borders with Norway, Finland, Estonia, Latvia, Lithuania and Poland (both via Kaliningrad Oblast), Belarus, Ukraine, Georgia, Azerbaijan, Kazakhstan, China, Mongolia, and North Korea. It also has maritime borders with Japan by the Sea of Okhotsk, and the US state of Alaska by the Bering Strait. At 17,075,400 square kilometres (6,592,800 sq mi), Russia is the largest country in the world, covering more than one eighth of the Earth's inhabited land area. Russia is also the ninth most populous nation with 143 million people as of 2012.

Extending across the whole of northern Asia and most of eastern Europe, Russia spans nine time zones and incorporates a wide range of environments and landforms. Russia has the world's largest reserves of mineral and energy resources and is the largest producer of oil and natural gas globally. Russia has the world's largest forest reserves and its lakes contain approximately one-quarter of the world's fresh water.

The nation's history began with that of the East Slavs, who emerged as a recognizable group in Europe between the 3rd and 8th centuries AD. Founded and ruled by a Varangian warrior elite and their descendants, the medieval state of Rus arose in the 9th century. In 988 it adopted Orthodox Christianity from the Byzantine Empire, beginning the synthesis of Byzantine and Slavic cultures that defined Russian culture for the next millennium. Rus' ultimately disintegrated into a number of smaller states; most of the Rus' lands were overrun by the Mongol invasion and became tributaries of the nomadic Golden Horde.

The Grand Duchy of Moscow gradually reunified the surrounding Russian principalities, achieved independence from the Golden Horde, and came to dominate the cultural and political legacy of Kievan Rus'.

By the 18th century, the nation had greatly expanded through conquest, annexation, and exploration to become the Russian Empire, which was the third largest empire in history, stretching from Poland in Europe to Alaska in North America.

Following the Russian Revolution, Russia became the largest and leading constituent of the Soviet Union, the world's first constitutionally socialist state and a recognized superpower, which played a decisive role in the Allied victory in World War II. The Soviet era saw some of the most significant technological achievements of the 20th century, including the world's first human spaceflight. The Russian Federation was founded following the dissolution of the Soviet Union in 1991, but is recognized as the continuing legal personality of the Soviet state.

The Russian economy is the world's ninth largest by nominal GDP and sixth largest by purchasing power parity, with the 3rd largest nominal military budget. Russia is one of the world's fastest growing major economies. It is one of the five recognized nuclear weapons states and possesses the largest stockpile of weapons of mass destruction.

Russia is a great power and a permanent member of the United Nations Security Council, a member of the G8, G20, the Council of Europe, the Asia-Pacific Economic Cooperation, the Shanghai Cooperation Organisation, the Eurasian Economic Community, the Organisation for Security and Cooperation in Europe (OSCE), the World Trade Organisation (WTO), and is the leading member of the Commonwealth of Independent States.

Background:	Founded in the 12th century, the Principality of Muscovy, was able to emerge from over 200 years of Mongol domination (13th-15th centuries) and to gradually conquer and absorb surrounding principalities. In the early 17th century, a new Romanov Dynasty continued this policy of expansion across Siberia to the Pacific. Under PETER I (ruled 1682-1725), hegemony was extended to the Baltic Sea and the country was renamed the Russian Empire. During the 19th century, more territorial acquisitions were made in Europe and Asia. Repeated devastating defeats of the Russian army in World War I led to widespread rioting in the major cities of the Russian Empire and to the overthrow in 1917 of the imperial household. The Communists under Vladimir LENIN seized power soon after and formed the USSR. The brutal rule of Josef STALIN (1928-53) strengthened Russian dominance of the Soviet Union at a cost of tens of millions of lives. The Soviet economy and society stagnated in the following decades until General Secretary Mikhail GORBACHEV (1985-91) introduced glasnost (openness) and perestroika (restructuring) in an attempt to modernize Communism, but his initiatives inadvertently released forces that by December 1991 splintered the USSR into 15 independent republics. Since then, Russia has struggled in its efforts to build a democratic political system and market economy to replace the strict social, political, and economic controls of the Communist period. While some progress has been made on the economic front, recent years have seen a recentralization of power under Vladimir PUTIN and an erosion in nascent democratic institutions. A determined guerrilla conflict still plagues Russia in Chechnya.

GEOGRAPHY

Location:	Northern Asia (that part west of the Urals is included with Europe), bordering the Arctic Ocean, between Europe and the North Pacific Ocean
Geographic coordinates:	60 00 N, 100 00 E
Map references:	Asia
Area:	total: 17,075,200 sq km land: 16,995,800 sq km water: 79,400 sq km
Area - comparative:	approximately 1.8 times the size of the US
Land boundaries:	total: 20,017 km border countries: Azerbaijan 284 km, Belarus 959 km, China (southeast) 3,605 km, China (south) 40 km, Estonia 294 km, Finland 1,340 km, Georgia 723 km, Kazakhstan 6,846 km, North Korea 19 km, Latvia 217 km, Lithuania (Kaliningrad Oblast) 227 km, Mongolia 3,485 km, Norway 196 km, Poland (Kaliningrad Oblast) 206 km, Ukraine 1,576 km
Coastline:	37,653 km
Maritime claims:	territorial sea: 12 nm exclusive economic zone: 200 nm continental shelf: 200-m depth or to the depth of exploitation

Climate:	ranges from steppes in the south through humid continental in much of European Russia; subarctic in Siberia to tundra climate in the polar north; winters vary from cool along Black Sea coast to frigid in Siberia; summers vary from warm in the steppes to cool along Arctic coast

For additional analytical, business and investment opportunities information,
please contact Global Investment & Business Center, USA
at (202) 546-2103. Fax: (202) 546-3275. E-mail: rusric@erols.com

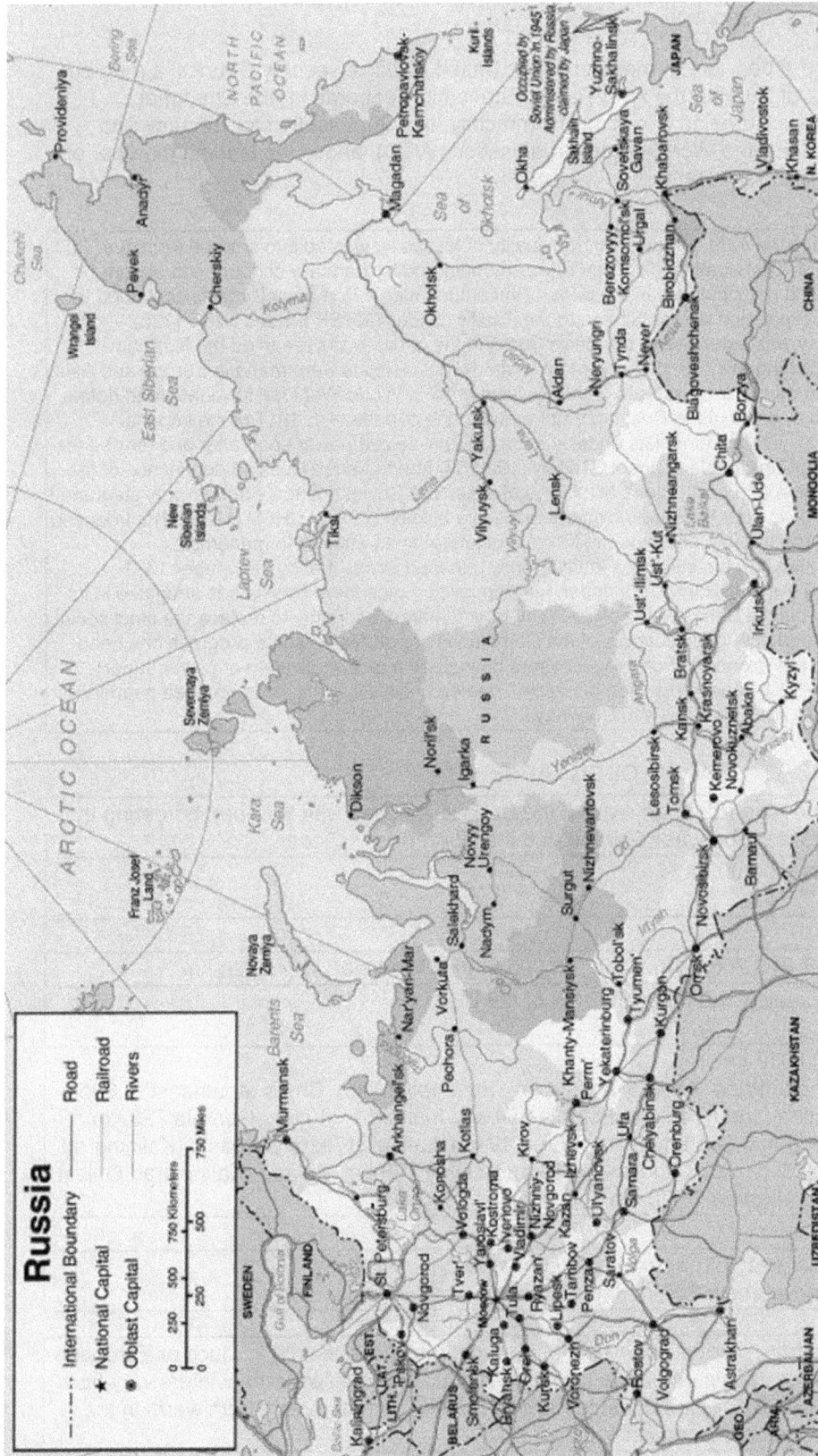

Russia

International Boundary ----
★ National Capital
● Oblast Capital

Road ———
Railroad ———
Rivers ———

0 250 500 750 Kilometers
0 250 500 750 Miles

For additional analytical, business and investment opportunities information,
please contact Global Investment & Business Center, USA
at (202) 546-2103. Fax: (202) 546-3275. E-mail: rusric@erols.com

Terrain:	broad plain with low hills west of Urals; vast coniferous forest and tundra in Siberia; uplands and mountains along southern border regions

Elevation extremes:	lowest point: Caspian Sea -28 m highest point: Gora El'brus 5,633 m

Land use:	arable land: 7.33% permanent crops: 0.11% other: 92.56%
Irrigated land:	46,630 sq km (1998 est.)
Natural hazards:	permafrost over much of Siberia is a major impediment to development; volcanic activity in the Kuril Islands; volcanoes and earthquakes on the Kamchatka Peninsula; spring floods and summer/autumn forest fires throughout Siberia and parts of European Russia

Environment - current issues:	air pollution from heavy industry, emissions of coal-fired electric plants, and transportation in major cities; industrial, municipal, and agricultural pollution of inland waterways and seacoasts; deforestation; soil erosion; soil contamination from improper application of agricultural chemicals; scattered areas of sometimes intense radioactive contamination; groundwater contamination from toxic waste; urban solid waste management; abandoned stocks of obsolete pesticides
Environment - international agreements:	party to: Air Pollution, Air Pollution-Nitrogen Oxides, Air Pollution-Sulfur 85, Antarctic-Environmental Protocol, Antarctic-Marine Living Resources, Antarctic Seals, Antarctic Treaty, Biodiversity, Climate Change, Endangered Species, Environmental Modification, Hazardous Wastes, Law of the Sea, Marine Dumping, Ozone Layer Protection, Ship Pollution, Tropical Timber 83, Wetlands, Whaling signed, but not ratified: Air Pollution-Sulfur 94, Climate Change-Kyoto Protocol
Natural resources:	wide natural resource base including major deposits of oil, natural gas, coal, and many strategic minerals, timber note: formidable obstacles of climate, terrain, and distance hinder exploitation of natural resources
Geography - note:	largest country in the world in terms of area but unfavorably located in relation to major sea lanes of the world; despite its size, much of the country lacks proper soils and climates (either too cold or too dry) for agriculture; Mount El'brus is Europe's tallest peak

PEOPLE

Population:	143,782,338
Age structure:	0-14 years: 15% (male 11,064,109; female 10,518,595) 15-64 years: 71.3% (male 49,534,076; female 52,958,107) 65 years and over: 13.7% (male 6,177,580; female 13,529,871)
Median age:	total: 37.9 years male: 34.7 years female: 40.7 years
Population growth rate:	-0.45%
Birth rate:	9.63 births/1,000 population

For additional analytical, business and investment opportunities information, please contact Global Investment & Business Center, USA at (202) 546-2103. Fax: (202) 546-3275. E-mail: rusric@erols.com

Death rate:	15.17 deaths/1,000 population
Net migration rate:	1.02 migrant(s)/1,000 population
Sex ratio:	at birth: 1.06 male(s)/female under 15 years: 1.05 male(s)/female 15-64 years: 0.94 male(s)/female 65 years and over: 0.46 male(s)/female total population: 0.87 male(s)/female
Infant mortality rate:	total: 16.96 deaths/1,000 live births male: 19.58 deaths/1,000 live births female: 14.18 deaths/1,000 live births
Life expectancy at birth:	total population: 66.39 years male: 59.91 years female: 73.27 years
Total fertility rate:	1.26 children born/woman
HIV/AIDS - adult prevalence rate:	0.9%
HIV/AIDS - people living with HIV/AIDS:	700,000
HIV/AIDS - deaths:	9,000
Nationality:	noun: Russian(s) adjective: Russian
Ethnic groups:	Russian 81.5%, Tatar 3.8%, Ukrainian 3%, Chuvash 1.2%, Bashkir 0.9%, Belarusian 0.8%, Moldavian 0.7%, other 8.1% (1989)
Religions:	Russian Orthodox, Muslim, other
Languages:	Russian, other
Literacy:	definition: age 15 and over can read and write total population: 99.6% male: 99.7% female: 99.5%

GOVERNMENT

Country name:
conventional long form: Russian Federation
conventional short form: Russia
local long form: Rossiyskaya Federatsiya
local short form: Rossiya
former: Russian Empire, Russian Soviet Federative Socialist Republic
etymology: Russian lands were generally referred to as Muscovy until PETER I officially declared the Russian Empire in 1721; the new name sought to invoke the patrimony of the medieval eastern European Rus state centered on Kyiv in present-day Ukraine; the Rus were a Varangian (eastern Viking) elite that imposed their rule and eventually their name on their Slavic subjects

Government type:
semi-presidential federation

Capital:

name: Moscow
geographic coordinates: 55 45 N, 37 36 E
time difference: UTC+3 (8 hours ahead of Washington, DC, during Standard Time)
note: Russia has 11 time zones, the largest number of contiguous time zones of any country in the world; in 2014, two time zones were added and DST was dropped

Administrative divisions:
46 provinces (oblasti, singular - oblast), 21 republics (respubliki, singular - respublika), 4 autonomous okrugs (avtonomnyye okrugi, singular - avtonomnyy okrug), 9 krays (kraya, singular - kray), 2 federal cities (goroda, singular - gorod), and 1 autonomous oblast (avtonomnaya oblast')

oblasts: Amur (Blagoveshchensk), Arkhangel'sk, Astrakhan', Belgorod, Bryansk, Chelyabinsk, Irkutsk, Ivanovo, Kaliningrad, Kaluga, Kemerovo, Kirov, Kostroma, Kurgan, Kursk, Leningrad, Lipetsk, Magadan, Moscow, Murmansk, Nizhniy Novgorod, Novgorod, Novosibirsk, Omsk, Orenburg, Orel, Penza, Pskov, Rostov, Ryazan', Sakhalin (Yuzhno-Sakhalinsk), Samara, Saratov, Smolensk, Sverdlovsk (Yekaterinburg), Tambov, Tomsk, Tula, Tver', Tyumen', Ul'yanovsk, Vladimir, Volgograd, Vologda, Voronezh, Yaroslavl'

republics: Adygeya (Maykop), Altay (Gorno-Altaysk), Bashkortostan (Ufa), Buryatiya (Ulan-Ude), Chechnya (Groznyy), Chuvashiya (Cheboksary), Dagestan (Makhachkala), Ingushetiya (Magas), Kabardino-Balkariya (Nal'chik), Kalmykiya (Elista), Karachayevo-Cherkesiya (Cherkessk), Kareliya (Petrozavodsk), Khakasiya (Abakan), Komi (Syktyvkar), Mariy-El (Yoshkar-Ola), Mordoviya (Saransk), North Ossetia (Vladikavkaz), Sakha [Yakutiya] (Yakutsk), Tatarstan (Kazan'), Tyva (Kyzyl), Udmurtiya (Izhevsk)

autonomous okrugs: Chukotka (Anadyr'), Khanty-Mansi-Yugra (Khanty-Mansiysk), Nenets (Nar'yan-Mar), Yamalo-Nenets (Salekhard)
krays: Altay (Barnaul), Kamchatka (Petropavlovsk-Kamchatskiy), Khabarovsk, Krasnodar, Krasnoyarsk, Perm', Primorskiy [Maritime] (Vladivostok), Stavropol', Zabaykal'sk [Transbaikal] (Chita)

federal cities: Moscow [Moskva], Saint Petersburg [Sankt-Peterburg]
autonomous oblast: Yevreyskaya [Jewish] (Birobidzhan)
note 1: administrative divisions have the same names as their administrative centers (exceptions have the administrative center name following in parentheses)
note 2: the United States does not recognize Russia's annexation of Ukraine's Autonomous Republic of Crimea and the municipality of Sevastopol, nor their redesignation as the Republic of Crimea and the Federal City of Sevastopol

Independence:
24 August 1991 (from the Soviet Union); notable earlier dates: 1157 (Principality of Vladimir-Suzdal created); 16 January 1547 (Tsardom of Muscovy established); 22 October 1721 (Russian Empire proclaimed); 30 December 1922 (Soviet Union established)

National holiday:
Russia Day, 12 June (1990)
Constitution:
history: several previous (during Russian Empire and Soviet era); latest drafted 12 July 1993, adopted by referendum 12 December 1993, effective 25 December 1993
amendments: proposed by the president of the Russian Federation, by either house of the Federal Assembly, by the government of the Russian Federation, or by legislative (representative) bodies of the Federation's constituent entities; proposals to amend the government's constitutional system, human and civil rights and freedoms, and procedures for

amending or drafting a new constitution require formation of a Constitutional Assembly; passage of such amendments requires two-thirds majority vote of its total membership; passage in a referendum requires participation of an absolute majority of eligible voters and an absolute majority of valid votes; approval of proposed amendments to the government structure, authorities, and procedures requires approval by the legislative bodies of at least two-thirds of the Russian Federation's constituent entities; amended 2008, 2014 (2017)

Legal system:
civil law system; judicial review of legislative acts
International law organization participation:
has not submitted an ICJ jurisdiction declaration; non-party state to the ICCt

Citizenship:
citizenship by birth: no
citizenship by descent only: at least one parent must be a citizen of Russia
dual citizenship recognized: yes
residency requirement for naturalization: 3-5 years

Suffrage:
18 years of age; universal

Executive branch:

chief of state: President Vladimir Vladimirovich PUTIN (since 7 May 2012)

head of government: Premier Dmitriy Anatolyevich MEDVEDEV (since 8 May 2012); First Deputy Premier Igor Ivanovich SHUVALOV (since 12 May 2008); Deputy Premiers Arkadiy Vladimirovich DVORKOVICH (since 21 May 2012), Olga Yuryevna GOLODETS (since 21 May 2012), Aleksandr Gennadiyevich KHLOPONIN (since 19 January 2010), Dmitriy Nikolayevich KOZAK (since 14 October 2008), Vitaliy Leontyevich MUTKO (since 19 October 2016), Dmitriy Olegovich ROGOZIN (since 23 December 2011), Sergey Eduardovich PRIKHODKO (since 22 May 2013); Yuriy Petrovich TRUTNEV (since 31 August 2013)

cabinet: the "Government" is composed of the premier, his deputies, and ministers, all appointed by the president; the premier is also confirmed by the Duma

elections/appointments: president directly elected by absolute majority popular vote in 2 rounds if needed for a 6-year term (eligible for a second term); election last held on 4 March 2012 (next to be held in March 2018); note - term length extended to 6 years from 4 years in late 2008, effective after the 2012 election; there is no vice president; premier appointed by the president with the approval of the Duma

election results: Vladimir PUTIN elected president; percent of vote - Vladimir PUTIN (United Russia) 63.6%, Gennadiy ZYUGANOV (CPRF) 17.2%, Mikhail PROKHOROV (CP) 8%, Vladimir ZHIRINOVSKIY (LDPR) 6.2%, Sergey MIRONOV (A Just Russia) 3.9%, other 1.1%; Dmitriy MEDVEDEV (United Russia) approved as premier by Duma; vote - 299 to 144

note: there is also a Presidential Administration that provides staff and policy support to the president, drafts presidential decrees, and coordinates policy among government agencies; a Security Council also reports directly to the president

Legislative branch:

description: bicameral Federal Assembly or Federalnoye Sobraniye consists of the Federation Council or Sovet Federatsii (170 seats; 2 members in each of the 83 federal

For additional analytical, business and investment opportunities information, please contact Global Investment & Business Center, USA at (202) 546-2103. Fax: (202) 546-3275. E-mail: rusric@erols.com

administrative units (see note below) - oblasts, krays, republics, autonomous okrugs and oblasts, and the federal cities of Moscow and Saint Petersburg - appointed by the top executive and legislative officials; members serve 4-year terms) and the State Duma or Gosudarstvennaya Duma (450 seats; as of February 2014, the electoral system reverted to a mixed electoral system for the 2016 election, in which one-half of the members are directly elected by simple majority vote and one-half directly elected by proportional representation vote; members serve 5-year terms)

elections: State Duma - last held on 18 September 2016 (next to be held in fall 2021)

election results: State Duma - United Russia 54.2%, CPRF 13.3%, LDPR 13.1%, A Just Russia 6.2%, Rodina 1.5%, CP 0.2%; seats by party - United Russia 343, CPRF 42, LDPR 39, A Just Russia 23, Rodina 1, CP 1, independent 1

note: the State Duma now includes 3 representatives and the Federation Council 2 each from the Republic of Crimea and the Federal City of Sevastopol, two regions that Russia occupied and attempted to annex from Ukraine and that the US does not recognize as part of Russia

Judicial branch:

highest court(s): Supreme Court of the Russian Federation (consists of 170 members organized into the Judicial Panel for Civil Affairs, the Judicial Panel for Criminal Affairs, and the Military Panel); Constitutional Court (consists of 19 members); note - in February 2014, Russia's Superior Court of Arbitration was abolished and its former authorities transferred to the Supreme Court, which in addition to being the country's highest judicial authority for appeals, civil, criminal, administrative, and military cases, and the disciplinary judicial board now has jurisdiction over economic disputes

judge selection and term of office: all members of Russia's 3 highest courts nominated by the president and appointed by the Federation Council (the upper house of the legislature); members of all 3 courts appointed for life

subordinate courts: Higher Arbitration Court; regional (kray) and provincial (oblast) courts; Moscow and St. Petersburg city courts; autonomous province and district courts; note - the 21 Russian Republics have court systems specified by their own constitutions

Political parties and leaders:
A Just Russia [Sergey MIRONOV]
Civic Platform or CP [Rifat SHAYKHUTDINOV]
Communist Party of the Russian Federation or CPRF [Gennadiy ZYUGANOV]
Liberal Democratic Party of Russia or LDPR [Vladimir ZHIRINOVSKIY]
Rodina [Aleksei ZHURAVLYOV]
United Russia [Dmitriy MEDVEDEV]
note: 72 political parties are registered with Russia's Ministry of Justice (as of August 2017), but only six parties maintain representation in Russia's national legislature, and two of these only have one deputy apiece

Political pressure groups and leaders:
Committees of Soldiers' Mothers
Confederation of Labor of Russia or KTR
Federation of Independent Trade Unions of Russia
Golos Association in Defense of Voters' Rights
Memorial
Movement Against Illegal Migration

For additional analytical, business and investment opportunities information, please contact Global Investment & Business Center, USA at (202) 546-2103. Fax: (202) 546-3275. E-mail: rusric@erols.com

Russkiye
Solidarnost
The World Russian People's Congress
Union of Russian Writers
other: business associations; environmental organizations; religious groups (especially those with Orthodox or Muslim affiliation); veterans groups

International organization participation:
APEC, Arctic Council, ARF, ASEAN (dialogue partner), BIS, BRICS, BSEC, CBSS, CD, CE, CERN (observer), CICA, CIS, CSTO, EAEC, EAEU, EAPC, EAS, EBRD, FAO, FATF, G-20, GCTU, IAEA, IBRD, ICAO, ICC (national committees), ICRM, IDA, IFAD, IFC, IFRCS, IHO, ILO, IMF, IMO, IMSO, Interpol, IOC, IOM (observer), IPU, ISO, ITSO, ITU, ITUC (NGOs), LAIA (observer), MIGA, MINURSO, MONUSCO, NEA, NSG, OAS (observer), OIC (observer), OPCW, OSCE, Paris Club, PCA, PFP, SCO, UN, UNCTAD, UNESCO, UNHCR, UNIDO, UNISFA, UNMIL, UNMISS, UNOCI, UNSC (permanent), UNTSO, UNWTO, UPU, WCO, WFTU (NGOs), WHO, WIPO, WMO, WTO, ZC

Diplomatic representation in the US:
chief of mission: Ambassador Anatoliy Ivanovich ANTONOV (since 8 September 2017)
chancery: 2650 Wisconsin Avenue NW, Washington, DC 20007
telephone: [1] (202) 298-5700, 5701, 5704, 5708
FAX: [1] (202) 298-5735
consulate(s) general: Houston, New York, Seattle

Diplomatic representation from the US:
chief of mission: Ambassador Jon HUNTSMAN (since 3 October 2017)
embassy: Bolshoy Deviatinskiy Pereulok No. 8, 121099 Moscow
mailing address: PSC-77, APO AE 09721
telephone: [7] (495) 728-5000
FAX: [7] (495) 728-5090
consulate(s) general: Saint Petersburg, Vladivostok, Yekaterinburg

Flag description:
three equal horizontal bands of white (top), blue, and red
note: the colors may have been based on those of the Dutch flag; despite many popular interpretations, there is no official meaning assigned to the colors of the Russian flag; this flag inspired several other Slav countries to adopt horizontal tricolors of the same colors but in different arrangements, and so red, blue, and white became the Pan-Slav colors

National symbol(s):
bear, double-headed eagle; national colors: white, blue, red

National anthem:
name: "Gimn Rossiyskoy Federatsii" (National Anthem of the Russian Federation)
lyrics/music: Sergey Vladimirovich MIKHALKOV/Aleksandr Vasilyevich ALEKSANDROV
note: in 2000, Russia adopted the tune of the anthem of the former Soviet Union (composed in 1939); the lyrics, also adopted in 2000, were written by the same person who authored the Soviet lyrics in 1943

ECONOMY

Russia has undergone significant changes since the collapse of the Soviet Union, moving from a centrally planned economy towards a more market-based system. Both economic growth and reform have stalled in recent years, however, and Russia remains a predominantly statist economy with a high concentration of wealth in officials' hands. Economic reforms in the 1990s privatized most industry, with notable exceptions in the energy, transportation, banking, and defense-related sectors. The protection of property rights is still weak, and the state continues to interfere in the free operation of the private sector.

Russia is one of the world's leading producers of oil and natural gas, and is also a top exporter of metals such as steel and primary aluminum. Russia's reliance on commodity exports makes it vulnerable to boom and bust cycles that follow the volatile swings in global prices.

The economy, which had averaged 7% growth during 1998-2008 as oil prices rose rapidly, has seen diminishing growth rates since then due to the exhaustion of Russia's commodity-based growth model.

A combination of falling oil prices, international sanctions, and structural limitations pushed Russia into a deep recession in 2015, with the GDP falling by close to 4%. Most economists expect this downturn will continue through 2016. Government support for import substitution has increased recently in an effort to diversify the economy away from extractive industries. Although the Russian Ministry of Economic Development is forecasting a modest growth of 0.7% for 2016 as a whole, the Central Bank of Russia (CBR) is more pessimistic and expects the recovery to begin later in the year and a decline of 0.5% to 1.0% for the full year. Russia is heavily dependent on the movement of world commodity prices and the CBR estimates that if oil prices remain below $40 per barrel beyond 2016, the resulting shock would cause GDP to fall by up to 5%.

GDP (purchasing power parity):

$3.745 trillion (2016 est.)
$3.774 trillion (2015 est.)
$3.92 trillion (2014 est.)
note: data are in 2016 dollars
country comparison to the world: 7

GDP (official exchange rate):
$1.268 trillion (2015 est.)

GDP - real growth rate:
-0.8% (2016 est.)
-3.7% (2015 est.)
0.7% (2014 est.)
country comparison to the world: 201

GDP - per capita (PPP):
$26,100 (2016 est.)
$26,300 (2015 est.)
$27,300 (2014 est.)
note: data are in 2016 dollars
country comparison to the world: 73

Gross national saving:
24.7% of GDP (2016 est.)
23.8% of GDP (2015 est.)
23.7% of GDP (2014 est.)
country comparison to the world: 52

For additional analytical, business and investment opportunities information,
please contact Global Investment & Business Center, USA
at (202) 546-2103. Fax: (202) 546-3275. E-mail: rusric@erols.com

GDP - composition, by end use:
household consumption: 55.8%
government consumption: 19.9%
investment in fixed capital: 21.6%
investment in inventories: -3.2%
exports of goods and services: 25.8%
imports of goods and services: -19.9% (2016 est.)

GDP - composition, by sector of origin:
agriculture: 4.7%
industry: 33.1%
services: 62.2% (2016 est.)

Agriculture - products:
grain, sugar beets, sunflower seeds, vegetables, fruits; beef, milk
Industries:
complete range of mining and extractive industries producing coal, oil, gas, chemicals, and metals; all forms of machine building from rolling mills to high-performance aircraft and space vehicles; defense industries (including radar, missile production,

Industrial production growth rate:
0.7% (2016 est.)
country comparison to the world: 159

Labor force:
77.41 million (2016 est.)
country comparison to the world: 8

Labor force - by occupation:
agriculture: 9.4%
industry: 27.6%
services: 63% (2014)

Unemployment rate:
8.2% (2016 est.)
5.6% (2015 est.)
country comparison to the world: 93

Population below poverty line:
11.2% (2014 est.)

Household income or consumption by percentage share:
lowest 10%: 5.7%
highest 10%: 42.4% (2011 est.)

Distribution of family income - Gini index:
42 (2014)
41.7 (2011)
country comparison to the world: 54

Budget:
revenues: $186.5 billion
expenditures: $236.6 billion (2016 est.)

For additional analytical, business and investment opportunities information, please contact Global Investment & Business Center, USA at (202) 546-2103. Fax: (202) 546-3275. E-mail: rusric@erols.com

Taxes and other revenues:
14.7% of GDP (2016 est.)
country comparison to the world: 190

Budget surplus (+) or deficit (-):
-4% of GDP (2016 est.)
country comparison to the world: 136

Public debt:
13.7% of GDP (2016 est.)
9.4% of GDP (2015 est.)
note: data cover general government debt, and include debt instruments issued (or owned)
by government entities other than the treasury; the data include treasury debt held by foreign
entities; the data include debt issued by subnational entities, as well as in
country comparison to the world: 169

Fiscal year:
calendar year

Inflation rate (consumer prices):
7.2% (2016 est.)
15.5% (2015 est.)
country comparison to the world: 189

Central bank discount rate:
11% (31 December 2015 est.)
17% (31 December 2014)
note: this is the so-called refinancing rate, but in Russia banks do not get refinancing at this
rate; this is a reference rate used primarily for fiscal purposes
country comparison to the world: 20

Commercial bank prime lending rate:
12.7% (31 December 2016 est.)
15.73% (31 December 2015 est.)
country comparison to the world: 62

Stock of narrow money:
$199.7 billion (31 December 2016 est.)
$151.5 billion (31 December 2015 est.)
country comparison to the world: 23

Stock of broad money:
$926.8 billion (31 October 2014 est.)
$1.087 trillion (31 December 2013 est.)
country comparison to the world: 19

Stock of domestic credit:
$818.5 billion (31 December 2016 est.)
$603.9 billion (31 December 2015 est.)
country comparison to the world: 17

Market value of publicly traded shares:
$393.2 billion (31 December 2015 est.)

For additional analytical, business and investment opportunities information,
please contact Global Investment & Business Center, USA
at (202) 546-2103. Fax: (202) 546-3275. E-mail: rusric@erols.com

$385.9 billion (31 December 2014 est.)
$770.7 billion (31 December 2013 est.)
country comparison to the world: 25

Current account balance:
$38.56 billion (2016 est.)
$69 billion (2015 est.)
country comparison to the world: 11

Exports:
$259.3 billion (2016 est.)
$341.5 billion (2015 est.)
country comparison to the world: 20

Exports - commodities:
petroleum and petroleum products, natural gas, metals, wood and wood products, chemicals, and a wide variety of civilian and military manufactures
Exports - partners:
Netherlands 11.9%, China 8.3%, Germany 7.4%, Italy 6.5%, Turkey 5.6%, Belarus 4.4%, Japan 4.2% (2015)

Imports:
$165.1 billion (2016 est.)
$193 billion (2015 est.)
country comparison to the world: 25

Imports - commodities:
machinery, vehicles, pharmaceutical products, plastic, semi-finished metal products, meat, fruits and nuts, optical and medical instruments, iron, steel
Imports - partners:
China 19.2%, Germany 11.2%, US 6.4%, Belarus 4.8%, Italy 4.6% (2015)

Reserves of foreign exchange and gold:
$365.5 billion (31 December 2016 est.)
$368.4 billion (31 December 2015 est.)
country comparison to the world: 8

Debt - external:
$514.8 billion (31 December 2016 est.)
$520.2 billion (31 December 2015 est.)
country comparison to the world: 22

Stock of direct foreign investment - at home:
$348 billion (31 December 2016 est.)
$342.9 billion (31 December 2015 est.)
country comparison to the world: 21

Stock of direct foreign investment - abroad:
$359.3 billion (31 December 2016 est.)
$336.3 billion (31 December 2015 est.)
country comparison to the world: 20

Exchange rates:
Russian rubles (RUB) per US dollar -

68.06 (2016 est.)
60.938 (2015 est.)
60.938 (2014 est.)
38.378 (2013 est.)
30.84 (2012 est.)

ENERGY

Electricity - production:
1.057 trillion kWh
country comparison to the world:
4

Electricity - consumption:
1.038 trillion kWh
country comparison to the world:
4

Electricity - exports:
19.14 billion kWh
country comparison to the world:
11

Electricity - imports:
2.661 billion kWh
country comparison to the world:
50

Electricity - installed generating capacity:
223.1 million kW
country comparison to the world:
5

Electricity - from fossil fuels:

67.7% of total installed capacity
country comparison to the world:
112

Electricity - from nuclear fuels:
17.8% of total installed capacity
country comparison to the world:
12

For additional analytical, business and investment opportunities information,
please contact Global Investment & Business Center, USA
at (202) 546-2103. Fax: (202) 546-3275. E-mail: rusric@erols.com

Electricity - from hydroelectric plants:
15.1% of total installed capacity
country comparison to the world:
100

**Electricity - from other renewable
sources:**
0% of total installed capacity
country comparison to the world:
117

Crude oil - production:
10.44 million bbl/day
country comparison to the world:
3

Crude oil - exports:
4.72 million bbl/day
country comparison to the world:
2

Crude oil - imports:
16,380 bbl/day
country comparison to the world:
69

Crude oil - proved reserves:

80 billion bbl
country comparison to the world:
8

**Refined petroleum products -
production:**
4.812 million bbl/day
country comparison to the world:
4

**Refined petroleum products -
consumption:**
3.196 million bbl/day
country comparison to the world:
6

For additional analytical, business and investment opportunities information,
please contact Global Investment & Business Center, USA
at (202) 546-2103. Fax: (202) 546-3275. E-mail: rusric@erols.com

**Refined petroleum products -
exports:**
2.92 million bbl/day
country comparison to the world:
1

**Refined petroleum products -
imports:**
24,300 bbl/day
country comparison to the world:
97

Natural gas - production:

669.7 billion cu m
country comparison to the world:
2

Natural gas - consumption:
457.2 billion cu m
country comparison to the world: 2

Natural gas - exports:

196 billion cu m
country comparison to the world: 1

Natural gas - imports:

32.5 billion cu m
country comparison to the world:
17

Natural gas - proved reserves:
47.8 trillion cu m (1 January 2013 est.)
country comparison to the world:
1

**Carbon dioxide emissions from
consumption of energy:**
1.788 billion Mt

For additional analytical, business and investment opportunities information,
please contact Global Investment & Business Center, USA
at (202) 546-2103. Fax: (202) 546-3275. E-mail: rusric@erols.com

COMMUNICATIONS

Telephones - main lines in use
:
42.9 million
country comparison to the world:
6

Telephones - mobile cellular:

261.9 million
country comparison to the world: 5

Telephone system:

general assessment:
the telephone system is experiencing significant changes; there are more than 1,000 companies licensed to offer communication services; access to digital lines has improved, particularly in urban centers; Internet and e-mail services are improving; Russia has made progress toward building the telecommunications infrastructure necessary for a market economy; the estimated number of mobile subscribers jumped from fewer than 1 million in 1998 to more than 235 million in 2011; fixed line service has improved but a large demand remains
domestic:
cross-country digital trunk lines run from Saint Petersburg to Khabarovsk, and from Moscow to Novorossiysk; the telephone systems in 60 regional capitals have modern digital infrastructures; cellular services, both analog and digital, are available in many areas; in rural areas, the telephone services are still outdated, inadequate, and low density
international:
country code - 7; Russia is connected internationally by undersea fiber optic cables; satellite earth stations provide access to Intelsat, Intersputnik, Eutelsat, Inmarsat, and Orbita systems

Broadcast media:

6 national TV stations with the federal government owning 1 and holding a controlling interest in a second; state-owned Gazprom maintains a controlling interest in a third national channel; government-affiliated Bank Rossiya owns controlling interest in a fourth and fifth, while the sixth national channel is owned by the Moscow city administration; roughly 3,300 national, regional, and local TV stations with over two-thirds completely or partially controlled by the federal or local governments; satellite TV services are available; 2 state-run national radio networks with a third majority-owned by Gazprom; roughly 2,400 public and commercial radio stations

Internet country code:
.ru; note - Russia also has responsibility for a legacy domain ".su" that was allocated to the Soviet Union and is being phased out

Internet hosts:
14.865 million
country comparison to the world:
10

For additional analytical, business and investment opportunities information,
please contact Global Investment & Business Center, USA
at (202) 546-2103. Fax: (202) 546-3275. E-mail: rusric@erols.com

Internet users:
40.853 million
country comparison to the world:
10

TRANSPORTATION

Airports
:
1,218
country comparison to the world:
5

Airports - with paved runways:
total:
594
over 3,047 m: 54
2,438 to 3,047 m: 197
1,524 to 2,437 m: 123
914 to 1,523 m: 95
under 914 m: 125

Airports - with unpaved runways:
total: 624
over 3,047 m: 4
2,438 to 3,047 m: 13
1,524 to 2,437 m: 69
914 to 1,523 m: 81
under 914 m: 457

Heliports:
49

Pipelines:
condensate 122 km; gas 163,872 km; liquid petroleum gas 1,378 km; oil 80,820 km;
oil/gas/water 40 km; refined products 13,658 km; water 23 km (2013)

Railways:
total: 87,157 km
country comparison to the world: 2
broad gauge: 86,200 km 1.520-m gauge (40,300 km electrified)
narrow gauge: 957 km 1.067-m gauge (on Sakhalin Island)
note:an additional 30,000 km of non-common carrier lines serve industries (2006)

Roadways:
total: 1,283,387 km
country comparison to the world: 5
paved: 927,721 km (includes 39,143 km of expressways)

For additional analytical, business and investment opportunities information,
please contact Global Investment & Business Center, USA
at (202) 546-2103. Fax: (202) 546-3275. E-mail: rusric@erols.com

unpaved: 355,666 km (2012)

Waterways:
102,000 km (including 48,000 km with guaranteed depth; the 72,000 km system in European Russia links Baltic Sea, White Sea, Caspian Sea, Sea of Azov, and Black Sea) (2009)
country comparison to the world:
2

Merchant marine:
total: 1,143
country comparison to the world: 11

by type: bulk carrier 20, cargo 642, carrier 3, chemical tanker 57, combination ore/oil 42, container 13, passenger 15, passenger/cargo 7, petroleum tanker 244, refrigerated cargo 84, roll on/roll off 13, specialized tanker 3
foreign-owned: 155 (Belgium 4, Cyprus 13, Estonia 1, Ireland 1, Italy 14, Latvia 2, Netherlands 2, Romania 1, South Korea 1, Switzerland 3, Turkey 101, Ukraine 12)
registered in other countries: 439 (Antigua and Barbuda 3, Belgium 1, Belize 30, Bulgaria 2, Cambodia 50, Comoros 12, Cook Islands 1, Cyprus 46, Dominica 3, Georgia 6, Hong Kong 1, Kiribati 1, Liberia 109, Malaysia 2, Malta 45, Marshall Islands 5, Moldova 5, Mongolia 2, Panama 49, Romania 1, Saint Kitts and Nevis 13, Saint Vincent and the Grenadines 11, Sierra Leone 7, Singapore 2, Spain 6, Vanuatu 7, unknown 19) (2010)

Ports and terminals:
major seaport(s):
Kaliningrad, Nakhodka, Novorossiysk, Primorsk, Vostochnyy
river port(s):
Saint Petersburg (Neva River)
oil terminal(s):
Kavkaz oil terminal
container port(s) (TEUs):
Saint Petersburg (2,365,174)

MILITARY

Military branches:
Ground Troops (Sukhoputnyye Voyskia, SV), Navy (Voyenno-Morskoy Flot, VMF), Air Forces (Voyenno-Vozdushniye Sily, VVS); Airborne Troops (Vozdushno-Desantnyye Voyska, VDV), Missile Troops of Strategic Purpose (Raketnyye Voyska Strategicheskogo Naznacheniya, RVSN) referred to commonly as Strategic Rocket Forces, and Aerospace Defense Troops (Voyska Vozdushno-Kosmicheskoy Oborony or Voyska VKO) are independent "combat arms," not subordinate to any of the three branches; Russian Ground Troops include the following combat arms: motorized-rifle troops, tank troops, missile and artillery troops, air defense of the Ground Troops (2014)

Military service age and obligation:
18-27 years of age for compulsory or voluntary military service; males are registered for the draft at 17 years of age; service obligation is 1 year (conscripts can only be sent to combat zones after 6 months of training); reserve obligation for non-officers to age 50; enrollment in military schools from the age of 16, cadets classified as members of the armed forces
*note:*the chief of the General Staff Mobilization Directorate announced in May 2013 that for

health reasons, only 65% of draftees called up during the spring 2013 draft campaign were fit for military service, and over 12% of these were sent for an additional medical examination (by way of comparison, 69.9% in 2012 and 57.7% in 2011 were deemed fit for military service); approximately 50% of draft-age Russian males receive some type of legal deferment each draft cycle (2014)

Manpower available for military service:
males age 16-49: 34,765,736
females age 16-49: 35,410,779 (2013 est.)

Manpower fit for military service:
males age 16-49: 22,597,728
females age 16-49: 23,017,006 (2013 est.)

Manpower reaching militarily significant age annually:
male: 696,768
female: 664,847 (2013 est.)
Military expenditures:
4.47% of GDP (2012)

country comparison to the world: 8
4.13% of GDP (2011)
4.47% of GDP (2010)

TRANSNATIONAL ISSUES

Russia remains concerned about the smuggling of poppy derivatives from Afghanistan through Central Asian countries; China and Russia have demarcated the once disputed islands at the Amur and Ussuri confluence and in the Argun River in accordance with the 2004 Agreement, ending their centuries-long border disputes; the sovereignty dispute over the islands of Etorofu, Kunashiri, Shikotan, and the Habomai group, known in Japan as the "Northern Territories" and in Russia as the "Southern Kurils," occupied by the Soviet Union in 1945, now administered by Russia, and claimed by Japan, remains the primary sticking point to signing a peace treaty formally ending World War II hostilities; Russia's military support and subsequent recognition of Abkhazia and South Ossetia independence in 2008 continue to sour relations with Georgia; Azerbaijan, Kazakhstan, and Russia ratified Caspian seabed delimitation treaties based on equidistance, while Iran continues to insist on a one-fifth slice of the sea; Norway and Russia signed a comprehensive maritime boundary agreement in 2010; various groups in Finland advocate restoration of Karelia (Kareliya) and other areas ceded to the Soviet Union following World War II but the Finnish Government asserts no territorial demands; Russia and Estonia signed a technical border agreement in May 2005, but Russia recalled its signature in June 2005 after the Estonian parliament added to its domestic ratification act a historical preamble referencing the Soviet occupation and Estonia's pre-war borders under the 1920 Treaty of Tartu; Russia contends that the preamble allows Estonia to make territorial claims on Russia in the future, while Estonian officials deny that the preamble has any legal impact on the treaty text; Russia demands better treatment of the Russian-speaking population in Estonia and Latvia; Lithuania and Russia committed to demarcating their boundary in 2006 in accordance with the land and maritime treaty ratified by Russia in May 2003 and by Lithuania in 1999; Lithuania operates a simplified transit regime for Russian nationals traveling from the Kaliningrad coastal exclave into Russia, while still conforming, as an EU member state with an EU external border, where strict Schengen border rules apply; preparations for the demarcation delimitation of land boundary with Ukraine have commenced; the dispute over the boundary between Russia and Ukraine through the Kerch Strait and Sea of Azov is suspended

For additional analytical, business and investment opportunities information, please contact Global Investment & Business Center, USA at (202) 546-2103. Fax: (202) 546-3275. E-mail: rusric@erols.com

due to the occupation of Crimea by Russia; Kazakhstan and Russia boundary delimitation was ratified on November 2005 and field demarcation should commence in 2007; Russian Duma has not yet ratified 1990 Bering Sea Maritime Boundary Agreement with the US; Denmark (Greenland) and Norway have made submissions to the Commission on the Limits of the Continental shelf (CLCS) and Russia is collecting additional data to augment its 2001 CLCS submission

Refugees and internally displaced persons:
IDPs: at least 34,900 (armed conflict, human rights violations, generalized violence in North Caucasus, particularly Chechnya and North Ossetia) (2013)
stateless persons: 178,000 (2012); note - Russia's stateless population consists of Roma, Meskhetian Turks, and ex-Soviet citizens from the former republics; between 2003 and 2010 more than 600,000 stateless people were naturalized; most Meskhetian Turks, followers of Islam with origins in Georgia, fled or were evacuated from Uzbekistan after a 1989 pogrom and have lived in Russia for more than the required five-year residency period; they continue to be denied registration for citizenship and basic rights by local Krasnodar Krai authorities on the grounds that they are temporary illegal migrants

Trafficking in persons:
current situation: Russia is a source, transit, and destination country for men, women, and children who are subjected to forced labor and sex trafficking, although labor trafficking is the predominant problem; people from Russia and other countries in Europe, Central Asia, and Asia, including Vietnam and North Korea, are subjected to conditions of forced labor in Russia's construction, manufacturing, agriculture, repair shop, and domestic services industries, as well as forced begging and narcotics cultivation; North Koreans contracted under bilateral government arrangements to work in the timber industry in the Russian Far East reportedly are subjected to forced labor; Russian women and children were reported to be victims of sex trafficking in Russia, Northeast Asia, Europe, Central Asia, and the Middle East, while women from European, African, and Central Asian countries were reportedly forced into prostitution in Russia
tier rating: Tier 3 - Russia does not fully comply with the minimum standards for the elimination of trafficking and because it is not deemed to be making significant efforts to do so was downgraded to Tier 3 after the maximum of two consecutive annual waivers; the number of prosecutions remains low compared to estimates of Russia's trafficking problem; the government did not develop or deploy a formal system for the identification of trafficking victims or their referral to protective services, although some victims were reportedly cared for through ad hoc efforts; the government has reported minimal efforts to identify or care for the large number of migrant workers vulnerable to labor exploitation and has not investigated allegations of slave-like conditions in North Korean-operated timber camps (2013)

Illicit drugs:
limited cultivation of illicit cannabis and opium poppy and producer of methamphetamine, mostly for domestic consumption; government has active illicit crop eradication program; used as transshipment point for Asian opiates, cannabis, and Latin American cocaine bound for growing domestic markets, to a lesser extent Western and Central Europe, and occasionally to the US; major source of heroin precursor chemicals; corruption and organized crime are key concerns; major consumer of opiates

TELECOM SECTOR IN RUSSIA: STRATEGIC INFORMATION AND DEVELOPMENTS

Russia was among the first countries to introduce radio and television. Due to the enormous size of the country Russia leads in the number of TV broadcast stations and repeaters. There were few channels in the Soviet time, but in the past two decades many new state-run and private-owned radio stations and TV channels appeared. In 2005 a state-run English language Russia Today TV started broadcasting, and its Arabic version Rusiya Al-Yaum was launched in 2007. The governmental agency responsible for telecommunications is Ministry of Communications and Mass Media.

The telecommunications system in Russia have undergone significant changes since the 1980s, resulting in more than 1,000 companies licensed to offer communication services today. The foundation for liberalization of broadcasting was laid by the decree signed by the President of the USSR in 1990. Communication is mainly regulated through the Federal Law "On Communications" and the Federal Law "On Mass Media"

The Soviet-time "Ministry of communications of the RSFSR" was through 1990s transformed to "Ministry for communications and informatization" and in 2004 it was renamed to "Ministry of information technologies and communications (Mininformsvyazi)", and in 2008 – "Ministry of connections and mass commnunications (Minkomsvyaz)".

The "Ministry of press and information of the RSFSR" was in 1990s renamed to "Ministry of Press, Broadcasting and Mass Communications (Minpechati)" and in 2004 it was turned into the "Federal Agency on Press and Mass Communications (Rospechat)" which was no longer a standalone ministry but a subdivision to the "Ministry of Culture and Mass Communications" (originally "Ministry of culture of the RSFSR"). In 2008 it was re-subordinated back to "Minvsyazi".

Fiber to the x infrastructure has been expanded rapidly in recent years, principally by regional players including Southern Telecom Company, SibirTelecom, ER Telecom and Golden Telecom. Collectively, these players are having a significant impact of fiber broadband in regional areas, and are enabling operators to take advantage of consumer demand for faster access and bundled services.

Retrospectively, "networking" of "data" in the Russian language can be traced to the spread of mail and journalism in Russia, and information transfer by technical means came to Russia with the telegraph and radio (besides, a 1837 sci-fi novel *Year 4338*, by the 19-century Russian philosopher Vladimir Odoevsky, contains predictions such as *"friends' houses are connected by means of magnetic telegraphs that allow people who live far from each other to talk to each other"* and *"household journals" "having replaced regular correspondence"* with *"information about the hosts' good or bad health, family news, various thoughts and comments, small inventions, as well as invitations"*[1]).

Computing systems became known in the USSR by the 1950s. Starting from 1952, works were held in the Moscow-based Institute of Precision Mechanics and Computer Engineering (headed by Sergei Lebedev) on automated missile defense system which used a "computer network" which calculated radar data on test missiles through central machine called M-40 and was interchanging information with smaller remote terminals about 100—200 kilometers distant.[2] The scientists used several locations in the USSR for their works, the largest was a massive test range to the West from Lake Balkhash. In the meantime amateur radio users all over USSR were conducting "P2P" connections with their comrades worldwide using data codes. Later, a massive "automated data network" called *Express* was launched in 1972 to serve needs of Russian Railways.

From early 1980s the All Union Scientific Research Institute for Applied Computerized Systems (*VNIIPAS*) was working to implement data connections over the X.25 telephone protocol. A test

For additional analytical, business and investment opportunities information, please contact Global Investment & Business Center, USA at (202) 546-2103. Fax: (202) 546-3275. E-mail: rusric@erols.com

Soviet connection to Austria in 1982 existed, in 1982 and 1983 there were series of "world computer conferences" at VNIIPAS initiated by the U. N. where USSR was represented by a team of scientists from many Soviet Republics headed by biochemist Anatoly Klyosov; the other participating countries were UK, USA, Canada, Sweden, FRG, GDR, Italy, Finland, Philippines, Guatemala, Japan, Thailand, Luxembourg, Denmark, Brazil and New Zealand.[3]

Also, in 1983 the *San Francisco Moscow Teleport (SFMT)* project was started by VNIIPAS and an American team which included George Soros. It resulted in the creation in the latter 80s of the data transfer operator *SovAm* (Soviet-American) *Teleport*. Meanwhile, on April 1, 1984 a Fool's Day hoax about "Kremlin computer" Kremvax was made in English-speaking Usenet. There are reports of spontaneous Internet (UUCP and telnet) connections "from home" through X.25 in the USSR in as early as 1988. In 1990 a *GlasNet* non-profit initiative by the US-based Association for Progressive Communications sponsored Internet usage in several educational projects in the USSR (through Sovam).

The telecommunications infrastructure in Russia is being reformed and modernized; this project is expected to be finished in 2012. Prior to completion, all cities and settlements in the Russian Federation will have a modern landline-telephone infrastructure. Use of '0' and '00' as the long-distance call and international call prefixes will become standard (this was scheduled for 2008, but authorities are first introducing the soon-to-be-universal emergency '112' number and cancelling special numbers starting with '0'). Domestic regulators plan to have this scheme in place by early 2012. Their intent is to increase the number of regions connected to 112 year by year: 2 in 2007, 6 in 2008, 24 in 2009, 44 in 2010, etc. These changes are aimed at bringing local regulations into compliance with ITU and EU recommendations.

1998 FINANCIAL CRISIS

When the Russian economy's collapse came about in August 1998, the market shrank drastically and the ruble fell several cellular operators were squeezed between low traffic and huge foreign currency denominated credits and telecommunications equipment bills. In 1998, prepaid subscriptions were made at a loss and infrastructure investments fell. NMT450 operator Moscow Cellular communications was hardest hit due to its about 50 % corporate users. The 1998 crisis also caused many regional operators tariff and payment problems with accumulated debt to vendors; large debts were restructured and foreign investors lost out.[4]

TELEPHONE

See also: Telephone numbers in Russia

Telephones – main lines in use: 25.019 million

Telephones – mobile cellular: 161,000,000

The telephone systems in the 60 regional capitals have modern digital infrastructures; cellular services, both analog and digital, are available in many areas. In the rural areas, the telephone services are still outdated, inadequate, and low density.

Until the end of 1991 (the end of the USSR), the sole fixed-line telephone operator in the country was the Ministry of Communications of the USSR. The state possessed all telecommunications structure and access networks. In 1994, the investment communication company (OJSC "Sviazinvest") was established by the Presidential Decree #1989 dated 10 October 1994 "*On the specific features of the state management of the electric communication network for public use in Russian Federation*". The authorised capital of OJSC "Sviazinvest" was formed by the consolidation of federal shares of joint stock companies acting in the area of electric communications and established during the privatisation of the state enterprises for electric communications. The seven regional incumbents

For additional analytical, business and investment opportunities information,
please contact Global Investment & Business Center, USA
at (202) 546-2103. Fax: (202) 546-3275. E-mail: rusric@erols.com

which make up Svyazinvest, majority-owned by the government, in early 2011 merged with the key subsidiary Rostelecom. The move created an integrated company based on Rostelecom which will be better placed to exploit economies of scale in coming years.[5]

Cross-country digital trunk lines run from Saint Petersburg to Vladivostok, and from Moscow to Novorossiysk.

Liberalization of the long distance communication market is another market driver. Rostelecom lost its monopoly when new players obtained licences for the provision of long-distance communication services. Currently,[when?] there are about 32 active companies in this space, including MTT, Golden Telecom, TransTeleCom and Synterra. Russian regulation stipulates that new players must build their own networks. The growth of traffic between Europe and Asia is an additional opportunity; more than 6,000 km of international communication cables were built during the first nine months of 2007, representing a 48.5% increase on 2006, according to the Russian Ministry of Communication and Mass Media.[6]

RUSSIAN PSTN (PUBLIC SWITCHED TELEPHONE NETWORK)

Russian public switched telephone network (PSTN) has specific features. The lowest part of this model is example of the local network in the middle and large cities. The central office (CO) is connected to the tandem exchange (TE). In some cases, COs are connected by the directly. Such possibility is shown by the dotted lines for three COs connected to the TEIII. COs may be directly connected with the toll exchange. This option is shown by the dotted line for the COII1. Automatic Branch Exchange (PABX) is served by the nearest CO. All TEs are forming the meshed network. Up to the 1990s, TE was independent element of the local network. Operators did not use the equipment combined functions Tandem and Toll Exchanges. So, TE provided connections between COs of the local network, and access to the toll exchange. A function of the toll exchange is to establish connections for the long-distance and international calls. Last type of calls is served by the Gateway (GW). Processing of the local calls is performed by the COs and TEs. If a subscriber dials digit "8" (prefix of the long-distance connection in the national PSTN) all further processing of the call is a function of a toll exchange. The numbering plan for the cellular networks based on the Area Code (three digits) and number of mobile terminal (seven digits). In this case, the Area Code defines the concrete cellular network.[7]

MOBILE PHONE

There are three mobile phone service brands that cover all Russia: Beeline, MegaFon and Mobile TeleSystems. The access points (AP) are built in long-distance telephone exchanges (LDTEs), Russian fixed-line communication infrastructure which is present in every province. As a result, interconnecting mobile operator only needs to create "last kilometer" circuits to the regional LDTE, the requirement already imposed by its mobile license.

In May 2008, 3G network was deployed in St. Petersburg, in Kazan in June of that year, and in Sochi in July of that year. By 2010, 3G networks covered largely most of Russia.

In April 2011, MegaFon deployed high-definition voice services on its Moscow and Sochi GSM and UMTS networks. As the key supplier of core and access networks to MegaFon, Nokia Siemens Networks was responsible for the HD voice implementation, which is also a world first for a commercial GSM network.

In early 2011, Rostelecom signed a memorandum of understanding with the three main MNOs to develop a joint LTE network using the infrastructure to be built by Yota. The network will expand LTE availability to 70 million Russians in 180 cities by 2014, vastly improving regional broadband availability in coming years.

For additional analytical, business and investment opportunities information,
please contact Global Investment & Business Center, USA
at (202) 546-2103. Fax: (202) 546-3275. E-mail: rusric@erols.com

In December 2011, Rostelecom signed an agreement with Yota, a Russian mobile broadband provider, to jointly develop and use 4G wireless networks. The agreement will facilitate the development and expansion of advanced communications technologies in the Russian Federation, including the latest 4G-LTE system. Both companies will make full use of each other's telecommunications infrastructures and advanced telecommunications services will be made more accessible to Russian residents. As part of the agreement, Rostelecom will have the right to use Yota's wireless networks and to provide customers with telecommunications services as a MVNO. The agreement will also provide Rostelecom with access to Yota's existing telecommunications equipment sites and its wire communications channels at these sites. In return, Yota will use Rostelecom's wire communications channels at their telecommunication equipment sites; it will gain access to Rostelecom's Internet connection and inter-city backbone links and the company's existing telecommunication equipment sites and data centres.[10]

RADIO

Radio Rossii is the primary public radio station in Russia. Digital radio broadcasting is developing fast with the Voice of Russia announced on 1 July 2004, the successful implementation, and planned expansion, of its DRM broadcasts on short-wave and medium-wave. In September 2009 the Radio Frequency Service, the national regulator of broadcasting, has decided on the DRM has the standard for mediumwave and shortwave services.[11]

Radios: 61.5 million (1998)

Radio broadcasting stations: AM 420, FM 447, shortwave 56 (1998).

TELEVISION

Privately owned stations are often owned by industrial groups either controlled by the State or with close connections to the government so that they can be called semi-state. Both state and private stations can have a national status (broadcasters that reach over 70% of the national territory), or a regional, district or local status. Local partners are often united in bigger networks.

In the 1970s and 1980s, television become the preeminent mass medium. In 1988 approximately 75 million households owned television sets, and an estimated 93 percent of the population watched television. Moscow, the base from which most of the television stations broadcast, transmitted some 90 percent of the country's programs, with the help of more than 350 stations and nearly 1,400 relay facilities.

There are about 15,000 TV transmitters. Development of domestic digital TV transmitters, led within "Multichannel" research program, had already been finished. New domestic digital transmitters have been developed and installed in Nizhniy Novgorod and Saint Petersburg in 2001–2002.

The state public television broadcaster is Pervy kanal (Channel One).[citation needed]

INTERNET

Broadband internet access is becoming more readily available in Russia, and as a result the internet is growing as an avenue for Russian commerce, with 42% of internet users in Russia shopping online, and 38% using online banking services.[12]

IPTV

The IPTV developing fast as a cheap alternative to regular television. On July 2011 Rostelecom started a plan to unify IPTV services in Russia's regions offering standard features such as linear and

For additional analytical, business and investment opportunities information,
please contact Global Investment & Business Center, USA
at (202) 546-2103. Fax: (202) 546-3275. E-mail: rusric@erols.com

on-demand TV along with new interactive and OTT services provided by the operator to various mobile devices. For this Russian company SmartLabs was chosen.[13]

Country code top-level domain: RU (Also SU – left from Soviet Union)

INTERNATIONAL CONNECTION

Russia is connected internationally by three undersea fiber-optic cables; digital switches in several cities provide more than 50,000 lines for international calls; satellite earth stations provide access to Intelsat, Intersputnik, Eutelsat, Inmarsat, and Orbita. In May 2006, Rostelecom launched a new fiber-optic data transmission line linking Russia's Far Eastern cities of Belogorsk and Blagoveshchensk with the Chinese city of Heihe on the Russian border.[14] On May 2006 TransTeleCom Company and North Korea's Ministry of Communications have signed an agreement for the construction and joint operation of a fiber-optic transmission line (FOTL) in the section of the Khasan–Tumangang railway checkpoint. This is the first direct land link between Russia and North Korea. TTC's partner in the design, construction, and connection of the communication line from the Korean side to the junction was Korea Communication Company of North Korea's Ministry of Communications. The technology transfer was built around STM-1 level digital equipment with the possibility of further increasing bandwidth. The construction was completed in 2007.[15]

On February 2012 the national operator Rostelecom has selected TeliaSonera International Carrier to operate and manage its new backbone network between Kingisepp, Russia and Stockholm. The next-generation managed optical network provides connectivity between the cable landing points of the Baltic Cable System, Kingisepp and Kotka, implemented over TeliaSonera International Carrier's wholly owned fibre-optic infrastructure to Stockholm.[

MOBILE PHONE INDUSTRY IN RUSSIA

The **mobile phone** industry in **Russia** has expanded rapidly to become one of the largest in the world.

Russian Federation has 226.2 million subscribers in total, or a 162% penetration rate.

In 1963, Russia's first mobile phone network using the car phone came into operation. [1]

Initial selection of technological mobile standard in Russia had been left for market forces by issuing licenses for different standards. Later, regulatory authorities have developed stricter policy. However, there still exists a great variety of both analogue and digital standards. NMT standard was a first generation analogue mobile technology that still has footstep in Russia, employed by commercial mobile operators since the early 90s.[2]

Regional operators have deployed the GSM[3] networks in Russia since 1995, originally in the 900 MHZ frequency band. GSM standard is dominating in Russian mobile market with small number of NMT-450, AMPS/DAMPS subscribers.

In 1994, a joint venture of Moscow City Telephone Network, T-Mobile and Siemens, which later became part of Mobile TeleSystems, offered Russia's first mobile phone service for the public in Moscow. [4] In the same year in June, VimpelCom also started Beeline mobile phone service. [5]

In 2002, MegaFone was formed to provide all-Russia service, amalgamating Sonic Duo of Moscow, Mobikom-Novosibirsk, and other companies. [6] In 2007, MegaFon started Russia's first 3G service in Saint Petersburg.

For additional analytical, business and investment opportunities information, please contact Global Investment & Business Center, USA at (202) 546-2103. Fax: (202) 546-3275. E-mail: rusric@erols.com

Russian WiMAX operator Scartel (Yota brand), finished in 2010 its implementation of a trial LTE network in Kazan and plans to deploy LTE networks in Novosibirsk and Samara. In July 2010 Scartel received approval from regulator Roskomnadzor to abandon WiMAX for LTE, re-using its existing spectrum. the regulator had however previously insisted that the frequencies allocated to Scartel for WiMAX could not be used for other access types.

MOBILE PHONE SERVICE PROVIDERS

Rank	Operator	Technology	Subscribers (in millions)	Ownership
	Mobile Network Operators
1	MTS	GSM, GPRS, EDGE UMTS, HSDPA, HSUPA, HSPA+	69.375 (March 2012)	Sistema (50.8%)
2	MegaFon	GSM, GPRS, EDGE UMTS, HSDPA, HSUPA, HSPA+ LTE (test)	61.63 (March 2012)	TeliaSonera 35.6%, MegaFon Invesments Ltd. 14.4%, Garsdale Services 50%
3	Beeline	GSM, GPRS, EDGE UMTS, HSDPA, HSUPA, HSPA+	55.62 (March 2012)	VimpelCom (100%: Telenor (39.51%), Alfa Group (24,998%), Weather Investments II (18.276%), Bertofan Investments Ltd. (5.995%), 11,221% in minoritaries)
4	Tele2	GSM, GPRS, EDGE	20.94 (March 2012)	Tele2
5	Rostelecom	GSM, CDMA2000 1x, 450 MHz CDMA2000 EV-DO Rev. A, 450 MHz	12.5 (March 2012)	Svyazinvest (45,7%)
6	Sotovaja Svjaz MOTIV	GSM, GPRS, EDGE	2.24 (March 2012)	?
7	SMARTS	GSM, GPRS, EDGE	1.92 (March 2012)	?
8	SkyLink	CDMA2000 1x, 450 MHz CDMA2000 EV-DO Rev. A, 450 MHz	1.34 (March 2012)	Svyazinvest 50%, Rostelecom 50%
9	Yota	LTE	0.68 (2010)	Garsdale Services 100% (82% AF Telecom, 13,482% Telconet Capital, 4,518% Rostechnology)
	Mobile Virtual Network Operators

For additional analytical, business and investment opportunities information, please contact Global Investment & Business Center, USA at (202) 546-2103. Fax: (202) 546-3275. E-mail: rusric@erols.com

10	Prosto dlya obscheniya (using MegaFon)	GSM		
11	Matrix Telecom (using MegaFon)	GSM		
12	Allo inkognito (using MegaFon & SkyLink)	GSM, CDMA2000 1x, 450 MHz		
13	MegaTel (using MegaFon)	GSM		
14	Gars Telecom (using MegaFon & SkyLink)	GSM, CDMA2000 1x, 450 MHz		
15	EuroNet (using SMARTS)	GSM		
16	A-Mobile (using MTS)	GSM		
17	Yo (using SMARTS)	GSM		
18	MTT.Mobile (using Synterra))	CDMA2000 1x, 450 MHz	///	Multiregional Transit Telecom (MTT)
19	X5 Retail Group (using MTS)	GSM		

INTERNET IN RUSSIA

Internet in Russia (also **Russian Internet** (Russian: российский Интернет), sometimes Runet - by state officials) is a part of the Internet, which related to Russia. Currently Internet access in Russia is available to businesses and home users in various forms, including dial-up, cable, DSL, FTTH, mobile, wireless and satellite

In September 2011, Russia overtook Germany as the European market with the highest number of unique visitors online.[1]

Internet in Russia is also sometimes called by government as Runet, but Runet mostly describe Russian-language Internet.

Retrospectively, "networking" of "data" in the Russian language can be traced to the spread of mail and journalism in Russia, and information transfer by technical means came to Russia with the telegraph and radio (besides, a 1837 sci-fi novel *Year 4338*, by the 19-century Russian philosopher Vladimir Odoevsky, contains predictions such as *"friends' houses are connected by means of magnetic telegraphs that allow people who live far from each other to talk to each other"* and *"household journals"* *"having replaced regular correspondence"* with *"information about the hosts' good or bad health, family news, various thoughts and comments, small inventions, as well as invitations"*[2]).

Computing systems became known in the USSR by the 1950s. Starting from 1952, works were held in the Moscow-based Institute of Precision Mechanics and Computer Engineering (headed by Sergei Lebedev) on automated missile defense system which used a "computer network" which calculated radar data on test missiles through central machine called M-40 and was interchanging information with smaller remote terminals about 100—200 kilometers distant.[3] The scientists used several locations in the USSR for their works, the largest was a massive test range to the West from Lake Balkhash. In the meantime amateur radio users all over USSR were conducting "P2P" connections

For additional analytical, business and investment opportunities information, please contact Global Investment & Business Center, USA at (202) 546-2103. Fax: (202) 546-3275. E-mail: rusric@erols.com

with their comrades worldwide using data codes. Later, a massive "automated data network" called *Express* was launched in 1972 to serve needs of Russian Railways.

From early 1980s the All Union Scientific Research Institute for Applied Computerized Systems (*VNIIPAS*) was working to implement data connections over the X.25 telephone protocol. A test Soviet connection to Austria in 1982 existed, in 1982 and 1983 there were series of "world computer conferences" at VNIIPAS initiated by the U. N. where USSR was represented by a team of scientists from many Soviet Republics headed by biochemist Anatoly Klyosov; the other participating countries were UK, USA, Canada, Sweden, FRG, GDR, Italy, Finland, Philippines, Guatemala, Japan, Thailand, Luxembourg, Denmark, Brazil and New Zealand.[4]

Also, in 1983 the *San Francisco Moscow Teleport (SFMT)* project was started by VNIIPAS and an American team which included George Soros. It resulted in the creation in the latter 80s of the data transfer operator *SovAm* (Soviet-American) *Teleport*. Meanwhile, on April 1, 1984 a Fool's Day hoax about "Kremlin computer" Kremvax was made in English-speaking Usenet. There are reports of spontaneous Internet (UUCP and telnet) connections "from home" through X.25 in the USSR in as early as 1988. In 1990 a *GlasNet* non-profit initiative by the US-based Association for Progressive Communications sponsored Internet usage in several educational projects in the USSR (through Sovam).

MASS USAGE

In 1990—1991 Relcom's network was rapidly expanding, it joined EUnet and was used to spread news about the Soviet coup attempt of 1991 worldwide while coupers through KGB were trying to suppress mass media activity on the subject.[5] After the fall of the USSR many former Soviet state-controlled structures were inherited by the Russian Federation, vast telephone networks among them.[6] With the transformation of the economy, market-based telecommunication industries grew quickly, various ISPs appeared.

Meanwhile, the first Russian FidoNet node reportedly started in October 1990 in Novosibirsk, and the USSR was included in FidoNet's *Region 50*. Russian FidoNet activity did contribute to development of Runet, as mass-networking over BBSes was for a time more popular than over the Internet in the early 90s.

By the mid 1990s, computer networks (where TCP/IP was replacing UUCP) appeared in many branches of regular life and commerce in Post-Soviet states. The Internet became a popular means of communication for anyone in the world who spoke Russian. National so-called *Nets* of former Soviet Republics began to occur (e.g. *Uznet*, *Kaznet* and others).

In October 2007 then Deputy Prime Minister Dmitry Medvedev announced that all of the schools in Russia (about 59,000) were connected to the Internet, but later concerns were publicized that there were problems with a contractor to serve them. Also in December 2007, as a follow-up to the noted Ponosov's Case, which dealt with the use of illegal software in a Russian school, plans were announced to officially test Linux in the schools of Perm Krai, Tatarstan and Tomsk Oblast to determine the feasibility of further implementing Linux-based education in the country's other regions.[7] In subsequent years test results were considered successful, but new organizational problems appeared, including obscurities with distribution of funds assigned by state.[8]

The prominent Public Opinion Foundation *FOM* (ФОМ) in March 2007 issued a report that found 28 million people 18+ in Russia (25%) had used the internet within the last six months (monthly users 23.9/21%; daily 10.1/9%).[9] In November 2006 *TNS Gallup Media* in a report called by some sources "first quality Internet audience research in Russia" put a monthly Russian audience at more than 15 million.[10] The *Rukv.ru* monitoring project found 1,001,806 WWW-addresses within .ru and .su responding in March 2008.[11] The national domain registration service RU-Center announced

For additional analytical, business and investment opportunities information, please contact Global Investment & Business Center, USA at (202) 546-2103. Fax: (202) 546-3275. E-mail: rusric@erols.com

creation of millionth .ru domain on September 17, 2007 (about 200 thousand of domains are thought to be 'parked' by squatters).

On April 3, 2008, the RIF-2008 was opened by president-elect of Russia Dmitry Medvedev who said in the opening address to the forum that he estimates Runet to be populated by 40 million users, or 28 percent of the population. He also stated that Russian sites do $3 billion in annual transactions and have $370 million in advertising revenue.[12]

In October 2008 President Medvedev started his own video blog which in April 2009 was expanded with the separately moderated version in LiveJournal.[13]

In June 2009 FOM issued results of its new survey that found "half-year audience" of people 18 years old and over was 33%, or 37.5 million.[14]

CIA World Factbook states there were 10.382 million internet hosts in 2008 and 40.853 million internet users in 2010.[15]

By March 2011 the total number of broadband subscribers reached 16.5 million with penetration almost 30%. These numbers increased within two years by 180% against 9 million in 2009. The highest penetration rate above 70% is in Moscow and Saint-Petersburg, these two cities also makes up a quarter of all subscribers (3.2 and 1.2 million respectively).[16]

BACKBONE

The development of Internet infrastructure in Russia began with development analog modem-based computer networks in Soviet cities, primarily in scientific institutions. The first one to connect UNIX email hosts country-wide (including Soviet Republics) was the *Relcom* organization which formed on August 1, 1990 at the Kurchatov nuclear physics institute in Moscow. They were functioning together with partner programming cooperative *Demos*, named after the Soviet-made DEMOS Unix-like operating system. In August 1990 they established regular email routing with an Internet node in Helsinki University over a paid voice line.

Back in the 1990s, Rostelecom built international fiber optic cable systems - "Zapadny" (Denmark-Russia), "Yuzhny" (Italy-Turkey-Ukraine-Russia) and "Vostochny" (Russia-Japan-Korea) - as well as "Moscow-Khabarovsk" Trans-Russian Fiber Optic Line. The situation favored Russia's entry to the international telecommunication transit market. However, low transmission capacity (560 megabits per second) of all the three systems designed mainly for voice communication became the principal obstacle that hindered international expansion.

In 2005 the Chelyabinsk-Khabarovsk Fiber-Optic Communication Line was laid-down which extends for 10 thousand kilometers. The minimum transmission rate is 120 Gigabits per second.[17]

Plenty of local commercial ISPs function in large cities, but most of the existing country-wide cable lines are held by small number of large operators such as former "monopolist", the state-controlled Rostelecom and the railways-affiliated Transtelecom, which operates country biggest DWDM fiber backbone. Cell phone coverage with the digital services such as GPRS is almost ubiquitous. In year 2007 the Golden Telecom company has constructed a massive Wi-Fi network in Moscow for commercial use which is recognized as the largest urban wireless network in the world.[18] The Black Sea coast of Russia has became an important area for the fiber-optic networks, as it will serve as a backbone of communication during the Winter Olympic Games in 2014.

On October 2010 mobile operator MegaFon has selected Huawei NE5000E routers to construct backbone nodes for a 40-Gbit/s IP/MPLS network in Russia' s largest cities, including Moscow and St. Petersburg, Huawei says. Meanwhile, Megafon also announced the opening of what it touts as Russia's largest data center in Samara.[19]

For additional analytical, business and investment opportunities information, please contact Global Investment & Business Center, USA at (202) 546-2103. Fax: (202) 546-3275. E-mail: rusric@erols.com

In 2011 Rostelecom started implementation of WDM-based equipment on the backbone network for data transmission in the Republic of Dagestan. Due to WDM introduction the fiber-optic communication lines bandwidth increased to 2.5 Gbit/s. Rostelecom invested about 48 million rubles in the project

Public **Internet exchange points in Russia** are *MSK-IX* in Moscow, *SPB-IX* in Saint-Petersburg, *SAMARA-IX* in Samara, *Ix-NN* (Nizhny Novgorod), *NSK-IX* in Novosibirsk, and *KRS-IX* in Krasnoyarsk and in Kazan.

The most popular of these is the MSK-IX, with over 320 members and over 140 Gbit/s steady throughput during peak hours of the weekdays. On the territory of NSK-IX, RIPE operates a mirror of its k.root-servers.net.

For additional analytical, business and investment opportunities information, please contact Global Investment & Business Center, USA at (202) 546-2103. Fax: (202) 546-3275. E-mail: rusric@erols.com

RUSSIAN TELECOM SECTOR DEVELOPMENT AND OPPORTUNITIES

REGULATION OF ELECTRONIC COMMUNICATIONS

A significant proportion of the fixed communications market remains in state ownership. (Notably 75 percent plus one share in Svyazinvest, the company that groups together regional carriers. Svyazinvest, in turn, also owns 51 percent of Rostelecom, which provides long-distance and international services). As yet, it is unclear when the government will sell its remaining shares; there were plans to privatise in 2006 but this has not happened and no new timescale has been announced. The Parliament passed amendments to the Law on Communications in July 2006 in order to facilitate the sale. There is also no independent telecommunications regulatory authority and there are no plans to set one up.

As Russia opens its markets, the regulation of competition and liberalisation is being addressed by the government on a ongoing, if gradual, basis. For example, interconnection, where there had traditionally been little regulation, with prices and conditions being based on contractual agreements, is now subject to far more comprehensive legislation – although mobile interconnection is not as strictly regulated as fixed. There are no immediate plans to reorganise the management of Russian numbering resources, which remain under the responsibility of the Ministry for Communications and Informatisation. However, work is underway to assess the possibilities for mobile, but not fixed, number portability.

There are no procedures for facilities sharing and no appeals procedure in the case of disputes. An order imposing cost accounting on SMP operators was introduced in 2006. Tariff rebalancing is underway, while elements of universal service legislation were introduced in 2003 and again in 2005. A tender process is now well underway for the provision of phone and Internet access nationwide. Tenders are being awarded on a regional rather than a national level. Companies can bid simply for one region and are not obliged to bid nationwide.

Leased line provisioning varies widely – ranging from very active competition and low prices in profitable urban areas to higher prices in less developed regions – with no specific regulatory provisions in place for this sector.

The situation regarding licensing in the telecommunications sector has become considerably less complex since the introduction of the 2003 Federal Law on Communications: one licence is required for mobile operators, two for Internet access and service providers, and up to five for fixed telephony service providers. Licences are generally issued on a regional basis.

New data protection legislation was passed at the end of 2005, ratifying the Council of Europe Convention on the Automatic Processing of Personal Data (ETS 108).

REGULATION OF ELECTRONIC SERVICES

Digital signature legislation is in force in Russia (Russian Federal Law on the Electronic Digital Signature of 2001). Licensing requirements that had been in place for service providers are now in the process of being removed. New legislation, based on the current German law, has been adopted, which should greatly improve the ease with which digital signatures can be used.

For online intermediaries, such as Internet access and hosting providers, the legal situation regarding liability for illegal content has become more clear. The new Law on Information, Information Technology and the Protection of Information, which was adopted in July 2006, gives ISPs protection

For additional analytical, business and investment opportunities information, please contact Global Investment & Business Center, USA at (202) 546-2103. Fax: (202) 546-3275. E-mail: rusric@erols.com

similar to that offered in the EU by the E-Commerce Directive. With regard to the legal framework concerning illegal content, progress is being made with regard to legislation on intellectual property rights infringements. On the other hand, while the procedures and laws concerning online child abuse images need further development, for example in relation to "notice and takedown" procedures, there appears to be increasing industry pressure (from Microsoft, in particular) for a comprehensive solution. However, the absence of a representative body for ISPs in the country makes implementation of such a measure very difficult.

E-payment systems have developed very slowly due to a variety of factors, including lack of trust in online systems, the absence of comprehensive legislation on e-payments, and the low purchasing power of the population.

According to the traffic measurement website http://rumetrica.rambler.ru , there were 3,888 online shops in Russia in May 2006. According to the National Association of Participants in Electronic Trade,[1] the Russian e-commerce market was worth 3,714 million Euro in 2005, shared between B2G (1,797 million Euro), B2B (1,074 million Euro) and B2C (843 million Euro) services.

USE OF INFORMATION AND COMMUNICATIONS TECHNOLOGIES

Fixed line telephone penetration varies considerably from urban to rural regions, although the number of towns and settlements without fixed telephone access has been decreasing rapidly. According to the Ministry for Communications and Informatisation of the Russian Federation, the overall penetration rate was 30.0 percent at the end of 2005

[1] Quoted in "Online Trade Still Unregulated", Alina Travina, Moscow News, N 46, 2005 5

and 30.4 in the middle of 2006.[2] Similarly, mobile take-up, as elsewhere in the region, is booming, with a growth in penetration rate from 86.5 to 98.8 percent[3] from 2005 to 2006. This is calculated on the basis of active SIM cards, as reported by mobile operators. Most mobile operators define active SIM cards as those which have been used in the past six months, the exception being Megafon, where it is three months. However, high churn rates combined with high numbers of prepaid customers reduce the accuracy of this methodology. Nonetheless, the rapid growth rate is duplicated (albeit with a lower penetration rate) when other methodologies are used, such as Euroset's calculations based on the number of handsets on the market.[4]

The wireless Internet access market grew steadily in 2005. Mobile communications operators remain the main providers of wireless Internet access: the number of GPRS-users grew 250 percent and surpassed 10 million.[5] 3G licences have yet to be issued, although the tendering process is expected to be launched in early 2007. The number of wireless hotspots also grew by 250 percent. The first pre-WiMAX (Unitline)[6] and WiMAXnetworks (Synterra)[7] appeared in the country in 2005.

The number of personal computers in use is rising steadily, with a 6.9 PCs per 100 inhabitants in 2000 to 12.1 PCs per 100 inhabitants in 2006. Taking the average cost of a basic personal computer as approximately 420 Euro,[8] this equates to approximately 8 percent[9] of an average yearly salary, indicating that income levels remain a significant barrier to the take-up of both Internet access and e-commerce services. Nonetheless, one study estimated the number of people who accessed the Internet in a six month period at 23 percent[10] of the population aged 18 and over. Again, this hides a major disparity between urban and rural regions, with Svyazinvest calculating that Moscow accounts for 58 percent of Russia's aggregate Internet traffic.

The proportion of electronic trade as a percentage of total turnover of wholesale and retail trade volumes in Russia was only 0.6 percent in 2005[11] which still represented an increase from 0.5 percent in 2004 and 0.2 percent in 2003.

For additional analytical, business and investment opportunities information,
please contact Global Investment & Business Center, USA
at (202) 546-2103. Fax: (202) 546-3275. E-mail: rusric@erols.com

E-government services have been developing slowly. In 2006, Russia was ranked 43 (out of 198) in a global league table[12] of e-government services. At the moment, e-government services have limited interactivity and are predominantly at the national

[2] http://www.inforegion.ru/ru/main/infrastructure/activities/ [3] There are widely varying statistics regarding mobile penetration, although, all measures show significant increases, regardless of methodology. These figures are from the Ministry of Information Technology and Communications [4] See http://www.cellular-news.com/story/14431.php , for example. [5] http://www.iks-consilting.ru; http://www.synterra.ru/presscentre/press/43 [6] http://www.unitline.ru/eng/ [7] http://www.synterra.ru/english/ [8] In the study, a figure of 420 Euro is taken as an estimate from our local experts of the cost of a standard (permitting use of Internet and standard office applications) new computer in their countries. This figure is purely indicative in order to gain an insight into the accessibility of computer ownership for the average citizen. [9] Based on income data from the Russian State Statistics Committee from the first half of 2005, quoted in "Consumer Issues in Tomsk, Russia. http://www.bisnis.doc.gov/bisnis/bisdoc/0507IndustryTomsk.htm - last visited 15 March 2006. [10] Data collected by the Public Opinion Foundation (http://www.fom.ru) in the summer of 2006. [11] According to the National Association of E-Commerce Participants [12] Global E-Government 2004, http://www.insidepolitics.org

rather than regional government level. Russia raised its score from 3.74 (out of 10) to

3.98 from 2004 to 2005 in the Economist E-readiness rankings, attaining its best mark for its business environment (6.16) and worst for consumer and business adoption (2.0). In 2006, Russia's score went up significantly, reaching 4.30, although its overall place in the ranking system did not change, remaining in 52nd place.

GENERAL ENVIRONMENT

REGULATION AND POLICY

There are a number of trade associations representing enterprises working in the telecommunication sphere, among them the GSM Association, Electronic Data Interchange Association, and the Association of Telephone Operators and Cable Television Association.[13] Industry experts unanimously assess their role as being very limited. There are three groups that have real lobbying power: AFK Systema, AlfaGroup/Altima and Telecominvest (more specifically, the group of companies connected with the Telecominvest–Petersburg group[14]). These groups own large shares of the telecommunications business (including a substantial share in the three major mobile operators) and largely determine the direction of the development of the telecoms industry in Russia. Another influential party is Svyazinvest,[15] a 75 percent state-owned holding company that brings together traditional operators of fixed-line local and long-distance telephone communication networks. The limited effectiveness of trade associations in Russia is a direct result of the significant positions held by the most important domestic companies.

There are no limitations or restrictions for establishing trade associations (for example, minimum quotas on the number of participating companies).

There are also telecoms-specific user groups (for instance, mobile network users); however, they are also considered to be of limited effectiveness and lacking substantial influence. The Association for the Protection of Consumer Rights, on the other hand, is a household name and does have real political power. This association covers the telecommunications market as part of its wider activities, which extend to all consumer markets.

The Union of Internet Operators,[16] an Internet trade body, is focussed on network-related issues, rather than telecommunications or content regulation and is currently inactive.

For additional analytical, business and investment opportunities information,
please contact Global Investment & Business Center, USA
at (202) 546-2103. Fax: (202) 546-3275. E-mail: rusric@erols.com

NATIONAL DEVELOPMENT PLAN

The "electronic Russia" (also known as e-Russia) Plan was launched in 2000, as a ten-year programme to improve Russia's ICT infrastructure, improve the legislative framework and improve publicly available databases. The programme was approved by Parliament in 2002 and revised in 2006. The initiative was planned in four stages, a planning stage in 2002, an initial development stage in 2003-2004 and an implementation stage from 2005 to 2010. Total investment for the project is estimated at 25.5 billion RUB for the second stage and 49 billion RUB for the third stage.

Since its launch, the focus of e-Russia appears to have shifted to promoting the use of advanced information society products to improving government efficiency. The aim was to achieve this by both improving back- and front-office procedures in government as well as by boosting the amount of information available to citizens via the Internet. Examples of initiatives undertaken are the modernisation of budget planning and accounting by the Finance Ministry (a project worth 220 US$ million or 181.8 million Euro), and a major programme to improve IT use by the customs service, currently being carried out with support from the World Bank.

The e-Russia initiative has successfully led to significant regional development plans such as the e-Moscow, e-Petersburg and e-Altai programmes.

Government spending on IT is high. Indeed, spending levels have been reached which are comparable with countries such as Germany in terms of share of GDP (0.3 percent for Russia and 0.32 percent for Germany in 2004[17]). However, while there have been improvements in the level of funding devoted to e-Russia, the amounts spent fall significantly short of the intended budgets. The overall spend amounted to 20 percent of the initially planned budget in 2002 and 2003, and 28 percent in 2004. Research by Rand[18] suggests that this is due to the lack of "a powerful champion" for e-government, with lack of clarity between the Ministry for Communications and Informatisation and the Ministry for Economic Development regarding overall responsibility for the project.

In 2005, the Ministry for Communications and Informatisation developed a Concept for the Development of the Information Technologies Market in the Russian Federation. However, this has yet to be adopted.

The Concept of Regional Informatisation up to 2010 was approved by the Federal Government in July 2006. Its provisions focus on the development of regional informatisation programmes. The Concept defines the main areas in ICT development and use in the Russian regions, the procedure for the participation of the federal government bodies in the funding of regional programmes and projects and the need for development of regional e-government standard solutions including the methodological support, hardware and software.

DATA PROTECTION

The Russian parliament passed the draft Law on the Ratification of the European Convention on Automatic Processing of Personal Data[19] in November 2005, and this was signed into law by the President on 20 December 2005. This Convention

[17] Peterson, D.J,, "Russia and the Information Revolution", Rand National Security and Research Division, 2005, p.53 [18] Idem [19] Council of Europe Convention for the Protection of Individuals with regard to Automatic Processing of Personal Data: ETS No.: 108

establishes key principles, which overlap with the 1995 EU Data Protection Directive with regard to definitions in this policy area ("personal data", "processor", etc) and establishes key obligations regarding data security and special categories of data. In addition, in July 2006 the Parliament adopted the laws on Personal Data and on Information, Information Technology and Information

Protection, which aim to develop the concept of protection of personal data in the Russian Federation.

However, Russia has yet to sign the additional Protocol to that Convention which deals with "*Supervisory Authorities and Transborder Data Flows.*"[20] The Council of Europe has recognised the ratification of both the Convention and Protocol as key elements in the development of the information society and has encouraged its adoption through the World Summit on the Information Society.

CYBERCRIME AND SPAM

Russia has neither signed nor ratified the Council of Europe Cybercrime Convention and has also neither signed nor ratified the Optional Protocol to the Convention on the Rights of the Child on the Sale of Children, Child Prostitution and Child Pornography. According to the UK's Internet Watch Foundation, 37 percent of pay per view sites for child pornography that it identified appeared to be located in Russia.[21] Very little action has been taken in response to complaints about such sites forwarded from European hotlines.

Intellectual property organisations have also made complaints regarding allegedly illegal material or activities of Russian websites. Fortunately, some action can be reported on this front. In 2004, with the support of the International Federation of the Phonographic Industry (IFPI), a site selling pirated CDs was closed down and criminal charges brought against the owners.[22]

While the necessary laws appear to be in place to deal with intellectual property rights infringements, there are still gaps in legislation regarding child pornography, particularly regarding possession. Moreover, no hotline has been established to deal with reports of any kind of illegal[23] content in Russia. Business representatives, particularly Microsoft, which has taken a proactive and wide-ranging interest in dealing with illegal content in Russia, are now promoting the concept of hotlines.

The situation regarding hosting providers' liability for illegal content has become more clear. The new Law on Information, Information Technology, and the Protection of Information adopted in July 2006, should serve to give ISPs similar protection to that which they enjoy in the EU under the E-Commerce Directive (2000/31/EC).

[20] Additional Protocol to the Convention for the Protection of Individuals with regard to Automatic Processing of Personal Data, regarding supervisory authorities and transborder data flows. ETS No 181 [21] It can be disputed how many of those sites are, in fact, based in Russia. However, it does appear likely that a significant proportion is actually hosted in Russia. [22] IFPI, "International Recording Industry Applauds Action Against Russian Website Offering Pirate Discs for Sale", 23 June 2004. [23] The Russian Law of 8 December 2003 on Sexual Exploitation and Abuse prohibits the exploitation of children for pornographic purposes.

There is no specific legislation regarding the sending of unsolicited electronic communications. However, communications service providers do have the right to terminate the accounts of spammers, while civil cases for damages can also be taken, including by providers whose mail servers have been damaged or overloaded by unsolicited messages. Independently of its privacy laws, the Russian Parliament is also reviewing proposals for a strict opt-in regime for electronic messages sent for the purpose of advertising, with the burden of proof on advertisers to show that prior consent was obtained.

REGULATORY ENVIRONMENT FOR ELECTRONIC COMMUNICATIONS

INTERCONNECTION

Currently, prices for call termination in the Russian market can vary considerably, since payments between operators are governed exclusively by contractual agreements. Legislation on interconnection was, however, approved in March 2005 and came into effect on 1 January 2006 (although freedom of contract will be maintained for agreements between mobile networks).

1 FIXED LINE

Prior to the adoption of the new law on interconnection, Rostelecom had a monopoly over the provision of international long-distance services. Rostelecom provided long-distance services to Svyazinvest regional operators[24] and other communications companies. The regional and local operators would bill their customers for international and long distance services and pay Rostelecom the appropriate fee for providing the service. They would also charge Rostelecom for call termination services.

Under the new, more competitive system, providers of both domestic long-distance and international long-distance services can provide services directly to subscribers of local network operators. Operators of inter-regional telephone networks can offer interregional termination and origination of calls to long-distance operators. Moreover, local network operators are able to provide inter-regional network operators with local call origination and termination. These new rights are only available to long-distance operators if they are in technical conformity with the local and long-distance network operators, with a point of presence in every Russian administrative region, and are operationally ready to provide long-distance services to any local network subscriber. Any VoIP traffic either originating or terminating on the public switched network must be processed through a licensed long-distance operator.

In view of these changes, extensive building of networks is currently taking place, as operators prepare to take advantage of the new situation as soon as possible. Industry players have indicated to the study team that calls for proposals for suppliers generally designate January 2007 as the deadline for delivery of services. As a result, it appears that most of the new, competitive services will be launched at approximately that time. So far, only MTT Telecom has launched long-distance services in competition with Rostelecom. Nine long-distance operators were granted licences in November 2005, meaning that both alterative operators and the legal framework are now in place to boost competition in the long-distance market.

[24] The joint-stock company Svyazinvest was created during the transition to market economy mechanisms by merging a majority of the regional State telecommunications enterprises. Svyazinvest covers seven inter-regional communications companies (ICC), integrating 72 regional operators, and holds a 51 percent stake in Rostelecom (an operator of international and inter-regional telecommunications).

There are industry concerns, however, that technical conformity procedures are generally cumbersome in Russia and could be detrimental to the introduction of competition. For instance, concerns were expressed by market players regarding the Russian conformity assessment procedures for interconnection billing systems, which are considered expensive, time-consuming and significantly in excess of requirements in other countries. Due to the unpredictability of the procedures, concerns were raised that this could result in delays to the launch of the new services.

Rostelecom has also had concerns with billing procedures. In a press release[25] in December 2005, Rostelecom explained that it had difficulties in organising its activities to bill subscribers directly and, consequently, announced its intention to enter into contracts with local Svyazinvest and other network operators to act as their agents. Rostelecom also expressed concerns regarding the compatibility of billing and traffic measurement and general worries regarding the impact of these new arrangements on its business.

Further competition is expected to be introduced into the market with the implementation of carrier preselection. Legislation facilitating carrier preselection is now in force, with codes having been allocated to two providers and licences having been provided to a further 18, according to the Ministry for Communications and Informatisation. The preselection code is 8-NN

In total, about 3,300 fixed line communications licences have been issued: 3,200 for local services and 100 for interregional services. 20 long-distance licences have also been issued. The inter-regional and international telephony market had a combined value of 3 billion US$ /2.48 billion Euro in 2005 according to the Ministry for Communications and Informatisation. This represents 13 percent of telecoms revenues. IKS Consulting estimates that 10 percent of this market consists of VoIP services.

SMP Obligations

The 2003 Law on Communications states (in Article 19(1) and (2)):

In order to guarantee non-discriminatory access to the communication services market, the operator having significant market power in the communication market must, in comparable circumstances, establish equal interconnection agreements and traffic conditions with the network operators providing similar services, as well as supply information and provide connection and traffic services to these operators on the same terms and with the same quality as for its structural divisions and/or affiliated unit.

Refusal by the operator having significant market power to conclude a network interconnection agreement is prohibited, except for cases wherein the network interconnection and interaction contradict the network operator licence conditions or regulatory acts determining the establishment and functioning of the unified electronic communication network in the Russian Federation.

[25] "Rostelecom to switch to a new system of interaction with Russian operators and end users in providing long-distance services," 15 December, 2005, http://www.rustocks.com/index.phtml/Pressreleases/0/1/8647 .

The Law on Communications also includes a provision requiring the operator with significant market power, but not the other operators, to publish a reference interconnection offer (RIO). Article 19 of the Law about Communications declares in this regard:

Based upon the rules of network interconnection and interaction, the operators having Significant Market Power in the communication market shall establish the conditions for connecting other communication networks to their own network, which specify the usage of the network resources and traffic and include general technical, economic, and information conditions as well as property relations.

The conditions for connecting communication networks should stipulate:

Technical requirements pertinent to the network interconnection;

Volume, procedure, and timeline of network interconnection activities and their distribution between the interacting operators;

Traffic procedure for the interacting operators' networks;

Location of the connection points for the communication networks;

Register of connection and traffic services provided;

Cost of connection and traffic services and the payment schedule;

Procedure of interaction between the communication networks' management systems.

SMP operators are required to publish the aforementioned conditions within seven days of determining the network connection conditions and to submit them to the regulator, RosSvyazNadzor.

Order no. 127 on the Organisation of Activities Concerned with the Consideration of Telecommunications Carriers' Requests Concerning the Issues of Telecommunication Networks Interconnection and Interaction issued by the Minister of Information Technologies and Communications on 10th November 2005 came into force on 1st of January 2006. The new rules place obligations on companies which, on their own or with partners, control 25 percent of capacity or traffic – a ruling very similar to the initial SMP threshold imposed by the first EU telecommunications regulatory framework. Operators under this category need to publish a basic list of prices for interconnection and data transmission services within 20 days of having received its notification from the RosSvyazNadzor. The latter then approves or rejects the prices (see the section below on cost accounting for more details).

Under this law, operators may complain about the refusal to provide interconnection, the prices offered and/or the technical requirements for interconnection, and appeal for clarification of other issues concerned with the relationships between the networks and the operators. If the demands of the regulated operator are inconsistent with the current regulatory framework, the Federal Service for Telecommunications Supervision has the power to make a ruling imposing an alterative solution. Under the procedure foreseen by the new rules, the Federal Service requests (and must receive within 10 days) all necessary documents and information (written explanation, network interconnection specifications, contracts in force, technical and organisational information about the operation of networks, etc.) from the regulated operators. Decisions should be made within 60 days if at least one of the parties to the network interconnection is a regulated operator, or within 30 days in other cases.

The illegal termination of VoIP calls on fixed or mobile networks has not emerged as a significant problem in Russia.

ISPs cannot normally share dial-up revenue with fixed line telephony providers.

2 MOBILE

In January 2006, new arrangements for mobile-fixed interconnection were also implemented. Up until January 2006, the tradition in Russia had been for the mobile operator to pay all the expenses incurred during interconnection with fixed telecommunications operators. Under the newly implemented regime, mobile operators are permitted to terminate domestic calls from the fixed line network without incurring charges that have to be passed on to their customers. The current call termination price for mobile-to-fixed interconnection is about 1 Eurocent. A few years ago, the price reached 4 Eurocents. Call termination for fixed-to-mobile is free for the fixed operator. With regard to interconnection between mobile operators, the mobile operators pay the cost of the traffic to their partners. As of 1 July 2006, mobile subscribers no longer have to pay to receive incoming calls.

The Russian mobile market is relatively active. There are about 200 companies licensed to provide mobile services in Russia. Currently, there are 56 Russian members of the GSM Association, of which 49 are active and seven have services planned. A complete, up-to-date list with links to network maps can be accessed at: http://www.gsmworld.com/roaming/gsminfo/cou_ru.shtml

NUMBERING

RosSvyazNadzor, working under the jurisdiction of the Ministry for Communications and Informatisation, is responsible for allocating numbering resources in Russia.

Numbering resource allocation in Russia is conducted purely on an "on application" basis; therefore each network service provider has equivalent access to these resources. There have never been any problems or complaints from operators regarding access to numbering resources.

Number portability is not currently available. However, the Ministry for Communications and Informatisation has created a taskforce on mobile number portability, which includes representatives of the Ministry, the telecommunications sector and the scientific community. This taskforce is looking at possibilities for the introduction of, and procedures for, the provision of number portability. The Ministry for Communications and Informatisation published draft documents on general provisions and engineering procedures for the implementation of mobile number portability in April 2006. End-user fees for portability are not currently envisaged. As a consultation on the draft documents is still underway and the legislative basis has yet to be established, it is unlikely that portability will be available for several years. The deputy IT and Telecommunications Minister is quoted as saying that it is not expected before 2012.[26] Certain issues that have been experienced elsewhere, such as problems with price transparency, will need to be addressed for this to be implemented successfully.

There are no non-geographic numbers available for fixed providers, apart from the special codes used by the emergency services.

The applicable national rule for numbering is Government Resolution 350, which was adopted in 2004. Work is underway at the moment to change the Russian numbering plan to bring it more into line with international ITU standards, with some changes already made and the final alterations currently being implemented.

RIGHTS OF WAY AND FACILITIES SHARING/COLLOCATION

At present, about 89 percent of Russia's telecommunications infrastructure belongs to Svyazinvest, with the remaining 11 percent divided among alternative operators. The alternative service providers and their infrastructure successfully compete with the traditional providers on the fixed telephony market in the corporate segment, which creates competition primarily in large cities. In the home user segment of the fixed-line communications market, the de facto monopolists in Russia are the service providers that are part of the Svyazinvest holding group (75 percent+1 shares are owned by the state). This is due to the lack of effective, competition-conducive regulation and the subsidisation of local call charges (at the expense of long-distance calls, which are therefore relatively expensive), as well as the incumbent providers' inherited advantages, namely the entire, extensive infrastructure created in the Soviet era.

The free and equal rights of providers to access infrastructure and network facilities are stipulated in the Federal Law on Communication (2003). In theory, there are equal rights for building new infrastructure; however in practice, operators often experience difficulties when it comes to receiving permission for building work.

Procedures for facilities sharing are more or less non-existent. However, a Decision has been under discussion since 2005 to address this issue and to regulate in favour of nondiscriminatory access to network infrastructure. Discussions have yielded a Government Resolution developed by the Federal Antimonopoly Service, although at the time of writing in December 2006, agreement has not yet been reached with the other relevant government bodies (the Ministry of Justice, the Ministry of Information Technologies and the Ministry for Communications and Informatisation).

As for an appeals procedure for any disputes, there is unlikely to be any formal process until an independent regulator is established, which will almost certainly not happen for several years.

TARIFF POLICY

The Government of the Russian Federation plans to remove current price regulation. This will ultimately lead to increased prices for local calls and reductions in the prices of long-distance calls. The new Rules on Interconnection,[27] in force since 1 January 2006, require that, by 1 January 2008, the price for the local and zonal origination of calls should include be rebalanced.

Clear progress has already been made towards tariff rebalancing, as can be seen in the relationship between Rostelecom's traffic growth and revenue from 2000 to 2004: while revenue from international calls fell from 193 million US$ to 126 million US$ (159.5 million to 104 million Euro) from 2000 to 2003 (-34 percent), traffic increased in the same period from 897 million to 1,207 million minutes (+34 percent).[28] On the other hand, local tariffs are on the rise: local tariffs increased by 30 percent in the second half of 2005.

As regards the difference between the total number of minutes for incoming and outgoing international calls, outgoing international traffic is by far the more dominant. A significant proportion of outgoing traffic is through IP–telephony, illustrating the importance of the development of the IP-telephony market in the general growth of the Russian telecommunications market. Moreover, a shift is taking place in the price of international calls due to the use of VoIP technologies, with heavy losses to traditional international telephony being estimated by some analysts.[29]

COST ACCOUNTING

The Ministry for Communications and Informatisation issued an Order on Cost Accounting in March 2006.[30] Subsequently, in May 2006, it has issued an Order by which it approved the methodology for the calculation of economically justified costs and standard profit for interconnection and traffic transmission as well as universal communication services. This methodology is intended for the operators designated as holding significant market power as well as for universal services operators. It defines the procedure for cost and profit calculation basing on book-keeping and accounting separation, the recommendations for which were also approved by the above-mentioned order.

The adoption of these documents is an important step towards ensuring that pricing mechanisms for the provision of the telecommunication services and interconnection will

[27] Rules for State Regulation of Prices for Interconnection Services and Traffic Transmission Services provided by Operators having Significant Market Power in the General Use Telecommunication Networks [28] Anton Klimenko, Rostelecom, Brunswick UBS Telecom Conference, March 2005 [29] See http://www.gii.co.jp/press/ir30302_en.shtml for more information. [30] Order on methodological recommendations for separate accounting for telecommunications operators' revenues and expenditures by the types of their business activities, telecommunications services provided, and the parts of the telecommunications networks used for providing said services be more transparent and more cost oriented. These documents were developed on the basis of EU experience in this field.

For additional analytical, business and investment opportunities information, please contact Global Investment & Business Center, USA at (202) 546-2103. Fax: (202) 546-3275. E-mail: rusric@erols.com

UNIVERSAL SERVICE

The Government's policy on universal service is articulated in the 2003 Law on Communication, which introduced new rules relating to universal service.

Universal service is also regulated by five Government Resolutions adopted in April 2005:

On the measures for organising universal network communication service provision;

On establishing the rules for state regulation of tariffs for universal communication services;

On establishing the rules for reimbursing the losses incurred by universal service providers when providing universal network communication services;

On establishing the rules for the tendering process for the right to provide universal services;

On establishing the rules for accumulating and spending the resources of the universal service fund.

The Order on Cost Accounting (detailed above) also covers costs related to the provision of universal communication services.

The national system for the provision of universal service in Russia is, insofar as can be assessed, absolutely unique and its implementation has only just begun. The four key elements of universal service in Russia can be described as follows:

(1) Definition of Universal Service. The Law on Communications introduces the following definition of universal service and its scope (which is narrower than in the EU):

(a) Universal networked communication services include:

Telephone communication services, including the use of public phone booths; and

Data transfer services and Internet access services through public access points.

(b) The procedure and the starting time for communication service provision as well as the tariff regulations for universal services are determined by the Government of the Russian Federation based upon a report from the RosSvyazNadzor and taking into account the following aspects:

The time it takes for a user to access a phone booth, without using any means of transportation, should not exceed one hour;

Each settlement should have at least one phone booth providing free access to emergency services;

All settlements with over five hundred people should have at least one public access point providing access to the Internet.

(2) In order to reimburse the losses incurred by universal service providers for providing universal network communication services, the universal service fund has been established. All public network service providers are obliged to pay into this fund.

(3) Universal service providers are selected in open competitions, which are conducted on a municipal or regional basis.

(4) The prices charged for universal service are regulated.

For additional analytical, business and investment opportunities information, please contact Global Investment & Business Center, USA at (202) 546-2103. Fax: (202) 546-3275. E-mail: rusric@erols.com

The five Resolutions specify mechanisms for the creation of the Universal Service Fund. This is funded through a direct levy on communications companies, which is currently

1.2 percent of income from end users (i.e. not including revenue from interconnection and routing).

The regulator has declared the legislation should take into consideration all concerns expressed by those providers who may qualify for the provision of services under the universal service regime.

The adopted regulatory acts stipulate neutral, non-biased conditions for the provision of universal service. There has not yet been any test to see whether this will be accurately implemented, as the regime was only recently initiated.

The tendering process for the provision of universal services is being undertaken under the authority of the Ministry for Communications and Informatisation. The tenders for the last 14 regions are to be conducted in January - July 2007 (two tenders per region, one for pay phones and a second for Public Internet Access Points).[31] Regional Svyazinvest companies are among the winners in the first round of this process for telephony services, while the Russian Postal Service (Pochta Rossii) has won a significant number of PIAP tenders, others being won by local and interregional ISPs. No significant problems regarding the tendering process have so far been reported.

Minister Reiman stated in the Federal Assembly in July 2005 that there were still 46,000 population centres in Russia without fixed line telephone services. (By the end of 2005 this number had fallen to 42,000.[32]) The Minister stated that the intention was to provide access to all population centres with more than 500 inhabitants.

Unlike the European Union's current regulatory framework, other universal service concepts, such as calling line ID and competition in directory services, are not regulated by national legislation, nor are they covered by other relevant regulation. Whilst the selective barring of incoming calls is possible, and is indeed used by subscribers, there is no regulation in place that provides for its availability.

Existing regulatory acts do not include any special provisions regarding disadvantaged users (such as Braille bills for blind users). However, the general rules on service provision mention the necessity of providing access to services for disadvantaged users (this is specifically mentioned in the general rules of the Russian Law on Consumer Rights). However, there has been no follow-up to this principle within the framework of sector-specific electronic communications legislation.

LOCAL LOOP UNBUNDLING

Local loop unbundling has not been implemented in Russia and there appears to be little prospect of it being introduced in the foreseeable future. Nonetheless, some recent legislation appears to be edging in this direction. For example, a subscriber can request that his line be used by two different operators (i.e. shared access). This, together with the first tentative steps towards the introduction of comprehensive cost accounting rules, is helping to create a framework within which LLU could more easily be introduced.

LEASED LINES

Leased lines are available in almost all regions in Russia. However, there are significant differences in terms of price and choice between rural settlements and large cities. In the former, prices are high and competition is severely limited; while in the latter prices are lower, with significant competition between suppliers. There is no legislative support to ensure that *all* areas are covered by at least one supplier. The high-speed, dedicated Internet access market is supplemented by DSL providers, particularly in Moscow and St Petersburg.

For additional analytical, business and investment opportunities information, please contact Global Investment & Business Center, USA at (202) 546-2103. Fax: (202) 546-3275. E-mail: rusric@erols.com

No obligatory cost accounting schemes have been adopted within the framework of current rules or regulations, with the exception of operators designated as having SMP. In those cases where leased lines are provided by the incumbent operator, its activity is controlled by the anti-monopoly authority, which regulates the price using rules for calculating the appropriate price on a case-by-case basis.

There are no specific regulatory requirements for leased lines (e.g. transparency, nondiscrimination and cost orientation). The provision of leased lines is regulated by antimonopoly legislation and there are only general principles relating to the provision of non-discriminatory access to telecommunications infrastructure. However, there are plans to adopt sector-specific legislation on leased lines in a joint act of two authorities: the Ministry for Communications and Informatisation and the Anti-monopoly Authority.

On average, a leased line can be provided within one to two weeks in Russia. The situation varies in certain cases: for instance, the technical work for the provision of a DSL line can be completed within hours; however when a new physical line must be laid, it can take several months, as it depends on the time it takes to obtain all the necessary permits.

Overall, leased lines of any standard speed are available; price is usually the only limiting factor in their use.

According to Rosstat data, 19.8 percent of medium-sized and large businesses used leased lines at the beginning of 2006. It should be noted, however, that the statistical questionnaire used by Rosstat for collecting this data uses the term "leased line" in a generic sense, making no distinction between xDSL lines and leased lines in the traditional sense.

The most common leased lines in Russia have 2 mbps capacity and cost the end user from 300 US$ (249 Euro) to 500 US$ (419 Euro per month). The leased lines market between operators is closed and prices are not published, as they are usually subject to confidentiality agreements between the parties.

There are no inherent technical limitations for interconnection between leased lines and public telecommunications networks.

MOBILE SERVICES

There are about 250 mobile operators in the Russian market. The mobile market represents about 40 percent of telecoms market revenue and breaks down (in September 2006) as follows: MTS has 34 percent, Vimpelcom 32 percent, Megafon 19 percent and others 15 percent.

Third generation (3G) services are non-existent in the country and no 3G licences have been issued in Russia to date. UMTS was selected as a 3G top priority standard in Russia. Minister Reiman stated in October 2006 that 3G licences will begin to be issued in 2007. 3G networks are developing in Russia de facto due to the efforts of CDMA-450 operators: since late 2005. SkyLink[33] is providing high-speed data transmission services (SkyTurbo) based on CDMA2000 1xEV-DO technology in Moscow and St. Petersburg.

Telephone retailer Euroset has announced plans to launch an MVNO in 2006, although this had not happened at time of writing (December 2006). The study team has not been able to identify any specific regulatory barriers to the creation of MVNOs.

According to Rosstat, in 2005 there were 104 mobile phones per 100 households (55 phones in 2004).

According to official data,[34] the national level of mobile penetration in Russia, at the end of 2004, was 50 subscribers per 100 people - in the Moscow Region it exceeded 100 subscriptions per 100 people.

Government figures[35] from the end of 2005 indicated that there were 123.5 million mobile subscribers (86.5 subscriptions per 100 people), with

[33] http://www.skylink.ru [34] http://www.minsvyaz.ru/site.shtml?id=2753 [35] Widely quoted, for example at TMCNet, "Daily News Headlines for 30 December 2005", 31 December 2005

134 subscriptions per 100 inhabitants in Moscow and 118 subscriptions per 100 inhabitants in St Petersburg[36]. According to the J'Son & Partners Agency (a consultancy), the number of subscribers reached 147.2 million and the official nationwide penetration rate went up to 103 percent, reaching 151% in Moscow region in September 2006[37].

It should be noted that the official number of subscriptions does not reflect the true proportion of the population using mobile phones. Data from a special study by Euroset[38] (which looked at the number of handsets in use) indicates there are 38 percent fewer actual mobile subscribers than is reported by the mobile service providers, market analysts and the Ministry for Communications and Informatisation.

Market researchers and consultancies offer various further insights into the level of mobile phone use in Russia. According to the Levada Centre, a market research agency, the proportion of the population that uses mobile phones reached 58 percent at the end of 2006 compared with 2 percent in 2000.[39] The ROMIR consultancy suggests that penetration reached 56 percent[40] at the end of 2005. The Sotovik Agency indicates that 65 percent of the population used a mobile phone at least once in April 2006. While Russia uses essentially the same methodological basis as EU countries to establish the penetration rate, the fact that the vast majority of Russian users are prepay customers[41] and ongoing high churn rates means that this methodology produces less reliable results in Russia.

Pre-paid mobile users represent more than 80 percent of mobile consumers.

The cost of an SMS is about five times less than a one minute mobile-to-mobile call, therefore SMS is a popular means of communication. On average, around 15-25 SMS are sent by mobile subscribers per month. The highest recorded number of outgoing and incoming SMS via any service was through one of the youth-targeted tariffs from Sonic Duo (the Moscow branch of Megafon) which reached 120 SMS per month (on average for subscribers of this tariff).

GPRS services are expanding quickly. In Russia, there are currently over ten million GPRS users and since the beginning of 2004, the number of GPRS users has grown exponentially. Taking Megafon North West[42] as an example, GPRS services are included in the basic subscription, with downloads charged at 0.40 US$ (0.33 Euro) per megabyte from 8am until midnight and 0.10 US$ (0.08 Euro) from midnight until 8am. MTS launched iMode services in late 2005.

It is estimated that ten to fifteen percent of mobile users in Russia avail of GPRS services. Megafon is the most advanced in rolling out EDGE services, covering 39 regions, followed by Vimpelcom in 13 regions and MTS in eight regions.

As experienced in a number of European Union Member States, there is a steady trend of migration of traffic from the fixed telecommunications network to the mobile communications network, which has begun to influence the wider development of fixed-line telephony.

Geographically, the proportion of the country's territory covered by mobile networks is negligible; however, according to different estimates, between 80 percent and 95 percent of the country's population reside in those areas covered by mobile networks, according to operators.

Revenues from Mobile Communication Services.

	2002		2003	2004	2005

For additional analytical, business and investment opportunities information, please contact Global Investment & Business Center, USA at (202) 546-2103. Fax: (202) 546-3275. E-mail: rusric@erols.com

Revenues from mobile communication services (billion USD / billion Euro)		3.2 / 2.6	4.9 / 4	7.9 / 6.5	10.5 / 8.7
ARPU (total), USD / Euro including:		20.5 / 16.9	15.1 / 12.5	11.9 / 9.8	8.7 / 7.2
	ARPU (voice), USD / Euro	19.5 / 16.1	13.8 / 11.4	10.4 / 8.6	7.6 / 6.3
	ARPU (value added services), USD / Euro	1.0 / 0.83	1.3 / 1.07	1.5 / 1.23	1.1 / 0.8

In terms of market leaders, by the end of August 2005, VimpelCom was the leading company in the Volga Region, Siberia and the Central Region (excluding the Moscow Licence Area); MTS remains the leader in the Far East and the regions of the Northern Caucasus and the Urals; and Megafon enjoys the largest subscriber base in the North-West.

The top local operators are Baykalwestcom[44] (10.6 percent of the mobile market in the Far East), SMARTS[45] (over 15 percent of the market share in the Volga region), Uralsvyazinform[46] (22 percent of the market in the Urals region), and Yeniseytelecom[47] (8.4 percent in the Siberian market).

SATELLITE SERVICES

NTV+[49] is the only operator in the market providing satellite TV connection services for home users in Russia. There are widely differing estimates of the penetration rate for such services, ranging from less than 1 percent of households (according to the consulting company MIS-Inform,[50] which equates to about 520,000 subscriptions) to 360,000 subscriptions (according to the international television company Zone Vision[51]). Several companies, such as IP Net,[52] offer satellite connection services for the business sector.

A range of services, which include IP uplink/downlink, telephony, and IP connection are on offer for resale by ISPs.

The costs of satellite services can be very attractive in comparison with fixed-line charges in remote regions and telephones with a satellite connection are likely to become increasingly competitive in remote regions.

The satellite communications providers' market share is very small, representing about 0.7% of total Russian telecoms revenues in 2005[53]. The Ministry for Communications and Informatisation's figures show that in 2005, "*radio networks, radio and televised broadcasting, and satellite connection,*" accounted for 3.6% of the telecommunications and broadcasting industry's overall revenues.[54]

As far as universal service is concerned, there are territories that will certainly require satellite connections for their local universal service provision. As explained above, the parameters of universal service are currently being developed and, as yet, there are no in-depth estimates of the geographical extent to which satellite connections will be used.

NRENs are supported by satellite. In Russia, two of the eleven science and educational networks use satellite channels as their communication means: RADIO-MSU,[55] which was created as the research network focusing on nuclear physics; and the university network RUnet.[56]

According to satellite data and telephony service provider Globalstar, the cost of 1 minute call by satellite mobile phone from Russia to a fixed line in Russia is $1.40 / 1.16 Euro,[57] whereas Rostelecom's maximum intercity communications tariff is about $0.30 / 0.25 Euro per minute.[58]

For additional analytical, business and investment opportunities information, please contact Global Investment & Business Center, USA at (202) 546-2103. Fax: (202) 546-3275. E-mail: rusric@erols.com

Problems regarding licensing for using services from foreign-owned satellites are described in the licensing and authorisation chapter (above).

STATUS OF THE NATIONAL REGULATORY AUTHORITY (NRA)

Russia does not have an independent National Regulatory Authority. Regulation of the ICT sector is managed primarily by the Ministry for Communications and Informatisation through RosSvyazNadzor (Federal Telecommunications Agency), which reports directly to it. This Ministry covers post, telecommunications, radio, TV and satellite communications, licensing, standardisation, international cooperation, research, investment strategy and information technologies.

LICENSING AND AUTHORISATION

Licensing in Russia is governed principally by the 2003 Federal Law on Communications. This law has greatly simplified procedures for obtaining communications licences in Russia.

There is only one licence required for a public switched mobile network operator to operate lawfully. This is called the Mobile Network Communication licence.

Public fixed-line telephone operators, however, require an array of licences, depending on the service provided: a licence for the local network, for the regional network, for the long-distance network, for the public phone booth network, and for the pubic access nodes.

Internet access providers must obtain two licences: one for data transfer and another for "telematic" (data transmission and storage) services.

According to the Law on Communications, the cost of licences for the provision of most communication services including mobile network communications, local fixed-line telephone network, regional network, long-distance network, and mobile satellite communication, is set at 15,000 roubles or 435 Euro (for any licence), multiplied by the number of regions where services are to be provided.

The cost of licences for other communication services, including the provision of network channels within the territory of one region, data transfer (excluding the transfer of voice information), telematic services and telegraph communication services is set at 1,000 roubles or 30 Euro (for any licence), multiplied by the number of regions where services are to be provided.

Currently, operators that wish to avail of services provided by a Russian satellite have a waiting period of up to six weeks for a licence to be awarded. However, foreign satellite providers complain that an equivalent licence to use a foreign satellite can take up to six months.

According to the Law on Communications, where tenders are issued for the provision of communication services (in case of frequency spectrum shortage etc.) the cost of a licence for the provision of such services is fixed by the terms of the tender.

RUSSIAN COMMUNICATIONS LICENCES

Fixed	Mobile	Data
1. fixed-line local telephone networks, excluding public pay-booth networks and public access nodes	1. personal paging networks	1. data transfer services (excluding transfer of voice information)

For additional analytical, business and investment opportunities information, please contact Global Investment & Business Center, USA at (202) 546-2103. Fax: (202) 546-3275. E-mail: rusric@erols.com

2. long-distance fixed-line telephone networks	2. public mobile radio networks	2. telematic communications services
3. dedicated fixed-line telephone networks	3. dedicated mobile radio networks	
4. regional fixed-line telephone networks	4. switched public cellular mobile networks;	
5. public pay-booth telephone networks	5. mobile satellite radio communications	
6. public access telephone nodes.		

SPECTRUM

The State Commission on Radio Frequencies, part of RosSvyazNadzor (which is part of the Ministry for Communications and Informatisation of the Russian Federation), oversees spectrum management and allocation, produces a table of prospective spectrum allocation, and monitors spectrum utilisation.

The Directive on the Procedure for Allocating Radio Frequencies for Radio-Electronic Devices of Various Purposes in the Russian Federation regulates frequency allocation.

Any plans for spectrum liberalisation and trading focus primarily on the issue of spectrum conversion. The 2004 report of the Minister for Information Technology and Communication and the corresponding programme for activities in 2005 included provisions to substantially expand the segment of the spectrum allocated for civil use. Most of the available spectrum is reserved for military use. Less than 10 percent of spectrum is currently available for civil use.

As in most countries, frequency ranges available for public use include the 2.4 GHz band, which is used for Wi-Fi.

REGULATORY ENVIRONMENT FOR ONLINE SERVICES

DIGITAL SIGNATURES

In contrast to the EU Directive, the current Russian Federal Law on the Electronic Digital Signature of 2002 defines specific parameters for digital signatures: a digital signature must be received using one of the cryptographic algorithms in use at the time of the law's enactment, making it completely technology specific. No other forms of electronic document verification are included in the provisions and no other federal laws stipulate the possibility to use other forms of digital personal signatures.[59] On the other hand, insofar as signatures meet the requirements of the law, they are recognised as functionally equivalent to handwritten signatures.

A new law, which overhauls the existing legislation, is currently going through the legislative process. As it is based on the German digital signatures law, the new Russian law is in line with EU legislation and appears to resolve many of the existing legislation's shortcomings. The draft has been agreed by the relevant ministries and is (at time of writing in December, 2006) awaiting Parliamentary approval. Plans are also underway to remove provision of digital signatures from the list of activities subject to licensing requirements.

The current law's principle of dividing information systems into general-use and corporate systems essentially transfers the legal basis regarding the use of an electronic signature into the domain of general contractual regulations. These regulations do not allow for the establishment of general conditions for recognising the legal status of a document signed with an electronic digital signature, thus leading to additional legal complications.

Only one article of the current law addresses the issue of recognising foreign electronic digital signatures. However, the legislation does not specify the criteria to be met for a foreign digital signature to be recognised in the Russian Federation as having legal status – these are to be assessed on a case-by-case basis. The use of foreign electronic signatures therefore remains uncertain.

Despite these shortcomings, which substantially limit the use of electronic digital signatures in all potential sectors, recent changes to public procurement rules encourage the use of electronic documentation in Russia. The Federal Law on the Placement of Orders for the Procurement of Commodities, Execution of Works, and Provision of Services for Public and Municipal Needs was adopted in July 2005. This law replaced the 1999 law, which was considered by industry to suffer from a number of omissions, and includes important amendments covering the usage of ICT. In particular, article 16 deals with publishing public information on tenders on the government website; article 23 regulates the provision of tender documentation upon request (made

[59] The new law "On the information, information technologies, and protection of information," adopted in July 2006, in addition to digital signature, provides for the use of 'other analogues of manual signature', the use of which equals electronic documents to paper documents unless otherwise specified in the federal legislation.

in an electronic form); and other clauses regulate the submission and processing of electronic applications, etc. This Law is important in that it is one of the only laws that stipulate the equality of electronic and paper documents. In addition, this law provides for the regional authorities to independently regulate the usage of electronic documentation before the introduction of such regulation at the federal level. However, the new procurement rules have not lead to the use of e-procurement yet, due to the need to pass additional implementing legislation, which has not yet been done.

PAYMENT SYSTEMS

The somewhat limited use of electronic channels for financial services in Russia is partially caused by the relatively low availability of banking payment cards. According to the Institute for the Information Society (IIS), only 16.7 percent of Muscovites possess such cards. Payment mechanisms using banking cards have not yet been fully established or implemented, associated transaction costs are relatively high for the vendor, and payments (even through the Internet banking systems) are time-consuming. Debit and credit cards are only accepted by 8.1 percent of Internet trade companies, and the same number use other electronic payment systems (PayCash, WebMoney, etc.). The transfer from offline payments to online systems is also hindered by insufficient critical mass and inconvenience of use of the Russian payment systems, Webmoney[60] and "Yandex-Den'gi,"[61]. Consumers also have concerns about the security of electronic payment systems. All of these factors lead to a situation in which the domestic B2C system has adopted the "cash to courier" payment scheme.

According to research company MASMI's April 2006 survey, only 10.5 percent of Russian Internet users had made payments with electronic money over the Internet and 5.1 percent had conducted other financial operations online.[62]

In summary, the following factors impede the expansion of individual use of online financial transactions in Russia:

Underdeveloped online financial services infrastructure (both in terms of the range of services and the number of credit and other financial institutions providing such services);

Low general level of trust in Russian financial organisations;

Lack of an adequate legislative basis regulating online financial transactions, which would reduce the potential risks for the user; and

Low purchasing power of the population, leading to low demand for financial services (due to the majority of the population's lack of substantial disposable income).

USE OF ELECTRONIC COMMUNICATIONS SERVICES

FIXED TELEPHONY PENETRATION

According to the Ministry for Communications and Informatisation of the Russian Federation, in 2005, the number of telephones on the public network reached 42 million, compared with 38 million in 2004, 36 million in 2003 and 23 million in 1992. Telephone density (the number of subscriber lines per 100 people) amounted to 28.8 percent in 2004 and 30.0 percent at the end of 2005.[63]

Telephone density across the country is extremely disparate. As one would expect, cities have the main share of telephone lines. Although all constituent parts of the Russian Federation have access to the main networks, a considerable number of rural zones still do not have automatic intercity and international communications. The number of towns and settlements without access to the telephone network dropped from 54,000 in 2000 to 42,000 in 2005.[64] Determined efforts to improve access are likely to have significantly reduced this figure in the meantime.

There are considerable differences between the federal regions. The situation in the north-western and central regions is more favourable – their average exceeds the mean value for Russia (for example, Moscow has 58.3 telephone sets per 100 people) whilst the lowest telephone density is in the southern regions (2.8 – in Ingushetia).[65]

MOBILE USAGE

Number of Subscribers to the Mobile Communications Network in Russia

	1995	1996	1997	1998	1999	2000	2001	2002	2003	2004	2005	2006*
Number of subscribers (million people)	0.09	0.22	0.49	0.75	1.37	3.4	7.84	17.8	35.6	71.3	123.5	141.1
Number of connections (per 100 people)	0.06	0.15	0.33	0.51	0.93	2.33	5.37	12.4	24.7	49.7	86.5	98.8

According to IKS-Consulting,[66] there are currently over 4.6 million GPRS users in Russia. Since the beginning of 2004, the number of GPRS users has grown by more than 1200 percent. The proportion of GPRS users among the total number of mobile subscribers is 6.2 percent.[67] However, according to J'son & Partners, a consultancy, the mobile Internet audience still remains rather small (see the table below).

Mobile Internet Users

Parameter	Number of users, '000
WAP	
Weekly WAP audience*	~850
GPRS (2.5G)	
GPRS-enabled handsets in use	~32 000
GPRS services subscribers	~6 500
GPRS weekly audience**	~900
Internet over GPRS weekly audience	~250
EDGE (2.75G)	
EDGE-enabled handsets in use	~1 000
EDGE weekly audience	< 10
IMT-MC-450 (2.75G)	
IMT-MC-450 handsets in use	~240
Internet over INT-MC-450 weekly audience	~70

* Including WAP over GPRS users ** Including access both to WAP (view on handset screen) and HTML (view on PC) sites *Source*: J'son&Partners research

CABLE SERVICES

According to data from the World Bank, in 2003 there were 43.6 out of 1000 people subscribed to cable networks in Russia. Data from MIS-Inform, a consultancy, shows actual use of cable television services standing at 3 percent. According to IKS-Consulting, the percentage of households connected to commercial cable TV networks grew from 1 percent in 1998 to 8 percent in 2005.[68]

In terms of cable television penetration, Russia is already ahead of Southern European (countries such as Portugal), but is still behind Northern and Central Europe (countries such as Sweden and Hungary).

COMPUTER AVAILABILITY

By the beginning of 2006, the total number of personal computers in the Russian Federation had reached 17.4 million (26 computers per 100 households),[69] having grown by 16 percent compared with the previous year and over 70 percent compared with 2000. Ministry for Communications and Informatisation figures show that the number of personal computers per 1,000 inhabitants had reached 121 by the end of 2005, compared with only 69 in 2000.[70]

For additional analytical, business and investment opportunities information, please contact Global Investment & Business Center, USA at (202) 546-2103. Fax: (202) 546-3275. E-mail: rusric@erols.com

With regard to other types of electronic equipment, data is only available for Moscow. The IIS[71] reports that 5 percent of private households own PDAs and 8 percent own satellite set-top boxes.

Rosstat reports that the informatisation of Russian enterprises is progressing rapidly:

88.7 percent of medium-sized and large businesses had computer equipment[72] at the end of 2004; this figure rose to 90.1 percent by the end of 2005. The sectors of the economy exhibiting the highest levels of engagement in the information society include network communications, academia (higher and professional education), the finance sector, and information services.

With the average price of a basic computer at 420 Euro, the equivalent of 14,420 roubles, and with the average annual income in the first half of 2005 equal to 83,580 roubles (6,965 roubles per month), the cost of a computer comprises 17.25 percent of an average, annual salary. Purchasing a PC at this time is a serious burden for the typical family budget and is unaffordable for many households. This is clearly demonstrated by the limited percentage of PC owners among the Russian population. A poll covering various aspects of Russian life[73] conducted by the Public Opinion Foundation in May 2005, showed that only 20 percent of respondents (47 percent in Moscow) had ever worked on a PC while only 8 percent considered themselves familiar with the Internet. This poll also indicated that purchasing a PC was not high on the list of priorities of most Russians.

INTERNET ACCESS

According to the Public Opinion Foundation (POF)[74], in summer 2006, 57 percent of people who used the Internet at least once over the previous six months had accessed it from home. The six month Internet audience accounted for 23 percent of the population (18+) in summer 2006, compared with 19 percent in summer 2005, 16.9 percent in summer 2004 and 12.1 percent in summer 2003. The equivalent 3-monthly figures were 21 percent, 18.9 percent, 15.5 percent and 10.8 percent respectively.

Women are less active in using the Internet: 19 percent, compared with 27 percent of men.

At the same time, a significant digital divide in using the Internet persists, which is particularly apparent in the regions going through the earlier stages of Internet development. According to POF data (Georating project), in October 2005, the share of Internet users (persons who used Internet during the last 2-3 years) among the adult population varied from 42 percent in Moscow to 4 percent in areas such as the Mordovia and Severnaia Osetia republics. .

As an indication of the cost of Internet access, dial-up access services provided by one of the largest providers, MTU-Intel,[75] costs 20US$ (16.50 Euro) for 50 hours per month, and 60US$ (49.50 Euro) per month for unlimited access.

The cost of ADSL services from MTU-Intel varies between 15 US$ (12.40 Euro) and 75 US$ (62 Euro) per month for private users. Businesses pay monthly subscribers' fees varying from 60 US$ (49.60 Euro) plus 0.14US$/Mb (0.12 Euro) to 720 US$ (595 Euro), with 30 Gb of traffic included (plus 0.01 US$/Mb (0.008 Euro) for additional traffic).[76] The speed of ADSL access provided by MTU-Intel for private users varies between 160/128 and 7500/768 Kbit/sec (for upstream/downstream traffic).

Unlimited Internet access via cable is provided in Moscow by Komkor TV[77] and costs from 20 US$ (16.52 Euro) up to 90 US$ per month (74.38 Euro) depending on the speed, while the monthly fee for prepaid traffic costs 50 US$ (41.32 Euro) for 15 Gb. The speed of access by cable, provided in Moscow by Komkor TV varies from 256/128 Kbit/sec to 3000/512.[78]

Komkor (Moscow Telecommunications Corporation, also spelt COMCOR) also provides broadband access services in Moscow by fibre-optic lines at speeds of up to 100 Mbit/sec (collective access). Fixed transmission capacity of dedicated digital channels varies from 64 Kbit/sec to 622 Mbit/sec.

When using a ATM/Gigabit Ethernet network as a mainline transport network, the speed of data transmission reaches 40 Gb/sec.[79]

PUBLIC INTERNET ACCESS POINTS (PIAPS)

According to data obtained by the Ministry for Communications and Informatisation, there were 8,600 public Internet access points in Russian post offices in 2005, used by a total of 3.5 million people.[80] In 2004, there were 2,311 public Internet access points in post offices with 3,271 workstations available. Accordingly, without taking Internet cafes, and educational institutions into account (no statistical data is available for those access points), there were 0.06 public Internet access points per 1,000 people in the first quarter of 2006. However, this figure is expected to grow significantly with the rollout of PIAPs across the country as part of the government's universal service plans.

The total number of PIAPs in Russia increased from 2,493 in 2000 up to 12,004 at the end of 2005 and 13,587 in the middle of 2006.[81]

According to a 2005 IIS survey of Moscow's Internet use, only 0.3 percent of the Moscow adult population uses libraries for Internet access and 0.2 percent use government buildings for such purposes. The same survey revealed that the majority of commercial centres are connected to the Internet by high speed fibre-optic transmission systems (37.8 percent). Others are connected via xDSL (11.1 percent), LAN (27.4 percent), or cable (4.4 percent).

According to the POF survey,[82] in summer 2006, 9 percent of the half-year audience (i.e. those who accessed the Internet once over the past 6 months), or 2.1 percent of Russia's population, accessed the Internet at Internet cafes.

WIRELESS INTERNET ACCESS

J'son & Partners, a consultancy, estimates that the Wi-Fi market is developing very dynamically, having grown in 2004 by 285 percent. At the end of 2004, there were seven market leaders with ten or more hotspots (see the table below).[83]

Top Wi-Fi Providers

	Company	City	Number of public hot-spots	
1.	Tascom84	Moscow	40	
2.	Quantum85	St. Petersburg	22	
3.	Moscom86		Moscow	20
4.	Stelcom87		Moscow	17
5.	Golden Telekom88		Moscow	15
6.	Peterstar89		St. Petersburg	11
7.	EWI-FI90		Moscow	10

Source: J'son&Partners. http:/ /www.json.ru

For additional analytical, business and investment opportunities information, please contact Global Investment & Business Center, USA at (202) 546-2103. Fax: (202) 546-3275. E-mail: rusric@erols.com

Service provision is continuing to grow: In 2005 the total number of hot-spots in Russia reached 662. In 2006, the market displayed 165% growth, so it is expected that the number of hotspots will exceed 1,000 by the end of the year.[91]

Enforta (run by Prestige Internet) announced plans in early 2006 for a 50 million US$ (41.32 million Euro) investment plan to roll out WiMAX services in 28 Russian cities. Rollout should be completed by the end of 2007.

According to a 2005 IIS survey, only 0.8 percent of Moscow households used wireless access to connect to the Internet.

GENERAL STRUCTURE OF THE ICT SECTOR

In order to provide a more accurate assessment of the Russian ICT sector's state of development, it is necessary to study its structure. The following sections therefore examine the key ICT sector statistical indicators by major fields of activity (telecommunications, production and other services). A more detailed analysis of the structure of the products and services produced by this sector is then provided. The overall Russian data can then be compared with specific Moscow and St Petersburg data, as well as some international and other countries' statistics.

PRODUCTION BY MAJOR TYPES OF ECONOMIC ACTIVITY

In Russia, electronic network communications account for the majority of ICT production. The share of this segment in overall ICT production exceeds its share in the number of people employed in the ICT industry and its share of the gross salary, which indicates high productivity levels.

Interestingly, the production shares for both products and services are less than the proportion of those employed in the corresponding sectors. A conclusion can be drawn that relative labour productivity in other sectors is not as high as in the telecommunications sector (although it is necessary to compare the absolute values of this statistic for more detailed conclusions).

DISTRIBUTION OF THOSE EMPLOYED IN THE ICT SECTOR BY MAJOR ACTIVITY FIELDS

40 percent of all those employed in the ICT sector work in the equipment production sector. Notably, in Moscow, the percentage of those employed (of all those people working in the ICT sector) in service provision is much higher than the total number for the whole country (it is also much higher than the figure for St Petersburg) – 67 percent of those employed in the ICT sector in Moscow work in the telecommunications sector.

The Russian ICT industry's structure is similar to countries such as Turkey. It is different from the majority of developed countries, in terms of the lower share of ICT hardware compared with IT service provision.

DETAILED STRUCTURE OF THE ICT SECTOR: PRODUCT AND SERVICE PRODUCTION

As was highlighted above, and illustrated in the diagram below, in Russia the absolute leader in ICT products and services is the telecommunications field. Its share of total production levels is higher than its equivalent employment or gross salary shares.

Software production and IT services comprise only 5 percent of the whole ICT sector, which is substantially lower than in EU countries. Telecommunications production is mostly concentrated in Moscow, which accounts for 53 percent of all Russian production of telecommunications products

For additional analytical, business and investment opportunities information,
please contact Global Investment & Business Center, USA
at (202) 546-2103. Fax: (202) 546-3275. E-mail: rusric@erols.com

and services, and represents 19 percent of the total number of those employed throughout Russia and 31 percent of the gross salary total figures.

AVAILABILITY OF ONLINE SERVICES

Russia was placed 52nd in the 2006 Economist's E-Readiness Report list of 64 countries ranked using a system of over one hundred criteria measuring infrastructure, available services and e-skills[92] and the highest among the four countries in this study included in the report. Its overall score was 4.3 (up from 3.98 in 2005), scoring highest in business environment and lowest in consumer and business adoption.

E-COMMERCE

Rosstat estimates that only 16.9 percent of Russian businesses had their own websites at the beginning of 2006. This is an extremely low figure in comparison with the EU where the figure is on average 62 percent (from 29 percent in Latvia, to 85 percent in Sweden).[94] Such a small proportion of companies with websites represents a considerable obstacle to e-commerce development, as product marketing, electronic sales and subsequent client support via companies' websites are limited. Russian Internet stores have also adopted little of the best-practice witnessed on American or European sites; there is limited product information and the catalogue structures and navigation can be difficult.

According to Rosstat, by the beginning of 2006, the share of all businesses that used the Internet to communicate with their customers varied significantly depending on the purposes of that usage: 24.9 percent of the surveyed enterprises used the Internet to provide information about the organisation and its products; 16.3 percent to receive orders; 9.9 percent for e-settlements with customers; and 3.0 percent for after-sales customer service.

The share of all businesses that used the Internet for communication with suppliers also differed depending on the purposes of that usage: 34.5 percent of the surveyed enterprises obtained information about goods and services; 20.8 percent provided information concerning the business's product requirements; 19.4 percent placed orders; 10.1 percent paid for products.

According to Rosstat, by the beginning of 2006, 57.8 percent of businesses used e-mail (compared to 53 percent a year before).

With regards Russian consumers, according to MASMI[95] (an international social and marketing research agency), in a population survey conducted in spring 2006, 85.8 percent of Internet users regularly used e-mail and 90 percent used the Internet for information retrieval. Respondents to the survey were asked what they had recently used the Internet for. 72.4 percent had browsed the news, 65.4 percent had browsed weather forecasts, 53.3 percent had used ICQ, 47.2 percent had updated/loaded software, 18.7 percent had made purchases and 10.5 percent had made electronic payments for purchased goods and services.

According to Rambler's Top 100,[96] there were 3,510 online news and mass media sites (out of a total of 169,000 websites registered .RU sites) as of 16 May 2006 and, according to the same source, about 3,888 Russian online-shops. According to the National Association of the Participants of e-Trade (NAUET) 18.6 percent of Internet users made at least one online purchase during 2005.[97]

PROPORTION OF BUSINESSES PLACING AND RECEIVING ORDERS OVER THE INTERNET

According to Rosstat data, 19.4 percent of Russian enterprises use the Internet to place orders for materials or products. The IIS[98] reports that in the Moscow area 19.3 percent of businesses with

For additional analytical, business and investment opportunities information,
please contact Global Investment & Business Center, USA
at (202) 546-2103. Fax: (202) 546-3275. E-mail: rusric@erols.com

more than 10 employees make purchases through the Internet. This statistic is considerably lower than the EU average (29 percent) and significantly lower than the highest level (50 percent, in Great Britain). Russia also lags behind some countries with transitional economies, including Slovenia and the Czech Republic; however, the use of the Internet for placing orders for products and services in Russia is higher than in Spain (3 percent) and Portugal (8 percent).

Percentage of enterprises having purchased online in EU*, 2004, countries and Russia, 2005,** (% of all enterprises) Proportion of businesses receiving orders over the Internet

* Enterprises with 10 employees or more ** Excluding small business as of 1 January 2006 *Sources:* Eurostat NewCronos (http:/ /www.europa.eu.int) ; Rosstat survey, Form No 3 - INFORM

According to Rosstat data, 16.3 percent of Russian enterprises use the Internet for receiving orders. The IIS survey demonstrated that 16.7 percent of the capital's businesses with more than 10 employees sell their products and services via the Internet. Despite the lower overall Internet penetration in the business sector, international comparisons demonstrate that Russia has intensive rates of adoption of online sales technologies, exceeding not only the Spanish and Portuguese rates, but also those of Hungary and Lithuania. As could be expected, this remains far below the leading EU figures, such as Great Britain, for example, where the figure is 27 percent. Overall, there are encouraging signs for the development of online commercial transactions by Russian businesses.

ENTERPRISE E-COMMERCE TURNOVER

The National Association of E-Commerce Participants[99] reports that in 2004 Russian e-commerce turnover was three times the level achieved in 2003. Total volumes stood at

2.658 billion Euro and was mainly driven by the business to Government segment (B2G) and connected to the rapid increase in the amount of public contracting and use of electronic tendering. The B2G segment levelled off from 2004 to 2005, growing from 1.76 billion Euro to 1.79 billion Euro, having grown at a very high rate for the previous three years. The Russian e-commerce market was worth 3,714 million Euro in 2005.

Despite the growth of the retail trade in the Russian segment of the Internet, RUnet's overall registration levels (sites registered within the .RU ccTLD) are still far behind Europe and the US.

The share of online sales in the total revenues of Russian businesses is predictably low. The proportion of electronic trade in the total turnover of the wholesale and retail markets in Russia is only 0.6 percent. According to an IIS study, in Moscow, this indicator is substantially higher: in 2004, for businesses with more than 10 employees, the share of product and service sales conducted through the Internet amounted to 3.4 percent of total sales transactions of the capital's businesses, exceeding even the EU's average level of 2.2 percent, but remaining well below Irish (at 12.8 percent, the highest in the EU in 2004) levels. Russia falls even further behind the EU in terms of online sales transactions completed through the Internet or other networks, as such transactions in the EU in 2004 averaged 9.3 percent of total business sales (the highest figure was 13.7 percent in Great Britain).[100]

B2C/B2B TURNOVER RATIO

According to data from the National Association of E-Commerce Participants, the total volume of e-commerce in 2005 was distributed among the following market segments: business to Government (B2G) accounted for 48.38 percent (2174 million US$/ 1,797 million Euro), business-to-customer (B2C) totalled 22.7 percent (1020 million US$ / 843 million Euro) and business-to-business (B2B) made up 28.9 percent (1,300 million US$ / 1,074 million Euro). This represents a significant increase

For additional analytical, business and investment opportunities information, please contact Global Investment & Business Center, USA at (202) 546-2103. Fax: (202) 546-3275. E-mail: rusric@erols.com

in the proportion of B2B and a significant decrease in the proportion of B2G, with all segments rising overall.

Russian e-commerce market (million dollars / million Euro)

	2001	2002	2003	2004	2005
B2C	218.3 / 180.4	317.9 / 262.73	480.4 / 397.03	662 / 547.11	1,020 / 843
B2B	99 / 81.82	189 / 156.20	316.2 / 261.32	442 / 365.29	1,300 / 1,074
B2G	-	10.8 / 8.92	141 / 116.52	2,130 / 1760.33	2,174 / 1,797

Source: National Association of E-Commerce Participants, www.nauet.ru

PERCENTAGE OF ENTERPRISES HAVING MADE PURCHASES VIA SPECIALISED B2B INTERNET MARKETPLACES

The basic platforms for conducting inter-corporate business through the Internet are B2B-trading spaces, where purchase and sales transactions between enterprises can take place.[101] The advantages of using such marketplaces include the possibility of saving time on completing agreements, reducing direct costs and reducing administrative and operational expenditures.

IB Partners,[102] a consultancy, report that in March 2004, there were 154 electronic marketplaces in Russia, which encompassed virtually all spheres of business activity. By the end of that year, their number had grown to around 200. The most active participants are market pioneers, especially from the metallurgical and construction sectors, as well as market newcomers, such as from the chemicals and food industries. A number of major marketplaces have been successfully operating in the RUnet space, including b2b-energo.ru (energy), platts.ru (oil and gas products), lesprom.ru (forest industry), metall-trade.ru and metalltorg.ru (metallurgical industry), medprom.ru (medical equipment) and ematrix.ru (IT products).[103]

There are few Russian Internet marketplaces that allow the full completion of transactions online (i.e. from "browsing" to submitting an electronic payment). The exceptions are marketplaces such as b2b-energo.ru, ematrix.ru and faktura.ru. The latter, for example, provides a range of financial and security services, such as secure e-mail and digital signature services. The majority of Russian B2B marketplaces actually

[101] In general, in addition to the possibility of submitting sales/purchasing requests, a number of other services are offered to market participants free of charge, or for an additional fee: news and analysis, importing product catalogues directly from the participating company's inventory, marketing services (advertisements, e-mail lists, etc.), financial services (online payment systems, applications for financial services, such as insurance, loans and leasing), and other services. There are three types of these B2B marketplaces:

Corporate marketplaces, which are established by the selling party to keep in contact with clients and/or for the enterprise to contact its suppliers;

Industry and product marketplaces, which are generally established by a third party, created for businesses of the same industry or buying/selling similar or related products; and

Universal portals, which support the trade of a large range of products and services. There are also three groups of B2B websites in respect of their functional capabilities:

For additional analytical, business and investment opportunities information, please contact Global Investment & Business Center, USA at (202) 546-2103. Fax: (202) 546-3275. E-mail: rusric@erols.com

Catalogues enabling customers to find the providers of certain products in a certain price range;

Electronic exchanges used mainly for trading a wide range of consumer products;

Universal portals, which support the trade of a large range of products and services. [102] http://www.ibpartners.cl [103] See http://www.cnews.ru.

only amount to online searchable product and service catalogues, with subsequent transactions conducted offline.

As opposed to online marketplaces in other countries, only 20 percent of Russian online marketplaces are integrated with corporate management information systems. This is largely due to the low level of ICT usage in business processes.

According to the National Association of E-Commerce Participants, the majority of online trade transactions originate directly on businesses' websites.

ONLINE PAYMENTS AND BANKING

Electronic payments are not yet widespread in Russian e-commerce. The major share of banking operations is still conducted through traditional systems. The Russian Banking Association reports that, in 2003, 90 percent of banks still only used the traditional Client-Bank systems.[104]

According to CNews Analytics estimates, by early 2004 only 150 Russian banks provided fully-fledged Internet services for business clients – this represents approximately 17 percent of the total number of Russian banks. Very few banks have switched completely from the traditional banking systems to an Internet-based system.

Rosstat estimates that by the end of 2005 10.1 percent of Russian enterprises used the Internet for online payment purposes. 9.9 percent of businesses received electronic payments for products sold online. The IIS 2005 survey demonstrates that even among Moscow companies engaged in online sales, only 11.4 percent receive payments electronically,[105] whereas in the EU-15 the average is 23 percent, ranging from 10 percent in Italy to 44 percent in Great Britain.

The major obstacles to the widespread use of online payments and e-commerce development, including in the B2B sector, include the insufficient supply of reliable electronic payment technologies and businesses' lack of readiness to use them. Currently, payment services for B2B-market participants in Russia are provided by the multibanking system faktura.ru, the NIKoil bank,[106] Menatep SP Banks and Impeksbank.

NUMBER OF ONLINE RETAILERS

Although the first electronic stores only appeared in Russia in 1999, by early 2005, according to Rambler's TopShop, there were around 4,000 Internet stores, including their separate departments, offering electronic showcases, price-lists and possibilities to place orders online. Of the total number, 2,900 are located in Moscow and 334 are in St Petersburg. According to a SpyLog (online statistics service) study, there are 1,500 online shops, which offer Internet sales only (i.e. not including electronic showcases of their departments).

Rambler's statistics demonstrate that the Russian stores generally offer household and family goods, home electronics and appliances, computers and software, and sports and leisure goods.

For additional analytical, business and investment opportunities information, please contact Global Investment & Business Center, USA at (202) 546-2103. Fax: (202) 546-3275. E-mail: rusric@erols.com

Internet Sales Volumes of the Leading Online Stores in 2004

Store	Volume of Internet sales, million dollars (Euro)	Share of Internet sales as a proportion of total sales volumes, %
M-Video109	10 (8.26 million Euro)	2
eHouse Holding Group stores110	39 (32.23 million Euro)	N/a
Ozon111	6.21 (5.13 million euro)	53 (47- through catalogues) (44 million Euro with 39 million Euro through the catalogue)

Source: National Association of the E-Commerce Participants, http:/ /www.nauet.ru and http:/ /www.e-commerce.ru .

E-COMMERCE USE BY INDIVIDUALS

Expert studies have shown that the number of customers using Internet stores in Russia is growing much faster than the number of Internet users in general. Spylog, an online statistics service, reported that, at the end of 2004, the total number of users of Internet stores in Russia was 8.6 million people per month (this number accounts for all those visiting websites and not only those who have completed transactions). This figure represented a 10 percent increase compared with the beginning of that year. According to the results of a study conducted by the Internet-Projects company in 2004, amongst four thousand Internet store visitors, around 11 percent made regular online purchases (one or more purchases a month), while 49 percent had experience of online purchases, but not on a regular basis.[112] The customers of Internet stores comprise around 7 percent of the total monthly RUnet audience.[113] Of this number, 70 percent are from Moscow and St Petersburg, which substantially exceeds the share of these cities in the weekly audience of the Russian Internet (which is less than 50 percent).

The reasons for such concentrations of e-commerce customers in the two main Russian cities are related to a corresponding concentration of computers, Internet access (41 percent of Moscow households had Internet access in Spring/Summer 2004 according to an IIS study) and credit card users in these areas. Other Russian provinces also have lower computer literacy rates. However, there is another significant reason: delivering orders to these other regions presents practical difficulties. Most Russian online stores are registered in the capital, where their warehouses are also located. The delays in the delivery of products to remote regions are substantial, courier services are very expensive and returning purchases is therefore very complicated. The appearance of regional Internet stores, such as in the Volga region, Siberia and the Urals, does contribute to solving this problem. But, in general, the regional nodes of e-commerce development are large economic centres with a large number of affluent Internet users: Yekaterinburg, Novosibirsk, Nijny Novgorod, Rostov-on-Don and Samara, for example.

According to a Moscow population survey conducted by the IIS in 2004, 24.1 percent of the capital's Internet users purchased products and services online in the previous year. The proportion of online buyers in the EU15 in 2004 averaged 38 percent. This varied from 4 percent in Greece to 47 percent in Germany (and from 2 percent in Lithuania to 12 percent in Slovenia in the newest Member States).

The low proportion of online customers and the relatively low total volume of Internet purchases are caused by the following factors:

**For additional analytical, business and investment opportunities information,
please contact Global Investment & Business Center, USA
at (202) 546-2103. Fax: (202) 546-3275. E-mail: rusric@erols.com**

the novelty of e-commerce;

a low level of ICT and Internet access;

the population's low purchasing power; and

customers' anxiety regarding the risks of electronic trade (perceived problems of security, delivery, product quality, guarantee, and purchase returns).

According to a Romir Monitoring 2006 survey, the main reasons for not buying online were a lack of information about the goods (44% of internet users who had no experience of online purchases), lack of need (42%), delivery problems (27%) and that the process of buying online was too complicated (25%) [114].

E-GOVERNMENT

According to Rosstat, by the beginning of 2006, 27,6 percent of Russian federal authorities (including the regional offices of federal executive authorities in the regions, cities and districts, 24.2 percent of regional authorities, and 4.6 percent of local authorities had a website (compared with 10.6 percent, 18.6 percent and 2.9 percent respectively at the beginning of 2004). The federal e-Russia programme (launched in 2002 and due to run until 2010) focuses mainly on ICT usage by public authorities and the government hopes the programme will boost these figures. The Russia sits at the 50th position in the 2005 UN e-Government readiness ranking[115].

Russia's regions vary dramatically with regard to e-Government readiness. While leading regions' indices are comparable with those of European countries, the more remote regions demonstrate e-readiness which is comparable with that of some African and Latin American countries. Thus, the Moscow score corresponds to 28th position in the 2004 UN e-Government readiness ranking (between Slovenia and Czech Republic), while Ingushetia is at 122 (after Lesoto, Algeria, Tunis and Nicaragua). In other words, the gap between Russia's regions with regard to e-Government readiness is very nearly 100 countries (there are 200 countries included in the rating). There is a trend towards Russia's regions having index values corresponding to higher positions with regard to ICT infrastructure and human capital and lower positions with regard to web-presence. An example of this trend (for Moscow) is illustrated in the table below.

UN e-Government readiness ratings for Moscow[116]

Index	UN ratings corresponding to Moscow's values of indices (scores)
e-Government Readiness Index	28
Human Capital index	1
Telecommunication Infrastructure Index	22
Web-Presence index	53

Russia's comparative weakness in the use of the Internet for providing information and communicating with citizens can be explained in more detail by reviewing assessments of regional authorities' websites according to the stages of e-Government implementation (based on UN methodology). Thus, the table below shows Moscow's and Mordovia's scores with regard to the development of web-presence when compared with the highest possible scores according to UN methodology. The gap is most prominent for the indices regarding interactive, networked and, in particular, transactional presence; while the information presence (emerging and enhanced presence) of Russian authorities is more mature.

Assessment of Moscow and Republic of Mordovia authorities' web-sites in terms of the main stages of web-presence development (according to UN methodology)[117]

	Highest possible score	Moscow		Republic of Mordovia	
		Score	% of highest possible score	Score	% of highest possible score
Emerging presence	8	8	100.0%	8	100.0%
Enhanced presence	87	63	72.4%	10	11.5%
Interactive presence	68	24	35.3%	25	36.8%
Transactional presence	41	0	0%	0	0%
Networked presence	54	16	29.6%	0	0%

E-HEALTH

The remarkable achievements of global medicine in the last 20 years were made possible largely by the implementation of new, ICT-based medical technologies. The developments in the ICT field became a driving force in modern medicine and rapidly changed existing methods of diagnosis and treatment, the principles of interaction between doctors and patients and the organisation of therapy and health recovery.

Medical Institutions' Access to ICT

According to Russian Federation Ministry of Health data, in 2003 the proportion of health institutions with personal computers was 76.1 percent, those having e-mail 24.5 percent, and those with Internet access 20.8 percent. The number of computers used (i.e. as opposed to a simple figure representing a computer to doctor ratio) by health institutions reached 36 per 100 doctors in 2003; overall, there was one computer for every 10.2 medical staff.

According to Rosstat, by the end of 2005, the proportion of health institutions with personal computers was 95 percent, while 59.9 percent had Internet access. The number of computers used by health institutions was 8.5 per 100 persons employed (all staff) in those institutions.

Such levels of technical equipment availability, which remain much lower than EU averages, preclude modern ICT use both in modern medical information systems and various telemedicine technologies (see below).

Digital equipment and computer availability in medical institutions is also highly uneven, both in terms of region and institution type. There are a number of well-equipped diagnostic centres, hospitals, and polyclinics. Nonetheless, the overwhelming majority of municipal medical institutions have insufficient access to modern equipment and computers.

Computers are primarily used by medical institutions for undertaking organisational and financial tasks (accounting, personnel, medicine inventory maintenance, medical and statistical reporting, registering services provided), and to a lesser extent for supporting treatment and therapy processes.

For additional analytical, business and investment opportunities information, please contact Global Investment & Business Center, USA at (202) 546-2103. Fax: (202) 546-3275. E-mail: rusric@erols.com

Internet Resources and Services in the Medical Sphere: Use by the Population and Medical Personnel

Use of Health-related Internet Resources by the Population

According to the Rambler's Top 100 rating, a web traffic tracker, only 3.7 percent of all informational resources in RUnet were devoted to health issues in 2006.[118] This small percentage limits possibilities for citizens and specialists to use the Internet for medical research. It should also be noted that the proportion of health website visitors as a proportion of all web users amounts to only one percent. While insufficient demand for online health-related resources could explain why the figure is so low, the lack of high-quality resources also plays a role.

The 2005 IIS survey of Moscow residents demonstrated that the popularity of health and medicine related Internet resources is markedly higher in the capital; over 40 percent of the city's three-month Internet audience use these resources. For comparison, EU resident surveys conducted by the European Opinion Research Group showed that the proportion of Internet users searching for health information online amounts on average to 37-40 percent, although the timeframe for most of these users (less often than once a month) is somewhat vague.

Proportion of people who have used the Internet for health related purposes during the last three

These results should be analysed in conjunction with information and service availability factors:

The majority of visited Internet resources in the field of medicine and pharmaceuticals are dedicated to descriptions of medicines. There are over a hundred such resources. Internet pharmacies offer services to residents of larger cities; for instance, they deliver medicines directly to an office or home (there are 30 such pharmacies in Moscow).

There is little availability (and hence use) of online doctors' appointment booking services. Almost no medical centres offer the option of making a doctor's appointment through the Internet. Even in Moscow, where the "Long-distance Registration" project is underway, full doctors' schedules are only listed by two medical centres (Centre Medicina and Centre of endosurgery and lithotripsy).

There is currently low demand for information about medical institutions. However, at the moment, only large, national, medical and scientific centres and some private medical centres have full-service websites. Municipal clinics do not have their own websites, probably due to the financial resources required for such an undertaking. Information about municipal medical institutions published on the website of the Department of Health of the Russian Federation,[119] and in various "yellow pages" databases, is limited to the name, address, one or two telephone numbers and, sometimes, a map with directions.

There are a few websites that provide patients with a basic long-distance medical consultation. However, the main aim of these websites is to lead patients to making a paid visit to a doctor. At the same time, the list of services provided by such doctors is limited to initial diagnoses, basic medical exams and basic treatment procedures, essentially because these are small, private medical centres with limited capacity.[120]

Use of health-related Internet resources and Services by Doctors

A large proportion of Russian Internet resources are geared towards medical professionals, including doctors:

Online medical references (primarily for drugs and medication and, to a lesser extent, for medical equipment);

Information on projects of large medical research centres and professional associations (publications targeted at medical specialists);

Thematic projects for medical professionals (dedicated to the various, specific medical fields or certain diseases and methods of their diagnoses and treatment);

Websites of companies (pharmaceutical producers, distributors, medical institutions, etc.), associations and non-profit organisations in the medical sphere;

Long-distance services for professionals (distance learning and consultation, forums, clinical practice experience exchange); and

Systems of reservation and ordering, marketplaces, tenders for purchases.

Currently, there are no Russian sites which provide more sophisticated online services, such as databases and expert systems, which could substantially assist a doctor in making a diagnosis or assigning treatment.

IIS survey data indicates that the main motivation for doctors to use the Internet is receiving professional information, distance learning, selecting medications and consulting with colleagues (see below).[121]

Out-patient observation via the Internet is undertaken by a negligible proportion of Moscow's doctors (according to the survey results, approximately only 6 percent). In Europe, only Luxemburg and Greece have lower indicators than Russia in this regard, whereas the average EU level of electronic out-patient observation is 26.5 percent – In Denmark this figure reaches 75.8 percent.

E-LEARNING

According to the Rambler's Top 100 rating, a web traffic tracker, only 3.3 percent of all informational resources in RUnet were devoted to education issues in 2006.[122] E-learning has not yet developed to an appreciable extent, despite the obvious potential in view of the country's size and geography. Distance learning is focussed primarily in the tertiary sector, with advanced services being provided by, for example, the Institute for Distance Education of Ulyanovsk State Technical University[123] and the Moscow State University of Economics, Statistics and Information.[124] According to Rosstat, by the beginning of 2006,

93.2 percent of universities and other higher education institutions used the Internet (compared to 89.5 percent in the previous year).

According to the Trans-European Research and Education Networking Association, 72 percent of Russian universities and 10 percent of secondary schools are served by the NREN.[125]

Total number of logical connections to the NREN, and the percentage breakdown for each usable bandwidth class[126]

Total number connected	% connected through ISDN or lower	% connected at up to 2 Mbit/s	% connected at >2 Mb and =< 10 Mb/s	% connected at > 10 Mb/s and =< 100 Mb/s	% connected at > 100 and < 1000 Mb/s	% connected at => 1 Gb and < 10 Gb/s above	% connected at 10 Gb or above

| 168 | 2.0 | 62.0 | 10.0 | 21.0 | 3.0 | 2.0 | 0.0 |

STRUCTURE OF THE COMMUNICATIONS INDUSTRY

The basic ownership structure of the Russian telecoms industry is represented in the tables below.

Share of different types of owners in the Russian telecom market *(%)

Type of owner	Total telecom market	Fixed	Fixed including Data & Internet	Cellular	Satellite**
State & municipal	27.0	36.4	28.6	2.6	61
Russian holdings	30.4	22.4	29.3	44.8	9
International telcos	10.0	2.6	10.5	20.3	8
Financial investors	2.4	3.2	3.5	1.9	1
Free float	28.3	33.4	20.7	28.2	17
Others ***	1.9	2.0	7.5	2.3	4

* The evaluation of the ownership structure was made on the basis of (a) information on ordinary shares distribution and (b) companies' shares in the overall revenue of the Russian telecom industry in 2004. Where possible, the shares (in telecoms operators) of Russian companies such as Svyazinvest, Gazprom, and Rostelecom were split between owner types according to the ownership structure of these companies to improve accuracy. ** Estimate *** Owners unaffiliated with large holdings and unknown owners Source: J'son&Partners research

Key assets for each type of owner

Type of owner	Key assets
State & Municipal	Rostelecom, Svyazinvest regional telcos and their cellular 'daughters', Transtelecom, MGTS (minority stock), 'independent' telcos (Bashinformsvyaz, Tattelecom and others), Central Telegraph, Postal service state enterprises, 'Russian satellites', broadcasting companies
Russian holdings	Shares in MTS, Vimpelcom, Megafon, MGTS, Golden Telecom, Comstar. Full or joint control of MTT, Skylink, PTT. Access Industries share in Svyazinvest assets
International telcos	Megafon (TeliaSonera), VImpelcom (Telenor), MTS (Deutsche Telecom), Equant (France Telecom), Golden Telecom (Telenor), Tele2, NTC (Korea telecom), Sonera Rus (TeliaSonera)
Financial investors	Minority stocks in Svyazinvest companies, Vimpelcom, Golden Telecom. Peterstar

For additional analytical, business and investment opportunities information, please contact Global Investment & Business Center, USA at (202) 546-2103. Fax: (202) 546-3275. E-mail: rusric@erols.com

Free float	Minority stocks in Svyazinvest companies, MTS, Vimpelcom, Golden Telecom, BashInformSvyaz

The Ministry for Communications and Informatisation reports that 1.8 percent of the workforce is active in specialist jobs in the ICT sector, producing 5 percent of GDP.

According to the Ministry, the Telecommunications market overall was worth 668 billion roubles or 19.4 billion Euro in 2005, which breaks down as follows:

Fixed line communications market – 340 billion roubles or 9.9 billion Euro.

Mobile communications – 305 billion roubles or 8.9 billion Euro

TV, radio broadcasting services and satellite communications – 23 billion roubles or 668 million Euro

FIXED NETWORKS

Traditional operators continue to control the majority of the telecommunications infrastructure (89 percent of access lines for the fixed-line network) and have a strong position in the fixed-line communications market (70 percent of total market revenue).[127]

The backbone and intercity networks, installed in Soviet times, still form the basis of the Russian public-switched telephone network. During the transition to market economy mechanisms, the joint-stock company Svyazinvest was created through the merger of most of the regional state telecommunications enterprises. The state holds a 75 percent+2 shares block in the company. Svyazinvest now comprises seven interregional communications companies (ICC), and an operator of international and intercity telecommunications, Rostelecom (in which Svyazinvest holds a 51 percent stake). Most of the remaining shares are owned by nominee shareholders such as ING Eurasia Bank.

The privatisation of state-controlled holding Svyazinvest was planned for 2006. However, this did not happen, and it is now very unclear when it is likely to take place. In addition, the final decision concerning the size of the block of shares to be sold (25 percent minus 2 shares, 50 percent plus 2 shares or all 75 percent plus 2 shares have been discussed) and the nature of that sale (by one lot or by several blocks) has not yet been made. It is also not clear whether Rostelecom, the most attractive asset for the investors, will be withdrawn from Svyazinvest in advance of the sale. The main candidates for acquiring the holding shares are Telecominvest, AFK Sistema, Alfa-Group/Altimo and Access Industries, which already owns 25 percent of Svyazinvest shares.

TransTeleCom (a major backbone provider) has no foreign investors.[133]

The market for local fixed communications services also includes operators building corporate networks and providing complex communications services to major clients (business centres, hotels, banks, etc.). These so-called alternative operators are described in the table, below. The "alternative (new) operators" are the telecommunications service providers who received licences for service provision after 1990 and whose tariffs are not regulated by the Ministry for Antimonopoly Policy and Entrepreneurial Support.

Largest Russian Alternative Providers of Fixed-Line Communication Services, 2003.

	Providers	Controlling Organisation
1.	Sovintel	Alfa Group/Altima
2.	Svyaztransneft	Transneft
3.	MTU-Inform	Systema
4.	Combellga	Alfa Group/Altimo
5.	Equant	France Telecom
6.	TransTeleCom Company	MPS
7.	MTT	Gamma Group
8.	ComStar	Systema
9.	Peterstar	Metromedia
10.	Central Telegraph	Svyazinvest
11.	PTT	Telecominvest
12.	MTU-Intel	Systema
13.	Comcor	Moscow Government
14.	RTComm.ru	Svyazinvest
15.	Telmos	Systema
16.	Cominkom	Alfa Group/Altima
17.	Metrocom	Antel Group
18.	Teleport TP	Grosco Holding
19.	Macomnet	TeliaSonera
20.	TeliaSonera	Antel Group

Source: Russian Telecommunication Market. Information Bulletin, February 2004. http://www.json.ru

According to J'son & Partners' data, about 60 percent of the alternative fixed-line operators' market is controlled by the major financial-industrial groups: Alfa Group/Altima (20 percent), AFK Systema (14 percent) and Telecominvest[136] (14 percent). A large group of operators is controlled by Svyazinvest holding companies and state-owned providers (11 percent), which have been actively promoting their services in the telecommunications market over the last two years.

For additional analytical, business and investment opportunities information,
please contact Global Investment & Business Center, USA
at (202) 546-2103. Fax: (202) 546-3275. E-mail: rusric@erols.com

There are substantial differences in the revenue structure of the traditional and alternative operators' clientele. The alternative providers prevail in the corporate sector, whereas the traditional operators are dominant in the consumer segment of the market, primarily due to the low local call tariffs regulated by the Ministry for Antimonopoly Policy and Entrepreneurial Support.

The majority of alternative operators use the traditional operators' public-switched telephone networks. Currently, some of them are building digital superimposed networks in order to provide a direct, high-quality connection between local subscribers and the international stations of Rostelecom. These networks provide voice mail services and high-speed data transfer services.

MOBILE NETWORKS

There are more than 250 mobile communications operators in Russia. Mobile communications companies are expanding, due both to the development of their own networks and consolidation (through mergers and acquisitions). Although up to seven mobile operators can operate simultaneously in several regions, the three operators with the largest subscriber bases are the national GSM operators MTS,[137] Beeline[138] and Megafon.[139]

The controlling block of MTS shares belongs to AFK Sistema. 47.4 percent of MTS shares belong to foreign investment funds.[140]

Beeline is owned by Vimpelcom, which is owned by Telenor (29.9% - 26.6% of voting shares) and Alfa Group (24.5% - 32.9% of voting shares), and 44.2% (39.3% of voting shares) are free float.

The Petersburg Telecominvest holding, together with Scandinavian group TeliaSonera, controls Megafon. Foreign shareholders of mobile operator Megafon are Telia International AB (6.37 percent), Sonera Holding B.V. (26 percent), IPOC International Growth Fund Limited (8.0 percent) and Telia International Management AB (1.73 percent).[141]

The Petersburg Telecominvest holding also owns part of Skylink[142] Company's fixed capital. Skylink is building a next generation mobile network in Russia, and Petersburg Telecominvest has a 50 percent stake in the project. The rest of the shares are owned by Sistema.

At present, the total share of direct foreign capital in the mobile communications sector is less than 50 percent.

These "big three" companies are present in virtually all Russian regions and also own the largest operators in many CIS countries. They are also starting to assess the possibilities for acquiring Eastern European and Central Asian mobile operators. The rapid and simultaneous expansion of the "big three" into the regions has fundamentally altered the business prospects for the majority of regional companies. These companies have settled on the necessity of quickly selling their assets to one of the largest operators before these market leaders have had a chance to build their own infrastructure and to consequently (and, they believe, inevitably) attract their customers. As a result, the Russian mobile communications market has been consolidating quickly since 2000-2001.

Competition in the consumer market is regulated by the Ministry of Antimonopoly Policy and Entrepreneurial Support. On the whole, the market situation can be characterised as quite sustainable for the leading players. For smaller players, however, the situation remains difficult, above all due to the limited possibilities of building new regional infrastructure.

Largest Cellular Network Operators in the Russian Federation

For additional analytical, business and investment opportunities information, please contact Global Investment & Business Center, USA at (202) 546-2103. Fax: (202) 546-3275. E-mail: rusric@erols.com

[142] http://www.deltatelecom.com/ [143] Very similar figures were reported in December 2006 by the Seekingalpha.com website, which said that MTS had a market share of 34.1%, Vimpelcom had 32.4% and Megafon had 19.1%, with the rest on 14.4%. See "MTS vs Vimpelcom: Russian Cellular Market Leaders' Q3 Results, 1 December, 2006

Operator	Number of subscribers on 30 September 2006.
MTS	49,990,000
Vimpelcom	47 651,000
Megafon	28,071,000
Теле2	5,644,000
Uralsvyazinform	4,251,000
SMARTS	3,525,000
Yenisejsktelecom	1,279,000
NSS	1,241,000
Baikalwestcom	1,120,000
Motiv	1,012,000
NTK	707,000

An analysis of operators' activities in setting up mobile communications networks of different standards shows that work to construct regional GSM-900 (GSM-900/1800) networks was conducted very quickly in almost every Russian Federation constituent member, regardless of their socio-economic development. This can be explained by the need of Russian GSM operators to implement existing federal licences within certain timeframes and the policy of these operators to cover regional markets as quickly as possible.

In 2005, Vimpelcom was a market leader in the Volga, Siberian, and Central regions; and MTS held its strong position in the Far Eastern, North-Caucasian and Ural regions. Among the regional players, Baikalwestcom[144] has a strong market position (a 12 percent market share) in the Far Eastern region; Smarts[145] takes up over 14 percent of the market share in the Volga region; Uralsvyazinform[146] has around 22 percent in the Ural region; and Yenisejsktelecom[147] accounts for 9.6 percent in the Siberian region.

In developing mobile communications networks, operators in the Russian Federation focused on two main areas of activity:

maximum coverage of the regions' territory, according to their demographic and geographic specifics and investment possibilities;

expansion of the range of services, including through emerging technologies.

For additional analytical, business and investment opportunities information, please contact Global Investment & Business Center, USA at (202) 546-2103. Fax: (202) 546-3275. E-mail: rusric@erols.com

CABLE NETWORKS

The leading players in this market are the state-owned, joint-stock company Mostelecom,[148] Komkor-TV[149] (Moscow), the state enterprise St Petersburg Cable Network, CJSC Arkhangelskoe Cable Television, and a number of other companies in almost every region of the country. At the same time, the fact that a very small number of operators operate in a specific region makes them de facto oligopolists, which means they can maintain quite high tariffs for subscriptions and monthly fees. This places a constraint on service development.

According to Iks Consulting, there were 500 cable operators in Russia at the end of 2005, connecting 8.0 percent of households to commercial cable television and providing Internet access for about 100,000 subscribers.

In 2005, the volume of mergers and acquisitions in the cable communication market totalled over 100 million US$ / 83 million Euro. Nafta-Moscow acquired National Cable Networks (HKC) and Mostelecom,[150] Renova group,[151] and Columbus Nova[152] acquired Kopbina Telecom[153] and Komkor-TV.

INTERNET ACCESS NETWORKS

Over the last two years, the Russian ISP market has been developing rapidly. The iKS-Consulting company[154] reports that, by the end of 2004, around two thousand Internet service providers offered access services in the country, with many offering a wide range of Internet-services: e-mail, hosting, collocation, applications leasing, etc. An IDC report has also indicated that, in the early part of this decade, the number of users logging on at home was growing faster than the number of corporate users.

The number of ISPs operating in the different segments of the Russian Internet market is presented in the table below.

Number of ISPs in Russian market

Type of ISPs	Number of ISPs*	National ISPs
Dialup	550	1
XDSL	60	-
other residential broadband	1 700	-
corporate broadband	1 400	4
wireless access	180	-
mobile access	25	3

* These estimations are approximate as there are few clear-cut borders between branches and subsidiaries *Source*: J'son&Partners research

Over 50 percent of dial-up access in the Russian telecommunications market is controlled by the ten largest operators, seven of which are members of the Svyazinvest holding group. The number of people using Svyazinvest dial-up access is about 990,000 users weekly. In comparison, Golden Telecom, via the only all-Russia brand ROL[155] has 390,000 users, and the leaders of the Moscow

For additional analytical, business and investment opportunities information, please contact Global Investment & Business Center, USA at (202) 546-2103. Fax: (202) 546-3275. E-mail: rusric@erols.com

and Saint Petersburg markets, MTUIntel[156] and Web-Plus, have 270,000 and 140,000 users respectively.

Broadband access using ADSL technology is mainly provided by MTU-Intel, Golden Telecom, WebPlus, Volga Telecom,[157] CenterTelecom[158] and Uralsvyazinform. There were 425,000 ADSL lines in Russia at the end of 2005, representing a penetration rate of approximately 0.3 percent.

The most widespread unlimited broadband access tariff plans cost 16.5 Euro per month or almost 200 Euro per year. This put the retail broadband price at approximately 4.5 percent of per capita GDP.

The market for wireless access grew strongly in 2005. The mobile communications operators still remain the main providers of wireless Internet: the number of GPRS-users grew by 250 percent and now exceeds 10 million.[159]

The first pre-WiMAX (Unitline)[160] and WiMAX-networks (Synterra)[161] have recently appeared in the country.

According to Rosstat, in 2005 14.3 percent of Russian households had access to the Internet at home.

According to J'son&Partners, at the end of 2005 over two thirds of Russian households connected to the Internet used dial-up. Some 1.3 million households used broadband.

In comparison with Europe (with ADSL as the dominant broadband technology) and North America (cable networks), broadband access in Russia is mostly provided through LANs. At the end of 2005 LAN (installed in office blocks or blocks of flats, for example) accounted for 62 percent of home broadband connections, while ADSL accounted for 32 percent and cable networks for only 6 percent.[162]

SATELLITE OPERATORS

The Russian satellite market includes three basic providers (which are also satellite owners) – Russian Satellites,[163] Gazcom,[164] Intersputnik Association,[165] as well as about 90 resellers of Russian and foreign satellite operators.

PRODUCTION OF IT SERVICES

The ICT sector does not have a prominent place in the Russian economy in terms of production volumes. However, it does exhibit a rapid pace of development and is attractive to investors. The sector, defined in accordance with OECD methodology, provides only 1.5 percent of the country's total employment. At the same time, however, gross salaries account for 2.35 percent, which signifies a relatively high income level in this sector. The production of ICT products and services forms 2.61 percent of the Russian economy's total production volume, which also indicates a relatively high level of productivity. The total volume of product and service production from the various types of ICT-related economic activity in Russia in 2003 exceeded 603 billion roubles, or around 17 billion Euro.

In general, the Russian ICT sector is very attractive to potential investors in relative terms, because the share of investment into fixed assets exceeds both the employment share and the production share of this sector, amounting to 4.76 percent of the corresponding indicators for the whole Russian economy. This means there is potential for advanced growth in the ICT sector in future compared with those sectors of the economy which have lower levels of investment.

For additional analytical, business and investment opportunities information,
please contact Global Investment & Business Center, USA
at (202) 546-2103. Fax: (202) 546-3275. E-mail: rusric@erols.com

The Russian ICT market grew by 30 percent in 2005, increasing from 27.7 billion US$ (22.89 billion Euro) in 2004 to 36.4 billion US$ (30 billion Euro) in 2005.[166] The Russian minister for IT and Communications Mr Reiman said that this was due to extensive domestic and foreign investment.

FINANCIAL DEVELOPMENT OF THE ICT SECTOR

Mergers and Acquisitions

According to information agency Sotovik, in 2004, 28 mergers and acquisitions (M&A) were announced in the mobile communications market, with MTS being most active in this sphere. The main goal of such transactions was the acquisition of regional operators or large blocs of their shares (Gorizont-RT, Sibintertelecom, Telesot-Alania, Far Eastern Cellular Communication Networks-900, Siberian Cellular Systems, Primtelephon, Digital Networks of Udmurtia, etc.), which allowed MTS to consolidate its position substantially in the Far East, Siberia and the Volga region.

The acquisition of the Far Eastern operator Daltelecom Inc. by VimpelCom is considered to be the largest mobile transaction of 2004 and one which ensured VimpelCom a 20 percent share in the Far Eastern market. The company also increased its stake in BeeLine–Samara capital.

MS Direct (owned by SkyLink) was rather active in acquiring the NMT-assets of the regional operators. In 2004, MS Direct and some other companies bought blocks of shares from Dalsvyaz, North-West Telecom, CenterTelecom, Uralwestcom and Sibirtelecom within the framework of the SkyLink project.

Russian companies have also been active in the foreign M&A market. In 2006, Alfa-Telecom acquired 13.22 percent of Turkcell for 1,593 million US$ / 1,316.5 million Euro. The other very large acquisition involving a Russian mobile company was the disputed purchase by Vimpelcom of the Ukrainian Radio Systems (URS) for 231 US$ million / 191 million Euro.

According to analysis from IKS-Consulting, a growth in the number of mergers and acquisitions in the fixed-line communications market is expected over the course of the next two to three years. Changes in regulation and plans for the liberalisation of the communications industry are among the principal catalysts for this change. Medium-sized and small operators are expected to attempt to band together to form associations or unions, and the consolidation of small operators will take place. However, Rostelecom, TransTeleCom and a group of large companies will remain in the market.

Production by Major Types of Economic Activity

In Russia, electronic network communications account for the majority of ICT production. The share of this segment in overall ICT production figures exceeds its share in the number of people employed in the ICT industry and its share in gross salary, which indicates high productivity levels.

Interestingly, the production shares for both products and services are less than the proportion of those employed in other corresponding sectors of the economy.

According to IDC, a research agency, the market for information security totals 140 million US$ / 116 million Euro. The software company Otkrytye Technologii estimates it at 300 million US$ / 248 million.

The Ministry for Communications and Informatisation reports that, in 2005, software exports reached 994 million US$ / 821.5 million Euro.

Distribution of those Employed in the ICT Sector by the Major Activity Fields 40 percent of all those employed in the ICT sector work in the equipment production sector.

For additional analytical, business and investment opportunities information, please contact Global Investment & Business Center, USA at (202) 546-2103. Fax: (202) 546-3275. E-mail: rusric@erols.com

Notably, in Moscow, the percentage of those employed (of all those people working in the ICT sector) in service provision is much higher than the total number for the whole country and it is also much higher than the figure for St Petersburg. 67 percent of those employed in the ICT sector in Moscow work in the telecommunications sector.

Detailed Structure of the ICT Sector: Product and Service Production

The absolute leader in ICT products and services in Russia is the telecommunications field. Its share of total production levels is higher than its equivalent employment or gross salary shares.

Content Industry & Information Services

Number of IT Companies

Type of company	2004	2005****
VoIP providers	570	600
Security service vendors *	70	80
Hosting providers **	750	770
Chargeable	660	680
Free of charge	90	90
Web-design companies ***	1150	1250

* There are very few "pure" security service providers in Russia. Usually, local systems integrators play the role of security service providers. This number represents the pure security service providers as well as the systems integrators which are focused on security services. ** Only hosting service providers (including ISPs and web-design companies) with their own location sites are included. *** Registered companies with full scale web-design services and whose bills average over $1000 / 827 Euro ****Estimated figures *Source*: J'son&Partners research

IMPORTANT LAWS AND REGULATIONS, AFFECTING TELECOM SECTOR

The Law on Telecommunications establishes general principles and rules which apply to telecommunications legislation in Russia. There are also a number of regulations adopted in furtherance of the Law on Telecommunications, eg by the Government of the Russian Federation and the Ministry of Communications.

Such regulations cover, *inter alia*, the following:

- Licensing requirements

- Rules for the provision of specific telecommunication services

- Rules for the operation of telecommunication networks

In addition, other ancillary considerations affecting the provision of telecommunications services in Russia are regulated by other laws including:

- The Federal Law 'On Personal Data' No. 152-FZ dated 27 July 2006

- The Federal Law 'On Combating Money Laundering and the Financing of Terrorism' No. 115-FZ dated 07 August 2001

- The Federal Law 'On Licensing on Certain Types of Activities' No. 99-FZ dated 04 May 2011

FEDERAL LAW NO. 126- FZ OF JULY 7, 2003 ON COMMUNICATIONS (with the Amendments and Additions of December 23, 2003, August 22, November 2, 2004, May 9, 2005, February 2, March 3, July 26, 27, December 29, 2006)

Passed by the State Duma on June 18, 2003 Approved by the Federation Council on June 25, 2003

The present Federal Law establishes the legal principles for activity in the sphere of communications on the territory of the Russian Federation and on the territories put under the jurisdiction of the Russian Federation, and defines the authority of the state power bodies in the sphere of communications, as well as the rights and the duties of the persons who are taking part in this activity or making use of communications services.

LAW ON COMMUNICATIONS

CHAPTER 1. GENERAL PROVISIONS

Article 1. Goals of the Present Federal Law The goals set in the present Federal Law are as follows:

- creation of conditions for rendering communications services on the entire territory of the Russian Federation;

- rendering assistance in the introduction of promising technologies and standards;

- protection of the interests of the users of communication services engaged in the activity of economic subjects in the sphere of communications;

- providing for efficient and fair competition on the market of communications services;

For additional analytical, business and investment opportunities information, please contact Global Investment & Business Center, USA at (202) 546-2103. Fax: (202) 546-3275. E-mail: rusric@erols.com

- creation of conditions for developing the Russian infrastructure of communications and for ensuring its integration with international communications networks;

- provisions for the centralised management of Russia's radio frequency resource, including the orbital- frequency resource and the numeration resource;

- creation of conditions for satisfying the requirements in the communications of the state administration, of the country's defence and of state security, as well as for ensuring law and order.

Article 2. Basic Concepts Used in This Federal Law The following basic concepts are used for the purposes of the present Federal Law:

- subscriber - the user of communications services with whom a contract for rendering such services is concluded, while assigning for these purposes a subscription number or a unique identification code;

- assignment of a radio frequency band - a written permit for:

the use of the particular radio frequency band, including for the development, modernisation and manufacture in the Russian Federation and/or for the import to the territory of the Russian Federation of radio- electronic appliances or high - frequency devices with particular technical characteristics;

- high- frequency devices - the equipment or instruments intended for generating and utilizing radio frequency energy for industrial, scientific, medical, everyday domestic and other purposes, with the exception of application in the sphere of telecommunication;

- use of the radio frequency spectrum - possession of a permit for the use and/or the actual use of a radio frequency band, a radio frequency channel or a radio frequency for rendering telecommunication services and for achieving other goals not prohibited by federal laws or other legal normative acts of the Russian Federation;

- conversion of the radio frequency spectrum - the aggregate of actions aimed at widening the application of the radio frequency spectrum through the use of radio- electronic facilities of the civilian profile;

- linear- cable communications structures - the electric communication (telecommunication) structures and other objects of the engineering infrastructure, created or adjusted for the placement of communication cables;

- communications lines - the transmission lines, physical chains and linear- cable communications structures;

- fitted capacity - the magnitude characterizing the technical possibilities of a communications operator for rendering telecommunications services and those involved in connection, as well as the services aimed at letting through traffic measured in accordance with the technical capacity of the equipment introduced into the network of the communications operator;

- numeration - the digital, letter or symbol designation or combinations of such designations, including the codes intended for a single- sign definition (for an identification) of the communication network and/or of its junction or end elements;

- user's equipment (the end equipment) - the technical facilities for the transmission and/or for the reception of telecommunication signals along the communications lines connected to the subscribers' lines and put into the subscribers' use, or intended for such purposes;

For additional analytical, business and investment opportunities information,
please contact Global Investment & Business Center, USA
at (202) 546-2103. Fax: (202) 546-3275. E-mail: rusric@erols.com

- operator occupying an important position in a general- use communications network - the operator who, jointly with the affiliated persons, has at his disposal in the geographically delineated zone of numeration or on the entire territory of the Russian Federation at least twenty- five per cent of the fitted capacity, or who is able to let through at least twenty- five per cent of the traffic;

- communications operator - the legal entity or individual businessman rendering communications services on the grounds of the corresponding licence;

- operator of the universal servicing - the communications operator rendering communications services in a general- use communications network upon whom is imposed the duty of rendering universal services in accordance with the procedure stipulated in the present Federal Law;

- communications organization - the legal entity performing an activity in the sphere of communications as the principal kind of activity. Provisions of the present Federal Law regulating the activity of communications organizations shall be correspondingly applied to the individual businessmen carrying out an activity in the sphere of communications as the principal kind of activity;

- user of the radio frequency spectrum - the person to whom a radio frequency band is assigned, or to whom a radio frequency or a radio frequency channel is awarded (assigned);

- user of communications services - the person ordering and/or utilizing communications services;

- awarding (assignment) of a radio frequency or of a radio frequency channel - the written permit for the use of the particular radio frequency or radio frequency channel with an indication of the particular radio- electronic appliance, as well as of the purposes and the terms for such use;

- radio interference - an impact of electromagnetic energy on the reception of radio waves called forth by a single emission or by several emissions, including radiation or induction, and manifesting itself in any deterioration of the communications standard, in the errors or in the losses of information which could have been avoided in the absence of the impact of this energy;

- radio frequency - the frequency of electromagnetic vacillations established for designating a unit component of the radio- frequency spectrum;

- radio- frequency spectrum - the aggregate of radio frequencies within the limits fixed by the International Telecommunications Union which may be used for the functioning of radio- electronic appliances or of high- frequency devices;

- radio- electronic appliances - the technical facilities intended for the transmission and/or for the reception of radio waves, consisting of one or of several transmitting and/or receiving appliances, or of combinations of such appliances incorporating auxiliary equipment;

- distribution of radio frequency bands - the definition of the purpose of the radio frequency bands by the entries in the Table for Distributing Radio Frequency Bands Between the Radio Services of the Russian Federation, on the basis of which the permit for the use of the particular radio frequency band is granted and the terms for such use are established;

- numeration resource - the aggregate or part of the numeration variants which may be used in the communications network;

- communications network - the technological system embracing communications facilities and communications lines intended for telecommunications or for postal communication;

- modern functional equivalent of a communications network - the minimum set of modern communications facilities providing for the standard and for the existing volume of services rendered in the communications network;

For additional analytical, business and investment opportunities information, please contact Global Investment & Business Center, USA at (202) 546-2103. Fax: (202) 546-3275. E-mail: rusric@erols.com

- communications installations - the objects of engineering infrastructure, including the buildings and structures created or adjusted for distributing communications facilities and telecommunications cables;

- communications facilities - the technical and software means used for the formulation, reception, processing, storage, transmission and delivery of telecommunications or postal dispatches, and the other technical and software means used in rendering communications services or in providing for the functioning of communications networks;

- traffic - the load created by the flow of calls, communications and signals falling onto the communications facilities;

- universal communications services - the communications services whose rendering to any user of communications services on the entire territory of the Russian Federation within a fixed term, of the established standard and at a reasonable price, is obligatory for operators of the universal servicing;

- management of the communications network - the aggregate of organizational and technical measures aimed at providing for the functioning of the communications network, including the regulation of traffic;

- communications service - activity involved in the reception, processing, storage, transmission and delivery of telecommunications or postal dispatches;

- connection service - activity aimed at meeting the communications operators' requirement in organizing interaction between communications networks, in which the establishment of the connection and the transmission of information between the users of the interacting telecommunications networks becomes possible;

- service for letting through the traffic - activity aimed at meeting the requirement of communications operators in letting through the traffic between the interacting telecommunications networks;

- telecommunications - any emission, transmission or reception of signs, signals, vocal information, written text, depictions, sounds or statements of any kind along the radio system or along the wire, optical and other electromagnetic systems;

- electromagnetic compatibility - the ability of radio - electronic appliances and/or of high- frequency devices to function in accordance with the fixed standard in the surrounding electromagnetic situation and not to create inadmissible radio interference for other radio- electronic appliances and/or high- frequency devices.

Article 3. Sphere of Action of the Present Federal Law

The present Federal Law regulates relations involved in the creation and operation of all communications networks and communications installations, and in the use of the radio frequency spectrum, as well as in rendering telecommunications and postal services on the territory of the Russian Federation and on the territories under the jurisdiction of the Russian Federation.

In respect of communications operators carrying out their activity outside the Russian Federation in conformity with the law of foreign states, the present Federal Law is applicable only as concerns regulating the procedure for their performance of communications works and rendering communications services on the territories under the jurisdiction of the Russian Federation.

Relations in the sphere of communications which are not regulated by the present Federal Law shall come under the regulation of other federal laws and of other legal normative acts of the Russian Federation in the sphere of communications.

For additional analytical, business and investment opportunities information, please contact Global Investment & Business Center, USA at (202) 546-2103. Fax: (202) 546-3275. E-mail: rusric@erols.com

Article 4. Legislation of the Russian Federation in the Sphere of Communications

The legislation of the Russian Federation in the sphere of communications is based on the Constitution of the Russian Federation and consists of the present Federal Law and other federal laws.

Relations involved in an activity in the sphere of communications are also regulated by the legal normative acts of the President of the Russian Federation, by the legal normative acts of the Government of the Russian Federation and by other legal normative acts of the federal executive power bodies issued in conformity with them.

If an international treaty of the Russian Federation has established the rules differing from those stipulated in the present Federal Law, the rules of the international treaty shall be applied.

CHAPTER 2. PRINCIPLES OF ACTIVITY IN THE SPHERE OF COMMUNICATIONS

Article 5. Ownership in Communication Networks and in Communication Facilities

1. Communication organizations are created and carry out their activity on the territory of the Russian Federation on the basis of the uniformity of the economic space and under the conditions of competition and of the multiplicity of the forms of ownership. The state ensures equal competition terms for communications organizations irrespective of their form of ownership.

Communications networks and communications facilities may be in federal ownership, in ownership of the subjects of the Russian Federation, in the municipal ownership and also in the ownership of citizens and legal entities.

The list of the communications networks and communications facilities which may only be in ownership is defined in the legislation of the Russian Federation. Foreign investors may take part in the privatization of the property of state and municipal unitary communications enterprises on the terms defined in the legislation of the Russian Federation.

2. The form of ownership in communications networks and communications facilities is altered in accordance with the procedure stipulated in the legislation of the Russian Federation, and shall be admissible under the condition that such alteration by no means deteriorates the functioning of the communications networks and the communications facilities, and does not infringe upon the right of citizens and legal entities to the use of communications services.

Article 6. Organizing an Activity Involved in the Placement of Communication Installations and Communication Facilities

In the town planning for the development of territories and settlements, and in building them over shall be determined the composition and the structure of the communications objects - of the communications installations, including the linear- cable installations, individual premises for the placement of communications facilities, as well as the necessary power capacities in the engineering infrastructures to provide for the functioning of the communications facilities.

The state power bodies of the subjects of the Russian Federation and local self- government bodies of municipal districts and urban circuits shall assist communications organizations rendering universal services to the population, in the receipt and/or in the construction of the communications installations and of the premises intended for rendering universal communications services.

For additional analytical, business and investment opportunities information, please contact Global Investment & Business Center, USA at (202) 546-2103. Fax: (202) 546-3275. E-mail: rusric@erols.com

Under a contract with the owner or with the other possessor of the buildings, of the supports for the power transmission lines, of the contact railway networks, pole supports, bridges, collectors, tunnels, including underground tunnels and railway and motor road tunnels, and of the other engineering objects and technological sites, as well as of the allocated strips of land, including those for railways and for motor roads, communications organizations may carry out on them the construction and the operation of communications facilities and of communications installations.

The owner or the other possessor of the above immovable property has the right to demand from the communications organization a proportionate payment for the use of this property, unless otherwise stipulated in federal laws.

If the immovable property belonging to a citizen or to a legal entity cannot be used in accordance with its purpose as a result of the performance of the construction or of the operation of communication facilities and of communications installations, the owner or the other possessor has the right to file a claim in court for the cancellation of the contract with the communications organization for the use of this property.

> If the communications lines and communications installations are shifted or rearranged as a result of construction, of expansion of the territory of populated centres, of capital repairs and reconstruction of the buildings, structures, installations, roads and bridges, or as a result of the development of new land, of the reconstruction of land reclamation systems, of the development of deposits of useful minerals and because of other requirements, the outlays involved in such shifting or rearrangement shall be compensated to the communications operator.

> Such compensation may be effected under the parties' agreement either in monetary form or by the customer of the construction shifting or rearranging the communications lines and communications installations at his own expense in accordance with the technical conditions supplied by the communications organization, and with standards.

Communications operators have the right to place communications cables in the communications linear- cable installations on a paid basis regardless of the ownership of these installations.

Article 7. Protection of Communications Networks and Communications Installations

Communications networks and communications installations are under the protection of the state.

In the construction and reconstruction of the buildings, structures and installations of communications networks and communications installations, communications operators and builders shall take into account the need to protect the communications facilities and the communications installations from unsanctioned access to them.

As they operate the communications networks and the communications installations, communications operators are obliged to provide for the protection of these communications networks and communications installations from unsanctioned access to them.

Article 8. Registration of the Right of Ownership and of Other Real Rights to Communications Objects

The communications installations closely connected with land the shifting of which is impossible without inflicting unproportionate damage to their purpose, including linear- cable communications installations, are referred to immovable property, state registration of the right of ownership and of other real rights to which is carried out in conformity with the civil legislation. The specifics of the state registration of the right of ownership and the other real rights to the linear- cable communications installations are established by the Government of the Russian Federation.

For additional analytical, business and investment opportunities information,
please contact Global Investment & Business Center, USA
at (202) 546-2103. Fax: (202) 546-3275. E-mail: rusric@erols.com

The procedure for the state registration of the right of ownership and other real rights to space communications objects (communications sputniks, including double- purpose ones) is established in federal laws.

The transfer of the right of ownership and of the other real rights to space communications objects does not entail the transfer of the right to the use of the orbital - frequency resource.

Article 9. Construction and Operation of Communication Lines on the Territory Adjacent to the State Frontier of the Russian Federation and within the Boundaries of the Territorial Sea of the Russian Federation

The procedure for the construction and the operation, including the servicing, of the communications lines crossing the State Frontier of the Russian Federation, on the territory along the State Frontier of the Russian Federation, in the inland sea waters of the Russian Federation and in the territorial sea of the Russian Federation, including for laying cables and for building linear- cable installations, as well as for carrying out construction, emergency and restoration works on the submerged linear- cable communications installations in the territorial sea of the Russian Federation, is defined by the Government of the Russian Federation.

Article 10. Communication Lands

In conformity with the land legislation of the Russian Federation, to communications lands shall be referred land plots allocated for the needs of communications into the permanent (the open- ended) or into the gratuitous fixed- term use or on lease, or those handed over by right of the restricted use of an alien land plot (the servitude) for building and operating communications facilities.

The allocation of land plots to communications organizations, the procedure (the regime) for the use thereof, including for establishment of protection zones for communications networks and communications facilities and for making through- cuts for the placement of communications networks, as well as the grounds the terms and the procedure for the withdrawal of these land plots are defined in the land legislation of the Russian Federation. The size of such land plots, including the land plots for establishment of protection zones and for making through- cuts, is determined in conformity with the norms for the allocation of land for the performance of the corresponding kinds of activity and with town- planning and design documentation.

CHAPTER 3. COMMUNICATIONS NETWORKS

Article 11. Federal Communications

Federal communications are formed by all the organizations and all the government bodies carrying out and providing for telecommunications and for postal communications on the territory of the Russian Federation.

The material and technical base for federal communications is comprised by the uniform telecommunications network of the Russian Federation and by the postal communications of the Russian Federation.

Article 12. Uniform Telecommunications Network of the Russian Federation

1. The uniform telecommunications network of the Russian Federation consists of telecommunications networks of the following categories situated on the territory of the Russian Federation:

- the general- use communications network;

- isolated communications networks;

- technological communications networks connected to the general- use communications network;

- special- purpose communications networks and other communications networks for transmitting information with the assistance of electromagnetic systems.

2. For the telecommunications networks comprising the uniform telecommunications network of the Russian Federation, the federal executive power body in the sphere of communications shall:

- determine the procedure for their interaction, and in the cases stipulated in the legislation of the Russian Federation - the procedure for centralized control of the general- use communications network;

- depending on the categories of communications networks (with the exception of special- purpose communications networks, as well as of isolated and technological communications networks, if these are not yet connected to the general- use communications network), establish the demands made on their construction, control or numeration, on the applied communications facilities, on the organizational and technical provisions for a stable functioning of the communications networks, including in emergency situations, and for protecting the communications networks against unsanctioned access to them and to information transmitted through them.

3. The communications operators of all the categories of communications networks in the uniform telecommunications network of the Russian Federation are obliged to create the systems for controlling their communications networks which would correspond to the established procedure for their interaction.

Article 13. General- Use Communications Network

The general- use communications network is intended for rendering the paid telecommunications services to any user of communications services on the territory of the Russian Federation; it includes both the telecommunications networks geographically defined in the framework of the serviced territory and of the numeration resource, and those not geographically defined within the boundaries of the territory of the Russian Federation and of the numeration resource, as well as the communications networks defined in accordance with the technology of rendering communications services.

The general- use communications network is a complex of interacting telecommunications networks, including the communications network for broadcasting television and radio programmes.

The general- use communications network is connected to the general- use communications networks of foreign states.

Article 14. Isolated Communications Networks

The isolated communications networks are telecommunications networks intended for rendering paid telecommunications services to a restricted group of users or to groups of such users. The isolated communications networks may interact between themselves. They are not connected either to the general- use communications network or to the general- use communications networks of foreign states. The communications technologies and facilities applied for organizing the isolated communications networks, as well as the principles for their building are laid down by the owners or by the other possessors of these networks.

An isolated communications network may be connected to the general- use communications network with its transfer into the category of the general- use communications network if the isolated communications network satisfies the demands, made on the general- use communications network. The isolated numeration resource shall in this case be withdrawn and the numeration resource from the numeration resource of the general- use communications network shall be assigned.

communications services shall be rendered by the operators of the isolated communications networks on the grounds of the corresponding licences within the boundaries of the territories indicated in them, and with the use of the numeration awarded to each isolated communications network in accordance with the procedure established by the federal executive power body in the sphere of communications.

Article 15. Technological Communications Networks

The technological communications networks are intended to provide for the production activity of organizations and for controlling the technological processes in the production.

The technologies and communications facilities applied for creating technological communications networks, as well as the principles for building such are established by the owners or by the other possessors of these networks.

If there are available resources in the technological communications network, part of this network may be connected to the general- use communications network with its transfer into the category of the general- use communications network for rendering the paid services to any user on the ground of the corresponding licence. Such connection is admissible if:

- the part of the technological communications network intended for connection to the general- use communications network may be separated by the owner, in technical or in software terms, or physically, from the technological communications network;

- the part of the technological communications network connected to the general- use communications network meets the demands made on the functioning of the general- use communications network.

The part of the technological communications network connected to the general- use communications network shall be assigned the numeration resource from the numeration resource of the general- use communications network in accordance with the procedure laid down by the federal executive power body in the sphere of communications.

The owner or other possessor of the technological communications network is obliged, after part of this communications network is connected to the general- use communications network, to keep separate records of the outlays on the operation of the technological communications network and of the part thereof connected to the general- use communications network.

Technological communications networks may be connected to the technological communications networks of foreign organizations only for the purpose of providing for a uniform technological cycle.

Article 16. Special Purpose Communications Networks

The special purpose communications networks are intended for the needs of the state administration, of the country's defence and state security, and for ensuring law and order. These networks cannot be used for rendering paid communications services unless otherwise envisaged in the legislation of the Russian Federation.

For additional analytical, business and investment opportunities information, please contact Global Investment & Business Center, USA at (202) 546-2103. Fax: (202) 546-3275. E-mail: rusric@erols.com

Communications for the needs of the state administration, including presidential communications, government communications and communications for the needs of the country's defence, of state security and of ensuring law and order, shall be effected in accordance with the procedure defined in the legislation of the Russian Federation.

The provision of communications for the needs of state power bodies, including communications for the President and the Government, communications for the needs of the country's defence and security and for maintaining law and order shall be an expense commitment of the Russian Federation.

The preparation and the use of the resources of the uniform telecommunications network of the Russian Federation in order to provide for the functioning of the special- purpose communications networks are effected in accordance with the procedure established by the Government of the Russian Federation.

The centres for controlling the special- purpose communications networks shall ensure their interaction with the other networks in the uniform telecommunications network of the Russian Federation in accordance with the procedure established by the federal executive power body in the sphere of communications.

Article 17. Postal Communications Network

The postal communications network is the aggregate of the objects of the postal communications and postal routes of the postal communications operators providing for the receipt, processing, shipment (transmission) and delivery (handing in) of postal dispatches, as well as for making postal transfers of monetary funds.

Relations in the postal communications sphere are regulated by the international treaties signed by the Russian Federation, by the present Federal Law, by the Federal Law on Postal Communications, by other federal laws and also by the other legal normative acts of the Russian Federation.

CHAPTER 4. CONNECTION OF COMMUNICATIONS NETWORKS AND THEIR INTERACTION

Article 18. Right to the Connection of Telecommunications Networks

Communications operators have the right to connect their own telecommunications networks to the general- use communications network. Connection of one telecommunications network to another telecommunications network and their interaction are carried out on the grounds of contracts for connecting the telecommunications networks concluded by the communications operators.

The operators of the general- use communication network are obliged to render connection services on the grounds of contracts for the connection of telecommunications networks in conformity with the Rules for Connecting Telecommunications Networks and for Their Interaction, approved by the Government of the Russian Federation.

The contracts for the connection of telecommunications networks in conformity with the Rules for Connecting Telecommunications Networks and for Their Interaction, approved by the Government of the Russian Federation, shall envisage:

- the rights and the duties of communications operators in the connection of telecommunications networks and in their interaction;

For additional analytical, business and investment opportunities information, please contact Global Investment & Business Center, USA at (202) 546-2103. Fax: (202) 546-3275. E-mail: rusric@erols.com

- the duties of the operators occupying an important position in the general- use communications network, as concerns the connection, if a party in the contract is an operator occupying an important position in the general- use communications network;

- the essential conditions for the connection of telecommunications networks and for their interaction;

- the list of the connection services and of the services for letting through traffic, which an operator occupying an important position in the general- use communications network, is obliged to render, and the procedure for rendering such;

- the procedure for the consideration of disputes between communications operators on the issues involved in the connection of telecommunications networks and in their interaction.

Unless otherwise stipulated in the present Federal Law, prices for connection services and for services for letting through traffic shall be defined by the communication operator on his own, proceeding from the demands of common sense and of honesty.

4. Disputes between the communications operators on the issues of signing contracts for connecting telecommunications networks shall be considered in court.

Article 19. Demands Made on the Procedure for Connecting Telecommunications Networks and on Their Interaction with the Telecommunications Network of an Operator Occupying an Important Position in the General- Use Communications Network

1. Towards a contract for connecting telecommunications networks, defining the terms for rendering connection services and the obligations on the interaction of telecommunications networks and on letting through traffic assumed in this connection shall be applied the provisions on the public agreement in respect of operators occupying an important position in the general- use communications network. Seen as the users of connection services and of the services involved in letting through the traffic for the purposes of the present Article shall be operators of the general- use communications network.

An operator occupying an important position in the general- use communications network, is obliged to establish, for the purposes of ensuring indiscriminate access to the market of communications services under similar circumstances, equal conditions for connecting telecommunications networks and for letting through traffic for communications operators rendering similar services, as well as to supply information and to render connection services and the services involved in letting through the traffic to these operators under the same terms and of the same standard, like for his own structural subdivisions and/or for the affiliated persons.

An operator occupying an important position in the general- use communications network on the territories of several subjects of the Russian Federation shall establish the terms for connecting telecommunications networks and for letting through traffic separately on the territory of each subject of the Russian Federation.

The refusal of an operator occupying an important position in the general- use communications network to conclude a contract for connecting telecommunications networks is seen as inadmissible, with the exception of cases when the connection of the telecommunications networks and their interaction contradict the terms of the licences issued to communications operators, or the legal normative acts determining the construction and the functioning of the uniform telecommunications network of the Russian Federation.

The procedure for connecting telecommunications networks and for their interaction with the telecommunications network of an operator occupying an important position in the general- use communications network, as well as his duties involved in the connection of telecommunications

For additional analytical, business and investment opportunities information, please contact Global Investment & Business Center, USA at (202) 546-2103. Fax: (202) 546-3275. E-mail: rusric@erols.com

networks and in the interaction with the telecommunications networks of the other communications operators are defined in accordance with the rules approved by the Government of the Russian Federation.

Operators occupying an important position in the general- use communications network shall establish the terms for connecting other telecommunications networks to their own telecommunications network on the ground of the Rules for Connecting communications Networks and for Their Interaction as concerns the use of the network resources and letting through traffic; these terms shall incorporate the general technical, economic and informational terms, as well as those defining property relations.

The terms for connecting telecommunications networks shall envisage:

- the technical demands made on the connection of telecommunications networks;

- the volume, the procedure and the time terms for the performance of works involved in connecting telecommunications networks and in their distribution among the interacting communications operators;

- the procedure for letting through traffic along the telecommunications networks of the interacting communications operators;

- the place of location of the points for connecting the telecommunications networks;

- the list of rendered connection services and of services for letting through the traffic;

- the cost of connection services and of those involved in letting through traffic, and the procedure for making settlements for these;

- the procedure for interaction between the control systems of telecommunications networks.

Operators occupying an important position in the general- use communications network are obliged to publish the above- said terms within seven days after the terms for connecting the telecommunications networks are established, and to direct them to the federal executive power body in the sphere of communications.

If the federal executive power body in the sphere of communications, on its own or at an application from the communications operators reveals a lack of correspondence of the terms for connecting other telecommunications networks to the telecommunications network of an operator occupying an important position in the general- use communications network, and for letting through the traffic to the Rules mentioned in the first paragraph of Item 3 of the present Article, or to the legal normative acts, the said federal body shall forward to the operator occupying an important position in the general- use communications network well- motivated instructions on eliminating these discrepancies. These instructions shall be accepted and fulfilled by the communications operator who has received them within thirty days as from the day of their receipt.

The newly established terms for the connection of other telecommunications networks to the telecommunications network of an operator occupying an important position in the general - use communications network, and for letting through the traffic along it shall be published by the operator occupying an important position in the general- use communications network, and shall be directed to the federal executive power body in the sphere of communicationss in accordance with the procedure envisaged in the present Article.

When new communications facilities are put into operation or new technological decisions in his own telecommunications network are implemented, or when the outmoded communications facilities are taken out of operation or are updated, which exerts a substantial impact upon the terms for connecting other telecommunications networks and for letting through the traffic along the telecommunications network of the operator, occupying an important position in the general- use communications network, the said operator has the right to establish new terms for connecting other telecommunications networks to his own network in accordance with the procedure envisaged in the present Article. The terms for connecting telecommunications networks cannot be amended more than once a year.

An operator occupying an important position in the general- use communications network is obliged to consider the applications of the communications operator for concluding a contract for connecting telecommunications networks within a term not exceeding thirty days as from the day of receiving such application. A contract for connecting telecommunications networks shall be concluded in writing by way of compiling, in conformity with civil legislation, a single document signed by the parties within a term not exceeding ninety days as from the day of receiving the application. Non- observation of the form for such contract shall entail its invalidation.

The federal executive power body in the sphere of communications shall keep and publish a register of operators occupying an important position in the general- use communications network.

The federal executive power body in the sphere of communications is obliged to consider the applications filed by the communications operators on issues of connecting telecommunications networks and of their interaction, in the course of sixty days as from the day of receiving the said applications, and to publish the decisions adopted on them.

If an operator occupying an important position in the general- use communications network fails to fulfil the instructions of the federal executive power body in the sphere of communications on the issues involved in the connection of telecommunications networks and of their interaction, and also if an operator occupying an important position in the general- use communications network, shirks the conclusion of a contract for connecting telecommunications networks, the other party has the right to turn to the court with a claim for the compulsion in signing the contract for the connection of the telecommunications networks and for the recompense of inflicted losses.

Article 20. Prices for Connection Services and for Services for Letting Through Traffic Rendered by Operators Occupying an Important Position in the General- Use Communications Network

Prices for connection services and for services involved in letting through traffic rendered by operators occupying an important place in the general- use communications network are subject to state regulation. The list of connection services and services for letting through the traffic, the prices for which are subject to state regulation, as well as the procedure for their regulation, are established by the Government of the Russian Federation.

The amount of the state- regulated prices for connection services and for services for letting through the traffic rendered by operators occupying an important position in the general- use communications network shall facilitate the creation of conditions for the reproduction of the modern functional equivalent of the part of the telecommunications network which is used as a result of an additional load caused by the network of the interacting communications operator, and shall also compensate for outlays made on the operational servicing of the used part of the telecommunications network and incorporate a substantiated norm of profit (profitability) from the capital made use of in rendering the given services.

Operators occupying an important position in the general- use communications network are obliged to keep separate records on the incomes and outlays in accordance with the carried out forms of activity, with the rendered communications services and the parts of the telecommunications network used to render these services.

The procedure for keeping such separate records in the cases established in the present Federal Law shall be defined by the federal executive power body in the sphere of communications.

CHAPTER 5. STATE REGULATION OF ACTIVITY IN THE SPHERE OF COMMUNICATIONSS

Article 21. Organizing the State Regulation in the Sphere of Communications

The state regulation in the sphere of communications in conformity with the Constitution of the Russian Federation and with the present Federal Law shall be carried out by the President of the Russian Federation, by the Government of the Russian Federation and by the federal executive power body in the sphere of communications, as well as by the other federal executive power bodies within the scope of their competence.

The Government of the Russian Federation establishes the authority of the federal executive power body in the sphere of communications.

The federal executive power body in the sphere of communications shall: exercise the functions of working out the state policy and of normative legal regulation in the area of communications;

on the basis and in pursuance of the Constitution of the Russian Federation, federal constitutional laws, federal laws, acts of the President of the Russian Federation and the Government of the Russian Federation shall independently carry on the legal regulation in the area of communications and computerization , except for the matters that are under the Constitution of the Russian Federation, federal constitutional laws, federal laws, acts of the President and the Government of the Russian Federation are solely regulated by federal constitutional laws, federal laws, acts of the President of the Russian Federation and the Government of the Russian Federation;

shall interact in respect of the matters and in the procedure established by federal laws with self-regulated organisations in the area of communications established in compliance with the laws of the Russian Federation (hereinafter referred to as self- regulated organisations);

shall exercise the functions of the communications administration of the Russian Federation, when exercising by the Russian Federation international activities in the area of communications;

shall have the right to inquire from communication operators information on the rendering of communication services for the needs of the defence of the country and the security of the State and of the protection of law and order, including on the technological possibilities of the communication operator for rendering communication services, on the prospects of the development of communication networks, on tariffs of communication services, and also to send to communication operators who concluded a government contract for rendering communication services to meet the needs of the defence of the country, the security of the State and the protection of law and order, which are compulsory for the fulfilment of the order in connection with the said contracts.

3. Abolished from January 1, 2005.

Article 22. Regulating the Use of the Radio Frequency Spectrum

Regulating the use of the radio frequency spectrum is the exclusive prerogative of the state and is provided for in conformity with the international treaties of the Russian Federation and with the legislation of the Russian Federation by carrying out the economic, organizational and technical measures involved in the conversion of theradio frequency spectrum and aimed at facilitating the introduction of promising technologies and standards, and at providing for the efficient use of the radio frequency spectrum in the social sphere and in the economy, as well as for the needs of the state administration, of the country's defence and of state security, and for the maintenance of law and order.

The use of the radio frequency spectrum in the Russian Federation is regulated by the interdepartmental collegiate radio frequencies body under the federal executive power body in the sphere of communications (hereinafter referred to as the State Radio Frequencies Commission), endowed with full powers in the state regulation of the radio frequency spectrum.

The Regulations on the State Radio Frequencies Commission and its composition are approved by the Government of the Russian Federation.

The Regulations on the State Radio Frequencies Commission shall establish the procedure for the distribution of radio frequencies. These Regulations shall contain, in particular, the procedure for adopting decisions by the Radio Frequencies Commission and the composition of the Commission with the participation of representatives from all interested federal executive power bodies.

If a representative from one of the above- mentioned bodies has an interest which may exert an impact on the objectivity in the decision- making on an issue under the Commission's consideration, this representative shall not take part in the voting.

The organizational and technical measures providing for proper use of radio frequencies or of radio frequency channels, and of the corresponding radio- electronic appliances or high-frequency devices for civilian uses in the execution of the decisions of the State Radio Frequencies Commission, shall be implemented by the specially authorized service for ensuring the regulation of the use of radio frequencies and of radio- electronic appliances under the federal executive power body in the sphere of communications (hereinafter referred to as the radio frequencies service), the regulations on which are approved by the Government of the Russian Federation.

The use of the radio frequency spectrum in the Russian Federation is carried out in accordance with the following principles:

- permissive procedure for the users' access to the radio frequency spectrum;

- rapprochement of the distribution of radio frequencies and of the terms for their use in the Russian Federation with the international distribution of radio frequency bands;

- the right of access for all users to the radio frequency spectrum, taking into account state priorities, including the provision of the radio frequency spectrum for the radio services of the Russian Federation to ensure citizens' safety, presidential and government communications, the country's defence and state security, the ecological welfare and the prevention of technogenic emergency situations;

- the paid character of the use of the radio frequency spectrum;

- inadmissibility of a free- end allocation of radio frequency bands and assignment of radio frequencies or of radio frequency channels;

- conversion of the radio frequency spectrum;

- transparency and openness of the procedures for the distribution and the use of the radio frequency spectrum;

5. The communications facilities and the other radio - electronic appliances and high- frequency devices which are the sources of electromagnetic emission, are subject to registration. The list of the

For additional analytical, business and investment opportunities information, please contact Global Investment & Business Center, USA at (202) 546-2103. Fax: (202) 546-3275. E-mail: rusric@erols.com

radio- electronic appliances and of the high- frequency devices subject to registration, and the procedure for their registration are defined by the Government of the Russian Federation.

The radio- electronic appliances used for individual reception of teleradio broadcasting programmes, of personal signals for radio calls (the radiopagers), electronic items for personal use and means of personal radio navigation not containing any radio emission devices are used on the territory of the Russian Federation taking account of the restrictions envisaged in the legislation of the Russian Federation, and are not subject to registration.

The use without registration of radio- electronic appliances and high- frequency devices subject to registration in accordance with the rules formulated in the present Article is inadmissible.

Article 23. Distribution of the Radio Frequency Spectrum

The radio frequency spectrum is distributed according to the Table for Distributing Frequency Bands Between the Radio Services of the Russian Federation and to the Plan for the Future Use of the Radio Frequency Spectrum by Radio - Electronic Devices which are developed by the State Radio Frequencies Commission and are approved by the Government of the Russian Federation.

The Table for Distributing Frequency Bands Between the Radio Services of the Russian Federation shall be revised at least once every four years, and the plan for the future use of the radio frequency spectrum, at least once in ten years.

Once every two years the State Radio Frequencies Commission shall consider proposals lodged by the self- regulated organizations and by the individual communications operators on revising the Table for Distributing Frequency Bands Between the Radio Services of the Russian Federation and the Plan for the Future Use of the Radio Frequency Spectrum by Radio - Electronic Devices.

3. The radio frequency spectrum incorporates the following categories of radio frequency bands:

- for the priority use of radio- electronic devices for the needs of state administration, including for presidential and government communications, for the needs of the country's defence and of the state security, and for ensuring law and order;

- for the priority use of civilian- purpose radio - electronic devices;

- for a joint use of radio- electronic devices of any profile.

4. For the users of the radio frequency spectrum is fixed a single- time payment and an annual payment for its use to provide for the radio frequencies control system, for the conversion of the radio frequency spectrum and for financing measures for shifting the operating radio- electronic devices to other radio frequency bands.

The procedure for fixing the amount of a one- off payment and of an annual payment, for the collection of such payment, as well as for its distribution and use is defined by the Government of the Russian Federation, proceeding from the fact that the amount of a one- off payment and of an annual payment shall be fixed in a differentiated way, depending on the utilized range of the radio frequencies and on their number, as well as on the applied technologies.

Article 24. Setting Aside Radio Frequency Bands and Assignment (Awarding) of Radio Frequencies or of Radio Frequency Channels

The right to the use of the radio frequency spectrum is presented by setting aside the radio frequency bands and by the assignment (awarding) of radio frequencies or of the radio frequency channels.

The use of the radio frequency spectrum without a corresponding permit is inadmissible.

In the radio frequency bands of the categories for the joint use of radio- electronic devices of any profile and for the priority use of civilian- purpose radio- electronic devices, the radio frequency bands for radio- electronic devices of any profile, and in the radio frequency bands for the priority use of radio- electronic devices used for the needs of the state administration, the radio frequency bands for civilian- purpose radio- electronic devices shall be assigned by the State Radio Frequencies Commission.

In the radio frequency bands of the category for the priority use of radio electronic devices applied for the needs of the state administration, the radio frequency bands for radio electronic devices providing for the presidential and government communications, for the country's defence, state security and maintaining law and order, shall be set aside in the Russian Federation by the specially authorized federal executive power body in the sphere of government communications and informatics, and by the federal executive power body in the sphere of defence.

Radio frequency bands are assigned for ten years or for a shorter declared term. At the request of the user of the radio frequency spectrum, this term may be extended or reduced by the bodies which have assigned the radio frequency band.

The right to the use of radio frequency bands granted in conformity with the present Article cannot be handed over by one user of the radio frequency spectrum to another user without the decision of the State Radio Frequencies Commission or of the body which has granted this right.

3. A radio frequency or a radio frequency channel for the civilian- purpose radio- electronic devices shall be awarded (allocated) by the federal executive power body in the sphere of communications at the conclusion of the radio frequencies service on the grounds of applications from the citizens of the Russian Federation or from Russian legal entities.

Decisions on the assignment (allocation) of a radio frequency or of a radio frequency channel for the civilian - purpose radio- electronic appliances, as well as those at the other applications from citizens shall be adopted by the federal executive power body in the sphere of communications not later than one hundred and twenty days as from the day of filing such application.

A radio frequency or a radio frequency channel for the radio- electronic appliances used for the needs of the state administration, including the presidential communications and government communications, for the needs of the country's defence and state security, and for maintaining law and order shall be assigned (allocated) by the specially authorized federal executive power body in the sphere of government communications and informatics, and by the federal executive power body in the sphere of defence.

A radio frequency and a radio frequency channel shall be assigned (allocated) for ten years or for a shorter declared term. The term for the assignment (allocation) of a radio frequency or of a radio frequency channel for the orbital - frequency resource may be extended with an account for the guaranteed service life of the space objects used for the creation and functioning of communications networks.

The decision on setting aside radio frequency bands and on the assignment (allocation) of radio frequencies or of a radio frequency channel shall be adopted in accordance with Items 2 and 3 of the present Article in case of a positive expert conclusion on the possibility of applying the declared radio- electronic devices. The procedure for carrying out an expertise shall be established by the State Radio Frequencies Commission.

The procedure for considering the materials and for adopting the decision on setting aside radio frequencies and for the assignment (allocation) of radio frequencies or of radio frequency channels within the scope of the set aside radio frequency bands shall be established and published by the State Radio Frequencies Commission.

The assignment (allocation) of a radio frequency or of a radio frequency channel may be altered in the interests of providing for the needs of the state administration, including for the presidential and government communications, for the needs of the country's defence and state security, and for maintaining law and order, with the recompense of the losses caused by an alteration of the radio frequency or of the radio frequency channel, to the owners of the radio- electronic appliances.

A compulsory alteration of the radio frequency or of the radio frequency channel of the user of the radio frequency spectrum by the federal executive power body in the sphere of communications is admissible only for the purposes of preventing a threat to human life or health and of providing for state security, and also to fulfil the obligations stemming from the international treaties of the Russian Federation. Such alteration may be appealed against by the user of the radio frequency spectrum in court.

The refusal to set aside radio frequency bands for the civilian- purpose radio- electronic devices to the users of the radio frequency spectrum is admissible for the following reasons:

- non- correspondence of the declared radio frequency band to the Table for Distributing Radio Frequency Bands Between the Radio Services of the Russian Federation;

- non- correspondence of the radiation parameters and of the reception of the declared radio-electronic devices to the demands, norms and national standards in the sphere of providing for the electromagnetic compatibility of radio - electronic appliances and of high- frequency devices;

- negative expert conclusion on the electromagnetic compatibility with the radio- electronic devices currently in use and planned for use.

8. Refusal to assign (allocate) radio frequencies or a radio frequency channel to the users of the radio frequency spectrum for civilian- purpose radio- electronic appliances is admissible on the following grounds:

- absence of the documents for the radio- electronic appliances declared for use confirming their correspondence in the cases when such confirmation is obligatory;

- non- correspondence of the declared activity in the sphere of communications to the demands, norms and rules established for the given kind of activity;

- negative expert conclusion on the electromagnetic compatibility with the radio- electronic devices currently in use and planned for use;

- negative results of carrying out an international procedure for coordinating the use of a radio frequency appropriation, if such procedure is envisaged in the Radio Communication Regulations of the International Telecommunications Union and in the other international treaties of the Russian Federation.

The refusal to assign (allocate) radio frequencies or radio frequency channels for the radio- electronic appliances used for the needs of the state administration, including for the presidential and government communications, for the needs of the country's defence and of state security, as well as for

providing for law and order, shall be made in accordance with the procedure defined by the specially authorized federal executive power body in the sphere of government

For additional analytical, business and investment opportunities information, please contact Global Investment & Business Center, USA at (202) 546-2103. Fax: (202) 546-3275. E-mail: rusric@erols.com

communications and information, and by the federal executive power body in the sphere of defence.

If a violation of the terms established when setting aside a radio frequency band or when allocating (assigning) a radio frequency or a radio frequency channel is exposed, a permit for the use of the radio frequency spectrum by the users of the radio frequency spectrum for civilian-purpose radio- electronic devices may be suspended by the body which has set aside the radio frequency band or which has assigned (allocated) the radio frequency or the radio frequency channel in conformity with Items 2 and 3 of the present Article for a term necessary for eliminating this violation, but for no longer than ninety days.

A permit for the use of the radio frequency spectrum shall be terminated out of court, or the term of validity of such permit shall not be extended for the following reasons:

- an application from the user of the radio frequency spectrum;

- the cancellation of the licence for the performance of an activity in the sphere of rendering communications services, if such activity is connected with the use of the radio frequency spectrum;

- an expiry of the term fixed when the radio frequency or the radio frequency channel was assigned (allocated), if this term was not extended in the established order or if an application for its extension was not filed in good time, that is, at least thirty days before the end of the said term;

- the use of the radio- electronic appliances and/or of the high- frequency devices for illegal purposes, causing harm to the interests of the person, state and society;

- the failure on the part of the user of the radio frequency spectrum to fulfil the terms formulated in the decision on the assignment (allocation) of the radio frequency or of the radio frequency channel;

- non- making by the user of the radio frequency spectrum of the payment for the use thereof within thirty days as from the day of the term fixed for the payment;

- the liquidation of the legal entity to which the permit for the use of the radio frequency spectrum was issued;

- the failure to eliminate the violation which has served as a ground for suspending the permit for the use of the radio frequency spectrum.

If in the documents submitted by the applicant there is unauthentic or distorted information which has exerted an impact on the decision- making on setting aside a radio frequency band or on assigning (allocating) a radio frequency or a radio frequency channel the body which has set aside the radio frequency band or which has assigned (allocated) the radio frequency or the radio frequency channel, has the right to turn to the court with a claim for the termination or for the non-extension of the term of validity of the permit for the use of the radio frequency spectrum.

If the permit for the use of the radio frequency spectrum is terminated or suspended, the payment made for its use shall not be returned.

Article 25. Control over the Emissions of Radio- Electronic Appliances and/or of High- Frequency Devices

1. Control over the emissions of radio- electronic appliances and/or of high- frequency devices (radio control) shall be exerted for the following purposes:

- checking the observation by the user of the radio frequency spectrum of the rules for its use;

For additional analytical, business and investment opportunities information, please contact Global Investment & Business Center, USA at (202) 546-2103. Fax: (202) 546-3275. E-mail: rusric@erols.com

- exposure of the radio- electronic devices not permitted for use, and termination of their operation;

- identifying the sources of radio interferences;

- revealing a violation of the procedure and of the rules for the use of the radio- electronic spectrum, of the national standards and of the demands for the emission parameters (reception) of the radio-electronic appliances and/or of the high- frequency devices;

- providing for electromagnetic compatibility;

- ensuring the operational preparedness of the radio frequency spectrum.

2. The radio control is a component part of the state management of the use of the radio frequency spectrum and of the protection of the assignment (allocation) of radio frequencies or of radio frequency channels by international law. Radio control over civilian- purpose radio - electronic appliances is exerted by the radio frequencies service. The procedure for the exertion of radio control shall be defined by the Government of the Russian Federation.

In the process of exerting radio control, a record may be made of the signals of the controlled emission sources for the study of the radiation parameters of the radio- electronic appliances and/or of the high- frequency devices, and also for confirming a violation of the established rules for the use of the radio frequency spectrum.

This record may serve only as proof of the violation of the procedure for the use of the radio frequency spectrum and shall be destroyed in accordance with the procedure established by the legislation of the Russian Federation.

The use of this record for any other purposes is inadmissible, and persons guilty of such use shall bear the responsibility established in the legislation of the Russian Federation, for violating the inviolability of private life and of personal, family, commercial and other law- protected secrets.

Article 26. Regulation of the Numeration Resource

1. The regulation of the numeration resource is the prerogative of the state.

The Government of the Russian Federation lays down the procedure for the distribution and use of the numeration resources of the uniform telecommunications network of the Russian Federation, including of the Russian segments of the international communications networks, taking account of the recommendations of the international organizations of which the Russian Federation is a member, in conformity with the Russian system and with the plan of numeration.

When distributing the numeration of the Russian segments of the international communications networks, the generally accepted international practice of activity of the self - regulated organizations in this sphere shall be taken into account.

2. For the receipt of a numeration resource, from the communication operator shall be collected the state duty in compliance with the legislation of the Russian Federation on taxes and fees.

The federal executive power body in the sphere of communications has the right in the cases established in the present Federal Law to alter and to completely or partially withdraw the numeration resource set aside for a communications operator. Information on the forthcoming change of the numeration and on the term for effecting it is subject to publication. In case of the complete or partial withdrawal of the numeration resource assigned to the communications operator, the communications operator is not entitled to any compensation.

The numeration resource which was earlier set aside for the communication operators shall be withdrawn on the following grounds:

- an application from the communications operator to whom the corresponding numeration resource is assigned;

- the end of the validity of the licence issued to the communications operator;

- the use of the numeration resource by the communications operator with a violation of the system and of the plan of numeration;

- the failure on the part of the communications operator to make use of the numeration resource in the course of two years as from the day of its assignment;

- the failure on the part of the communications operator to fulfil the obligations he has assumed at the bidding envisaged in the present Federal Law;

The communications operator shall be notified about the adopted decision to withdraw from him the numeration resource in writing, thirty days before the time of the withdrawal sets in, with the substantiation of the reasons behind the adoption of such decision.

3. The federal executive power body in the sphere of communications is obliged:

1) to present to the Government of the Russian Federation the procedure for the distribution and use of the numeration resources of the uniform telecommunications network of the Russian Federation for approval;

2) to ensure organizing the work for the distribution and for recording the numeration resources, as well as for setting aside the numeration resources;

3) to establish normative demands to be made on the communication networks as concerns the activation of the numeration resources, thes demands obligatory for the communications operators connected with building communications networks, with controlling the communications networks, with the numeration and with protecting the communications networks from an unsanctioned access to information transmitted through them, as well as the demands made on the use of the radio frequency spectrum, on the procedure for letting through the traffic and on the terms for interaction of communications networks and for rendering communications services;

4) to approve the Russian system and the plan of numeration;

5) to alter in the technically substantiated cases the numeration of communications networks with the preliminary publication of the reasons and the terms for the forthcoming changes in accordance with the procedure for the distribution and use of the numeration resources of the uniform telecommunications network of the Russian Federation;

6) to ensure the existence of an available numeration resource;

7) to present information on distributing the numeration resource at the enquiries from the interested persons;

8) to control correspondence between the use by the communication operators of the numeration resource set aside for them, and the established procedure for the use of the numeration resources of the uniform telecommunications network of the Russian Federation, including the fulfilment by the communications operator of the obligations he has assumed at the bidding, stipulated in the present Federal Law.

For additional analytical, business and investment opportunities information,
please contact Global Investment & Business Center, USA
at (202) 546-2103. Fax: (202) 546-3275. E-mail: rusric@erols.com

Information on the allocation, the alteration and the withdrawal of the numeration resource of the particular communications operator is not a commercial secret.

A numeration resource for the communications networks is set aside by the federal executive power body in the sphere of communications by application from the communications operator within a term of sixty days at the most, if the volume of the numeration set aside for all communications operators on the concrete territory comprises less than ninety per cent from the available resource. When determining the numeration resource presented for the bidding, the applications which have come in for the bidding, envisaged in Article 31 of the present Federal Law shall be taken into account.

The communications operators for whom the numeration resource is set aside or altered are obliged to start the use of the set aside numeration resource or to change the numeration of the network within the established term and to cover all the necessary expenditures.

The subscribers shall not bear the expenditures involved in setting aside and in altering the numeration of the communications network, with the exception of those involved in replacing the subscribers' numbers or identification codes in the documents and in the informational materials.

The communications operator has the right to hand over the numeration resource set aside for him, or a part thereof to another communications operator only with the consent of the federal executive power body in the sphere of communications.

When a legal entity is reorganized in the form of merger, affiliation or transformation, the law-establishing documents on the numeration resource assigned to it shall be reformalized at an application from its legal successor.

When a legal entity is reorganized in the form of division or branching off, the law- establishment documents on the numeration resource shall be reformalized by applications from the legal successors. If other successors put in doubt the rights of the interested legal successor to the use of the numeration resource, the dispute between the parties shall be resolved in court.

Article 27. State Supervision of Activity in the Sphere of Communications

The Government of the Russian Federation shall determine the procedure for exercising the state supervision over the activities in the area of communications. The state supervision over the activities in the area of communications shall be exercised by the federal executive body in charge of supervision in the area of communications.

Ensuring the state supervision over the activities in the area of communications shall be an expense commitment of the Russian Federation.

Official persons from the federal executive body in charge of supervision in the area of communications authorized to compile protocols on the administrative law offences in the sphere of communications and informatics, shall be seen as state inspectors for supervision over the communications.

A state inspector for supervision over communications shall discharge the functions imposed upon him in accordance with the legislation of the Russian Federation.

In accordance with the procedure and in the cases established in the legislation of the Russian Federation, a state inspector for supervision over communications shall apply measures of impact against the perpetrators or shall make the corresponding presentation to the body endowed with the right to draw to responsibility.

**For additional analytical, business and investment opportunities information,
please contact Global Investment & Business Center, USA
at (202) 546-2103. Fax: (202) 546-3275. E-mail: rusric@erols.com**

If a violation of obligatory demands in the sphere of communications is exposed which has been established in federal laws or in other legal normative acts of the Russian Federation adopted in conformity with them, the federal executive body in the area of communications shall issue an instruction on the elimination of this violation at the presentation of the state inspector for supervision over the communications. This instruction is subject to obligatory execution within the time term fixed in it.

The decisions of the state inspector for supervision over communications may be appealed against in accordance with the procedure laid down in the legislation of the Russian Federation.

Article 28. Regulating Tariffs on Communication Service

Tariffs on communications services are established by the communications operator on his own, unless otherwise stipulated in the present Federal Law and in the legislation of the Russian Federation on natural monopolies.

Tariffs on the services of the generally available telecommunications and of generally available postal communications are subject to state regulation in conformity with the legislation of the Russian Federation on natural monopolies. The list of services of the generally available telecommunications and generally available postal communication, the tariffs on which are regulated by the state, as well as the procedure for their regulation, are established by the Government of the Russian Federation. Tariffs on the universal communications services are regulated in accordance with the present Federal Law.

The state regulation of tariffs on communications services (with the exception of the regulation of tariffs on the universal communication services) shall create conditions ensuring for the communication operators the compensation for their economically substantiated expenses involved in rendering communications services, as well as the recompense of the substantiated norm of profit (the profitability) from the capital used in rendering the communications services, the tariffs on which are established by the state.

CHAPTER 6. LICENSING ACTIVITY IN THE SPHERE OF RENDERING COMMUNICATIONS SERVICES AND CONFIRMATION OF THE CORRESPONDENCE OF COMMUNICATIONS FACILITIES

Article 29. Licensing Activity in the Sphere of Rendering Communications Services

The activity of legal entities and individual businessmen in the paid rendering of communications services is carried out only on the grounds of a licence for the performance of an activity in the sphere of rendering communications services (hereinafter referred to as the licence). The list of the names of communications services entered in the licences, and the corresponding lists of licensing terms are established by the Government of the Russian Federation.

The activity in the sphere of rendering communications services is licensed by the federal executive power body in the sphere of communications (hereinafter referred to as the licensing body), which:

1) establishes the licensing terms in conformity with the lists of licensing terms mentioned in Item 1 of the present Article, and introduces amendments and addenda into them;

2) registers the applications for granting licences;

3) issues licences in conformity with the present Federal Law;

4) exerts control over the observation of the licensing terms and issues instructions on the elimination of the exposed violations and warnings about the suspension of the licences' validity;

5) refuses in issue of licences;

6) suspends the licences' validity and reinstates their validity;

7) cancels the licences;

8) reformalizes the licences;

9) keeps a register of licences and publishes information from this register in conformity with the

present Federal Law.

3. Licences are issued in accordance with the results of considering the applications, and in the cases envisaged in Article 31 of the present Federal Law - in accordance with the results of bidding (of an auction or a tender).

Article 30. Demands Made on an Application for Granting a Licence

1. To obtain a licence, the licence seeker shall file an application to the licensing body, in which he shall indicate: 1) the name (the official designation), the legal organizational form, the place of location of the legal entity and the name of the bank, with an indication of the account (for a legal entity); 2) the surname, name and patronymic, the place of residence and the data from the document

identifying the person (for an individual businessman);

3) the name of the communications service;

4) the territory on which the communications service will be rendered and the communications network will be created;

5) the category of the communications network;

6) the time term in the course of which the licence seeker intends to perform an activity in the

sphere of rendering communications services.

2. To the application shall be enclosed:

1) the copies of the constituent documents contained in the registration file of the legal entity certified by the state bodies keeping the uniform state register of legal entities, and a copy of the document confirming that an entry on the legal entity is made in the uniform state register of legal entities certified by the body which has issued the said document, or by a notary (for legal entities);

2) a copy of the certificate on the state registration in the capacity of an individual businessman certified by the body which has issued the said document, or a notarially certified copy of this document (for individual businessmen);

3) a notarially certified copy of the certificate on the legal entity or the individual businessman being put onto the records in the tax body; 4) the plan for the construction of the communications network and a description of the communications service;

5) the document confirming the payment of the fee for considering the application for being granted a licence.

For additional analytical, business and investment opportunities information,
please contact Global Investment & Business Center, USA
at (202) 546-2103. Fax: (202) 546-3275. E-mail: rusric@erols.com

If in the course of rendering communications services it is supposed to use the radio frequency spectrum, including for the purposes of telecasting and radio broadcasting; to carry out the cable telecasting and the wire radio broadcasting; to transmit vocalinformation, including along the network for transmitting the data; and to present communications channels going beyond the territory of one subject of the Russian Federation (to perform an activity in the sphere of postal communications), the licence seeker shall submit, alongside with the documents mentioned in Items 1 and 2 of the present Article, also a description of the communications network and of the communication facilities, with the use of which communications services are going to be rendered, as well as the plan and the economic substantiation for the development of the communications network. The demands made on the content of such description shall be formulated by the federal executive power body in the sphere of communications.

To receive a licence, envisaging the use of the radio frequency spectrum in rendering the communications service, the decision of the State Radio Frequencies Commission on the assignment of a radio frequency band shall also be required.

To obtain a licence for rendering communications services for the purposes of the telecasting, of the radio broadcasting and of broadcasting additional information, the licence seeker shall also submit a notarially certified copy of the licence for the broadcasting.

To demand from the licence seeker any other document in addition to those pointed out in the present Article, is inadmissible.

The licence seeker bears responsibility in conformity with the legislation of the Russian Federation for the supply to the licensing body of unauthentic or distorted information.

Article 31. Bidding (an Auction or a Tender) for Obtaining a Licence

1. Licences shall be issued in accordance with the results of the bidding (of the auction or the tender), if:

1) the communications service is going to be rendered with the use of the radio frequency spectrum, while the State Radio Frequencies Commission has it established that the radio frequency spectrum available for rendering communications services restricts the possible number of communications operators on the given territory. The winner in the bidding (in the auction or in the tender) shall be issued a licence and shall be assigned the corresponding radio frequencies;

2) the resources of the general- use communications network on the territory are restricted, including the restricted numeration resource, and the federal executive power body in the sphere of communications hasit established that the number of communications operators on the given territory shall also be restricted.

The procedure for holding the bidding (the auction or the tender) is established by the Government of the Russian Federation. The decision on holding the bidding (the auction or the tender) shall be adopted by the federal executive power body in the sphere of communications in accordance with the established procedure.

Arrangements for holding the bidding (the auction or the tender) shall be made by the federal executive power body in the sphere of communications not later than six months after such decision is passed.

Before the decision is adopted on the possibility of the issue of a licence (on the grounds of the decision taken in accordance with the results of considering an application for granting a licence

For additional analytical, business and investment opportunities information, please contact Global Investment & Business Center, USA at (202) 546-2103. Fax: (202) 546-3275. E-mail: rusric@erols.com

or with the results of holding the bidding /the auction or the tender/), a licence envisaging the use of the radio frequency spectrum in rendering communications services shall not be issued.

The provisions of the present Article shall not be spread to relations, involved in the use of radio frequencies for the purposes of the telecasting and of the radio broadcasting.

Article 32. Procedure for Considering an Application for Granting a Licence and for the Issue of a Licence

1. The decision on the issue of a licence or on the refusal of its issue shall be adopted by the licensing body:

- within a term not exceeding thirty days as from the day of the decision- making in accordance with the results of the held bidding (auction or tender);

- in the cases pointed out in Item 3 of Article 30 of the present Federal Law, within a term not exceeding seventy five days as from the day of receiving an application from the licence seeker with all the necessary documents named in Items 1- 3 of Article 30 of the present Federal Law, with the exception of cases when the issue of the licence takes place in accordance with the results of holding the bidding (the auction or the tender);

- in the other cases within a term not exceeding thirty days as from the day of receiving an application from the licence seeker with all the necessary documents indicated in Items 1 and 2 of Article 30 of the present Federal Law, in accordance with the results of considering the application.

The licensing body is obliged to notify the licence seeker about taking the decision on the issue of the licence or about the refusal to issue such within ten days as from the day of passing the corresponding decision. The notification of the issue of the licence shall be directed or handed in to the licence seeker in written form, with an indication of the requisites of the bank accounts and of the term fixed for the payment of the licence fee. The notification of the refusal to issue the licence shall be forwarded or handed in to the licence seeker in writing, pointing out the reasons behind the refusal.

For considering an application for the issue of a licence, a fee shall be collected in the amount of three hundred roubles.

For the issue of a licence shall be collected a licence fee. After receiving the notification on the issue of a licence, the licence seeker is obliged to pay the licence fee. The licence shall be issued within three days after the licence seeker submits the document confirming the payment of the licence fee.

4. For the issue of a licence is established the payment of a licence fee in the amount of:

- 15,000 roubles, multiplied by the number of subjects of the Russian Federation on whose territories (parts of territories) communications services will be rendered in accordance with this licence - in the cases mentioned in Item 3 of Article 30 of the present Federal Law;

- that fixed in the terms of the bidding (of the auction or of the tender) - if the licence is issued in accordance with the results of the held bidding (auction or tender);

- 1,000 roubles, multiplied by the number of subjects of the Russian Federation on whose territories (parts of territories) communications services will be rendered in accordance with this licence - in the other cases.

The sums of the licence fee and of the fee for considering an application for the issue of a licence shall be entered in the federal budget.

For additional analytical, business and investment opportunities information,
please contact Global Investment & Business Center, USA
at (202) 546-2103. Fax: (202) 546-3275. E-mail: rusric@erols.com

If the licensee has not paid the licence fee within three months, the licensing body has the right to cancel the licence.

The territory on which it is permitted to render communications services in accordance with the licence shall be pointed out in the licence by the licensing body.

The licensee has no right to hand over, fully or in part, the licence or any rights it grants to another legal entity or natural person.

Article 33. Term of the Licence Validity

1. A licence may be issued for a term of three to twenty five years, which is established by the licensing body with an account for:

- the time term the license seeker has indicated in his application;

- the content of the communications services, for rendering which the licence is sought;

- the time term pointed out in the decision of the State Radio Frequencies Commission on the assignment of a radio frequency band, if the communications service is rendered with the use of the radio frequency spectrum;

- the technical restrictions and technological conditions in accordance with the rules for connecting telecommunications networks and for their interaction.

A licence may be issued for a term of less than three years at the request of the licence seeker.

The term of the licence's validity may be extended at the licensee's application for the same term for which it was issued, or for a different term, which shall not exceed that established in Item 1 of the present Article. An application for an extension of the term of the licence validity shall be filed with the licensing body not later than two months, and not earlier than six months, before the end of the licence validity. For extending the term of the licence's validity, the licensee shall submit the documents named in Article 30 of the present Federal Law. The decision on the extension of the term of the licence validity shall be adopted by the licensing body on the basis of the submitted documents within a term not exceeding forty five days as from the day of arrival of the said documents.

An extension of the term of the licence's validity may be refused, if violations of the licensing terms have been established but have not been eliminated.

Article 34. Refusal to Issue a Licence

1. The following are seen as the grounds for refusal to issue a licence: 1) non- correspondence of the documents enclosed to the application, to the demands formulated in Article 30 of the present Federal Law; 2) non- presentation of the documents which are necessary in conformity with the present Federal Law;

3) existence of unauthentic or of distorted information in the documents submitted by the licence seeker;

4) non- correspondence of the activity the licence seeker has declared, to the standards, demands and rules established for the given kind of activity;

5) non- recognition of the licence seeker as the winner in the bidding (in the auction or tender), if the licence is issued in accordance with the results of the bidding (of the auction or of the tender);

6) cancellation of the decision of the State Radio Frequencies Commission on the assignment of a radio frequency band;

7) absence of the technical possibility for implementation of the declared communications service.

2. The licence seeker has the right to appeal in court against the refusal to issue a licence or against the licensing body's inaction.

Article 35. Reformalizing a Licence

1. A licence may be reformalized for the legal successor at an application from its holder.

In this case, the legal successor is obliged to submit, in addition to the documents mentioned in Items 1 and 2 of Article 30 of the present Federal Law, also the documents confirming that the communication networks and communications facilities necessary for rendering communications services in accordance with the licence under reformalization have been handed over to him and that to his name has been reformalized the permit for the use of the radio frequencies, if these have to be used for rendering communications services on the grounds of the reformalized licence.

If the legal entity is reorganized in the form of the merger, affiliation or transformation, the licence shall be reformalized by application from its legal successor. To the application shall be enclosed the documents mentioned in Items 1 and 2 of Article 30 of the present Federal Law.

If the legal entity is reorganized in the form of division or branching off, the licence shall be reformalized at an application from the interested legal successor or legal successors. The interested legal successor or legal successors are in this case obliged to present, in addition to the documents indicated in Items 1 and 2 of Article 30 of the present Federal Law, also the documents confirming that to them have been handed over the communications networks and communications facilities necessary for rendering communications services in conformity with the reformalized licence and that to their name has been reformalized the permit for the use of the radio frequencies if these have to be used for rendering communications services on the grounds of the reformalized licence.

If the other legal successors call into question the rights of the interested legal successor or legal successors to the reformalization of the licence, the dispute between the parties shall be resolved in court.

In case of the reorganization of the legal entity or of an alteration of the requisites of the legal entity or of the individual businessman named in the licence, the licensee is obliged to file within thirty days an application for reformalizing the licence, with an enclosure of the documents confirming the changes pointed out in this application. If such application is not lodged within the fixed time term, the licence validity shall be stopped.

A licence shall be reformalized by the licensing body within thirty days as from the day of receiving the corresponding application.

For reformalizing a licence a fee shall be collected in the amount of one thousand roubles, which shall be entered to the federal budget.

If the licence is reformalized, the licensing body shall introduce the corresponding changes into the register of licences in the sphere of communications.

If he refuses to reformalize the licence, the licensee shall bear responsibility to the users of communications services in conformity with the legislation of the Russian Federation and with the

For additional analytical, business and investment opportunities information, please contact Global Investment & Business Center, USA at (202) 546-2103. Fax: (202) 546-3275. E-mail: rusric@erols.com

contracts for rendering communications services concluded with the users of communications services.

Article 36. Introduction of Amendments and Addenda into a Licence

A licensee may apply to the licensing body for an introduction of amendments and addenda into the licence, including into the licence terms. The licensing body is obliged to consider such application and to notify the applicant of the adopted decision within a term not exceeding sixty days.

For the actual introduction of the amendments and addenda into the licence shall be collected a fee in the amount of one hundred roubles, which shall be entered into the federal budget.

If it is necessary to introduce into the licence the amendments and addenda concerning the name of the communications services, the territory on which the licence is valid or the use of the radio frequency spectrum, a new licence shall be issued in accordance with the procedure envisaged for the issue thereof.

If the legislation of the Russian Federation is amended, the licensing body has the right to introduce the amendments and addenda into the licensing terms at its own initiative, while notifying to this effect the licensee within thirty days. In the notification shall be explained the grounds for the adoption of such decision. In this case, the amendments and addenda are introduced into the licence free of charge.

Article 37. Suspension of the Licence Validity

1. Before the licence validity is suspended, the licensing body has the right to issue a warning about the suspension of the licence validity, if:

1) the duly authorized state bodies have exposed a violation connected with the failure to observe the norms established in the federal laws and in the other legal normative acts of the Russian Federation in the sphere of communications;

2) the duly authorized state bodies have revealed that the licensee has violated the licence terms; 3) no communications services have been rendered for over three months, including as from the day of the start for rendering such services indicated in the licence.

2. The licensing body has the right to suspend the licence validity if:

1) violations are exposed which may entail infliction of damage upon the man's rights, lawful interests, life and health, or upon the provisions for the needs of the state administration, including of presidential and government communications, for the needs of the country's defence and of state security, as well as for ensuring law and order;

2) cancellation of the permit of the State Radio Frequencies Commission for the use by the licensee of radio frequencies, if such cancellation makes the rendering of communications services impossible;

3) the licensee's failure to fulfil on time the instruction of the licensing body which has obliged him to eliminate the exposed violation, including an instruction issued as a warning about the suspension of the licence validity.

A warning about the suspension of the licence validity, as well as the decision on the suspension of the licence validity shall be brought up by the licensing body to the licensee's knowledge in writing, with an indication of the reasons behind passing such decision or behind making the

For additional analytical, business and investment opportunities information, please contact Global Investment & Business Center, USA at (202) 546-2103. Fax: (202) 546-3275. E-mail: rusric@erols.com

warning, not later than ten days after the adoption of such decision or of the issue of such warning.

The licensing body is obliged to establish a reasonable term for the licensee to eliminate the violation which has entailed the issue of a warning about the suspension of the licence validity. The said term shall not exceed six months. If the licensee has not eliminated this violation within the given term, the licensing body has the right to suspend the licence validity and to file a claim to the court for the cancellation of the licence.

Article 38. Resumption of the Licence Validity

If the licensee has eliminated the violation which has entailed the suspension of the licence validity, the licensing body is obliged to take the decision on the resumption of its validity.

Seen as the confirmation of the elimination by the licensee of the violation which has entailed the suspension of the licence validity is the conclusion of the state body for supervision over the communications issued not later than ten days as from the date of eliminating the above-mentioned violation. The decision on the resumption of the licence validity shall be adopted not later than ten days as from the day of receipt of this conclusion by the licensing body.

Article 39. Cancellation of the Licence

A licence shall be cancelled in court at the claims filed by the interested persons or by the licensing body, if: 1) unauthentic data has been exposed in the documents which have served as the grounds for taking the decision on the issue of the licence; 2) the circumstances which have caused the suspension of the licence validity have not been eliminated within the fixed term;

3) the licensee has failed to fulfil the obligations he has assumed upon himself as he was taking part in the bidding (in the auction or in the tender) (if the licence is issued in accordance with the results of the held bidding (auction or tender).

The licensing body shall cancel a licence, if: 1) the legal entity is liquidated or its activity is terminated as a result of the reoganization, except for its reorganization in the form of transformation; 2) the validity of the certificate on the state registration of the citizen in the capacity of an

individual businessman has ended;

3) the licensee has filed an application with a request to cancel the licence;

4) the licence fee has not been paid in the course of three months as from the day of notification

of the licence seeker about the issue of the licence.

3. If a licence is cancelled, the licence fee shall not be returned.

4. The licensing body's decision on the cancellation of a licence shall be brought to the licensee's knowledge within ten days as from the day of its adoption and may be appealed against in court.

Article 40. Formation and Maintenance of a Register of Licences in the Sphere of Communications

1. The licensing body shall form and maintain a register of licences in the sphere of communications. In this register shall be contained the following information:

1) information on the licensees;

For additional analytical, business and investment opportunities information,
please contact Global Investment & Business Center, USA
at (202) 546-2103. Fax: (202) 546-3275. E-mail: rusric@erols.com

2) the names of the communications services for rendering which the licence is issued, and the territory on which the rendering of the corresponding communications services is permitted;

3) the date of issue and the number of the licence;

4) the term of the licence validity;

5) the grounds for and the time term of the suspension and of the resumption of the licence validity;

6) the grounds for and the date of the cancellation of the licence;

7) other information established by the licensing body depending on the names of the

communications services.

2. Information supplied in the register of licences in the sphere of communications, is subject to publication in the volume, in the form and in the order to be defined by the licensing body, with an account for the amendments introduced into this register.

Article 41. Confirmation of the Correspondence of Communication Facilities and of Communication Services

To provide for the integrity, stability in the functioning and security of the uniform telecommunications network of the Russian Federation, it is obligatory to confirm the correspondence to the established demands made on the communications facilities, applied:

1) in the general- use communications network; 2) in the technological communications networks and in the special- purpose communications networks, if they are connected to the general- use communications network.

Confirmation of the fact that the communications facilities mentioned in Item 1 of the present Article correspond to the technical regulations adopted in conformity with the legislation of the Russian Federation on technical regulation, and to the demands envisaged in the legal normative acts of the federal executive power body in the sphere of communications on the issues involved in the application of communications facilities shall be effected by way of their obligatory certification or by the adoption of a declaration on correspondence.

The communications facilities, subject to obligatory certification, shall be presented for the performance of the certification by the manufacturer or by the seller.

The documents on the confirmation of the correspondence of communications facilities to the demands and the protocols of the tests of communications facilities received outside the territory of the Russian Federation, shall be recognized in conformity with the international treaties of the Russian Federation.

The manufacturer has the right to adopt a declaration on correspondence on those communications facilities which are not subject to obligatory certification.

3. The list of communications facilities subject to obligatory certification, which is approved by the Government of the Russian Federation, incorporates:

- communications facilities fulfilling the function of commutation systems, of digital transportation systems and of control and monitoring systems, as well as the equipment for recording the volume of rendered communications services in general- use communications networks;

For additional analytical, business and investment opportunities information, please contact Global Investment & Business Center, USA at (202) 546-2103. Fax: (202) 546-3275. E-mail: rusric@erols.com

- end equipment which may lead to a fault in the functioning of the general- use communications network;

- communications facilities of the technological communication networks and of the special- purpose communications networks as concerns their connection to the general- use communications networks;

- radio- electronic communications facilities;

- communications facilities equipment, including software which provides for the performance of established actions in carrying out the operational- search measures.

As he modifies the software which is a part of a communications facility, the manufacturer may adopt in accordance with the established procedure a declaration on the correspondence of the given communication facility to the demands of the earlier issued certificate of conformity or of the earlier issued declaration on correspondence.

Communication services and the systems for controlling the standard of communications services are certified on the voluntary basis.

The Government of the Russian Federation defines the procedure for organizing and carrying out work for obligatory confirmation of the correspondence of communications facilities and the procedure for the accreditation of the certification bodies and the testing laboratories (centres) carrying out certification tests, and approves the rules for carrying out the certification.

Exertion of control over the observation by the holders of the certificates and by the declarants of their obligations to provide for the correspondence of the supplied communications facilities to the certification demands and terms, and the registration of declarations on correspondence adopted by the manufacturers shall be imposed upon the federal executive power body in the sphere of communications.

Onto the federal executive power body in the sphere of communications shall also be imposed the duty to organize the certification system in the sphere of communications, which would incorporate the certification bodies and testing laboratories (centres) regardless of legal organizational forms and of the forms of ownership.

For registering a declaration of correspondence the state duty shall be collected in compliance with the laws of the Russian Federation on taxes and fees.

The holder of the certificate of conformity or the declarant is obliged to provide for the correspondence of the communications facility, of the system for controlling the standard of the communications facility, of the communications service or of the system for controlling the standard of the communications service to the demands of the normative documents for correspondence to which the certification was carried out or the declaration was adopted.

If it is discovered that the operated communications facility, while possessing the certificate of conformity or the declaration on correspondence, does not satisfy the established demands, the holder of the certificate or the declarant is obliged to eliminate the exposed non- correspondence at his own expense. The term for the elimination of the exposed non- correspondence shall be fixed by the federal executive power body in the sphere of communications.

Article 42. Issue and Termination of the Operation of Certificates of Conformity When Carrying out Obligatory Certification of Communications Facilities

For carrying out obligatory certification of a communication facility, the seeker shall forward to the certification body an application for the certification and a technical description of this facility in the Russian language, making it possible to identify the communications facility and containing technical parameters by which the correspondence of the communications facility to the established demands may be estimated.

The applicant who is selling shall also present to the certification body the manufacturer's document confirming the fact of the manufacture of the communications facility he has submitted for the performance of the certification.

The term for considering an application for carrying out the certification shall not exceed thirty days as from the day of receipt by the certification body of the documents mentioned in Item 1 of the present Article.

After receiving the documentally formalized results of the certification tests, the certification body shall pass, within a term of no longer than thirty days, the decision on the issue or on the motivated refusal in the issue of the certificate of conformity. The certificate of conformity is issued for one year or for three years, depending on the certification scheme stipulated in the rules for carrying out the certification.

The refusal in the issue of the certificate of conformity or the termination of its validity shall take place, if the communications facility does not satisfy the established demands, or if the applicant has violated the rules for carrying out the certification.

The federal executive power body in the sphere of communications shall publish information on the entry of the certificate of conformity into the register of certificates of conformity of the certification system in the sphere of communications, or on the removal of the certificate of conformity from this register.

Article 43. Declaration on Correspondence and Registration of Declarations on Correspondence

The correspondence shall be declared by the adoption by the applicant of the declaration on correspondence on the basis of his own proof and of those obtained with the participation of an accredited testing laboratory (centre).

By way of his own proof the applicant shall make use of the technical documentation, of the results of his own studies (tests) and measurements and of the other documents serving as a motivated basis for confirming the correspondence of the communications facilities to the established demands. The applicant shall also include into such proving materials the protocols of the studies (tests) and measurements conducted in an accredited testing laboratory (centre).

The declaration on correspondence shall be formalized in the Russian language and shall contain:

the name and place of location of the applicant;

the name and place of location of the manufacturer of the communications facility;

- the technical description of the communications facility in the Russian language, making it possible to identify this communication facility;

- the applicant's statement that the given communications facility will not exert a destabilizing impact upon the integrity, stability of the functioning and security of the uniform telecommunications network of the Russian Federation, if it is used in accordance with its goal- oriented purpose and if the applicant takes measures to provide for the correspondence of the facility to the established demands;

- information on the carried out studies (tests) and measurements, as well as on the documents which have served as a ground for the confirmation of the fact that the communications facility satisfies the established demands;

- the term of validity of the declaration on correspondence.

The form of the declaration on correspondence shall be approved by the federal executive power body in the sphere of communications.

The declaration on correspondence formalized in accordance with the established rules, is subject to registration by the federal executive power body in the sphere of communications within three days.

The declaration on correspondence is valid as from the day of its registration.

The declaration on correspondence and the component proving materials shall be kept at the applicant's within the term of validity of this declaration and within three years after the end of the term of its validity. The second copy of the declaration on correspondence shall be kept in the federal executive power body in the sphere of communications.

CHAPTER 7. COMMUNICATIONS SERVICES

Article 44. Rendering Communications Services

On the territory of the Russian Federation, communication services are rendered by communications operators to the users of communications services on the grounds of a contract for rendering communications services, signed in conformity with the civil legislation and with the rules for rendering communications services.

The rules for rendering communications services are approved by the Government of the Russian Federation.

The rules for rendering communications services regulate relationships of the users of communications services with communication operators when concluding and when executing a contract for rendering communications services, as well as the procedure and the grounds for a suspension of rendering communications services under the contract and for the cancellation of such contract, the specifics in rendering communications services, the rights and the duties of communication operators and of the users of communications services, the form and the procedure for making settlements for the rendered communications services, as well as the procedure for filing and for considering the complaints and the claims of the users of communications services, and the parties' responsibility.

If the user of communications services violates the demands established in the present Federal Law, in the rules for rendering communications services or in a contract for rendering communication services, including the time terms fixed for the remuneration of communications services rendered to him, the communications operator has the right to suspend the rendering of communications services until the violation is eliminated, with the exception of the cases established by the present Federal Law.

If the said violation is not eliminated within six months as from the day when the user of communications services received a written notification from the communications operator about his intention to suspend the rendering of communications services, the communication operator has the right to unilaterally cancel the contract for rendering communications services, except for the cases established by the present Federal Law.

Article 45. Specifics in Rendering Communications Services to Citizens

A contract for rendering communications services signed with citizens is a public contract. The terms for such agreement shall correspond to the rules for rendering communications services.

In all cases of the replacement of a subscriber's number, the communications operator is obliged to notify the subscriber and to award him a new subscriber's number at least sixty days in advance, unless the necessity of the replacement was called forth by unforeseen or emergency circumstances.

The communications operator has no right to alter the connection scheme of the subscriber's end equipment working on a separate subscriber's line without the latter's written consent.

The subscriber has the right to demand the commutation of the subscriber's number, and the communications operator is obliged, if there is a technical possibility for doing so, to re- switch the subscriber's number onto the subscriber's line in premises situated at a different address and possessed by the given subscriber. The commutation of a subscriber's number is seen as an additional service.

If the subscriber's right to the possession and to the use of the premises in which the end equipment is installed (hereinafter referred to as the telephonized premises), is terminated, the contract for rendering communications services signed with the subscriber shall also be terminated.

In this case, the communications operator, a contract for rendering communications services with whom is terminated, is obliged to conclude a contract for rendering communications services with the new owner of the telephonized premises at the latter's demand within thirty days.

If the family members of the subscriber go on residing in the telephonized premises, the contract for rendering communications services shall be reformalized to the name of one of them in conformity with the rules for rendering communications services.

Until the term fixed in the Civil Code of the Russian Federation for the acceptance of an inheritance into whose composition are included the telephonized premises comes to an end, the communications operator has no right to dispose of the corresponding subscriber's number. If the said premises are inherited, a contract for rendering communication services shall be concluded with the heir. The heir is obliged to remunerate to the communications operator the cost of the rendered communications services for the period up to his entry into the rights of inheritance.

Article 46. Duties of Communications Operators

1. A communications operator is obliged:

- to render communications services to the users of communication services in conformity with the legislation of the Russian Federation, with the national standards, the technical norms and the rules, as well as with the licence and with the contract for rendering communication services;

- to be guided in the design, construction and reconstruction, as well as in the operation of communications networks and communications installations by the legal normative acts of the federal executive power body in the sphere of communications, and to build communications networks taking account for the demands for ensuring the stability and security of their functioning. The involved expenditures, as well as the outlays on the creation and operation ofcontrolling systems for their own communications networks and on their interaction with the uniform telecommunications network of the Russian Federation, shall be borne by the communications operators;

- to observe the demands concerning the organizational - technical interaction with the other communications networks, letting through traffic and defining its routes which are established by the federal executive power body in the sphere of communications, as well as the demands made on making mutual settlements and on obligatory payments;

- to submit statistical reports made out in accordance with the form and the procedure established in federal laws and other legal normative acts of the Russian Federation;

- to supply information at the enquiries from the federal executive power body in the sphere of communications for exercising the latter's powers, including on the technical condition and on the development prospects of communications networks and of communications facilities, on the terms for rendering communications services, connection services and those for letting through the traffic, as well as on the applied tariffs and settlement rates, which shall be made out in accordance with the form and the procedure established in the federal laws and in the other legal normative acts of the Russian Federation.

A communications operator is obliged to create conditions for an unobstacled access of invalids to the communications objects intended for work with the users of communications services, including to the places of rendering communications services and to the places for the remuneration thereof at the communications objects.

To inform the users of communications services about the numeration operating in his communications network, the communication operator is obliged to set up a system for a free of charge informational- reference servicing, and to supply on a paid basis proceeding from the economically substantiated outlays, information on the subscribers of his communications network to organizations interested in the establishment of their own systems for the informational - reference servicing.

Article 47. Privileges and Advantages in the Use of Communication Services

The international treaties of the Russian Federation, the federal laws and the laws of the subjects of the Russian Federation may establish privileges and advantages as concerns priority in rendering communication services, as well as in the procedure and the size of the remuneration thereof for the individual categories of the users of communication services.

The users of the communications services mentioned in Item 1 of the present Article are obliged to enter the payment for the communication services rendered to them in full volume, with the subsequent compensation for the outlays they have made directly at the expense of the funds from the budget of the corresponding level.

Article 48. The Use of Languages and of Alphabets in Rendering Communications Services

Office work in the sphere of communications is carried out in the Russian Federation in the Russian language.

Relationships of communications operators with users of communications services arising as communications services are rendered on the territory of the Russian Federation, are maintained in the Russian language.

Addresses of the senders and of the receivers of telegrams, postal dispatches and postal money transfers transferred within the boundaries of the Russian Federation shall be formalized in the Russian language. Addresses of the senders and of the receivers of telegrams, postal dispatches and postal money transfers transferred within the boundaries of the territories of the Republics in the composition of the Russian Federation, may be formalized in the state languages of the corresponding Republics under the condition that the addresses of the senders and of the receivers are doubled in the Russian language.

The text of a telegram shall be written in letters of the Russian alphabet or in letters of the Latin alphabet.

International communications transmitted along the telecommunications networks and along the networks of the postal communication, shall be processed in the languages defined in the international treaties of the Russian Federation.

Article 49. Recording- Accounting Time in the Sphere of Communications

In the technological processes for the transmission and receipt of communications in the telecommunications and postal communications, and for their processing within the boundaries of the territory of the Russian Federation, telecommunications operators and operators of postal communications shall apply the uniform recording- accounting time - Moscow time.

In international communications, recording- accounting time shall be determined in the international treaties of the Russian Federation.

The user or users of communications services shall be informed about the time of rendering a communications service requiring their direct participation, by the communications operator with an indication of the time operating in the time belt at the place of location of the user or of the users of communications services.

Article 50. Official Telecommunications

Official telecommunications is used for the purposes of the operational- technical and the administrative management of the communications networks, and cannot be used to render communication services under the terms of a contract for rendering communication services for a payment.

Communication operators shall provide the official telecommunications in accordance with the procedure defined by the federal executive power body in the sphere of communications.

Article 51. Rendering Communication Services to Meet State or Municipal Needs

Communication services to meet state or municipal needs shall be rendered on the basis of a contract of payable rendering of communication services to be made in the form of a state or municipal contract in the procedure, established by the civil legislation and the legislation of the Russian Federation on placement of orders to supply goods, carry out works and render services for meeting state or municipal needs, in the volume corresponding to the amount of financing outlays on payment for communication services provided for by the appropriate budgets.

Article 51.1. The Special Features of the Rendering of Communication Services to Meet the Needs of the Defence of the Country, the Security of the State and the Protection of Law and Order

The federal executive body in the sphere of communication, by agreement with the federal executive bodies in charge of the networks of special designation, intended for the needs of the defence of the country, the security of the State and the protection of law and order, shall have the right to make additional requirements for communication network, which are a part of the network of communication for public use and are used for rendering communication services to meet the needs of the defence of the country, the security of the State and the protection of law and order.

For additional analytical, business and investment opportunities information,
please contact Global Investment & Business Center, USA
at (202) 546-2103. Fax: (202) 546-3275. E-mail: rusric@erols.com

If the Government of the Russian Federation vests the communication operator with the duty of rendering such communication services in accordance with the legislation of the Russian Federation for placing orders in the deliveries of goods, the performance of works and the rendering services to meet state and municipal needs, the said requirements shall be fulfilled during the time fixed by the respective government contract to render communication services for the needs of the defence of the country, the security of the State and the protection of law and order.

Prices for communication services rendered to meet the needs of the defence of the country, the security of the State and the protection of law and order shall be determined by a government contract proceeding from the need to compensate the economically justified costs associated with the rendering of the given communication services and the reimbursement of the justified profit rate (profitability) from the capital used to render the given communication services.

Changes in the prices for communication services rendered to meet the needs of the defence of the country, the security of the State and the protection of law and order and in the terms of the payment for rendered communication services shall be allowed in the order established by a government contract at least once in a year.

During the fulfilment of a government contract for the rendering communication services to meet the needs of the defence of the country, the security of the State and the protection of law and order, the communication operator who concluded the said government contract shall not have the right to suspend and/or stop the rendering of services without the consent in written form of the government customer.

Article 52. Calling Emergency Operational Services

A communications operator is obliged to ensure for the user of communications services the free of charge possibility to call emergency operational services (the fire service, militia, medical first aid, emergency gas service and other services, the complete list of which is compiled by the Government of the Russian Federation) round the clock.

The free of charge calling of emergency operational services shall be ensured for every user of communications services by dialling a uniform number on the entire territory of the Russian Federation for all emergency operational services.

The outlays of the communications operators they have made to provide for calling emergency operational services including those involved in rendering services for connecting the communications network of emergency operational services to the general- use communication network and in the transmission and the reception of communications of these services, shall be recompensed on the ground of contracts signed by the communications operators with the bodies and organizations which have created the corresponding emergency operational services.

Article 53. Data Bases on the Subscribers of Communications Operators

Information on the subscribers and on communications services rendered by them which have become known to communications operators by force of execution of a contract on rendering communications services is in fact confidential information and is subject to protection in conformity with the legislation of the Russian Federation.

To information about the subscribers is referred the surname, name and patronymic, or the assumed name of the subscriber - a citizen, the name (official designation) of the subscriber - a legal entity, the surname, name and patronymic of the head and of the workers of this legal entity, as well as the address of the subscriber or the address of the installation of the end equipment, the subscription numbers and the other data, making it possible to identify the subscriber or his end equipment, and information of the data bases of the systems for settlements for the rendered communications services, including on the subscriber's connections, traffic and payments.

Communication operators have the right to make use of the data bases on the subscribers they have set up for the informational- reference servicing, including for preparing and disseminating information in various ways, in particular on magnetic carriers and with the use of telecommunications facilities.

When preparing the data for the informational- reference servicing may be used the surname, name and patronymic of the subscriber - a citizen and his subscriber's number, the name (official designation) of the subscriber - a legal entity, and the numbers and the addresses of the installation of the end equipment he has pointed out.

Information on individual subscribers without their consent in written form cannot be included in the data for the informational- reference servicing and cannot be used for rendering reference and other informational services by a communications operator or by a third person.

Supply to third persons of information on individual subscribers may be effected only with the written consent of the subscribers, with the exception of the cases stipulated in the federal laws.

Article 54. Remuneration of Communications Services

1. The payment for the communications services shall be carried out by cash or cashless settlements - either directly after the rendering of such services, or by way of paying an advance, or with a deferment of payment.

The procedure and form for the payment for communications services shall be determined by an agreement on the rendering of communications services, unless established otherwise by legislation of the Russian Federation. If the tariffs for the services of a telecom provider are subject to state regulation, then, at the demand of a subscriber- citizen, the telecom provider must give that subscriber- citizen the possibility of paying for the furnishing of access to the communications network with a deferment of payment of not less than for six months with the initial instalment of not more than thirty per cent of the established fee.

The subscriber shall not pay for a telephone connection established as a result of a call by another subscriber, except for cases when the telephone connection is established:

with the help of a telephone operator with payment at the expense of the communications services user being called up;

with the use of access codes to telecommunications services set by the federal body of executive power in the field of communications;

with a subscriber who is beyond the borders of the territory of an entity of the Russian Federation indicated in a decision on the assignment to the telecom provider of a numeration resource including the subscriber number assigned to the subscriber, unless the agreement on the rendering of communications services establishes otherwise.

The payment for local telephone communications shall be carried out at the option of a subscriber- citizen with application of the subscriber or the time system of payment.

2. Seen as a ground for making settlements for communications services are the readings of the communications equipment recording the volume of communications services rendered by the communications operators, as well as the terms of the contract for rendering communication services signed with the user of communications services.

3. Abolished from January 1, 2005.

Article 55. Filing Appeals and Presenting Claims, and Their Consideration

The user of communications services has the right to file appeals in the administrative order or in court against the decisions and the actions (inaction) of the body or of the official person, or of the communications operator involved in rendering communications services, as well as in providing for the operational fitness of the radio frequency spectrum.

The communications operator is obliged to keep a complaints and proposals book, and to present it at the first demand of the user of communications services.

Complaints of the users of communications services are considered in accordance with the procedure established in the legislation of the Russian Federation.

If the communications operator has failed to execute the obligations stemming from the contract on rendering communication services, or has executed them improperly, before turning to the court the user of communications services shall present a claim to the operator.

5. Claims shall be presented within the following terms:

1) within six months as from the day of rendering the communication service or of the refusal to render such, or as from the day of presenting a bill for the rendered communications service - on the issues involved in the refusal to render the communications service, in an untimely or an improper execution of obligations stemming from the contract for rendering communications services, or in the failure to fulfil or in an improper fulfilment of work in the sphere of telecommunications (with the exception of complaints connected with telegraph communications);

2) within six months as from the day of sending over a postal dispatch, of making a postal money transfer - on the issues involved in the non- delivery, untimely delivery, damage or loss of a postal dispatch, or in the non- payment out or an untimely payment out of the transferred monetary funds;

3) within a month as from the day of sending a telegram - on the issues involved in the nondelivery or untimely delivery of the telegram, or in the distortion of the text of the telegram, changing its meaning.

To the claim shall be enclosed a copy of the contract for rendering communication services or of another document certifying the fact of the conclusion of such contract (a receipt slip, an inventory of the enclosure, etc.), and other documents necessary for the consideration of the claim on merit, in which shall be supplied information on the non- execution or improper execution of obligations under the contract on rendering communications services, and if a claim for the recompense of a loss is presented - on the fact and on the size of the inflicted loss.

The claim shall be considered not later than sixty days from the day of its registration. The person who has filed a claim shall be informed about the results of the consideration of his claim in writing.

8. Special terms shall be fixed for the consideration of the individual kinds of claims:

1) the claims involved in postal dispatches and in postal money transfers sent over (transferred) within the boundaries of a single populated centre shall be considered within five days as from the day of the registration of the claims;

2) the claims connected with all the other postal dispatches, as well as with postal money transfers, shall be considered within a time term fixed in Item 7 of the present Article.

For additional analytical, business and investment opportunities information, please contact Global Investment & Business Center, USA at (202) 546-2103. Fax: (202) 546-3275. E-mail: rusric@erols.com

9. If a claim is rejected, fully or in part, or if no answer is received within the time term fixed for its consideration, the user of communications services has the right to lodge a claim in court.

Article 56. Persons Having the Right to Present Claims, and the Place for Presenting Claims

1. The right to present claims is possessed by:

- a subscriber concerning the obligations stemming from a contract for rendering communications services;

- a user of communications services who has refused rendering such services;

- a sender or the receiver of postal dispatches in the cases mentioned in Subitems 2 and 3 of Item 5 of Article 55 of the present Federal Law.

2. Claims shall be presented to a communications operator who has concluded a contract for rendering communications services or who has refused to conclude such contract.

The claims connected with the receipt or with handing in of postal or of telegraph dispatches may be presented both to the communication operator who has accepted the dispatch and to the communications operator at the place of destination of the dispatch.

CHAPTER 8. UNIVERSAL COMMUNICATIONS SERVICES

Article 57. Universal Communications Services

1. Rendering of universal communications services in the Russian Federation is guaranteed. In conformity with the present Federal Law, to universal communications services are referred:

- those of telephone communications with the use of coin- box telephones;

- those for transmitting data and for giving access to the Internet with making use of the points for collective access.

2. The procedure and terms for the start of rendering universal communications services, as well as the procedure for the regulation of the tariffs on universal communications services are defined by the Government of the Russian Federation at the presentation of the federal executive power body in the sphere of communications, proceeding from the following principles:

- the time in the course of which the user of communications services may reach a coin- box telephone without making use of a transportation facility shall not exceed one hour;

- in every settlement shall be installed at least one coin- box telephone with a free of charge access to emergency operational services;

- in settlements with the population of no less than five hundred people shall be organized at least one point for collective access to the Internet.

Article 58. Operator for Universal Servicing

Universal communications services shall be rendered by operators for universal servicing, who are selected in accordance with the results of a competition or are appointed in conformity with Item 2 of the present Article for every subject of the Russian Federation.

For additional analytical, business and investment opportunities information,
please contact Global Investment & Business Center, USA
at (202) 546-2103. Fax: (202) 546-3275. E-mail: rusric@erols.com

The number of operators for universal servicing functioning on the territory of a subject of the Russian Federation taking account of its specifics shall be determined proceeding from the need to supply universal services to all potential users of such services.

The right to render universal communications services is granted to operators of the general- use communications network in accordance with the results of the competition held in the order defined by the Government of the Russian Federation.

If there are no applications for taking part in the competition, or if it is impossible to identify the winner, rendering of universal communications service on a particular territory shall be imposed by the Government of the Russian Federation at the presentation of the federal executive power body in the sphere of communications upon an operator occupying an important position in the general- use communications network.

The operator occupying an important position in the general- use communications network has no right to refuse the duty involved in rendering universal communications services imposed upon him.

Article 59. Reserve of Universal Servicing

For the purposes of ensuring for the operators of universal servicing the recompense of the losses inflicted by rendering universal services, a reserve of universal servicing is formed.

The resources of the reserve of the universal service shall be spent exclusively on the purposes provided for by the present Federal Law in the order determined by the Government of the Russian Federation. The correctness and the timeliness of the making by the operators of the network of communication for general use of obligatory assignments (non- tax payments) to the reserve of the universal service shall be controlled by the federal executive body in the sphere of communication.

3. Abrogated from January 1, 2007.

Article 60. The Sources of the Formation of the Reserve of the Universal Service

Obligatory assignments (non- tax payments) by the operators of the network of communication for public use and other sources not prohibited by law shall be the sources of the formation of the reserve of the universal service.

The incomes received during a quarter from the rendered services of communication to subscribers and other users in the network of communication for public use, except for the sums of the taxes presented by the operator of the network of communication for public use to the subscribers and other users in the network of communication for public use in accordance with the legislation of the Russian Federation on taxation shall be the basis for the calculation of obligatory assignments (non- tax payments. Incomes shall be estimated in the order established in the Russian Federation for the procedure of keeping accountancy.

The rate of the compulsory assignment (non- tax payment) by the operator of the network of communication for public use shall be established at the rate of 1.2 per cent.

The amount of the obligatory assignment (non- tax payment) by the operator of the network of communication for public use shall be calculated by him independently as the percentage share of incomes estimated in keeping with the present Article as corresponding to the rate indicated in Item 3 of this Article.

Within 30 days since the end of the quarter in which incomes are received the operators of the network of communication for public use shall be obliged to make obligatory assignments (non-

For additional analytical, business and investment opportunities information,
please contact Global Investment & Business Center, USA
at (202) 546-2103. Fax: (202) 546-3275. E-mail: rusric@erols.com

tax payments) to the reserve of the universal service. The counting out of quarters shall be made since the beginning of a calendar year.

If obligatory assignments (non- tax payments) by the operators of the network of communication for public use to the reserve of the universal service are not made in the established times or are made not in a full scope, the federal executive body in the sphere of communication shall have the right to make recourse to a court of law with a suit on the recovery of compulsory assignments (non- tax payments).

Article 61. Recompense of the Losses Caused by Rendering Universal Communications Services

The losses of the operators for universal servicing caused by rendering universal communications services are subject to compensation in an amount not exceeding the amount for the compensation of losses established in accordance with the results of the competition or, if no competition was held, the maximum amounts of recompense of the losses and within a term not exceeding six months after the end of the financial year, unless otherwise envisaged in the terms of the competition.

The maximum amount of compensation for the losses caused by rendering universal communications services shall be defined as the difference between the incomes and the economically substantiated expenditures of the operator for universal servicing, and the incomes and the expenditures of the communications operator if no obligations for rendering universal services were imposed upon him, unless otherwise established in the present Federal Law.

The operator for universal servicing shall keep separate records on the incomes and on the expenditures in accordance with the performed kinds of activity, with the rendered communications services and with the parts of the telecommunications network used for rendering these services.

The procedure for the recompense of the losses inflicted by rendering universal communications services shall be defined by the Government of the Russian Federation.

CHAPTER 9. PROTECTING THE RIGHTS OF THE USERS OF COMMUNICATIONS SERVICES

Article 62. Rights of the Users of Communications Services

The user of communications services has the right to transmit a communication, to send over a postal dispatch or to make a transfer of the monetary funds, to receive a telecommunication, a postal dispatch or a postal transfer of the monetary funds, or to refuse their receipt, unless otherwise envisaged in federal laws.

Protection of the rights of the users of communications services when rendering telecommunications services and postal services, guarantees for the receipt of these communications services of the proper standard, the right to receive the necessary and authentic information on communications services and on communications operators, the grounds, size and procedure for the recompense of the losses inflicted as a result of the non- execution or of an improper execution of the obligations arising from a contract for rendering communication services as well as the mechanism for the exercise of the rights of the users of communications services, are defined in the present Federal Law, in civil legislation, in the legislation of the Russian Federation on the protection of consumers' rights and in other legal normative acts of the Russian Federation issued in conformity with them.

Article 63. Confidentiality of Communications

For additional analytical, business and investment opportunities information,
please contact Global Investment & Business Center, USA
at (202) 546-2103. Fax: (202) 546-3275. E-mail: rusric@erols.com

On the territory of the Russian Federation the confidentiality of correspondence, telephone conversations, postal dispatches, telegraph and other communications transmitted along telecommunications networks and along postal communications networks is guaranteed.

Restriction of the right to the confidentiality of correspondence, telephone conversations, postal dispatches, telegraph and other communications transmitted along telecommunications networks and along postal communications networks is admissible only in the cases stipulated in the federal laws.

Communications operators are obliged to provide for the observation of the confidentiality of communications.

Examination of postal dispatches by persons who are not the authorized workers of the communications operator, the opening of postal dispatches, the examination of the enclosures and getting acquainted with information and with the documental correspondence transmitted along the telecommunications networks and along the postal communications networks shall be made only on the grounds of a court decision, with the exception of the cases established in the federal laws.

Information on communications transmitted along telecommunications networks and postal communications networks, on the postal dispatches and postal transfers of monetary funds, as well as these communications, postal dispatches and transferred monetary funds themselves may be issued only to the senders and to the receivers, or to their authorized representatives, unless otherwise stipulated in federal laws.

Article 64. Duties of Communications Operators and Restriction of the Rights of the Users of Communications Services in Carrying Out Operational- Search Measures, Measures for Ensuring the Security of the Russian Federation and in Performing Investigatory Actions

Communications operators are obliged to supply to the authorized state bodies performing operational- search activity or ensuring the security of the Russian Federation, information on the users of communications services and the communications services rendered to them, as well as other information necessary for carrying out the tasks imposed upon these bodies, in the cases established in federal laws.

Communications operators are obliged to provide for the satisfaction of the requirements applicable to communication networks and facilities established by the federal executive power body in the sphere of communications in agreement with the authorized state bodies engaged in operational- search activity or ensuring the security of the Russian Federation, for the purpose of these bodies' implementing in the cases established by federal laws measures in order to fulfil the tasks vested therein, and to take measures aimed at precluding the revelation of the organizational and tactical methods applied in carrying out these measures.

Rendering communications services to legal and natural persons is suspended by communications operators on the grounds of a motivated written decision of one of the managers of the body performing operative investigation activity or ensuring the security of the Russian Federation in the cases established by federal laws.

Communications operators are obliged to resume rendering communications services on the grounds of a court decision or of the motivated written decision of one of the managers of the body engaged in operational- search activity or ensuring the security of the Russian Federation who has adopted the decision on the suspension of rendering communications services.

For additional analytical, business and investment opportunities information, please contact Global Investment & Business Center, USA at (202) 546-2103. Fax: (202) 546-3275. E-mail: rusric@erols.com

The procedure for the communications operators' interaction with the authorized state bodies carrying out operational- search activity or ensuring the security of the Russian Federation shall be established by the Government of the Russian Federation.

When the authorized state bodies are carrying out investigatory actions, communications operators are obliged to render assistance to these bodies in conformity with the demands of the criminal- procedural legislation.

CHAPTER 10. MANAGEMENT OF COMMUNICATIONS NETWORKS IN EMERGENCY SITUATIONS AND UNDER THE CONDITIONS OF A STATE OF EMERGENCY

Article 65. Management of the General- Use Communications Network

In emergency situations, the management of the general- use communications network shall be carried out by the federal executive power body in the sphere of communications in interaction with the centres for controlling the special - purpose communications networks, which have connections to the general- use communications network through the technical communications networks.

To coordinate the work aimed at the elimination of the circumstances which have served as a basis for the introduction of a state of emergency, and the consequences of their introduction, in conformity with the legal normative acts of the Russian Federation on the introduction of a state of emergency may be formed provisional special management bodies, to which shall be handed over the corresponding authority of the federal executive power body in the sphere of communications.

Article 66. Priority Use of Communications Networks and of Communications Facilities

During the states of emergency of natural and the technogenic character defined in the legislation of the Russian Federation, the state bodies authorized in accordance with the procedure laid down by the Government of the Russian Federation shall have the right to priority use of any communications networks and communications facilities, as well as suspension or to the restriction of the use of these communications networks and communications facilities.

Communications operators are obliged to provide for an absolute priority to all communications concerning man's safety on water, on land, in the air and in the cosmic space, as well as to the communications about serious accidents and catastrophes, about epidemics and epizootics, as well as about natural calamities connected with carrying out urgent measures in the sphere of the state administration, of the country's defence and of state security, and of ensuring law and order.

Article 67. Abolished from January 1, 2005.

CHAPTER 11. RESPONSIBILITY FOR VIOLATING THE LEGISLATION OF THE RUSSIAN FEDERATION IN THE SPHERE OF COMMUNICATIONS

Article 68. Responsibility for Violating the Legislation of the Russian Federation in the Sphere of Communications In the cases and in accordance with the procedure established in the legislation of the Russian Federation, the persons who have violated the legislation of the Russian Federation in the sphere of communications shall bear administrative and civil- law responsibility.

The losses inflicted as a result of illegal actions (inaction) of the state bodies, of local self-government bodies or official persons of these bodies are subject to the compensation to communications operators and to the users of communications services in conformity with the civil legislation.

Communications operators shall bear property responsibility for the loss or damage of a declared- value postal dispatch and for a shortage of the enclosures into postal dispatches in the amount of the declared value, and for the distortion of the text in a telegram which has changed its meaning, for failure to deliver a telegram or for handing over a telegram to the addressee after the expiry of twenty- four hours as from the moment of its submitting - in the amount of the made payment for the telegram except for telegrams, addressed to the populated centres where there is no telecommunications network.

The amount of responsibility for the non- execution or for an improper execution by communications operators of their duties involved in sending over or in the delivery of the other registered postal dispatches shall be determined in the federal laws.

The workers of communications operators shall be held materially responsible to their employers for the loss or for a delay in the delivery of all kinds of postal and telegraph dispatches and for the damage of the enclosures into the postal dispatches, which have taken place through their guilt as they performed their official duties, in the amount of the communications operator's responsibility to the user of communications services, unless a different measure of responsibility is envisaged in the corresponding federal laws.

A communication operator shall not be held responsible for the failure to fulfil or for an improper fulfilment of the duties involved in the transmission or reception of communications or in sending over or delivery of postal dispatches, if it is proved that such failure to fulfil or improper fulfilment of the duty has occurred through the guilt of the user of communications services or as a result of the action of a force- majeure.

In the cases envisaged in Item 3 of Article 44 of the present Federal Law, the user of communications services is obliged to compensate the communications operator for the losses he has inflicted upon him.

CHAPTER 12. INTERNATIONAL COOPERATION OF THE RUSSIAN FEDERATION IN THE SPHERE OF COMMUNICATIONS

Article 69. International Cooperation of the Russian Federation in the Sphere of Communications

1. The Russian Federation carries out international cooperation in the sphere of communications on the basis of the observation of the generally accepted principles and norms of international law, as well as of the international treaties of the Russian Federation.

In the international activity in the sphere of telecommunications and postal communications, the federal executive power body in the sphere of communications shall be the communications administration of the Russian Federation.

The communications administration of the Russian Federation represents and protects within the scope of its powers the interests of the Russian Federation in the sphere of telecommunications and of postal communications, interacts with the communications administrations of foreign states, with the intergovernmental and international non- governmental communications organizations, coordinates the questions of international cooperation in the sphere of communications carried out by the Russian Federation, and provides for the discharge of the obligations of the Russian Federation stemming from the international treaties of the Russian Federation in the sphere of communications.

2. Foreign organizations or foreign citizens performing an activity in the sphere of communications on the territory of the Russian Federation are entitled to the use of the legal regime established for the citizens of the Russian Federation and for Russian organizations in the same measure in which the said regime is granted in the corresponding state to the citizens of the Russian Federation and to

Russian organizations, unless otherwise established in the international treaties of the Russian Federation or in the federal laws.

Article 70. Regulation of the Activity in the Sphere of International Communications

Relations involved in the activity in the sphere of international communications on the territory of the Russian Federation are regulated by the international treaties of the Russian Federation; by the present Federal Law; by the other federal laws and by the other legal normative acts of the Russian Federation.

The procedure for making settlements between the operators of the international telecommunications is laid down on the basis of international operational agreements and taking account of the recommendations of the international telecommunications organizations of which the Russian Federation is a member.

For rendering communications services within the scope of the informational-telecommunications networks on the territory of the Russian Federation, it is obligatory:

- to create Russian segments of the world communications networks, to provide for interaction with the uniform communication network of the Russian Federation;

- to create Russian communications operators satisfying the demands made on them in the present Federal Law;

- to ensure the economic, public, defence, ecological, informational and other kinds of security.

Article 71. Taking the End Equipment Across the Customs Border of the Russian Federation

Taking the end equipment across the customs border of the Russian Federation, including the import of the end equipment to the customs territory of the Russian Federation by natural persons for the purposes of its operation in the communications networks for the personal, family, domestic and other needs not connected with the performance of business activity shall be effected in accordance with the customs legislation of the Russian Federation without obtaining a special permit for the import of the said equipment.

The list of the end equipment and the procedure for its use on the territory of the Russian Federation are defined by the Government of the Russian Federation.

Article 72. International Postal Communications

The communications administration of the Russian Federation shall organize the international postal communications and shall establish, among other things, the places for an international postal exchange on the territory of the Russian Federation.

CHAPTER 13. FINAL AND TRANSITIONAL PROVISIONS

Article 73. Adjustment of Legislative Acts to the Present Federal Law To recognize as invalidated as from January 1, 2004:

- Federal Law on Communications, No. 15- FZ of February 16, 1995 (Sobraniye Zakonodatelstva Rossiiskoi Federatsii, No. 8, 1995, Item 600);

- Federal Law on the Introduction of Amendments and Addenda into the Federal Law on Communications (Sobraniye Zakonodatelstva Rossiiskoi Federatsii, No. 2, 1999, Item 235);

For additional analytical, business and investment opportunities information, please contact Global Investment & Business Center, USA at (202) 546-2103. Fax: (202) 546-3275. E-mail: rusric@erols.com

- Item 2 of Article 42 of Federal Law on Postal Communications, No. 176- FZ of July 17, 1999 (Sobraniye Zakonodatelstva Rossiiskoi Federatsii, No. 29, 1999, Item 3697).

Article 74. Entry of the Present Federal Law into Force

1. The present Federal Law shall enter into force as from January 1, 2004, with the exception of Item 2 of Article 47 of the present Federal Law.

2. Item 2 of Article 47 of the present Federal Law shall enter into force as from January 1, 2005.

President of the Russian Federation

V. Putin

Moscow, the Kremlin July 7, 2003 No. 126- FZ

TELECOM LICENCING REGULATIONS

Certain types of activities are subject to mandatory licensing in Russia. Resolution No. 87 of the Russian Government on Titles of Telecommunication Services dated 18 February 2005 ('Resolution') outlines which types of telecommunications services require a licence. The Resolution currently lists 20 titles of licensable services. In particular, the following types of telecommunications activities are subject to licensing:

- Local telephone communications services except such services using payphones and means of collective access

- Intercity and international telephone communications services

- Telephone communications services in a dedicated communications network

- Intra-zone telephone communication services

- Local telephone communications services using payphones

- Local telephone communications services using the means of collective access

- Telegraphy communications services

- Personal radio paging communications services

- Mobile radio communications services in a public-use communications network

- Mobile radio communications services in a dedicated communications network

- Mobile radio telephone communications services

- Mobile satellite radio communications services

- Provision of communication channels

- Communications services in data-transfer, except for services in data communications for the purpose of voice information transfer

- Communications services in data transfer for the purpose of voice information transfer

For additional analytical, business and investment opportunities information, please contact Global Investment & Business Center, USA at (202) 546-2103. Fax: (202) 546-3275. E-mail: rusric@erols.com

- Telematics communications services

- Communications services for the purpose of cable broadcasting

- Communications services for the purpose of air broadcasting

- Communications services for the purpose of wired radio broadcasting

- Postal services

The listed titles are not clearly defined or exhaustively described in the Resolution or any other regulations. In practice, this sometimes makes it difficult to reach a clear conclusion on whether a certain business activity falls under any type of licensable service. Usually a Russian telecoms consultant is engaged for such purposes.

As mentioned above, apart from the telecommunication licence requirements, Russian law also requires obtaining state licences/permits for certain other types of activities.

INFORMATION TECHNOLOGY, COMMUNICATION AND INTERNET DEVELOPMENT IN RUSSIA: STRATEGIC INFORMATION

BASIC TRENDS AND DEVELOPMENTS

Population	147,000,000
Rural population (% of total population)	22.66%
GDP per Capita (PPP)	US$8,213
Main Telephone lines per 100 inhabitants	21.82
Internet hosts per 10,000 inhabitants	22.22
Personal computers per 100 inhabitants	4.29
Piracy Rate	79%
Percent of PCs connected to Internet	5.18%
Internet users per host	9.49
Internet users per 100 inhabitants	2.11
Cell phone subscribers per 100 inhabitants	2.22
Average monthly cost for 20 hours of internet access	US$14.83

*Key Stats are from source (12)

Total IT spending

- Domestic Internet Markets have grown 9% to more than $4 billion and will grow 2-3 times by 2005 (

- 3.7% of Russia's gross domestic product is invested in ICT

Telecommunication Infrastructure

- Phone lines per 1000: 218.20

- Cell phone usage per 1000: 22.21

Computing and Internet Diffusion

- Number of websites: 16,964,567

- Web Users as a percent of the population: 5%

- PCs per 1000 people: 48.3

For additional analytical, business and investment opportunities information, please contact Global Investment & Business Center, USA at (202) 546-2103. Fax: (202) 546-3275. E-mail: rusric@erols.com

IT Workforce

- Literacy: 99%

- Percent of adults who are college graduates: 20% (60)

- Number of CS/CE/MIS post secondary programs

    o Admissions in computer related degrees in 2000: 25,000 (60)

- Percent of Russian software companies who employ PhDs: 77.4%

    o In 45.8% of those, PhDs make up about 10% of staff (60)

Domestic Productions

- Software Exports for 2001 were close to $150M (57)

- Some estimate Russian IT Outsourcing to be close to $350M by 2005 (57)

Russia has such great potential to harness its ICT strengths and overcome its weaknesses. New economic conditions have truly created the opportunity to build its budding software industry into an international powerhouse. The Russians have one strength in particular that may prove to be their ticket to success – a well-educated, well-trained, and dynamic workforce focused on science, engineering and technology.

Studies suggest that the Russian market is following a similar pattern of internet adoption as occurred in North American and Western Europe. Although Moscow and St. Petersburg make up 44.2% and 10.6% of Russia's web users respectively, the regional penetration numbers are growing. (36) 40% of Runet citizens live in cities with populations of under 1 million people and Siberia and the Far East account for the largest share of the Runet regional audience. (38) In my opinion, the two biggest hindrances to penetration are infrastructure and disposable income. I think that once the government follows through on its eRussia initiative, the Russian penetration will explode, especially in the more educated populations.

Key Stats

- Number of websites: 16,964,567 (38)

- Web Users as a percent of the population: 5% (about 6 million) (36)

- PCs per 1000 people: 84 (40)

Broadband vs. Dial-up

In terms of household use, dial-up is really the only option for the Russian population. Less than 10% of Russian households have a PC and of those only 5.18% are connected to the Internet. Spending on ICT per month is about $4, the majority of which is most likely telephone costs.

Only 2% of the population has broadband access which is limited to large corporations and ISPs due to cost. (35) In 2001, 63% of Internet users in Russia accessed the Internet at work. (32)

Stimulus for IT growth & Attitudes toward IT diffusion

"While it took about 15 years for color TV to reach 5% of Russian urban population, it took less than eight years for the World Wide Web to reach the same number of users in Russia (www.km.ru)." (36) This penetration is attributable to several characteristics of the Russian population. First, a majority of Russians are technically savvy having advanced degrees in science and engineering. Second, Russians are learning that in a capitalist market, keeping up with technology is one key success factor. And finally, having access to global information is a relatively new concept.

ICT for development (mobile PCs, cybercafés, internet kiosks, etc.)

In the beginning of 2003, there were 2600 public internet access outlets in Russia. Under the CyberPost program, part of eRussia, the government plans to expand this to all Russian post offices by 2008 totaling 12,000 outlets

POTENTIAL

A Russian household spends only $4 per month on information technologies, Russian businesses hardly use e-mail for correspondence and the Russian government is relatively unsuccessful in promoting the sector, according to a report released this week.

These and other negative factors pushed Russia's ranking to 69th, down from last year's 61st-place showing, among the 82 countries surveyed by the World Economic Forum's annual Global Information Technology Report for 2002-2003.

Authors of the report, released for the first time last year, define the list's criteria as the degree to which a country is prepared to participate in and benefit from information and communication technology.

Because reliable data were not available for all countries, only 82 were included.Russia fared relatively poorly next to its former communist peers.

Latvia, Lithuania, Estonia, the Czech Republic, Hungary, Slovenia, Poland and Bulgaria ranked ahead of Russia. Of the countries evaluated, only Ukraine and Romania had lower scores.The list was topped by Finland, followed by the United States and Singapore.

The report's authors ranked countries based on 64 criteria, which were divided into three indexes -- environment, readiness and usage.

Russia ranked 68th in terms of its market, and political, regulatory and infrastructure landscape, 60th in openness toward new technologies and 78th in usage rates.

The report shows that Russia can tap only a limited supply of venture capital, suffers from low competition in the telecommunication sector. Only 3.7 percent of Russia's gross domestic product is invested in information and communication technology, compared to New Zealand's 13.6 percent, the highest rate among the countries surveyed.

Russia came in at a relatively impressive 29th in the number of skilled scientists and engineers, but the report went on to chide Russia's legal system for inadequate support of IT businesses.

Physical infrastructure also remains weak, the report said.

The country has only 218 telephone lines per 1,000 people, with a waiting list backlog stretching five years long. Luxembourg, by comparison, has 750 telephone lines per 1,000 people, while 22 countries have no telephone service backlog at all.

The country lacks good high-speed and public Internet access, the report said.

Estimates by ACM Consulting and J'son & Partners, both based in Moscow, show cellular penetration in Russia reached 12 percent of the population by the end of last year. A spokesman at J'son & Partners added that 2 percent of the Russian population has broadband access.Russia's IT spending has outperformed the global averages for the last three years running at about 20%. Spending in the ICT market is projected to reach almost $20B by 2005.

Foreign investment in ICT in Russia has been relatively flat from US companies. Despite this, there are several major US technology players that have had a strong presence in the market for the majority of market economy history including Intel, IBM, Sun, Dell, and HP. Russia has proven to be a high growth performer for several of these companies on an annual basis. Major factors preventing Russia from fully capitalizing on its human capital strengths are software piracy, poor infrastructure, and poor image.

Even though piracy rates have decreased significantly since the 1990s, Russia is still among the worst rated country in the world with a rate of 79%. Some legal reform has been enacted to significantly decrease this number but enforcement is key.

ICT BUSINESSE USE

Businesses in Russia are willing to take the risks to capitalize on the potential benefits of e-commerce. Several major industrial groups are going on and launching e-commerce initiatives. Following current Western trends, large corporations are using ventures to open new markets and to increase operational efficiency. Most significant is the commodity markets which have embraced the virtual marketplace concept. The companies that have projects currently are Zerno Online (grain), Oil Online, Grin.ru (universal exchange), Global Steel Exchange, Europ-Steel.com, Emetex (metals), and Business.ru (universal).

- 2001 Revenues (in US $ Millions)

    o Software: 6,007

    o ICT Hardware: 5,021

    o IT Services: 760

    o Data Communication Services: 391

    o Voice Telecom: 374

- B2C Retail Sales in 1999 were around $2M

- B2B sales totaled $90M in 1999

ICT applications in fuel and energy, metallurgy, banking, consumer goods protection, and trade are prominent. ERP providers are benefiting from the many Russian companies looking to attract foreign investment or float bonds on the European market and need to establish credible accounting practices. Several clients of IBS Company have taken advantage of their SAP implementation services including Rostelecom, Gazprom, the Ministry of railways, Lukoil, and Shell. (42)

Russia has proven a performer for several major players in the hardware market. It is Intel's fastest growing market, and "in the past year, software giant Microsoft's sales in Russia have grown 80%, while Sun's have doubled over the lat two years. Both cite their Russian divisions as their best performers companywide in 2002." (44)

There are several options for payment when conducting e-commerce in Russia.

For additional analytical, business and investment opportunities information,
please contact Global Investment & Business Center, USA
at (202) 546-2103. Fax: (202) 546-3275. E-mail: rusric@erols.com

- Cash on delivery

  - Most common means of payment

- Banking cards (credit or debit cards)

- Internet banking

- Prepayment or pre-paid cards

- Digital money

B2B prospects for E-Commerce are much more appealing at this point than B2C. B2C projects are significantly hindered by weak consumer purchasing power, low use of credit cards, lack of trust in the banking system, and a poor postal delivery system.

NATIONAL ICT POLICIES

Russia did little to establish an ICT policy prior to Putin's presidency and even he had a slow start. In 2000, Putin signed the Okinawa Charter of the Information Society. "Upon his initiative the Government of the Russian Federation has developed a number of programs aiming at wide dissemination of the modern computer technologies in all spheres of life."

It took another 2 years for the Russian Federation to take a closer look at its own policy. The "Electronic Russia 2002-2010" Program was created on January 28, 2002 with the aim "to increase the efficiency of the economy both in the public and private sectors, to make wider use of information technologies in government departments, and transfer much of the state's work online." (14) Currently, the Program is in its second phase and several pilot projects are in the works including the complete digitization of several oblast government agencies.

One of the major forces in bringing ICT policy to the forefront of Putin's agenda is its ongoing fight for WTO accession.

eRussia Program

- $2.6 Billion program intended to boost e-commerce and internet use in the country

  - Phase 1 - $230M

  - Phase 2 - $804M

  - Phase 3 - $1,595M

- Program addresses 4 key areas in ICT

  - Regulatory environment and institutional framework

  - Internet Infrastructure

  - E-Government

  - E-Education

- Timeline:

For additional analytical, business and investment opportunities information,
please contact Global Investment & Business Center, USA
at (202) 546-2103. Fax: (202) 546-3275. E-mail: rusric@erols.com

- o 2002 – refine the plan, identify necessary feasibility studies and define pilot projects

- o 2003-2004 – Studies and pilot projects conducted

- o 2005 – full implementation expected to begin

- Leadership:

  - o Implementation will be under the general management of the Interagency Commission headed by the Minister of Economic Development and Trade of the Russian Federation, German Gref

  - o The commission will form a Council of Experts made up of executives of IT companies, universities, scientific organizations, the Russian Academy of Sciences, and state and municipal bodies.

  - o Operational Management and technical support will be supervised by the Ministry of Telecommunications and Informatization

ICT WORKFORCE

Russian developers stand out for their ability to handle complex projects based on core engineering. "They are extremely creative; they are imaginative; they are disciplined," said Steve Chase, president of Intel Russia. "When it comes to solving mathematical algorithms, they are basically unbeatable." (53) They are also cheap, making only about 25% of what an American developer would make.

- Literacy: 99%

- Percent of adults who are college graduates: 20% (60)

- Number of CS/CE/MIS post secondary programs

  - o Admissions in computer related degrees in 2000: 25,000 (60)

- Percent of Russian software companies who employ PhDs: 77.4%

  - o In 45.8% of those, PhDs make up about 10% of staff (60)

Quality of IT Education

Russia has a long tradition of strong mathematical and scientific education. Software related disciplines contain heavy mathematical components sometimes at the cost of extensive programming practice. Yet Russian programmers learn a wide range of skills that can be applied to complex R&D situations. The emphasis on math may well help graduates deal with cutting edge domains and extremely challenging problems.

Supply and Demand of IT Professionals

"Russia is where India was 10 years ago," said Steve Chase, president of Intel Russia, "Information Technology makes up only 1% of Russia's gross domestic product. Although 1.3 million Russians have degrees in fields like computer science or engineering, only 70,000 currently work in information technology-related jobs." (53) In 2001, the Russian Offshore programming industry alone employed 5,000 to 8,000 programmers with totals for the industry ranging from 50,000 to 80,000 people. (56)

Praise for the Russian Programmer

For additional analytical, business and investment opportunities information, please contact Global Investment & Business Center, USA at (202) 546-2103. Fax: (202) 546-3275. E-mail: rusric@erols.com

Russian developers stand out for their ability to handle complex projects based on core engineering. "They are extremely creative; they are imaginative; they are disciplined," Chase said. "When it comes to solving mathematical algorithms, they are basically unbeatable." (53) They are also cheap, making only about 25% of what an American developer would make.

Colleges and Universities

Academy of the National Economy http://www.ane.ru/en/

Kaliningrad State University http://www.albertina.ru/eng/

Kazan State University http://www.kcn.ru/tat_en/university/index.php3

Moscow State Technical University http://www.bmstu.ru/mstu/English/

Moscow Institute of Physics and Technology http://www.mipt.ru/eng/

Moscow Engineering Physics Institute http://www.mephi.ru/eng/second.html

Moscow State Institute of Electronic Engineering

Moscow University Touro http://www.touro.ru/

Nizhni Novgorod State Universityhttp://www.unn.ru/main_eng.htm

Novgorod State University http://www.novsu.ac.ru/e-index.php3

Novosibirsk State Univeristy http://www.nsu.ru/english/

St Petersburg State Polytechnical Universityhttp://www.spbstu.ru/english/index.html

St Petersburg State University of Engineering and Economics http://www.engec.ru/eng/index.shtml

St Petersburg State University http://www.spbu.ru/e/

FEDERAL TARGET PROGRAM ELECTRONIC RUSSIA

It is evident that in order to bridge the economic development lag, the Russian government is to develop the high tech sector, ensuring the capital inflow to establish reliable processing capabilities. Such an objective requires a well developed high technology industry. Efficient national administration is a prerequisite for setting up the environment for process-oriented production growth. This perception prompted creation of a special federal program of the public administration development via high technologies. Besides, the investments into solving this problem will provide for the IT sector development.

The program provides for reforming the IT market legal environment, implementing new technologies in the public agencies and private sector, creating the education programs aimed at improving the computer competence of the Russian citizens and setting up a large-scale communications infrastructure. The program implementation would enable the Internet connection for all Russian higher education institutions and more than a half of schools, setting up the e-libraries, implementing the remote medicine system, etc.

The investments planned into the program total about $2.4 bln. They are investments proper, as the real return on investments is expected. For instance, according to the program, the share of the

For additional analytical, business and investment opportunities information, please contact Global Investment & Business Center, USA at (202) 546-2103. Fax: (202) 546-3275. E-mail: rusric@erols.com

information technologies (IT) sector products in the Russian GDP would grow from the current 0.5% up to 2% by 2007, and the high technologies exports would grow 15-20 times (Up to $2.5 bln)

IBS company, as a leader of consulting and system integration sector, is actively engaged in various stages and efforts of the Federal Target Program Electronic Russia. Today, the company works are parts of the following measures:

Development and implementation of the unified national data management and transmission system to serve the government agencies and local self-government, budget and non-budget funds and organizations. Connection of the federal executive authorities and federal budget-funded institutions to computer networks (Measure No 14)

Creation of a unified automated information system of monitoring the export of goods from the Russian Federation customs territory as a part of establishing a unified government system of data management and transmission, FTP Electronic Russia (2002-2010)

Launching, development and improvement of the dedicated information system Government Portal in the Internet. Launching the pilot project for its economic part (Measure No 7)

Launching the IS Government Portal, IS Economic Portal

Practical implementation of the measures aimed at supporting the openness of the Russian Federation constituents government authorities and local self-government activities (Measure No 10).

Developing the standard solution based methods to create the IS The Russian Federation Constituent Government Authorities Portal (Regional portal).

Developing the standard solutions and configurations for the computer networks connection nodes for budget organizations of various levels and the standard projects for Internet-enabled class rooms in educational institutions of different levels (Measure No 48).

Creating the unified protected software and hardware facility for the information technologies follow-up development and deploying the priority tasks of the FTP Electronic Russia. IBS acts as a subcontractor for this project.

E-GOVERNMENT IN THE RUSSIAN FEDERATION[1]

In the Russian Federation since 2002 the Federal target program "Electronic Russia 2002-2010" was launched. It will be finished in 2010. One of its components is creation of "the electronic government". Only in 2001 the first document of the Government of the Russian Federation obliging federal enforcement authorities to create official Web-sites was issued. Now all ministries have official Web-sites. One of requirements -to have means of interactive dialogue with citizens. All administrations of subjects of the Russian Federation (89) have the Web-sites. Many of them place cartographical images of controlled territories on the pages. Questions of normative displaying cartographical images in the Internet in Russia are not solved yet.

Development and wide application of information and communication technologies is the global tendency of world development of last decades. Application of modern technologies of processing and transferring information has crucial importance as for competitiveness of economy and expansion of opportunities for its integration in the

[1] Dr. R.B.Iakovleva [1], V.I.Jahimovitch [2] [1]Federal Service of Geodesy and Cartography of Russia, Moscow, Russia roskart@dol.ru , rb job@mail.ru [2]Kartgeocenter, Moscow, Russia vjahimovitch@mail.ru

For additional analytical, business and investment opportunities information, please contact Global Investment & Business Center, USA at (202) 546-2103. Fax: (202) 546-3275. E-mail: rusric@erols.com

world system, and for efficiency of processes of the government at all levels of authority, in the state and non-state sectors of economy.

Not less important result of distribution of information and communication technologies and their penetrations into all spheres of public life is creation of technological preconditions for development ofa civil society due to real maintenance of rights of citizens on free and operative access to the information through a global network of Internet.

In this connection in Russia the Federal target program "Electronic Russia 2002-2010" was developed. "The electronic government" -is one of priority directions of this program.

Under "The electronic government" the network of information-communication infrastructure supporting process of performance by federal enforcement authorities of the functions in a society is understood. The project "The electronic government" consists of two interconnected (and simultaneously independent) projects:

.an internal governmental information infrastructure, analogue of a corporate network; .the external information infrastructure cooperating with citizens and the organizations.

Within the framework of the project "The electronic government" information resources of the federal ministries and departments are integrated, access to them is provided, and also the system of on-line services is created.

The governmental network infrastructure should be aimed at the decision of actual political, economic and social problems of the state and provide:

realization of the right of citizens on access to the open state information; . finishing up to the public objective and trustworthy information about activity of bodies of the government strengthening trust to the state and to its policy; . interaction and constant dialogue of the state with citizens and institutes of a civil society, and also a necessary level of public control over activity of the state bodies and the organizations; . association of information resources and services of bodies of the government, bodies of the government of subjects of federation and bodies of local self-management with for strengthening national information space; . perfecting the government system , optimization of its structure , reduction financial and material inputs on it, stage-by-stage transferring of a part of the state services having cost expression in the system of the state network services answering to real needs of citizens and the organizations; . effective support of economic activities of the state enterprises being integrated in national and world economic space, -interaction and cooperation with the state bodies of foreign countries and the international nongovernmental organizations.

Since 2000 the official Web-site of the Government of the Russian Federation(www.pravitelstvo.gov.ru)is operating

There is the following information on the site :

. the Government of the Russian Federation (structure, news of the Government of the Russian Federation,federal bodies of executive power, the press centre); . Normative documents (current documents and the big database); . the Catalogue of network information resources; . Interactive services (the applications to the Government of the Russian Federation, discussion, the Internet of press -conference)

In July, 2001 Administration of the Government of the Russian Federation prepared the Recommendations containing the basic requirements to Web-sites of federal bodies of executive power.There should be following information on the Web-sites:

. the Official name and the contact information (addresses,the phone,e-mail); . Regulations about federal bodies of executive power; . Organizational structure (the central office, the territorial bodies, subordinated establishments and the enterprises); . the statutory Acts regulating activity of federal bodies of executive power; . the Normative legal acts touching the rights and duties of citizens and the organizations, accepted by federal bodies of executive power; according to its competence;

. the Information on economic branch,and state-of-the-art;
. the Information on federal target programs in which the federal body of executive powerparticipates;
. the Daily information of the press-services.
The obligatory requirement is presence of interactive communication with citizens, i.e. an opportunity of interactive applications to federal bodies of executive power;

For additional analytical, business and investment opportunities information,
please contact Global Investment & Business Center, USA
at (202) 546-2103. Fax: (202) 546-3275. E-mail: rusric@erols.com

Now practically all federal bodies of executive power have the sites -about 53.
The official site of Federal service of a geodesy and cartography of Russia is to the address:
International Symposium on GIS,September 23-26, 2002,Istanbul-TURKEY
www.roskart.ru also contains the following basic sections:

. Legislative bases;
. Structure of the Federal service of a geodesy and cartography of Russia;
. Directions of activity;
. Production ;
. News;
. Press;
. the Forum.

One of primary goals of Federal service of a geodesy and cartography of Russia is maintenance of wide access of legal and physical persons to the spatial data. For these purposes the base of metadata also will be placed on a site of Federal service of a geodesy and cartography of Russia .

authorities of subjects of the Russian Federation (89) have official sites also. On each of them the map of its territory is displayed.

In the Russian segment of the Internet it is possible to find about 130 sites containing the cartographical image. There is also a Internet -shop trading in maps and atlases

According to the current legislation "recording of creation in memory of computer is reproduction also" . In this connection accommodation of cartographical products in the environment the Internet may be adjusted by the general legislation under the intellectual property. So for accommodation of any cartographical products created with using of materials of federal cartographic-geodetic fund performance of all actions stipulated for creation of digital maps (or raster images) is necessary.

Now practically each accommodation of maps in the Internet is illegal. And on these facts it is possible to bring an action claims. A question of payment is open at present since more often cost of the contract on transfer of rights of use of the map depends on circulation of the created map, and in the Internet the concept of circulation does not exist.

Speaking about quality of the image of the cartographical information in the Internet, it is possible to say, that it substantially depends on availability of cartographical education at founders of sites.Frequently it is simply scanned traditional maps and plans. Now in Russia there are no the normative documents regulating display of the spatial information in the Internet, and the Federal service of a geodesy and cartography of Russia works under its creation..

E-COMMERCE DEVELOPMENT IN RUSSIA: IMPOTANT PRACTICAL INFORMATION

Small, specialised companies dominate e-commerce in Russia. The most popular goods ordered online are books, videocassettes, DVDs, CDs, computers and computer software, airline tickets and prepaid telephone cards. There are also a growing number of e-commerce companies in the grocery trade in Moscow and St Petersburg. Some supermarkets, including the Sedmoi Kontinent chain, now offer online ordering. But overall business-to-consumer (B2C) e-commerce in Russia is limited, mainly because of low Internet penetration rates, consumers' restricted purchasing power and limited use of credit cards.

The overwhelming majority of online sales are paid for in cash upon home delivery. Online debit- and credit-card transactions remain limited because Russians generally distrust retail banking. However, retail-banking services are rapidly developing with the arrival of several major foreign players in the market. Although there are around 30m plastic cards in Russia, only 300,000 of these are credit cards (the rest—the vast majority—are debit cards), and this restricts the growth of online sales. Other forms of online payment include direct bank transfers, pre-payment cards and digital money. A number of "virtual wallet" sites have been established to address Internet payment needs. These

For additional analytical, business and investment opportunities information,
please contact Global Investment & Business Center, USA
at (202) 546-2103. Fax: (202) 546-3275. E-mail: rusric@erols.com

sites receive bank transfers from Sberbank and other retail banks, and then hold the cash on deposit to be spent elsewhere on the Internet.

Business-to-business (B2B) e-commerce consists of distributors' outlets, marketplaces for small and medium-size enterprises and the first online marketplaces for industrial commodities. Computer and office-equipment sales dominate the first two categories. Industry-based marketplaces have recently begun to develop, notably in the metals sector. B2B trading consists of one-to-one transactions rather than online marketplaces.

GROWTH OF E-COMMERCE

A number of factors have traditionally restrained the growth of e-commerce in Russia. Obstacles include a poor telecommunications infrastructure, an underdeveloped banking system (including very low credit-card penetration rates) and an uncertain legal environment. According to J'son & Partners, a consultancy based in Moscow, there are more than 2,000 e-commerce businesses in Russia. Their sales volume in 2005 reached US$1.2bn, and the market is developing rapidly with annual growth of 45–50% expected in 2006, according to J'son. The National Association of Russian Electronic Trade Participants estimates local online sales at less than 1% of total retail-trade turnover.

J'son & Partners expects Internet penetration (weekly users) to reach 12.9m (or 9% of the total population) by the end of 2006. The firm estimates the annual growth of Internet users will be more than 20% over the next three years, and that one-fifth of the population will be using the Internet by 2010.

A number of factors should stimulate future growth in e-commerce. Russians are literate and well educated, and they will probably prove keen to use the Internet as an information resource. Moreover, the poor choice and regional distribution of goods outside the main cities creates a ready market for web-based retail sites, and limited access to fax and long-distance voice lines will stimulate demand for e-mail services.

The active Internet-consumer community is still almost exclusively in Moscow and St Petersburg, and this community accounts for about 60% of online transactions. If these two cities are taken alone for statistical purposes, and the rest of the country is ignored, then Internet penetration and spending figures more closely resemble those in other transition economies.

In 2001 the Russian government approved a US$2.4bn plan to fund Electronic Russia through 2010, as a means of promoting the use of the Internet, boosting e-commerce and providing equal access to electronic education, which should significantly stimulate the sector.

The first stage of Electronic Russia involved analyses of the use of information technology by the Ministries of Communications and Economic Development and Trade. Pilot projects were run in the regions to test the feasibility of programmes such as filing taxes online to judge whether they would work on a nationwide scale.

The second stage of Electronic Russia aims to make government bodies more transparent by opening their information resources to the general public. A series of pilot projects is planned within and among certain government bodies to assist the ongoing administrative, pension and housing-sector reforms. The ministry has proposed a legislative policy for the use and application of information technology in the economic and social spheres, spelling out what changes to laws are necessary and a timetable for adopting them.

FOREIGN INVESTMENT

There are no specific limitations on foreign participation in Russia's telecommunications industry, and investments are officially subject only to standard licensing and certification requirements. However, in the context of negotiations to enter the World Trade Organisation, the Russian government

**For additional analytical, business and investment opportunities information,
please contact Global Investment & Business Center, USA
at (202) 546-2103. Fax: (202) 546-3275. E-mail: rusric@erols.com**

presented a position paper in 2002 on plans for the telecoms industry after Russia's admission to the trade body, which would include a 49% limit on foreign ownership of telecoms companies. This plan is still subject to negotiations with Russia's trading partners, which have strongly objected to the proposed reversal of telecoms liberalisation.

Foreign investors have criticised the system of licensing telecoms companies. They complained about lack of transparency in licensing and about the five-year limitation of licences. The new amended version of the Law on Telecommunications, which came into force on January 1st 2004, lengthens the duration of licences up to 25 years. However, new licensing regulations still await adoption and publication.

INTELLECTUAL PROPERTY

The issue of cyber-squatters and trademark piracy in the realm of Internet domain names remains a major source of concern for both foreign and Russian companies. The Regional Network Information Centre (Ru-Centre, www.nic.ru) took over the registration of domain names from a previous entity, RosNIIRos, that performed the same function in 2000. Although RosNIIROS stop registering domain names in 2000, January 1st 2005 was the deadline for cancelling all registration agreements previously concluded with RosNIIRos.

The poaching of domain names continues, although some companies have successfully removed cyber-squatters. The practice hinders the development of e-commerce in Russia.
Important amendments made to the Trademark Law in October 2002 are expected to strengthen the protection of trademarks on the Internet. Unlike the previous law, the new law specifically identifies the unauthorised use of Internet domain names as an infringement of trademark law (Paragraph 2, Article 4 of the amended law).

This new provision has already been tested in practice. The Moscow Arbitration Court found on October 15th 2003 that the domain names gillette.ru and gilette.ru had been registered in breach of the trademark rights of the registered proprietor, The Gillette Company (US). The Gillette Company presented evidence of the appropriate trademark registrations for "Gillette" and "Gilette" for selling goods on the Internet.

The court ruled that to prove trademark infringement a trademark proprietor should present evidence that: (1) the mark and the sign in contest are identical or similar, (2) that the goods and/or services for which the contested sign is used on the Internet are similar to the goods/services for which the trademark has been registered, and (3) the sign has been used without the consent of the registered proprietor. All three of those elements were proved in court against the parasite user of gillette.ru and gilette.ru. The court ruled that the owner of the illegal domains should stop using gillette.ru and gilette.ru on the Internet.

In line with the trademark laws of many foreign states, the Russian Patent Office (Rospatent) allows the registration of trademarks in different classes if it believes there would be no confusion on the part of the consumer because of the different class of goods.

Copyright law was amended in July 2004 to increase the copyright term from 50 to 70 years after the author's death and to give enforcement bodies greater powers. Implementation of the law remains weak for images, music, videos and books. Better enforcement is a major criterion for entry to the World Trade Organisation, which Russia is coming closer to joining; however, Russia remains a producer of pirated CDs and DVDs on an industrial scale. Copyright protection clearly extends to material that has been converted to a digitised format and then placed on the web.
However, Russian copyright law emphasises the rights of the individual author rather than legal entities. Hence, companies that wish to use copyright protection must specifically conclude an "author's agreement" to transfer those rights from the creator of the material to the company. Russian law specifically regulates the form and content of this agreement.

For additional analytical, business and investment opportunities information,
please contact Global Investment & Business Center, USA
at (202) 546-2103. Fax: (202) 546-3275. E-mail: rusric@erols.com

CONSUMER PROTECTION

Consumers buying goods online in Russia will almost certainly have enforceable rights under the amended Law on Protection of Consumers' Rights of 1992. Where a product is sold or imported for sale in Russia, the product's description and instructions for use must be in Russian. Any goods that fail to include Russian language instructions are in breach of product-liability legislation. When goods are faulty, consumers are entitled to free repair of the defect, compensation for all costs incurred by the customer for such repair, a proportional decrease in the price of the product, replacement of the product or return of the purchase price. Relief in the form of damages and compensation for moral harm also is available to the consumer.

Improving the protection of personal data in e-commerce is an area that the Russian legislature wants to address. In accordance with the general privacy guarantees in the Russian Constitution (Articles 23 and 24), the specific provisions of Federal Law 24-FZ, On Information, Informatisation and Protection of Information (amended January 10th 2003) and Federal Law 85-FZ, On Participation in the International Exchange of Information (amended June 30th 2003), the collection, storage, use and dissemination of personal data to third parties is allowed only with the consent of the data subject or by court judgment. Under the Law on Information, personal data is defined as data on facts, events and circumstances of the life of an individual, which allows his/her identity to be revealed. This applies to anyone collecting or transferring personal data to third parties over the Internet.
These basic rights offer individuals strong protection in principle, though they have yet to be tested in court in relation to the Internet. Furthermore, unlike many other countries, Russia has not yet adopted regulations or guidelines covering these principles and their application to the new arena of the Internet and digital communications.

Russian websites are classified as advertisements under the present Advertising Law, and they are subject to considerations on such issues as bad faith, unfair, unethical and false advertising. Virtually all portals that sell their space for advertisements therefore carry meters to show figures on the number of visitors to their website. Since these figures largely determine the price of placing advertisements on a website, portals must be careful to avoid publishing false information.
The transparency of Russian Internet resources has increased with the research provided by four companies in particular. These are Rambler Group, Spylog, Gallup Media and Comcon-2. Rambler Group and Spylog place their meters on the pages of the sites being surveyed, whereas Comcon-2 and Gallup Media conduct public-opinion surveys. Rambler registers the number of hits for individual pages, and Spylog registers the number of visits an entire site receives.

The legal status of sites containing erotica remains unclear. In general, the law prohibits the distribution of pornography. The status of websites and the links found in them, however, is unclear since websites are arguably not categorised as mass media. Unlike in the United States, where individuals can be prosecuted for placing links to sites that contain illegal information, there are no laws regulating links in Russia, and everything depends on the individual court's discretion.

CONTRACT LAW AND DISPUTE RESOLUTION

The enactment of Federal Law 1–FZ, On Electronic Digital Signature (January 10th 2002) marked an important new development in Russian e-commerce.

The objective of any e-commerce legislation is to take established contract principles and apply them to Internet transactions. The electronic signature represents a crucial feature in this process. Articles 160(2) and 434(2) of the Russian Civil Code recognised electronic signatures but only where there was a prior mutual agreement between the parties to use them.

This had been understood to mean that a written agreement between contracting parties specifically agreeing to the future use of digital signatures, and establishing relevant procedures for future dispute resolution, would be needed to validate subsequent online transactions. This clearly

For additional analytical, business and investment opportunities information,
please contact Global Investment & Business Center, USA
at (202) 546-2103. Fax: (202) 546-3275. E-mail: rusric@erols.com

constituted an obstacle to the rapid growth of e-commerce, since most potential consumers lack such an agreement, and so their consumer rights would not be protected for purchases made via an electronic signature.

The latest law on digital signatures establishes specific rules on which types of electronic signatures will be recognised by law. Market participants have criticised it, however, because of its strict definition of an electronic signature. The biggest criticism is that the law recognises one technology (public-key technology) as the only acceptable basis for digital signatures. The law also requires the certification of both hardware and software used for digital signatures, and the establishment of certifying centres in Russia, licensed by the state, that would review electronic digital signatures. Such certifying centres have been created in Russia.

The State Duma considered several drafts of electronic-commerce law that could have further clarified the legal basis of e-commerce in Russia and added protection to participants in e-commerce transactions. However, all the drafts have so far failed to become law.

Where electronic signatures are recognised as legally binding, contracts are subject to the normal rules governing enforcement of contracts in Russia (in particular, the Russian Civil Code) and subject to enforcement through the Russian commercial courts.

Russia has not acceded to the Uniform Domain Name Dispute Resolution Policy (UDRP) established by the Internet Corporation of Assigned Names and Numbers (ICANN). This is the most common international method of dispute resolution in domain-name cases. Consequently, trademark law governs domain-name disputes in Russia through domestic courts.

TAXATION

The Russian Tax Code of January 1st 2001 does not impose any special tax burden on electronic transactions. Hence, taxation of e-commerce is comparable to that of similar transactions using non-electronic means. Even so, in practice, goods purchased and delivered via the web are often not taxed if paid through non-traceable means (not through a bank transfer), because there is no way to track and calculate such transactions.

Online purchases delivered to the consumer in material form are subject to all applicable excise taxes. Goods that are imported are also subject to customs duties. But customs officials maintain strict signed and stamped documentation requirements, and it is unclear whether online electronic contracts, which lack such formalities, would be sufficient for customs clearance.
Under present legislation, the main criteria in determining if a foreign company is subject to profits tax is whether that entity has a permanent establishment in Russia. Although there has been no specific legislative guidance on this issue, the tax authorities would probably consider a permanent establishment to exist only if the physical hardware necessary to support e-commerce is in Russia. A question remains over whether the registration of a domain name in Russia constitutes a permanent establishment for the purposes of profit taxation. With no legislative guidance or case law, this issue is unclear.

Value-added tax (VAT) of 18% (reduced in 2004 from 20%) applies on electronic transactions related to the sale of goods (work, services) in Russia and the import of goods into the customs territory of Russia. Services include the transfer of title, know-how, trademarks and other intellectual property, and certain consulting, legal, accounting, engineering, advertising and educational services. Liability for VAT will depend on the provider of goods or services having a permanent establishment in Russia. However, tax authorities will have difficulty monitoring online transactions and enforcing these obligations.

For additional analytical, business and investment opportunities information,
please contact Global Investment & Business Center, USA
at (202) 546-2103. Fax: (202) 546-3275. E-mail: rusric@erols.com

CLASSIFICATION OF E-COMMERCE TRANSACTIONS

On January 30th 1997, Russia voted in favour of a Model Law on E-Commerce at the 51st Session of the United Nations (Resolution A/51/628). This resolution treats e-commerce transactions as a service. Arguably under Russia's present media law (June 1998), the Internet is not classified as a mass medium. Therefore, it is much easier to set up an online business than to establish a mainstream media organisation, which requires far-more-cumbersome registration and accreditation. However, online businesses may voluntarily register as a media organisation to enjoy the incentives for mass-media companies that are offered under Russian law.

COMPLIANCE AND ENFORCEMENT

E-commerce in Russia is still at too early a stage to have attracted serious attention from the law-enforcement authorities. The main issues so far have been over the rights of the security services to monitor electronic correspondence, in the context of national-security concerns.

An amendment to the 1995 Law on Operational Investigations came into force on January 6th 2000. The original law gave the security services the right to monitor various correspondence (from postal deliveries to cell-phone conversations) if they first obtain a warrant. The amendment extends the access of the security services to electronic traffic, but the Russian constitution still requires these authorities to obtain a court warrant before opening e-mails. Nevertheless, the amendment caused concern among free-speech advocates because e-mail, e-commerce transactions and other Internet traffic can easily be monitored without anyone ever knowing, regardless of whether a court warrant has been obtained. With the growth of the Internet, the Federal Security Service and the State Communications Committee issued new regulations (based on their interpretation of the 1995 law) that forced Internet service providers (ISPs) to link their computers to those at the Federal Security Service's headquarters. However, a Supreme Court ruling in September 2000 overturned the requirement for ISPs to install the electronic eavesdropping equipment used by the security service.

As e-commerce develops, wider official scrutiny of electronic transactions can be expected, especially in the context of heightened official concern about money-laundering and illegal evasion of taxes and customs duties. Some Russian tax officials reportedly hope that the growth of e-commerce will improve their efforts to enforce compliance, since online commercial activity may be easier to track. But Russian officialdom is typically preoccupied with formal documentation rather than the substance of a transaction. Given the paperless nature of electronic commerce, it may take some time for the enforcement authorities to adapt to the new medium.

KEY CONTACTS

- Central Bank of the Russian Federation, 12 Ul Neglinnaya, Moscow 107016; Tel: (7.095) 771 9100; Fax: (7.095) 621 6425; Internet: http://www.cbr.ru.

- Chamber of Commerce and Industry, 6 Ilyinka Ul, Moscow 109012; Tel: (7.095) 929 0009; Fax: (7.095) 929 0360; Internet: http://eng.tpprf.ru. The federal chamber can provide information and contacts to members, as can Russia's regional chambers of commerce and industry. Representative offices are also in 19 foreign countries. Bulgaria, Canada, the Czech Republic, Finland, France, Iran, Italy, Poland, the UK and the United States also have joint chambers of commerce with the Russian Federation in Moscow.

- Directorate of the Ministry of Taxation for Moscow, Ul Bolshaya Tulskaya 15, Moscow 115191; Tel: (7.095) 980 5035; 957 6410; Fax: (7.095) 958 2558; Internet: http://www.mosnalog.ru (Russian only).

- Eurasia Patent Organisation, 2/6 Maly Cherkasskiy Pr, Moscow 109 GSP-9; Tel: (7.095) 928 5612; Fax: (7.095) 921 2423; Internet: http://www.eapo.org.

- Federal Anti-monopoly Service (FAS), 11 Ul Sadovaya-Kudrinskaya, Moscow 123995; Tel: (7.095) 252 7048; Fax: (7.095) 254 8300.Internet: http://www.fas.gov.ru/english. FAS can provide information about any restrictions on acquiring shares in Russian enterprises by foreign investors. It was known as the Anti-monopoly Ministry until early 2004.

- Government Investment Corp (Gosincor), Ul Myasnitskaya 35, Moscow 101990; Tel: (7.095) 204 1387, 208 9944; Fax: (7.095) 207 6936; Internet: http://www.gosincor.ru (Russian only). Gosincor, a state-owned company, was formed in 1993 to attract foreign investment to Russia and to insure foreign investors against political risk.

- Ministry of Economic Development and Trade, Ul Pervaya Tverskaya-Yamskaya 1/3, Moscow 125993; Tel: (7.095) 200 0353; Fax: (7.095) 251 6965; Internet: http://www.economy.gov.ru/wps/portal/english. The ministry provides general information on the government's foreign investment policy.

- Ministry of Natural Resources, 4/6, Bolshaya Gruzinskaya, Moscow 123812; Tel: (7.095) 254 4800; Fax: (7.095) 254 4310, 254 6610; Internet: http://www.mnr.gov.ru/.

- Ministry of Finance, 9 Ilyinka Ul, Moscow 100097; Tel: (7.095) 298 9101; Fax: (7.095) 925 0889; Internet: http://www.minfin.ru. The ministry prepares and implements the national budget and formulates taxation and investment policies. Its international tax relations division can be reached at the same address; Tel: (7.095) 925 2396.

- Rospatent (Russian Agency for Patents and Trademarks), Comp 1, 30 Berezhkovskaya emb, Moscow 123995; Tel: (7.095) 240 6015; Fax: (7.095) 243 3337; Internet: http://www.fips.ru/ruptoen/index.htm.

- Russian Authors' Society, 6A Bolshaya Bronnaya Ul, Moscow 103670; Tel: (7.095) 203 4599; Fax: (7.095) 200 1263; Internet: http://www.rao.ru.

- State Registration Chamber (SRC), Smolensky Bulvar 3/5, Moscow 119121; Tel/Fax: (7.095) 246 7200; Internet: http://www.palata.ru.

THE EXTERNAL FACTORS IN THE CREATION OF E-MARKETS IN RUSSIA[2]

1. INTRODUCTION

The legal globalization means that legal rules in different countries become homogenous, and the application of laws are standardized. This may occur within the global framework or inside a certain geographic area, such as European Union. The globalization can unfold in at least following ways:

- by international cooperation, where national states agree upon the harmonization of their legal systems. Vienna convention of international trade can be seen as an example of this development, as well as World Trade Organization treaties.

- through supranational system, such as European Union legal system

- legal systems can be harmonized also purely due economic reasons. In an increasingly open economy, this harmonization occurs without any formal international treaties or agreements. Contract law is one example of such development.[1]

---

[2] Mika Kärkkäinen University of Vaasa

For additional analytical, business and investment opportunities information, please contact Global Investment & Business Center, USA at (202) 546-2103. Fax: (202) 546-3275. E-mail: rusric@erols.com

Market economy and its structures is the leading force in formation of the global legal system. The legal system must be harmonized in order to meet the requirements of the market economy. The ratio of the market system requires certain level of openness, and global freedom of movement of goods, labor and services. The protectionism would lead to a economic stagnation International trade and international trade agreements have often gone on parallel tracks. Trade can not thrive without legal security and trust into the legal system. The traders throughout the history have sought to ensure that mechanisms of contract enforcements are applied. This can be accomplished through different kind of means, varying from full-fledged integration to free trade agreements. Discussion on international regulation on E-commerce follows the same lines. Electronic commerce in itself is a global form of trade, with a cross-border character of Internet in its core. Due to the logics of the market economy and economics of scale, a need for a harmonized legal environment for electronic commerce does exist.[2]

The accession to World Trade Organization has played an important role in the process of trade liberalization in the transition economies[3]. This applies also to Russian Federation; the on-going membership process has brought predictability and stability into the Russian foreign trade policies – two primary issues that the Russian legal system has had a lack of. The accession implies the adoption of WTO disciplines, and this poses a number of challenges and opportunities to Russian Federation. The external competition in Russian markets might increase, while the entrance of Russian products to foreign markets would become easier. The challenge is to ensure the competitiveness of Russian industry in the circumstances of hardening competition.

The lack of trust, uncertainty about the regulatory environment, gaining access and logistical problems can be seen as a barrier for the growth of the electronic commerce[4]. Global regulation, or at least guidelines are needed to increase the trust of internet users into the electronic commerce. At the same time, Russian legal system in general suffers from the lack of trust and consistency; these needs multiple the development of the electronic commerce system in Russia.

2. ELECTRONIC COMMERCE AND WTO

The search for global rules of electronic commerce at World Trade Organization was initiated in 1998, when WTO launched the Work Programme for Electronic Commerce. Since then, the enthusiasm and hype over the electronic commerce reached its peak and then slowly faded. From an outside perspective, it would seem like the electronic commerce has been caught in the sidetrack on the WTO agenda, since not much concrete developments have taken place. This is even more evident when one studies the research literature dealing with the World Trade Organization's stance on electronic commerce. The scholars interest has mostly died out in by the end of the year 2001, and most of the problems raised before that date, remain to be unsolved. However, as Wunch-Vincent notes, the World Trade Organizations influence on these matters may not be fully appreciated outside the realm of trade policy experts[5]. The World Trade Organization is the main forum of the world trade negotiations, and even though the negotiations since the events in Seattle, 1999, have been difficult and mostly unsuccessful, one can not put aside the strength of the WTO as an organization. As Schiavetta[6] states, WTO is arguably the only international organization with the required knowledge and political power to determine such a key issue of global electronic trade as how e-products should be classified for the purpose of collecting customs duties. World Trade Organizations competence in regulating the world trade is much larger than other global IGOs; one could argue, that in theory there are no formal limits to matters on which the WTO can make rules by concensus[7].

World Trade Organization has defined electronic commerce broadly as " production, advertising, sale and distribution of products via telecommunications networks. The most obvious examples of products distributed electronically are books, music and videos transmitted down telephone lines or through the Internet."

For additional analytical, business and investment opportunities information, please contact Global Investment & Business Center, USA at (202) 546-2103. Fax: (202) 546-3275. E-mail: rusric@erols.com

Even though a new technology is being used as a tool of electronic commerce, it still is just one way of conducting international trade. Even though WTO treaties were signed before the breakthrough of Internet and electronic commerce[8], their provisions apply also to the electronic commerce. The main principles of these treaties, such as Most Favoured Nation treatment, national treatment or transparency of regulations, apply also to the electronic commerce. WTO aims at technological neutrality; the WTO system should be applicable whatever the means of the trade are.

Technical neutrality is, however only a secondary target of the WTO regulation. The primary goal is the liberalization of the World Trade. The technical neutrality must not be used as protective measure. In other words, discriminatory liberalism is better than technically neutral protectionism.

The WTO regulation that applies to electronic trade is dependant on the type of the commodity being traded. The applicable WTO agreement varies between different types of e-commerce baskets. In basket number 1, the applicable WTO agreements are the agreements concerning the movement of goods – especially the GATT agreement, as well as the Information Technology agreement. The baskets 2 and 3 concern trade of services and are thus governed by the General Agreement on Trade In Services (GATS).

The basket 4 is more complicated; it is yet to be decided, whether digital products should be classified as goods or as services. The classification question is important, since it will determine the level of trade liberalization that exporters of these products can expect from WTO Members. Several WTO member countries (including European union) have taken a position that all electronic supplies should be classified as services while some members (namely USA) are asking whether some commodities should be classified as goods. These goods include software, which used to be in a physical form (a CD or a diskette) and are now downloadable. [9] If the digital products are set in the category of services, which seems to be the common consensus at the moment, another question appears. The treatment of the trade of digital products depends then on a question. The services transactions are classified in GATS agreement into four different modes. The electronic services may fall either into the mode 1, cross-border supply[10], or mode 2, consumption abroad. The distinction is relevant, since the levels of commitments made by WTO members on the two modes differ, and are often more liberal in mode 2[11]. Therefore the electronic deliveries would be subject to less restrictions if they were classified under the mode 2. GATS does not address which jurisdiction applies under mode 2; the question must be solved through other means of international private law. In European Union, the country of origin principle applies, unless the transaction is not a b-to-c trade. In most cases electronic services do, how ever, fall under the mode 1. [12]

WTO dispute settlement body (DSB) has so far processed one dispute concerning electronic commerce. Antigua and Barbuda requested formal consultations with the United States and WTO concerning United States' ban on cross-border and gambling services – services under the mode 1. The WTO Panel found that USA schedule for GATS commitments included specific commitments on gambling and betting services. According to the panel, US measures prohibit the cross-border supply of gambling and betting services in the United States in a manner, which is inconsistent with the GATS. Gambling services are a good example of services which can be offered cross the borders via the Internet, and which generate problems since they are usually a subject of specific national legislation.[13]

The decision is significant, since it clarifies the commitments made by the USA on the GATS schedule. Any uncertainty resulting from the vagueness of national commitments could inhibit the development of E-services as service suppliers would not be certain of their right to supply in a given country[14]. In Antigua case, Panel admitted that United States might have inadvertently undertaken specific commitments on gambling and betting services. The panel did not consider the moral or ethic point of views that the United States declared; the panel merely saw its role as to interpret and apply the GATS in light of the facts of the case instead of possible hidden intentions of the countries involved.[15]

For additional analytical, business and investment opportunities information,
please contact Global Investment & Business Center, USA
at (202) 546-2103. Fax: (202) 546-3275. E-mail: rusric@erols.com

In 1998 WTO declared a moratorium on customs tariffs on electronic products. Moratorium means that no custom duties shall be collected from the electronic delivery of digitized goods and services. This exemption has not been made permanent, but it is still in force. The outcome of the duty moratorium is to subsidy products that can be digitized. The moratorium does not extend to the goods ordered over the Internet. [16]

Several scholars and institutions have proposed that World Trade Organization should take more active role in the global regulation of electronic commerce. There are several suggestions for a framework agreement for electronic commerce regulation. The World Trade Organization has not, however taken further steps on the regulatory issues.

3. DEVELOPMENT OF ELECTRONIC COMMERCE LEGISLATION IN RUSSIA WITHIN THE FRAMEWORK OF THE WTO ACCESSION

In the development of a legal system in a country of an economic transition, one can distinct three problem areas relevant for the legal study. One is the influence of the external factors in the development of a legal system in general, and in development of legal hierarchy in particular; the second issue is the implementation of the legislation, and the third – which is connected to the second – is the practical aspect of the capability of the administrative machine to adapt to the changing circumstances. These problems occur also under the influence of the external factors - in this case Russian membership in World Trade Organization, when Russia is trying to adapt to the international regulation of the world trade. A fourth question, which is distinctive for the WTO accession, is the on-going debate on the protectionism and trade liberalization.

Russian federation applied to become a member of GATT-agreement in 1993 -shortly after the collapse of the Soviet Union. When WTO was established in 1995, Russia became the applicant for the WTO membership. At the moment, Russia is the most significant country in the world markets who is yet to join the World Trade Organization.

Accession to World Trade Organization is a complex issue, and requires thorough reform of the country's trading system and commitment to the liberalization of the foreign trade regime. The terms of the accession are eventually formulated through bilateral negotiations with the interested WTO member governments. Thus due to the economic and world politic realities, the final terms of accession are agreed with the major players of the world economy – in Russia's case European

Union, USA and Japan. On 21st of May 2004 European Union and Russia signed a bilateral agreement on the terms of the Russian WTO accession.

The WTO accession package goes well beyond the scope of the GATT treaty and traditional commitments of lowering the custom tariffs. The WTO treaties and the requirements set by the WTO members force the applicant country to make substantial legislative and institutional reforms. In Russian case, the mere undertaking of becoming a member in WTO has increased the stability and predictability in the Russian trade policy. WTO accession is an important, and perhaps the final, step on Russian transition to market economy. Conventional wisdom holds that Russian accession process is almost reaching the goal – accession may well conclude in 2006. Problems do still however exist.

WTO aims at lowering the customs tariff level globally. Russia applies at the moment tariff level that is significantly higher than the average in industrialized countries. In the course of the negotiations, Russia should agree to lower its tariff level. This is, however, difficult due to certain facts. First of all, custom duties, which equal almost 40 % of the tax income of Russian federation [17], are a significant source of income for Russian government, which is suffering in constant financial crises. As long as the internal taxation system in Russia does not function efficiently enough, it is unlikely that Russia would be willing to agree to lower its external customs tariff rates and thus reduce the money flow into the state budget. The tax reform, which was concluded in 2003, has significantly simplified the

For additional analytical, business and investment opportunities information, please contact Global Investment & Business Center, USA at (202) 546-2103. Fax: (202) 546-3275. E-mail: rusric@erols.com

taxation system in Russia, and the tax revenues have increased also due to the economic growth in Russia. This development might allow also the reducing of the customs tariff level.

Tax and customs duty implications of electronic commerce in Russia are unclear. Russian law defines the movement of goods over the "electronic border" to be subject to customs laws – and thus there is a possibility that the import of electronic products would be a subject of import duties in Russia, which would be against the current international customs duty moratorium. However, there is no method available to control this kind of importation.

Another matter is the government policy and its balancing between the path of further liberalization and protectionism; there have been demands from the side of Russian industry to maintain the high import tariff rate in order to protect the weak domestic industry from the foreign competition. This struggle between the liberal and protective regimes and, as a consequence, instability of the government's policies, has had its impact on the speed of the negotiations. During the last couple of years Russia has been able to develop its customs operation quite significantly, which has sped up the accession process. There are still some problems especially on the activities of the Customs administration and application of the lower level regulations.

Russia is yet to improve its legislation in trade in services in order to meet the WTO rules and to open its service markets to foreign competition. In principle, Russia has developed a basic legal framework for trade in services. However, also in the sphere of legislation regulating the service sector, the result of the legislative reforms has been a multitude of legal acts, with an unclear hierarchy of laws[18]. The GATS agreement is however somewhat limited, and does not mean, that all the services should be open to foreign competition. The commitment to open Russian service sectors to foreign competition does mean that Russia must develop its general economic legislation. The poor service sector is currently a weakness of the Russian economy, and it might prove to be a barrier for the economic growth Russia has enjoyed during the recent years, unless Russian government does not take sufficient actions in reforming the sector. Accession to WTO and meeting the requirements of the GATS-treaty would be the crucial factor in enhancing the structural reform of Russian economy.[19]

Electronic commerce is a growing form of trade also in Russia. Applications in trading and procurement operations have developed significantly, and electronic marketplaces, which provide online access to suppliers' information and offers are also being used. Most of the e-commerce has concentrated on Business-to-Consumers trade, but B-to-B trade has also increased its significance on Russian e-commerce. [20]

There are several factors that hold back the development of B-to-B e-marketplace in Russia. There is a lack of an efficient business model for creating an e-marketplace. Efforts that have been done by trading site organizers to inform the market participants about the site and provide training for them have been inadequate. The infrastructure which would enable the authentication centers to perform user identification is scarce, and there is a lack of confidentiality.[21]

At the moment, there are several laws that regulate electronic commerce in Russia. Electronic commerce is regulated in Russia by the civil code Russian federation, Law "about the protection of the rights of users", by federal law "about the electronic digital signature", federal law "about the technical regulation", and federal laws and normative lawful reports RF, which regulate owner's activity.

In 2001 State Duma of Russian Federation had its firs reading of the draft law on electronic commerce. The law was mainly based on the UNCITRAL model law on electronic commerce. The drafting of the e-commerce law lost then its momentum, and it took four years for the State Duma to have the second reading of the law, and finally reject the proposal. At March 2005, however, two new alternative legislative acts on the electronic commerce were introduced for the examination of the State Duma. The law was meant to be the general law regulating the electronic commerce in Russia, and was expected to simplify the legislative sphere on the electronic commerce. According to the official opinion of the government, the law was also crucial for the accession to the World Trade Organization [22]. The State Duma nevertheless rejected the proposed law at the first hearing.

The legal problems are also a barrier for development, in particular the difficulties in the electronic document validation. A law on electronic digital signatures was approved by the Duma in December 2001 and was signed into law by President Putin in January 2002. The law defines electronic signatures strictly, making public-key technology the sole acceptable digital signature technology.

This definition is in contradiction with the technical neutrality that the WTO is aiming at. The most probable reason for using such strict criteria is the Russian legislator's objective to increase reliability and trust in e-markets. The technological neutrality does not offer sufficient certainty in a country like Russia, and therefore Russia has moved to a more regulatory system. The strict criteria might, however, cause problems in the future, since it is tied in the existing technology, and technological developments would cause a need to amend the legislation. [23]

On the protection of the intellectual property rights Russia has already created legislation that is in most areas in conformity with the TRIPS, Agreement on trade related aspects of intellectual property rights. The implementation of the legislation is however problematic. Due to insufficient resources, Russia has not been able to stop the widespread sale of pirate music CD's and computer programs. Foreign companies have also faced problems with Russian companies that have already managed to register the trademark of a well-known foreign company to their own use. All in all, protection of intellectual property rights is still insufficient. To adjust Russian enforcement of intellectual property rights to meet the standards of international trading system is a time-consuming process, and certainly prolongs the negotiations since the WTO members in principle demand that this adjustment should be done before Russia enters the WTO. Russia, on the other hand, would like to have a possibility to adjust its policies during a transition period after the accession.

Some domain name problems have also occurred. RosNIIRos (administers the .ru zone) does not verify whether an applicant's proposed domain name might already be a registered trademark. This has played an important role in several cases, such as Eastman Kodak vs. Grundul, where Grundul registered the domain name Kodak.ru, and won the case. Subsequently, Eastman Kodak Subsidiary "OOO Kodak" sued Grundul. Decision was made for OOO Kodak. In court practice, the Russian courts have recognized the use of a identical or similar company name as a violation of the owner's rights. The company appealing for infringement must show that the defendant deliberately registered a domain name containing someone else's trade mark or a company name, and that the defendant is using the domain for commercial purposes in respect of similar goods or services with economic benefit from such use.[24]

Also Russia's administration of the trading system appears to be arbitrary and diverse. Partly due to the frequent changes in legislation, for instance, different customs officers may treat importers differently, and the whole customs system suffers from the lack of communication, which is complicated by the large amount of administrative rules introduced by state bodies like State Customs Committee. Widespread corruption is another well-known problem. The poor performance of the administration is closely linked to the fundamental problem of the Russian legal system in general: poor implementation of the legislation. Another fundamental problem is the lack of transparency in the actions taken by the administration.[25]

5. CONCLUSIONS

Electronic commerce regulation in a global level is yet to be developed. World Trade Organization could be the forum for such development, but it requires more active approach both from the WTO itself as from its Member States. Whether there is a need for a framework agreement concerning specifically electronic commerce is yet to be seen. The GATS treaty and its application needs more

For additional analytical, business and investment opportunities information, please contact Global Investment & Business Center, USA at (202) 546-2103. Fax: (202) 546-3275. E-mail: rusric@erols.com

clarifying, and the still open issues concerning the classification of electronic services need to be solved.

Russia is developing its national e-commerce legislation following the international models but adding also some characteristics from the Russian legal system and heritage. The same problems that are evident in the Russian legal system in general can be seen in the regulation of the electronic commerce as well. The World Trade Organization membership has its own impact on the creation of the electronic commerce legislation in Russia, even though there are no formal requirements set by the WTO on this specific issue. The accession procedure includes also the GATS schedule negotiations, and in the trade of services, the electronic commerce cannot be put aside.

For additional analytical, business and investment opportunities information, please contact Global Investment & Business Center, USA at (202) 546-2103. Fax: (202) 546-3275. E-mail: rusric@erols.com

RUSSIAN STATE PROGRAM "THE INFORMATION SOCIETY (2011 - 2020 YEARS)" AND BUSINESS OPPORTUNITIES

I. Characteristics of the current state of the sphere of creation and use of information and telecommunication technologies in the Russian Federation, the basic indicators and analysis of social, financial, economic and other risks of the Program

Industry information and communication technologies (hereinafter - IT) in 2000 - 2008, developed rapidly, the annual increase was about 25 percent, well above the average annual growth rate of gross domestic product and growth of individual industries. Information technology and information services have become quite a significant article of the Russian non-oil exports. However, the composite indexes and cross-country comparisons are still characterize Russia is not the best way, which means low level of development of the technology industry, the backlog of world leaders, as well as the unrealized potential of the existing infrastructures and technologies. On the other hand, the number of parameters, Russia is not very different from European countries where the share of information technology is about 5 percent of gross domestic product, about 30 percent of the population have never used the Internet and only 38 percent of citizens use the Internet for obtaining government services (mainly to obtain the application form).

Noted in this period are rather high growth rates have been demonstrated in many ways thanks to the new open markets, new products and services (cellular, computer hardware, consulting and other services) on the background of a low initial level of development of information technologies in Russia. At present, it is clear that to maintain the momentum of growth is necessary to eliminate a number of existing barriers.

One of the factors affecting the prevalence of information technologies and information society development in Russia is not a high level of socio-economic development in many regions of the Russian Federation. Thus, a high level of differences in the use of information technology in households regions. In assessing the rating of Russian regions according to their preparedness for the Information Society Index leader 22 times higher than in the region, an outsider. Problems remain for broadband access to end users. At the end of 2008, only about 21.5 percent of all Russian households (11.4 million households) had broadband Internet access, and the average access rate in the regions ranged from 128 kbit / s to 1 Mbit / s, which significantly lower than in Moscow (7.5 Mbit / s) and St. Petersburg (6 Mbit / s). In every other region of Russia the proportion of organizations using broadband does not exceed 27 percent. Even the leader of this indicator (Moscow) by 8 percentage points below the level of broadband use in the European Union. For accelerated development in the Russian Federation of the Information Society is necessary to ensure a significant reduction in the cost of services provided to citizens on the basis of information technology while enhancing their quality on the basis of competition between operators and equipment suppliers.

Another factor hindering the rapid development of information society in Russia, is the lack of spread in the society of basic skills in using information technology. This applies both to the general public, as well as state and municipal employees. Require adjustment and replacement personnel system in the area of information technology. Today, higher education is carried out mainly on old techniques. As a result of the higher educational institutions of the country often go professionals who do not understand modern technology and are unable to use them to improve the performance of the functions of state and municipal government.

For additional analytical, business and investment opportunities information,
please contact Global Investment & Business Center, USA
at (202) 546-2103. Fax: (202) 546-3275. E-mail: rusric@erols.com

It should be noted the high level of dependence on the Russian market of foreign products in the field of information technology. In the vast majority of information systems created in Russia today are used mostly foreign developments. There are a number of barriers to the successful development of the domestic industry in the field of information technology, including the critically important is the low level of legal protection of intellectual property.

A significant obstacle accelerated development of information society in Russia is the lack of mass interactivity of individuals and organizations with public authorities in providing the latest state services. It should be noted that so far Russia has not been approved by law, even the list of state and municipal services provided in an electronic form, respectively, state authorities and local authorities. Not resolved the question of recognition in law of an electronic document equivalent to a paper document.

Exploiting the potential of information technology prevents the fragmentation of state information resources, the inability to compare the data contained in these resources, as well as a considerable duplication of information. Necessary to ensure the completeness, accuracy, relevance and accessibility of official legal information in electronic form, including through the modernization of the mechanisms of the official publication of legal acts, integration of information and legal support of public authorities.

Obstacles for more effective use of information technology to improve the quality of life of citizens, the competitiveness of Russia's economic development, socio-political, cultural and spiritual spheres of society, improving the system of government decision-making are complex inter-agency in nature and can not be resolved at the the level of individual public authorities. Their elimination requires significant resources, coordinated organizational changes and to ensure coherence of action by public authorities.

As a result of the lack of a comprehensive approach to solving the problem of formation and development of information society as one of the necessary stages of modernization of Russian economy appeared negative trends, while maintaining that the current economic situation may be aggravated.

First, the results of the development and implementation of information technologies, conducted by order of state authorities, are not always systematic, in particular:

the introduction of information technology is mainly local, departmental in nature;

inadequate infrastructure is rapidly developing public access to the sites of public authorities and other means of reference and support services;

people and organizations to obtain government services, as well as information related to the activities of public authorities and other organizations, in most cases require treatment in their own state authorities, as well as providing queries and documents in hard copy. This leads to time consuming and creates significant inconvenience to the public;

lack the necessary legal framework, as well as standards and regulations granting public authorities the required information to the public, organizations and other bodies of state power, not formed infrastructure that provides information security of electronic forms of interaction between the public authorities themselves, and also with the people and organizations. For electronic forms of interaction are not implemented services such as notary services in electronic form, the official publication of electronic documents, and other services similar to services in the traditional forms of interaction through the use of paper documents.

For additional analytical, business and investment opportunities information, please contact Global Investment & Business Center, USA at (202) 546-2103. Fax: (202) 546-3275. E-mail: rusric@erols.com

Second, poorly co-ordinated use of public authorities of information technology, not the best experience using information technology to improve the efficiency of public administration, in particular:

there is an incompatibility of software and hardware solutions, the inability to exchange data between different information systems established by the state, there are no mechanisms and technologies of operational information between federal and regional information systems among themselves and with each other;

There are significant differences between the public authorities on the use of information technology in their work;

public authorities of the Russian Federation is seriously lagging behind the federal government in terms of information technology support administrative and management processes, as well as the development of information technology infrastructure and public information systems;

small number of public authorities using integrated electronic document management system;

no automated procedure for collecting and processing information necessary for planning and targets of public authorities, nor created a unified information system of control to achieve the planned values of indicators;

there is an uncontrolled growth of information about citizens, organizations and facilities of the economic circulation, contained in public information systems, that in the absence of effective mechanisms for monitoring its use also poses a threat to civil rights violations;

must provide the infrastructure, solutions and standards for data exchange in electronic form at the interagency level, and with the public and organizations, which becomes especially important with the further development of public information systems;

is still low level of computer literacy of government and municipal officials that determines the relevance of the organization of continuous training of civil servants and evaluation skills in using information technology in the statutory periodic evaluation.

Thirdly, there remains behind the Russian market of information technologies is not enough fast becoming the economy is carried out through information technology:

still low level of domestic production in the field of information and telecommunication technologies, the share of Russia in the global electronics market is 0.5 percent;

to reduce the backlog of the world's leading information technology sector requires the development of domestic developments in technology to create electronic components, formation of a national system of management of transport infrastructure and the construction of broadband wireless networks;

the level of competition in the Russian market of information technology remains low, including due to the presence of significant administrative barriers;

prerequisite for the development of the Information Society is to improve the quality of training, as well as a system of lifelong learning in the field of information technology.

Fourth, a high level of differences in the use of information technology regions, different sectors of society, and lack basic infrastructure of the information society, in particular:

differences in the level of regions in the use of information technology in households is high;

For additional analytical, business and investment opportunities information, please contact Global Investment & Business Center, USA at (202) 546-2103. Fax: (202) 546-3275. E-mail: rusric@erols.com

challenges remain for broadband access to end-users and low-quality access to the Internet.

Fifth, the increasing security threats in the information society, including:

one of the threats is to increase the number of computer crimes has increased their self-serving orientation, and caused material damage, increased the number of crimes, including cross-border computer crime committed by groups of individuals;

Information technology is increasingly used to commit traditional crimes, such as theft, extortion, fraud and terrorist activities;

remain a threat to national security associated with the active use by terrorists of the Internet and mobile telephony for the organization of covert channels of communication and promotion of its activities continue to operate and set up new sites and other illegal extremist orientation;

increasingly important issues of security of the national Internet segment.

Sixth, the actual threat to the preservation of the national library-in terms of electronic publications. So, check the reproducibility of retrospective electronic publications

(Until 2003) showed that about 28 percent of electronic publications have problems when playing due to the constant changing of hardware and software required to use them.

The main result of years of work on informatization of public authorities is the availability of computer and network equipment, and the level of development and utilization of applied information systems are inadequate, do not set up the infrastructure of e-government, in particular:

database containing account information on key government facilities, and cover a little sketchy time horizon;

in a small number of public authorities deployed and used comprehensive electronic document management system;

there is an incompatibility of software and hardware solutions and the impossibility of communication between different government information systems;

not formed infrastructure that provides information security of electronic forms of interaction between the public authorities themselves, with the people and organizations, there are no mechanisms available to ensure confidence in the digital signature is not established a complete system of certification authorities, and by certifying centers are not integrated into the domains of mutual trust and their services are not widespread;

no automated procedure for collecting and processing information;

inadequate means of rapidly evolving knowledge-management support and services;

uncontrolled growth of information about citizens, organizations and sites of economic turnover, contained in public information systems, in the absence of effective mechanisms to control its use poses a threat to civil rights violations.

The comprehensive nature of the state program of the Russian Federation, "The Information Society (2011 - 2020 years)" (hereinafter - the Program) gives rise to the following risks of its implementation:

irrelevance of planning and delay matching of the Program;

For additional analytical, business and investment opportunities information,
please contact Global Investment & Business Center, USA
at (202) 546-2103. Fax: (202) 546-3275. E-mail: rusric@erols.com

unbalanced distribution of funds for the activities of the Programme in accordance with the expected outcomes of the Programme;

lack of flexibility and adaptability to changes in the Programme worldwide trends in information technology, external factors and organizational changes in public authorities;

duplication and inconsistency of the work under the Program and other government programs and activities aimed at implementation of information technology in the activities of public authorities;

passive resistance to the use of public authorities e-government infrastructure and the spread of modern information technologies;

passive resistance of individuals and organizations conducting public events program for the creation of information databases, registries, qualifiers and single identifier citizens on ethical, moral, cultural and religious reasons.

II. Priorities and objectives of public policy in the sphere of information society development in the Russian Federation, the main goals and objectives of the Program, the forecast of development of the sphere of socio-economic development and the projected macroeconomic indicators for the results of the Program

In accordance with the Development Strategy for Information Society in the Russian Federation, approved by the President of the Russian Federation, February 7, 2008 № Pr-212 (further - Strategy), the objectives of the formation and development of information society in the Russian Federation is to improve the quality of life of citizens, ensuring the competitiveness of Russia's development economic, social, political, cultural and spiritual spheres of society, improving public administration through the use of information and telecommunication technologies. Thus, the creation of an information society is seen as a platform to meet the challenges of a higher level - economic modernization and social relations, and ensuring the constitutional rights of citizens and to release resources for personal development.

The concept of long-term socio-economic development of the Russian Federation until 2020, approved by the Federal Government on November 17, 2008 № 1662-r, defines as a public policy objectives in the field of information technology to create and develop the information society, improving the quality of life citizens, the development of economic, social, political and cultural spheres of life, improving governance, ensuring the competitiveness of products and services in information and telecommunication technologies. To achieve these objectives, in accordance with the Federal Government on November 17, 2008 № 1663-r of approved main activities of the Government of the Russian Federation until 2012 and a list of projects to implement the above directions, including projects in the field of information society and modernization of information processes and quality development of mass communications.

Thus, the public policy objectives determine the necessity of solving problems, not only in the sphere of information technologies, but also in other sectors of the economy, science and technology, social and governance. Among the indicators of information society development in the Russian Federation, the reference values are defined strategy, are also included indicators reflecting the level of development of information technologies and the extent of their use in various fields.

The current state of Russia's readiness to information society determines in accordance with the Strategy need not only the development of the technology industry, but also the priorities of its development, the creation on its base of services and to prepare citizens and organizations to the

For additional analytical, business and investment opportunities information,
please contact Global Investment & Business Center, USA
at (202) 546-2103. Fax: (202) 546-3275. E-mail: rusric@erols.com

use of technical capabilities. So, come to the fore the problem of coordination among various agents align their interests and resources.

International obligations of the Russian Federation, on the one hand, suggest that the provisions of relevant documents in the field of information society and on the other - provide participation in the development of international law and the mechanisms that regulate the relations in a global information infrastructure, international research projects in priority areas of science, technology and engineering, as well as create an opportunity to use the best experience. Need to create an atmosphere of interest in innovation, a willingness to innovate, openness and continuity of learning as the basis of the information society.

Strategy also found that the information society is characterized by a high level of development of information technologies and their intensive use by citizens, businesses and public authorities, that is to create an information society high level of development of information technologies is a necessary but not sufficient condition. Should be possible to implement technology and create the habit of using them in everyday life. As the information society by its very nature can not be local, then for all Russian citizens regardless of their place of residence and social status should be respected uniform minimum federal standards for accessibility of information technology.

In accordance with the aims and objectives of the formation and development of information society in the Russian Federation provided by the Strategy, as well as the scope of the current state of development and use of information technology in the Russian Federation to the Programme is to provide citizens and organizations benefit from the use of information technology by ensuring equal access to information resources, digital content development, innovative technologies and radically improve the efficiency of government in providing security in the information society.

Achieving the objectives of the Programme is provided through the implementation of measures, grouped by sub-program. The composition of activities can be corrected as targets of the Programme. For each subprogram defined tasks that ensures the achievement of the Programme.

Improving the quality of life of citizens and improving conditions for business development in the Information Society provides:

development of services for the facilitation of interaction between society and the state with the use of information technology;

translation of public and municipal services in an electronic form;

infrastructure access to electronic services of the state;

increased transparency of public authorities;

creation and development of electronic services in health, as well as in areas of housing and communal services, education and science, culture and sports.

Building e-government and improving governance includes:

formation of a single space electronic interaction;

creation and development of inter-state information systems for decision-making in real time;

the creation of directories and classifiers used in state and municipal information systems;

improving the efficiency of information technology at the level of the Russian Federation and municipal formations;

For additional analytical, business and investment opportunities information,
please contact Global Investment & Business Center, USA
at (202) 546-2103. Fax: (202) 546-3275. E-mail: rusric@erols.com

creation of spatial data infrastructure of the Russian Federation;

development of the accounting system of scientific research and development work carried out within the public order;

provision of translation into electronic form of government accounting;

creation and development of specialized information and information technology systems to ensure the activities of public authorities, including the protected segment of the Internet and inter-agency electronic document management system.

The development of the technology, providing a transition to an economy that are carried out through information technology, provides:

stimulation of domestic developments in information technology;

training of skilled personnel in the field of information technology;

development of economy and finance through the use of information technology;

the formation of socio-economic statistics of the Information Society;

development of industrial parks in the area of high technology.

Overcoming the high-level differences in the use of information technology regions, different sectors of society and the basic infrastructure of the Information Society provides:

development of broadcasting;

development of basic infrastructure of the information society;

promotion opportunities and benefits of the Information Society;

increased willingness of people and businesses to the opportunities of the information society, including training in the use of modern information technologies.

Security in the Information Society provides:

opposition to the use of the potential of information technology to threats to the national interests of the Russian Federation;

provision of technological independence of the Russian Federation in the information technology industry;

development of technologies to protect information, ensure privacy, personal and family secrets, as well as the security of restricted information;

ensuring the development of Russian legislation and improving law enforcement in the field of information technology.

The development of digital content and preservation of cultural heritage includes:

digitization of cultural heritage, including archival collections;

development of processing facilities and to provide remote access to digital content.

For additional analytical, business and investment opportunities information, please contact Global Investment & Business Center, USA at (202) 546-2103. Fax: (202) 546-3275. E-mail: rusric@erols.com

Forecast of development of information technologies based on the forecast of socio-economic development of the Russian Federation until 2020 and is made in two versions - inertia and innovation. In the inertial version of the volume of communication services in 2020 compared with 2007 at constant prices will rise by almost 6 times the volume of the information technology market - will increase by 2.7 times. In an innovative variant of projected growth in services in 2020 compared with 2007 at constant prices by almost 10 times the volume of the information technology market will grow to over 2007 by 5.9 times.

Macroeconomic indicators for planning and evaluation of the Program is not being used. However, first, the goal of the Programme indirectly affect macroeconomic performance. Thus, the gross domestic product is not an indicator of target programs, but one of the factors of change is to reduce costs through the use of information technology. Secondly, a number of targets and performance indicators for the Program are an integral part of macroeconomic indicators (eg indicators, reflecting the structure of gross domestic product and employment structure). Targets and indicators for the Programme are presented in Appendix № 1.

III. Forecast outcomes of the Program, describing the target state (change state) level and quality of life, social, economic, public safety, public institutions, the extent to which other public interest concerns and needs in the field of information society development, performance evaluation program

Program Outcomes are defined in accordance with the Strategy and reflect the goal of the program.

Effectiveness of the program is evaluated on the following parameters:

compliance with the planned values of final results of the Programme test values of indicators of information society development in Russia;

the degree of achievement of planned results.

The results of the implementation of the Program are responsible in accordance with the Strategy, the following problems:

the formation of modern information and telecommunications infrastructure, the provision on the basis of its quality services and high availability to the public of information and technology;

improving education, health care and social welfare on the basis of information technologies;

improving the system of state guarantees of constitutional human and civil rights in the information sphere;

Development of the Russian economy through the use of information technology;

improving the efficiency of public administration and local government, civil society and the interaction of business with public authorities, the quality and efficiency of public services;

development of science, technology and engineering, as well as skills training in information technology;

For additional analytical, business and investment opportunities information, please contact Global Investment & Business Center, USA at (202) 546-2103. Fax: (202) 546-3275. E-mail: rusric@erols.com

preservation of the culture of the multinational people of the Russian Federation, the strengthening of moral and patriotic principles in the public mind, as well as the development of cultural and humanitarian education;

opposition to the use of the potential of information technology to the threat to Russian interests.

Thus, the final result of the Programme will be the presence of a wide range of opportunities to use information technology in the industrial, scientific, educational and social purposes. These opportunities will be available to any citizen regardless of his age, health status, region of residence and any other characteristics. The possibilities of using information technologies provided by the creation of appropriate infrastructure, providing digital content, and user training.

Implementation of the Programme will create conditions for improving the quality of education, health care, social protection through the development and use of information technology.

Improving the quality of training is a prerequisite for the country's transition to innovative development. Increased speed of access to educational institutions on the Internet, training teachers to use information technology implementation in schools of the domestic software with a right to use, copy, modify it and distribute the source code (hereinafter - the free software), equipped with jobs for disabled children studying at home, with modern computers and the Internet connection will ensure the effective use of trainees and training educational information resources, not only Russia but the world community.

In health care and social assistance to the population increase in the use of information technology will improve the quality of diagnosis and rehabilitation and, therefore, provide a reduction in mortality, disability, increasing the share of active working population and life expectancy. Telecommunication tools allow you to organize the provision of high-tech medical care to people living far away from the scientific and medical centers. In the Russian Federation will create a new system of relations, and software and hardware solutions based on electronic recording technology in the treatment of reception time of booking specialists determine the budget treatment of electronic health records, automatic calculation of remuneration specialists and hospitals, depending on the objective evaluation of the complex result their activities.

In the field of social security capabilities of Information Technology will be actively used to support disadvantaged groups, persons with disabilities, as well as to promote a healthy lifestyle.

In addition, objective, accurate and prompt accounting and control activities in health care and social assistance, implemented by means of computer technology, will build confidence and reduce the traditional problems of feedback and citizen health.

A significant result of the Program will increase labor mobility and employment of the population. The use of modern information technology makes it possible not only to inform the public about current job openings, but also to information-analytical system for the assessment and socio-economic processes in the sphere of labor and employment, to form on the basis of these forecasts to support the program processes of internal migration.

Improving the system of state guarantees of constitutional human and civil rights in the information area will provide constant monitoring of the Russian Federation legislation, updating regulations, bringing them into line with the current needs of the information society and the international rule of law.

The next important result of the program will increase the efficiency of public administration and local government, civil society and the interaction of business with public authorities, the quality and efficiency of public services, as well as reducing the cost of providing government. For example, increasing the availability of public services will be expressed in lower costs for services for all

**For additional analytical, business and investment opportunities information,
please contact Global Investment & Business Center, USA
at (202) 546-2103. Fax: (202) 546-3275. E-mail: rusric@erols.com**

citizens regardless of their place of residence, health and employment. Orientation of the executive power to meet the needs of citizens will be expressed in a comprehensive and consolidated distribution services (for example, to prevent repeated appeals to the obvious cases).

The implementation of the development of the state system of legal information will create optimal conditions for maximizing the information needs of government and public organizations, enterprises, organizations, institutions and citizens in the use of instruments based on the effective organization and use of information and legal resources to the application of modern information technology.

In the field of science, technology and equipment, training of qualified personnel in the field of information technology activities of the Programme will ensure reduction in the backlog of the world leaders in this area, the development of technologies for creating databases, establishing the national system of management of transport infrastructure and the spread of broadband wireless networks.

Expected to reduce the shortage of skilled users of information technology, to provide training to employees in the use of information technology and increase the level of computer literacy of the state and municipal employees.

As a result of increasing development of information technologies and the creation of central registries, accumulating information about the subjects of entrepreneurial activity, a reduction of financial risks of economic entities, and their time costs associated with obtaining the relevant and available information of the counterparties.

Programme activities will ensure the prevention of threats to Russia's interests by ensuring the safety of the national segment of the Internet, reducing the vulnerability of the national domain management system, reducing the possibilities of access violation to the Russian information resources on the Internet and unleashing the Internet information warfare.

As a result of the implementation of the Program Information and telecommunications infrastructure of the Russian Federation will rise to a new level, providing an innovative scenario of socio-economic development.

In addition, as a result of implementation of the program will be worked out management mechanisms (such as project management, public-private partnership), the distribution of which will contribute to improving the investment climate and the development of market relations.

Extensive use of information technology will lead to a new quality of interaction among people especially through the electronic communications and the Internet, open up new opportunities for individual development and the development of all forms of business entities and public authorities and, consequently, increase productivity, efficiency and competitiveness of the economy.

Resource efficiency of government and public institutions are:

reducing time, organizational and financial costs of obtaining governmental and other services and the conduct of economic activity;

increase validity, responsiveness and flexibility in carrying out public policy;

reduction of administrative barriers and the burden of excessive regulation;

budget cuts on the activities of executive agencies, or improving the efficiency and transparency of these costs;

Distribution of social initiatives;

increased mobility of the population;

For additional analytical, business and investment opportunities information,
please contact Global Investment & Business Center, USA
at (202) 546-2103. Fax: (202) 546-3275. E-mail: rusric@erols.com

development of interregional cooperation.

Effects arising from the use of information technologies in various fields of activity, ultimately affect the quality of life of citizens regardless of their age, health status, and region of residence, as well as to increase the productivity and competitiveness of Russian goods.

The volume of temporary resources that citizens are spending for public services is about 25 million hours of working time. More than 10 percent of the goods and services of small businesses account for costs associated with additional administrative barriers. Accordingly, for the domestic economy, these costs become missed opportunities.

As a result of the implementation of the Program to any citizen, for example:

to get the public service, it will be enough to fill a time remotely request form, and after a certain time to obtain the necessary document to your mailbox or check for changes on their person in an appropriate database;

in order to express an opinion on a particular issue or create a group of like-minded people to implement any initiative, it will be enough to go to the corresponding site on the Internet;

to collect student in school, it is enough to download the complete set of textbooks and related materials from the regional educational portal and store them in an e-book;

in order to pass the tax returns, will not have to go to tax office;

to get professional advice, the patient will not have to go to the medical center, and it will be enough to keep their documents on the portal and at the appointed time to get in touch with the physician profile;

to get help in an emergency situation, it is enough to use one number for emergency pay phone connection located in close proximity;

in order to pick up literature on topics of interest, it will be enough to take advantage of electronic catalog of any library throughout the country;

to proceed with the implementation of certain types of professional activities, will not have to spend time on the road, it is enough to turn on the computer and log into the corporate network;

to enter into a contract with a partner from another region will not have to send him their representative, will be sufficient to certify the documents with digital signature;

to buy a train ticket, will not have to go to the cashier, will be sufficient to remotely select and pay for the right ticket, and landing controller called his name.

Carried out during the preparation program assessment of the likely effects showed the presence of both economic (the change in volume of value added and the structure of gross domestic product) and social (provision of information of citizens' equality) effects.

The source of economic effects is the impact of information technology on the socio-economic development processes of the country.

With the widespread use of information technology to create new models of knowledge sharing and the collective generation of ideas, transforming traditional services, acquire new forms and become more accessible, change management models, production and consumption, expanding economic (business) relationship between the actors of the business community and countries.

For additional analytical, business and investment opportunities information, please contact Global Investment & Business Center, USA at (202) 546-2103. Fax: (202) 546-3275. E-mail: rusric@erols.com

Possible economic effects of the Program are divided into direct and external. Direct effects of the Programme is made up of cost-effectiveness of individual interventions (projects in the action) and an increase in output and value added in the information technology sector.

External effects are in the impact of information technology on the structure and the costs in other sectors, changing skill requirements and training of workers in any industry, the expansion of communication capabilities of individuals and organizations.

Based on a preliminary assessment of the profitability measures (projects in the action) sets out a potentially attractive from a commercial point of view (eg, the creation of broadband access). To perform this kind of activities planned to raise funds from extrabudgetary sources. Performing activities that are mostly costly nature, is provided by the federal budget. Financing of the Program from the federal budget, the budgets of the Russian Federation and local budgets, partially offset by the following factors:

fiscal restraint in the execution of the Program for use of infrastructure and other results of the implementation of activities at the expense of budget sources;

increase in tax revenues due to growth of value added and expanding economic activity.

IV. Terms of the Program, milestones and deadlines for their implementation with an indication of milestones

The program is implemented in the 2011 - 2020, respectively.

To ensure the current control during the formation of passports of the Program and adjustment of activities as the Program Ministry of Communications of the Russian Federation shall determine the interim (control) for individual steps or routines of the Program. Proposals for the intermediate (control) stages of the routines are presented for approval to the Government Commission on the implementation of information technology in state agencies and local authorities before July 1, 2011, otherwise the intermediate stage for all the routines defined in 2015.

Targets and indicators for the Programme are presented in Appendix № 1 to the Program.

Reference values of the Information Society in the Russian Federation until 2015 to identify strategies for achieving them requires additional measures to coordinate activities on the use of information technology by public authorities, as well as incentives for spending at the expense of budget sources involved to achieve the goal the program.

V. List of main activities of the Programme

with a timetable for their implementation and expected results

Problems are solved within the framework of the Programme of six sub-programs. Routines are functional and can be implemented in every sphere of activity established by the authorized bodies of state power. Routines are interdependent, the implementation of the activities of one subroutine may depend on the performance of activities other routines. The sequence of the objectives and activities

For additional analytical, business and investment opportunities information,
please contact Global Investment & Business Center, USA
at (202) 546-2103. Fax: (202) 546-3275. E-mail: rusric@erols.com

defined by the Ministry of Communications and Mass Communications of Russian Federation in accordance with the procedures for managing the implementation of the program.

Programme activities funded from the federal budget in 2011 - 2013, respectively, are presented in Appendix № 2.

Activities Program, funded from other sources in 2011 - 2020, respectively, are presented in Appendix № 3.

SUB-PROGRAMS

SUBPROGRAMME 1. QUALITY OF LIFE OF CITIZENS AND CONDITIONS FOR BUSINESS DEVELOPMENT IN THE INFORMATION SOCIETY

Achieving this goal is impossible without a program to improve the quality and accessibility of public services, simplifying procedures and reducing the time of their delivery, increase the transparency of information about the activities of state and local governments.

The priorities of routines for the period up to 2015 are the following:

1) the development of federal government information system "single portal of public and municipal services (functions)" (hereinafter - a single portal), including:

modernization of the infrastructure of a single portal, providing access to information and services a single portal for all categories of consumers who use different software and hardware platforms;

development and implementation of technology standards to ensure integration with third-party information systems, development of appropriate interfaces for use with a single portal on the Internet, the introduction of paperless forms of remote interaction of citizens and legal persons with public authorities;

support services functional and technological components of a single portal, methodical support of the federal executive authorities and organs of state power of subjects of the Russian Federation, improving front-end solutions (navigation, search, notifications, and distribution, and other services) that are used on a single site;

development of a consolidated register of public and municipal services (functions);

implementation of a monitoring service prices for services in the field of housing and communal services on the basis of a single portal;

2) the creation and development of information systems to support small and medium-sized businesses, including:

implementation of interactive services for small and medium-sized enterprises on the basis of a single portal;

creation and development of automation processes in the interaction of small and medium-sized businesses with public authorities;

development of mechanisms to support small and medium-sized businesses;

For additional analytical, business and investment opportunities information, please contact Global Investment & Business Center, USA at (202) 546-2103. Fax: (202) 546-3275. E-mail: rusric@erols.com

3) ensuring that the transition to the provision of public and municipal services electronically, including:

normative, methodological and organizational support for the transition to the provision of public and municipal services in electronic form (design and implementation of standards for electronic services, standardization of inter-agency communication and public information systems used to deliver public services), the optimization of the order of realization of the state authority for the purpose of transferring them to electronic form;

normative, methodological, organizational and technical support of a consolidated register of public and municipal services (functions);

support the implementation and development of standard solutions (regional registries and portals of government and municipal services (functions), an automated information system to provide multi-functional center of state and municipal services);

4) optimization of the order of execution of public functions and services for the purpose of transferring them to electronic form, including the creation and development of an analytical system for optimization of state and municipal functions and services as a means of improving public administration and local self-government;

5) development of mechanisms to use mobile devices to access e-government services, including:

creation of a technological infrastructure for secure access to e-government infrastructure with mobile devices;

development of methodical and regulatory documents with a focus on mobile services;

6) the development of services, citizens' interaction with public authorities via e-mail created on the basis of a single portal, including:

infrastructure e-mail system and its integration into a single portal infrastructure, creating a single directory of users;

infrastructure and electronic services for issuing e-mail addresses citizens and public authorities;

7) the development of call centers, including:

provision of the reception of citizens in the delivery of public services on the basis of a single federal number (8-800);

creation of a federal call center, the creation of regional call centers with automatic switching to the nearest call center when calling on the federal number;

realization of the possibility of switching a call to the agency (service) that provides the appropriate public service (in case of questions that require examination agency (service));

creating a database of normative documents for use by operators call centers to answer questions about the procedure for providing public services;

formation on the basis of call centers to identify the mechanisms of incompleteness and irrelevance of the information contained in the consolidated register of state and municipal services (functions), other sources of normative documents, as well as ensuring they make the appropriate changes;

8) the development of electronic communication and information exchange within the framework of proceedings for bankruptcy, including:

For additional analytical, business and investment opportunities information, please contact Global Investment & Business Center, USA at (202) 546-2103. Fax: (202) 546-3275. E-mail: rusric@erols.com

refinement of an automated information system "Details for bankruptcy" in part enable the exchange of information and electronic documents in a proceeding in bankruptcy between the liquidator and the creditors;

development of draft regulations, explanatory notes thereto and other supporting documents required for electronic communication and information sharing within the production of the bankruptcy;

creating a single Federal Information Registry information on essential facts of the entities on the basis of the Uniform Federal Register information on bankruptcy, namely the organization of publishing reports of legally significant facts, in particular on the state registration;

9) To ensure transparency of information about the activities of public authorities and public availability of information resources for citizens and organizations, including:

formation requirements and guidelines to ensure the disclosure of public information on the official websites of state and local governments;

information resources to bring the official websites of the federal bodies of executive power in conformity with the requirements of the regulations;

Regular monitoring of compliance with regulatory legal acts of the official websites of federal executive bodies, executive bodies of subjects of the Russian Federation and local self-government;

methodological support of the federal bodies of executive power in terms of maintenance and development of their official websites;

10) optimization of design and operation of the official websites of federal executive bodies and executive bodies of subjects of the Russian Federation, including:

creation of a universal constructor official website, providing the design, function, content and technical support to federal, state and municipal Internet projects that do not require specialized technical training of the operators of sites;

development of common principles of operation and information sharing through technology services used on existing and newly created public authorities official websites;

official translation of existing sites on common principles of operation;

11) the creation of services for public debate and controlling the activities of public authorities, the creation of instruments of public management at the municipal level, including:

creation based on a single technological solution communication platform for the discussion of socially significant issues;

creation of tools to involve citizens and organizations in decision-making process at the municipal level, including the use of mobile devices;

creation of electronic services for public monitoring of government bodies and local authorities;

creation of electronic monitoring services to receive and review complaints of citizens and organizations to government bodies and local authorities;

12) the creation and implementation of integrated information systems in health care, including:

For additional analytical, business and investment opportunities information,
please contact Global Investment & Business Center, USA
at (202) 546-2103. Fax: (202) 546-3275. E-mail: rusric@erols.com

creation of a unified information system in healthcare, providing a personalized account of medical assistance to citizens of the Russian Federation in the framework of the state guarantees free medical care based on medical applications of the universal electronic cards;

preparation and presentation of structured information to citizens about the types of public health facilities, their addresses, contact information and other necessary information, the integration of the official websites of medical institutions into a single web portal for health care institutions;

development of technology and personal monitoring in real-time human health, information center, "Managing risks to health";

13) the development of electronic services to improve service delivery in education and science, including:

creating and maintaining a federal system of exceptions to access educational institutions in the Russian Federation to Internet resources that are incompatible with the objectives of education and training of students;

development of electronic educational resources of the new Internet generation, including cultural and educational services, remote education and job training, including for people with disabilities;

14), social adaptation and development of creative abilities of people with disabilities through the use of modern information technologies and distance learning technologies, including the organization of distance learning disabled children who need to study in general education programs at home;

15) improvement of urban planning, implementation and control, regulation and licensing functions and optimizing the delivery of public services in urban planning through the use of information technologies, including:

creation of the federal state of Geographic Information Systems Spatial Planning;

publication in the official sites on the Internet 100 percent of information on the availability of land and land owned by the state and municipal ownership, the rights to which are registered;

provision of services in electronic form at the stages of examination of project documentation, obtaining building permits, obtain a permit for commissioning of facilities;

16) improvement of enforcement and licensing functions and optimizing the delivery of public services in health, social, sanitary and epidemiological welfare of the consumer market through the use of information technologies, including:

transition from the licensing procedure for the start of the notification procedure of individual activities using the "e-mail notification";

formation and maintenance of the state register of notifications of commencement of business in the relevant field;

17) improvement of enforcement and licensing functions and optimizing the delivery of public services in the field of agriculture through the use of information technologies, including:

formation and maintenance of the official registry (database) phytosanitary requirements of the Russian Federation to the products subject to quarantine, regulated articles and consignments;

formation and maintenance of the registry information of phytosanitary requirements for regulated products exported from the territory of the Russian Federation, with the placement of relevant information on the official website on the Internet;

For additional analytical, business and investment opportunities information, please contact Global Investment & Business Center, USA at (202) 546-2103. Fax: (202) 546-3275. E-mail: rusric@erols.com

formation and maintenance of the official register for phytosanitary quarantine zones established in the territory of the Russian Federation, with the placement of relevant information on the official website on the Internet;

introduction of an electronic system of registration and issuance of veterinary accompanying documents;

forming and maintaining a register of notifications of commencement of business activity in agriculture.

SUBPROGRAMME 2. E-GOVERNMENT AND GOVERNMENT EFFECTIVENESS

Performing routines provide a transition to a new form of organization of state and local governments, a new level of speed and convenience of getting organizations and citizens of the state and municipal services, as well as information on the performance of government.

The priorities of routines for the period up to 2015 are the following:

1) formation of a common space of trust digital signatures (hereinafter - the electronic signature), including:

development of a nationwide infrastructure of public key certificates of electronic signatures (digital infrastructure of trust), which provides identification of the subjects of communication and content integrity of electronic documents;

establishing a system of certification of certification centers for entry into the single space of trust e-signature certification centers providing a single compliance requirements and standards;

creation of a register of certified (authorized) certification centers and access to it;

improvement of mechanisms for user authentication and authorization;

2) development of interagency electronic interaction (hereafter - the system of interactions), including:

development of infrastructure to ensure uninterrupted operation of the central nervous system interactions due to the growing number of connected public authorities and organizations, as well as subjects of the Russian Federation;

provision of electronic information between state authorities, local authorities and organizations in the processes of providing state and local government services electronically;

provision of electronic registration services of public and municipal services and functions, as well as electronic services implementation of interagency cooperation;

improvement of technologies and mechanisms of interaction between the central and regional systems of interaction;

implementation of control systems and monitoring services;

3) the formation and development of infrastructure of a universal e-cards, including:

development of common principles and approaches to the provision of public and municipal services in an electronic form using a universal electronic map in the Russian Federation;

organization of the process of production and circulation of a universal e-card;

For additional analytical, business and investment opportunities information, please contact Global Investment & Business Center, USA at (202) 546-2103. Fax: (202) 546-3275. E-mail: rusric@erols.com

normative legal support the introduction of universal electronic map on the whole territory of the Russian Federation;

4) methodological and organizational support for a unified system directories and classifiers used in the state (municipal) information systems, including:

adoption of regulations defining the basic parameters and a list of registers, common rules for the base register, the formalization of conditions and procedures for storage and disclosure of information contained in directories and classifiers;

the formation of uniform requirements for transfer of counts in an electronic form, including the requirements for obtaining the data base interface registers;

formation of a single federal registry of requisite regulatory and reference information, including the integration of nation-wide and departmental directories and classifiers;

5) creation of a unified system directories and classifiers used in the state (municipal) information systems, including:

development tools of the federal system of reference data, the creation of the bank's automated all-Russian classifiers of technical, economic and social information on computer media;

development of a unified federal interagency information exchange format data referenced data;

6) The creation of a unified accounting system of civil registration, including:

development of common principles and approaches to the integration of vital records in electronic form;

union account of civil status records maintained in the Russian Federation, at the federal level;

provision of public services on the basis of the accounting system of inter-agency electronic interaction;

7) development of a secure system of inter-agency electronic document, including:

integration of electronic document management systems of public authorities on the basis of a single standard, including the establishment of reporting systems for working with documents;

modernization of the departmental electronic document management systems of the Presidential Administration and the Government of the Russian Federation to ensure integration with the system of interdepartmental electronic document based on a single standard;

8) development of information technology support activities of the Russian Presidential Administration, Government of the Russian Federation and the Federal Assembly of Russian Federation;

9) development of information and analytical support for special purposes, including:

provide effective information and analytical support to the Russian Presidential Administration, Government of the Russian Federation and the federal government;

to create a custom universal system of converting data from various sources to fund the Main Information and Analytical Center;

modernization of information system "fund performance";

For additional analytical, business and investment opportunities information, please contact Global Investment & Business Center, USA at (202) 546-2103. Fax: (202) 546-3275. E-mail: rusric@erols.com

modernization of information and referral system, "The structure and management personnel of public authorities of the Russian Federation";

creation of an integrated repository of diverse information Main Information and Analytical Center;

development of an information system "Market of drugs";

creation of an information system for monitoring, analyzing and forecasting the socio-demographic processes in the Russian Federation;

creation of an information system for monitoring the action plan to implement the basic directions of foreign economic activity of the Russian Federation;

provision of an information system for monitoring the development of fuel-energy complex and the evaluation of the energy security of the Russian Federation;

development of complex software for the preparation of passports of the Russian Federation and federal districts in view of the ethno-religious, political, criminal, economic and social factors;

provision of special training center for the modernization of information;

10) development of a protected segment of the Internet for the public authorities of the Russian Federation in the federal districts and subjects of the Russian Federation, including:

infrastructure development segment of the Internet for the public authorities of the Russian Federation in the federal districts and subjects of the Russian Federation;

development of information between state authorities and ensuring the integration of state public information systems and resources in a segment of the Internet;

11) the development of the state automated system of "control", including:

integration of the central information system with the departmental information systems of the federal bodies of executive power;

implementation of regional segment of the state automated system of "control" in the executive branch of the Russian Federation;

creating a model of information system security manager of the federal agency (ensuring better control the implementation of the priorities of agencies and harmonize information systems departments based on a single information-analytical platform);

creation of an automated information system for the development and implementation of government programs (providing support progress in the development, adjustment and implementation of government programs, including the formation of a system for monitoring and analyzing the effectiveness of achieving expected results of state programs of the Russian Federation);

12) development of the project "E-region", including:

development of normative, methodological and technological solutions for implementing e-government at the level of the Russian Federation;

Develop a set of measures to introduce information technology in the region of the Russian Federation, development

relevant model of software solutions based on free software;

For additional analytical, business and investment opportunities information,
please contact Global Investment & Business Center, USA
at (202) 546-2103. Fax: (202) 546-3275. E-mail: rusric@erols.com

ensure cooperation in electronic form between the federal bodies of state power and bodies of state power of subjects of the Russian Federation;

13) development of a unified inter-agency information and statistical system, including:

development of an integrated statistical resource containing official statistical information;

provision of public services on the basis of statistical information in electronic form;

Integration with government information systems;

14) the creation and development of spatial data infrastructure of the Russian Federation, including:

development of a list of basic spatial data and spatial information base;

development of common rules and standards for creating and updating of spatial information;

creation of a state GIS portal, which provides publication basic spatial data and spatial information base, as well as metadata, provision of electronic public digital maps and plans;

15) the creation of organizational and technological infrastructure for electronic payments for government services, including:

creation of information and payment gateway for electronic payments;

Develop mechanisms to integrate a single portal with a single operator accounting charges and evidence of tax payments, government fees, cash payments (fines) and fees through the Federal Treasury;

16) development of a unified accounting system of the results of research and development work performed under government orders, including:

software incorporating the results of research and development work civil performed within the state order;

regulated to ensure the possibility of access to a single accounting system of the results of research and development activities and context of information search in the system;

17) the creation of a unified system of management cadre of civil service of the Russian Federation, including:

automation of receipt of tender procedures in the civil service;

providing opportunities for citizens to documents for the position of the civil service in electronic form through the federal portal of managerial personnel;

provision of a single register of civil servants based on the infrastructure of the federal portal of managerial personnel;

provision of planning and carrying out training activities and professional development of managerial personnel of state civil service;

18) monitoring the implementation of the program and examination results;

19) A system of monitoring the implementation of decisions of the Government Commission on the implementation of information technology in state agencies and local governments;

For additional analytical, business and investment opportunities information,
please contact Global Investment & Business Center, USA
at (202) 546-2103. Fax: (202) 546-3275. E-mail: rusric@erols.com

20) implementation of measures for the coordination of budget spending to the state government for information technology, including:

development of regulations and guidance documents for the implementation of measures for the Coordination of budget spending of public authorities for information technology;

development of automated information management system of departmental and regional information;

conduct an independent examination of information activities of public authorities;

ensuring interagency enforcement agencies to coordinate activities of state authorities on the spending of budget funds for information technology;

21) the creation of an integrated interagency automated system of federal executive authorities exercising control at checkpoints across the state border of the Russian Federation, including:

improve the effectiveness of regulatory bodies and reducing the time required for the control at the checkpoints;

interests and security of the Russian Federation in the border area to counter international terrorism and transnational crime, illegal migration, illegal movement across the border of the Russian Federation of drugs, arms and ammunition smuggling and plundering of natural resources;

22) the development of the state automated system of production, processing and control of passport and visa documents of new generation, including:

prevention of illegal migration through measures for preventing counterfeiting or fraudulent use of identity documents;

improving the efficiency of border controls and controls on issuance and circulation of passport and visa documents of new generation;

improvement and integration of state information resources used in the field of border and immigration control, as well as in the fight against criminal and terrorist manifestations;

increased protection of passport and visa documents of new generation from a fake by the use of modern methods and means of protection;

providing technical possibilities of information exchange in the process of inter-state law enforcement cooperation in combating illegal migration, criminal and terrorist manifestations;

more effective enforcement of foreign citizens and persons without citizenship requirements immigration legislation of the Russian Federation;

23) the creation of the state information system of technical regulation of the Customs Union, including:

remove excessive administrative barriers to the declaration of goods;

costs (time and money) on procedures for registration of the declaration of conformity;

creating conditions for free movement of goods within the Customs Union;

Raising awareness of purchasers and assistance in selecting a competent product.

For additional analytical, business and investment opportunities information,
please contact Global Investment & Business Center, USA
at (202) 546-2103. Fax: (202) 546-3275. E-mail: rusric@erols.com

SUBPROGRAMME 3. THE RUSSIAN MARKET OF INFORMATION AND TELECOMMUNICATION TECHNOLOGIES

The information technology industry is composed of several segments, among which are telecommunications, software and hardware, as well as the provision of services in information technology. The market of information technologies is not only one of the foundations of effective functioning of the existing world markets, but also performs the role of locomotive in the world economy, as recorded in the policy documents of governments of developed countries. The degree of implementation and use of information technologies in various areas of society is crucial to sustained economic and social development.

The main factors determining the availability to the population of modern information technology include:

prices for computer hardware and mobile communications;

prices for access to the Internet;

the price level of software and services in information technology;

penetration in the country the mobile;

penetration in the country broadband connection;

income level (this factor is the "landscape", which is difficult to influence directly);

availability of the Russian GIS platform;

availability of Russian navigation and information systems based on technologies of the global navigation satellite system GLONASS.

The priorities of routines for the period up to 2015 are the following:

1) create a national platform "cloud" including:

development of the Internet platform "cloud computing", to ensure safe working with standard software applications in the "software as a service";

development on the basis of a national set of standard software platform software services for use in government agencies, including the collaboration with the documents publicly available network storage, remote hosting of software applications, software development tools;

ensuring the integration of the national network of software services with the largest commercial resources that provide software services in the mode;

2) monitoring the transition to the provision of public and municipal services in electronic form in the Russian Federation and the evaluation of the authorities on translation services in electronic form;

3) creating conditions to increase transparency and efficiency of interaction between government and business entities in the field of public procurement through the introduction of information technologies, including the development of the Russian Federation official site for posting information about placing orders for goods, works and services for federal needs, the needs of the Russian Federation and municipal needs, including its completion in accordance with changes made to the legislation of the Russian Federation;

4) the operation and development of information systems in government procurement and bidding, including:

For additional analytical, business and investment opportunities information,
please contact Global Investment & Business Center, USA
at (202) 546-2103. Fax: (202) 546-3275. E-mail: rusric@erols.com

ensure synchronization and load sharing between the primary and backup sites of the Russian Federation official site for posting information about placing orders for goods, works and services for federal purposes, the needs of the Russian Federation and municipal needs;

development of an information system independent registrar electronic trading platforms and the official website on the Internet for placing orders for goods, works and services for federal purposes, the needs of the Russian Federation and municipal needs, as well as other needs, the legislation of the Russian Federation on the State Procurement ;

development of information systems for the analysis of information on state and local government tenders for realization (sale), including the Russian Federation official site for posting information on public tenders;

5) development of information technologies based on open source software for use in research and educational activities, including:

development of methodologies, standards, specifications and training materials for using the software in the educational activity;

the creation of a distributed system support of educational institutions;

6) the creation of national innovative technical products in the field of information technology, including:

devices based on natural interfaces, data entry;

devices in the integration of Internet access, public television and other electronic services;

detectors of explosives and narcotics for security systems;

RFID tags;

7) the creation of domestic telecommunications equipment, including:

implementation of complex program activities of the federal target program "Development of electronic components and electronics," in 2008 - 2015 years;

creation of a pilot area data network using Dense Wave Division Multiplexing equipment;

establishment of centralized service platform with a flexible softswitch;

creation of domestic equipment manufacture wireless broadband radio frequency 2.3 - 2.4 GHz;

devices in the field of network technologies, including services for the implementation of the "last mile";

8) the formation and development of socio-economic statistics of the Information Society, including:

modernization plan in the statistical monitoring of the addition of statistical process of technological modernization and economic processes, carried out through information technology, statistics, public e-services, statistics, civil society, regional and municipal statistics and other areas in which there are significant information gaps;

formation of a unified database of performance indicators, public authorities, targets to achieve the results of the government programs of the Russian Federation, which provides uniform standards within the public access to information and public control over the activities of government;

For additional analytical, business and investment opportunities information, please contact Global Investment & Business Center, USA at (202) 546-2103. Fax: (202) 546-3275. E-mail: rusric@erols.com

Development of State Statistics of information society development and creation of conditions for its effective application in accordance with international statistical standards;

monitoring and evaluation of the Strategy, the establishment of a comprehensive training program information for the formation of international rankings and interaction with international organizations in this field;

formation of a system for monitoring the development of human resources in information technology (qualitative and quantitative aspects).

SUBPROGRAMME 4. BASIC INFRASTRUCTURE FOR INFORMATION SOCIETY

To create an information society to improve access of citizens and organizations to modern information technologies, relevant information and knowledge.

Infrastructure development of information society promotes investments in the sector of information technology and ensures that the universal service obligations in areas where there are traditional market.

Measures aimed at ensuring the routines of universal, ubiquitous, equitable and affordable access to information technology infrastructure and services on the basis of information technologies.

The priorities of routines for the period up to 2015 are the following:

1) the creation of technological capabilities for Broadcasting Development (implementation of complex measures of the federal target program "Development of Broadcasting in the Russian Federation for 2009 - 2015"), including the development of system events to build a network of digital television broadcasting by region;

2) formation of a modern telecommunications infrastructure and telecommunications, including:

formation of a modern highway network;

creating conditions for the population of modern broadband services;

creation of satellite broadband Ka-band;

3) expanding the list of universal services;

4) arrangements for converting the radio frequency spectrum in order to release the frequency resource for the deployment of broadband access, including:

identification of promising radio technology and radio frequency bands for their implementation;

determine the possibility of using the selected frequency bands and the need for conversion and (or) the output of electronic civil to other radio frequency bands;

5) increased willingness of people and businesses to the opportunities of the information society, including:

creating conditions for increasing computer literacy of the population;

training and retraining of specialists in the field of information technology-based education centers, and developments in information technology;

For additional analytical, business and investment opportunities information,
please contact Global Investment & Business Center, USA
at (202) 546-2103. Fax: (202) 546-3275. E-mail: rusric@erols.com

a system of training highly qualified specialists in the field of supercomputing technology and specialized software;

creation of a multi-level federal system of electronic distance learning;

implementation of information system of continuous e-learning and reference methodology support for teachers of educational institutions on the use of information technologies and electronic educational resources in the educational process in the exchange of experiences and best practices in this area;

creation of a unified system of geographically distributed access to electronic educational resources developed in the framework of a unified educational Internet portal;

6) providing a high level to reduce the differences in the use of information technology subjects of the Russian Federation, including:

development of standards of security and accessibility to the public, businesses, government bodies and local government facilities information and telecommunication infrastructure of e-government;

funding for regional activities aimed at developing information society in order to eliminate the "digital divide" (annual competitions conducted under the Ministry of Communications of the Russian Federation and the Ministry of Economic Development).

SUBPROGRAMME 5. SAFETY ON THE INFORMATION SOCIETY

The condition for the transition of society in the Information Society is to provide the necessary and sufficient level of information security. Identify threats, ensure reliable counter malicious attacks in the information sphere, the elimination of the adverse consequences of violations of the protection of information resources, regular assessment of security infrastructure components, timely upgrading of systems of protection are implemented with the information security systems.

The priorities of routines for the period up to 2015 are the following:

1) a system of identifying and monitoring the level of actual security of the information society of the manifestations of terrorism in the information sphere, providing a continuous obtain information about the state of infrastructure and the possible manifestations of terrorism in the information sphere, as well as timely response to these manifestations;

2) the establishment and support of local protected storage technologies and processing large volumes of unstructured information, including the creation of national protected functional services, and technological components that provide storage and handling of large volumes of unstructured information, and their continued support and development that increase the amount of unstructured data being processed;

3) development and integration with other departmental and interdepartmental information and control systems of a single data bank on combating terrorism, including:

connectivity and inter-departmental information and management systems to a common data bank on combating terrorism;

modernization of the telecommunications component of a single data bank on combating terrorism;

development of specialized software and hardware systems interfacing with the requirements of information security and unique to each subscriber a single data bank on combating terrorism;

extend the warranty servicing of complex computing a single data bank on combating terrorism;

For additional analytical, business and investment opportunities information, please contact Global Investment & Business Center, USA at (202) 546-2103. Fax: (202) 546-3275. E-mail: rusric@erols.com

4) establishment of a national software platform (a set of domestic policy decisions - the modules built on the basis of common technologies that enable the development of new software products by the layout and configuration of ready modules, as well as the development of new modules), including:

development of the national assembly of the operating system free software;

creation of national database management system based on open development;

establishment of a Russian software development environment;

development of a set of architectural standards and standard components for software compatibility with each other;

creation of a basic package of application software, including drivers and tools to ensure information security;

establishment of a national fund of algorithms and programs (gospriklad.rf);

forming a package of standard solutions, and their placement in the national fund of algorithms and programs;

the formation of geographically distributed infrastructure, technical and methodological support of free software;

5) the formation of open interoperability standards information systems, including development and support of open standards architecture profile of public information systems, formats and communication protocols to ensure interoperability of government information systems and their components;

6) the development of supercomputing and grid technologies, including:

creation of mathematical models for domestic use in supercomputing;

create a basic number of domestic supercomputers with different performance characteristics;

construction of grid networks for high performance computing, including the benefit of the federal nuclear centers;

development of domestic software technology design and simulation on supercomputers;

a system of training highly qualified specialists in the field of supercomputing technology and specialized software.

SUBPROGRAMME 6. DIGITAL CONVENTION AND CULTURAL HERITAGE

The preservation of cultural diversity and traditions is one of the key objectives of the millennium. In this regard, there is a need to implement measures for the creation, dissemination and preservation of this information in electronic form, which will preserve cultural heritage for future generations.

Activities aimed at promoting sub production of and accessibility of information content - educational, scientific, cultural, and entertainment. A key role for translation of the existing cultural heritage in digital format.

The priorities of routines for the period up to 2015 are the following:

For additional analytical, business and investment opportunities information,
please contact Global Investment & Business Center, USA
at (202) 546-2103. Fax: (202) 546-3275. E-mail: rusric@erols.com

1) The development of means to find information on various types of content, including the creation of search engines with a range of highly relevant search on a particular subject;

2) establishment of national information and communication platform for the distribution of digital content (including audio-visual), including:

creation of a multifunctional platform for downloading, processing and distribution of digital content;

optimization of digital content to satisfy needs and geographic location of the user;

development of technologies to protect content owners from copying when viewed by placing a unique digital object labels in the digital copyright content;

development of geographically distributed content delivery network infrastructure to reduce the load on the channels of communication;

implementation of technologies for the collection of statistics, as well as the billing system to account for the legal acquisition of digital content;

development of tools categorization of content;

3) creation of a single web portal for the promotion of cultural heritage and traditions of Russia, including:

providing distributed access to various industry information resources on the Internet, to information about museum objects, collections, documents library fund public services in the fields of culture, site of the Office of Culture of the Russian Federation, cultural institutions, etc.;

generalization and systematization of modern information and knowledge about the culture by creating a multimedia version of the Russian National Atlas of Cultural and Natural Heritage, interactive maps of cultural and natural landscapes of Russia;

establishment of a national electronic museum of Russian history;

4) development of training digital media and interactive content, including the creation of stereoscopic 3D collections of significant events in the sphere of culture and cultural heritage of the peoples of Russia;

5) establishment of a national library resource, with a unified catalog of digitized assets on the basis of the Russian State Library, National Library of Russia, Boris Yeltsin Presidential Library, libraries, state academies of sciences of the Russian Federation, as well as state and municipal public libraries;

6) Internet connection of cultural institutions, particularly state and municipal public libraries;

7) The formation and maintenance of the State Catalogue of Museum Fund of the Russian Federation, the union catalog of libraries in Russia, creating a database of objects of cultural heritage of Russia to describe the monuments of history and culture of Russia.

VI. MANAGE THE IMPLEMENTATION OF THE PROGRAMME

The program is a system of measures (interconnected on the tasks and timing of resources) and the instruments of state policy, providing a framework of key government functions to achieve the priorities and objectives of public policy in the sphere of information society development in Russia.

Manage the implementation of the Programme shall be in accordance with the Procedure for the development, implementation and evaluation of the effectiveness of government programs of the Russian Federation, approved by the Government of the Russian Federation. Implementation of the Programme shall be in accordance with the plans of its implementation to be approved each year based on the priorities of the Programme.

Programme activities are implemented co-executors of the Programme in accordance with the passports of these activities, consistent with the Ministry of Communications and Mass Communications of Russian Federation.

Simultaneously with the implementation of the Programme of the Ministry of Communications of the Russian Federation organizes the analysis of emerging trends in the information society and the associated risks of the Program and forms the proposals for changes in the program.

In order to support the expert management of the implementation of the Programme is aimed at the examination specifications for projects under the Programme activities, as well as examination of proposals for changes in the program.

Executive in charge of coordination with subcontractors and taking into account the expertise to decide on amendments to the lists and the composition of events, the timing of their implementation, as well as in budgetary allocations for implementation of activities within the approved limits of budgetary allocations under the plan of the Program for the relevant year. If a decision to amend the plan to implement the Programme responsible contractor within 10 days notify the Ministry of Economic Development and the Ministry of Finance of the Russian Federation.

Disputes arising from the harmonization of the implementation plan of the Programme for the year, submitted by the Ministry of Communications of the Russian Federation to discuss the Government Commission on the implementation of information technology in state agencies and local governments.

Making other changes in the program have an impact on the parameters of the Programme, initiated by the Ministry of Communications and Mass Communications of Russian Federation, or pursuant to instructions of the Government of the Russian Federation (including the results of monitoring the implementation of the Programme) in the prescribed manner.

In order to ensure consistent implementation of the Programme of Action for the decision of the Ministry of Communications and Mass Communications of Russian Federation (on the proposals of subcontractors) may be set up temporary coordinating bodies (working groups) of the representatives of the responsible Executive, subcontractors, and higher executive bodies of subjects of the Russian Federation, scientific, expert and self-regulatory organizations.

VII. FINANCING OF THE PROGRAM

Programme activities funded from:

federal budget funds allocated for the implementation of measures contained in Annex № 2 to the Program (hereinafter - the direct costs of the Programme);

of different sources, including the federal budget allocated for the implementation of measures to develop the information society in the Russian Federation (including the computerization of government), contained in the federal programs, departmental targeted programs, regional programs, community programs and other instruments (hereinafter - the thematic program costs);

extra-budgetary funds.

For additional analytical, business and investment opportunities information,
please contact Global Investment & Business Center, USA
at (202) 546-2103. Fax: (202) 546-3275. E-mail: rusric@erols.com

The composition of the Program may include work, funded and due to the direct costs of the Programme, and through thematic expenses.

When co-financing of the Program by extra-budgetary sources may use different instruments of public-private partnership.

Resource support measures for the development of information society in the Russian Federation for 2011 - 2013 years and 2020 is presented in Annex № 4.

The amount of funding sub Programs

in 2011 - 2013 years in areas of expenditure are presented in Appendix № 5.

The amount of funding sub Programs in 2011 - 2013 years of co-executor presented in Annex № 6.

VIII. MONITORING THE IMPLEMENTATION OF THE PROGRAM

In order to monitor the implementation of programs can be created by the Supervisory Board of the Programme, which is a consultative body.

The rating impact of the proposed program activities on the performance of the Programme by the Ministry of Communications of the Russian Federation or a co-executor of the Programme in the preparation of annual plans approved by the Program.

Ministry of Communications and Mass Communications of Russian Federation in the implementation of the program analyzes the implementation of the Program and evaluate changes in the values of target indicators and targets. Passports of the Programme for which the Federal State Statistics Service does not conduct surveillance, are given in Appendix № 7.

Ministry of Communications and Mass Communications of Russian Federation in cooperation with subcontractors before March 1 of the year following the reporting year, prepare and transmit to the Government of the Russian Federation, Ministry of Finance and the Ministry of Economic Development's annual report on the implementation and evaluation of the effectiveness of the program.

As part of the program is formed as an information resource on the Internet, which publishes information on the implementation (of the stage, and interim results), projects and activities of the Programme, as well as the annual report.

IX. FEATURES OF THE ORGANIZATION WORKS ON PROJECTS FOR SUBJECTS OF THE RUSSIAN FEDERATION

The program is aimed at addressing the digital divide between the subjects of the Russian Federation and includes the following groups of activities in favor of the Russian Federation:

pilot event (an event aimed at identifying best practices and testing of software and technical and organizational solutions for the automation of health, education, culture, social welfare, security and rule of law, economy and industry, property, land and transport systems, housing and public economy in the region of the Russian Federation);

typical event (an event aimed at developing a consistent set of ready-to-implement software and technical and organizational solutions tested in the pilot activities in the Russian Federation);

For additional analytical, business and investment opportunities information,
please contact Global Investment & Business Center, USA
at (202) 546-2103. Fax: (202) 546-3275. E-mail: rusric@erols.com

innovative activity (activity initiated by state authorities, local authorities, organizations or citizens and aimed at obtaining new opportunities in the information society).

The pilot performs event responsible contractor or co-executor of the Programme in consultation with the supreme executive body of state power of subjects of the Russian Federation.

Types of activities implemented within the framework of regional programs of information, prepared in accordance with the Federal Government on July 3, 2007 № 871-p. Ministry of Communications of the Russian Federation annually generates recommendations for the inclusion of standard measures in the regional programs of information, as well as the expected results of implementation of these programs.

Innovative activity, corresponding to the aims and objectives of the Programme shall be included by the Ministry of Communications and Mass Communications of Russian Federation in the implementation plan for the program.

X. KEY MEASURES OF LEGAL REGULATION, AIMED AT ACHIEVING THE GOALS AND (OR) END RESULTS OF THE PROGRAMME

In forming and adjusting the plan of the Program as the identification of outstanding issues and regulatory legal executive in charge of the project forms the regulations and make them into a discussion of the Government Commission on the implementation of information technology in state agencies and local governments. Endorsed by the Government Commission on the implementation of information technology in state agencies and local government proposals are made in the prescribed manner to the Government of the Russian Federation.

When the activities of the Programme, as appropriate, the Ministry of Communications and Mass Communications of Russian Federation or collaborators programs take departmental regulations in accordance with its mandate.

The main regulatory measures aimed at achieving the goals and (or) the outcome of the program are presented in Annex № 8.

XI. A LIST AND BRIEF DESCRIPTION

Federal programs and subroutines

As a result of the federal target program "Electronic Russia (2002 - 2010 years)", approved by the Government of the Russian Federation on January 28, 2002 № 65, created a significant advance in the field of information technology in the activities of public authorities and organizations providing public services, including:

made the purchase, delivery, installation and commissioning of software and hardware for a number of information systems, including public services portal, the portal of state and municipal procurement portal for public sale, the network of certification centers, a network of public access to government services, the state automated system of "control" , an Internet site to ensure uninterrupted operation of information resources of the Russian President and Government of the Russian Federation, located on the Internet;

developed prototypes of hardware and software tools for analyzing and forecasting the progress of implementation of works on priority national projects, monitoring and evaluating the effectiveness of

For additional analytical, business and investment opportunities information, please contact Global Investment & Business Center, USA at (202) 546-2103. Fax: (202) 546-3275. E-mail: rusric@erols.com

budget resources management, information retrieval systems, storage and processing of multimedia information;

created software and hardware solution for managing the development and implementation of standard software and hardware solutions in the field of regional and departmental information;

prepared proposals for improving the regulatory framework, scientific and methodological, organizational and information-analytical maintenance processes information;

identified a list of issues (possible obstacles) to go to the provision of public services in electronic form, prepared proposals (including bills with supporting documentation) to remove from the regulations of all identified regulations that impede the transition to the provision of public services in electronic form;

analyzed the level of development of information technologies and their use by citizens, organizations and government bodies, as well as information processes of interagency cooperation, public administration and public service delivery;

developed a systematic project to create a technology platform and e-government infrastructure - defined objectives, participants, specific measures for building e-government infrastructure in terms of regulatory frameworks, technology components (telecommunications infrastructure, data centers, the major information resources, including the required lists, portals, technology systems), organizational measures;

established and put into effect a typical automated information system security of multi-service centers, including those organized in support of its introduction to the subjects of the Russian Federation;

Typical solutions are designed for operation of regional portals, and registries of public and municipal services;

developed technical requirements and solutions to create and develop the functionality of information systems (eg, interagency integrated automated information system of federal bodies of executive power, a unified system of information-analytical support of the President of the Russian Federation);

created a number of industry and functional solutions (eg, automated information system to provide public services electronically in real estate, automated information system for processing information on violations of traffic regulations, public information and analytical system control and audit bodies);

prepared and tested in the training of civil servants training techniques and the use of modern information technologies, including the highly applied nature;

analyzed the official websites of state and local governments for compliance with Federal Law "On Access to information about the activities of state bodies and local self-government."

The results of the federal target program "Electronic Russia (2002 - 2010 years)" determined the composition of tasks and activities for the sub program.

The activities of several federal targeted programs consistent with the objectives of the Programme, and the results of their activities are taken into account in planning the program.

XII. THE COMPOSITION AND SIGNIFICANCE OF THE INDICATORS AND TARGETS OF THE PROGRAMME OF THE STAGES OF ITS IMPLEMENTATION AND EVALUATION OF THE INFLUENCE OF

For additional analytical, business and investment opportunities information,
please contact Global Investment & Business Center, USA
at (202) 546-2103. Fax: (202) 546-3275. E-mail: rusric@erols.com

EXTERNAL FACTORS AND CONDITIONS FOR THEIR ACHIEVEMENT

The composition of indicators for each sub-program is defined in such a way as to ensure that:

observability values of the parameters during the period of implementation of the program (subroutine);

coverage of all the most important results of the implementation of activities;

minimize the number of indicators;

availability of formal methods for calculating the values of parameters obtained in the course of the research to build a system of indicators that characterize the main trends and factors of development of information society.

The structure of the Programme Strategy includes targets, indicators, which are formed on the basis of composite index for the international rankings of the Information Society and accessibility of information technology (adapted to the Russian statistical practice), and indicators that reflect regional differences.

The list of indicators includes indicators for statistical observation of the development and use of information technology and new indicators necessary for a comprehensive analysis of the main trends and factors in the development of information society, data for the calculation are missing in the current statistical practice.

The list of indicators is open and allows for adjustments in case of loss of information content index (reaching a maximum or saturation), changes in state policy priorities, the emergence of new technological and socio-economic circumstances, greatly influencing the development of information society.

Rationale for targets and assess the impact of external factors are held in the preparation of the relevant section of the socio-economic development of the medium term.

XIII. RESOURCE SUPPORT PROGRAM

Program costs are derived from the federal budget, the consolidated budgets of subjects of the Russian Federation and extrabudgetary funds. The expenditure of the federal budget is on two areas - the direct costs of program expenditures and thematic programs.

The amount of funding programs in 2011 - 2020 years will be:

costs associated with the implementation of the Program, funded through the federal budget - 88 billion rubles;

federal funds provided by the chief administrators of the federal budget for the implementation of measures on information, including federal and departmental targeted programs - an estimated 120 billion rubles a year;

expenditure budgets of the Russian Federation - an estimated 50 billion annually, including grants to encourage the achievement of the best indicators of the efficiency of executive bodies of subjects of the Russian Federation and intergovernmental transfers in support of the highest executive authorities of subjects of the Russian Federation of administrative reform, as well as subsidies for the implementation of regional programs to improve the efficiency of budget expenditures;

For additional analytical, business and investment opportunities information, please contact Global Investment & Business Center, USA at (202) 546-2103. Fax: (202) 546-3275. E-mail: rusric@erols.com

expenses from non-budgetary sources - approximately at least 200 billion rubles annually. Extrabudgetary funds are valued at current performance of official statistics, the information technology industry. In addition to those observed by the Federal Service of State Statistics figures take into account the information technology industry and other costs to the challenges of the Information Society.

More resource support program for 2011 - 2013 years and 2020 is presented in Annex № 4 for the program.

In order to improve the efficiency of budget spending in the planning, development and use of information technology in the activities of federal executive bodies, other state bodies and management of state budget funds the Ministry of Communications and Mass Communications of Russian Federation is coordinating these activities in accordance with the decision of the Government of the Russian Federation May 24, 2010 № 365 "On the coordination of information and communication technologies in government." In carrying out the coordination of activities on the use of information technology in the activities of public authorities the Ministry of Communications of the Russian Federation is guided by the purpose and objectives of the Programme.

To coordinate the implementation costs of the executive authorities of the Russian Federation and local self-government, as well as to stimulate the consumption of extra-budgetary resources to implement the objectives of the program requires additional measures of legal regulation in this area.

The direct costs of the Programme are reflected in the relevant chapters of the departmental structure of the federal budget by a unique code to the target line item without sharing a single sum at the event.

Expenditures in 2011, and the planning period is given in accordance with the draft federal budget for 2011 and for the planning period of 2012 and 2013, taking into account the need to complete the projects, which began under the federal target program "Electronic Russia (2002 - 2010)." The volume of spending years in the light of expert defined the start of full-scale infrastructure projects to achieve the reference values of indicators of information society development in Russia by the Strategy. This level of expenditure will be updated following the approval of the federal budget for the financial year and planning period.

Additional resource support of the Program at this time is possible due to redistribution of costs subject departments, conducted under the coordination of activities on the use of information technology in the activities of public authorities.

XIV. GOVERNMENTAL

risk management to minimize their impact

to achieve the objectives of the Programme

Governmental administrative nature to the section "Managing the implementation of the Programme."

The risk of irrelevance of planning, coordination of the Programme of delay is typical when the long-term and complex programs, and directed his steps to minimize the annual planning work, taking into account the analysis of global trends in information technology.

The other risks associated with industry-specific and measures taken to minimize them by the Ministry of Communications of the Russian Federation to the management of the Programme through measures to coordinate activities aimed at developing information society in the Russian Federation, as well as co-executors of the Programme in the planning and implementation activities.

For additional analytical, business and investment opportunities information, please contact Global Investment & Business Center, USA at (202) 546-2103. Fax: (202) 546-3275. E-mail: rusric@erols.com

XV. METHODS OF EVALUATING THE EFFECTIVENESS OF THE PROGRAM

The effectiveness of the Program is estimated as the degree of achievement of planned results (comparison of planned and actual values of the exponents of the Program), subject to reasonable expenditure.

Frequency of evaluating the effectiveness of the Program is determined by the frequency of data collection for monitoring indicators and targets of the Programme.

Evaluating the effectiveness of the Program is conducted to ensure the responsible executor of operational information on the progress and interim results of the actions and decisions

objectives of the Programme. The results of evaluating the effectiveness of the medium used to adjust the schedules of the Program and Plan for its implementation.

Information on the progress and interim results of the program is generic in nature, but is the result of the calculation, rather than a reflection of the final state (not reliable due to the presence of time lags, the accumulated actions of previous decisions, the impact of the actions of other entities) that is based on an array of raw data that allows the analysis in case of unsatisfactory ratings.

In assessing the effectiveness of the program separately analyzes information about achieving the target values of indicators (follow-up) and performance routines and activities (current control).

The calculation of integral index is carried out in the following sequence:

determination of the coefficients of importance of each activity in terms of problem solving routines Programme. The significance of each event is determined by an expert. The coefficient value activities (B) expressed as the number in the interval (0, 1]. Sum of the coefficients of the significance of events is equal to one;

calculation of the extent to which planned for the estimated period of performance indicators, measures of values. The degree of achievement of the planned evaluation period at the target value of the indicator (D) is calculated as the ratio of actual and planned values for each target indicator. If the actual value of the indicator more than planned, the extent to which shall be equal to unity;

calculation of the average degree of implementation of activities.

The average level of performance measures (DM) is defined as the sum of the weighted importance of the degree of achievement of indicators as follows:

where:

N - number of indicators;

i - number of indicators.

For target performance indicators and programs not included in the federal state statistical observation, the formation of passports of the Programme is provided by the responsible executor (developed passport of the Programme are presented in the annex to the program number 7). The passport program indicators reflect the name of the indicator, unit of measure, the algorithm is the formation of values, frequency of monitoring, collecting the names and order of the baseline.

For additional analytical, business and investment opportunities information, please contact Global Investment & Business Center, USA at (202) 546-2103. Fax: (202) 546-3275. E-mail: rusric@erols.com

IMPORTANT REGUALTIONS RELATED TO ICT DEVELOPMENT

E-GOVERNMENT POLICY, LAW AND REGULATION IN RUSSIA: IMPORTANT INFORMATION

NATIONAL E-GOVERNMENT MASTER PLAN

The 8-year program "Electronic Russia," is designed to implement a wide range of e-Government applications, using the public sector as a catalyst to spearhead development of e-commerce and the Internet in the wider economy. It aims to make wide use of information technologies in government departments, and transfer much of the state's work online. During 2002, an interagency taskforce was to define e-Government pilot projects and studies to be conducted between 2003-4 at the federal and regional level.

Full implementation was expected to begin in 2005. A government portal http://www.gov.ru has been created and several regions have participated in pilot e-Government initiatives including e-mail and document management systems. The third phase, from 2005 to 2010, will see the implementation of e-Government across all public sector agencies. The government hopes that the e-Russia program will both reduce bureaucracy for citizens and businesses when dealing with the government and make the federal and local government more efficient. The lack of more recent information on this, suggests that progress may not be on track.

The E-Russia federal program specifies various tasks, timing and responsible agencies for its implementation. For example, one of the tasks is to review the existing legislation, prepare proposals for implementation of information technology program and draft necessary legislation (including civil, administrative and criminal legislation). The timeframe for this task is from 2002 to 2004 and the responsible agencies include the Ministry of Economic Development, the Ministry of Justice and the Ministry of Communications.

According to the news report (of 21 March 2006), the Ministry of Information and Communications is going to present a proposal to introduce certain changes to the E-Russia federal program to the government's session at the end of March 2006. In particular, it is going to be proposed to centralize all coordination among the governmental agencies and to concentrate the efforts of the E-Russia federal program on its e-Government component (making all other components separate programs).

On 27 September 2004 the government has adopted a regulation (Order of the Government of the Russian Federation of 27.09.04,. _ 1244-r) on "Use of Information Technology in Government Operations by 2010" (the "2004 Order").[1] It was adopted to:

"1. approve enclosed proposals on use of information technologies in the activity of federal governmental bodies by 2010;

1. approve enclosed plan of measures for implementation and use of information technologies in the activity of federal governmental bodies by 2010; and

2. recommend interested federal governmental bodies to take into account concept regulations on use of information technologies in the activity of federal governmental bodies by 2010 in formation and implementation of projects and programs, containing the measures for the development and use of information technologies."

For additional analytical, business and investment opportunities information,
please contact Global Investment & Business Center, USA
at (202) 546-2103. Fax: (202) 546-3275. E-mail: rusric@erols.com

The 2004 Order was prepared by the Ministry of Information Technologies and Communication of the Russian Federation. The 2004 Order suggests to create an interdepartmental agency to supervise and coordinate the process.

The 2004 Order outlines the need to amend the existing, or to adopt new, legislation, that is necessary for the implementation of the e-Government program. For example, it suggests to amend the 1995 federal "Law on Information, Informatisation and Protection of Information" and the 2001 "Law on Electronic Digital Signature", to introduce certain changes to the various regulations dealing with public procurement and to adopt new "Law on Right to Information" and "Law on Electronic Document Circulation".

GOVERNMENT ACTIVITIES

The 1995 federal "Law on Information, Informatisation and the Protection of Information", Article 12 provides:

Users --citizens, agencies of state authority, agencies of local self-government, organizations, and public associations --possess equal rights to access to state information resources and are not required to substantiate to the possessors of those resources the need to obtain the information that they are requesting. Information with limited access constitutes an exception.

The access of individuals and legal entities to state information resources is the basis for carrying out public monitoring of the activities of the agencies of state authority, the agencies of local self-government, public, political, and other organizations, as well as the monitoring of the state of the economy, ecology, and other spheres of public life.

Article 13 provides:

Agencies of state authority and agencies of local self-government create resources that are accessible for everyone on questions of the activities of those agencies and their subordinate organizations, and also, within the limits of their competency, carry out the mass informational support of the users with regard to questions of citizens' rights, freedoms, and obligations, their safety, and other questions that are of public interest. Refusal to provide information can be appealed in court.

The 2004 Order outlines the need to adopt a new federal "Law on Right to Information", which should define the concept of "official information", regulate access to, and storage and protection of, such "official information", and provide for disclosure of information in respect of operations of various local self-government agencies.

The 2001 "Electronic Russia" program speaks about filing of various forms and documentation electronically and exchange of forms and documentation among various governmental bodies. For example, the program envisages electronic submission of tax forms to the Ministry of Taxation and Collections and filings with the Ministry of State Statistics, The Antimonopoly Ministry, customs, etc. However, it is unclear if any progress has been made in this field or any legislation passed. The 1995 federal "Law on Information, Informatisation and the Protection of Information", recognized electronic signatures (Article 5).

A new law on electronic signatures came into force in 2002 (Federal Law No. 1FZ "On Electronic Digital Signature" adopted on 11 January 2001). The underlying concept of the Law establishes encryption as the only method whereby a valid (from the standpoint of Russian law) electronic digital signature may be created. The Law is drafted to intentionally omit other analogues of personal signatures and exclude the use of other technologies for electronic digital signature creation. Further, the Law limits the scope of use of electronic digital signatures to civil law transactions and transactions where electronic digital signatures are specifically permitted under other Russian

For additional analytical, business and investment opportunities information,
please contact Global Investment & Business Center, USA
at (202) 546-2103. Fax: (202) 546-3275. E-mail: rusric@erols.com

legislation; as of today, such specific references only exist in the Russian Civil Code. Accordingly, an electronic digital signature can be used for any civil law contract (with a few exceptions specified below), but cannot be used for signing of any electronic documents submitted to the government authorities. Equally, it cannot be used for signing of any civil law documentation that will subsequently need state registration (or notarization).

Baker & McKenzie commented that this new law will not create enough confidence to drastically increase the use of electronic documents in Russia. In fact, the impact of the Law on IT business and commerce in Russia would be far more significant if a draft Law on Electronic Trade was also adopted, since this draft law contains important provisions with respect to the use of electronic documents (including use as evidence in court), as well as, other provisions relating to transactions concluded over the Internet.

The 2004 Order stresses the need to amend the 2001 "Law on Digital Signature" and emphasizes the importance of harmonization of this law with similar legislation on e-signature which has been adopted internationally.

The 2001 "Electronic Russia" program envisages that the tender notices and documents and other tender information should be posted on the internet. It is unknown if any law has been adopted to require thins. According to the 2004 Order, the existing legislation on public procurement for goods, works and services has to be amended to allow use of new information technology in, for example, bidding process.

Presently, there is no comprehensive data protection law in Russia. Certain data protection provisions can be found in the Constitution of the Russian Federation of 1993, the 1995 federal "Law on Information, Informatisation and the Protection of Information" and the "Law on Participation In International Information Exchange" of 1996. In addition, a draft "Law on Personal Data" has been pending in the Russian Duma (the lower chamber of the Russian parliament) since 1996, however, I have not been able to establish if such law has been passed.

Constitutional Provisions

The Constitution of the Russian Federation recognizes the right to privacy: data protection and secrecy of communications (articles 23, 24), inviolability of the home (article 25), freedom of speech and access to information (article 29). The Constitution of the Russian Federation states that "[c]ollection, storage, usage and dissemination of information about the private life of an individual without his consent are not permitted" (Art. 24.1). This provision has direct effect and can be invoked in court if implementing legislation is developed.

Federal Legislation

The two federal laws, the 1995 federal "Law on Information, Informatisation and the Protection of Information" and the "Law on Participation In International Information Exchange" of 1996 implement parts of the constitutional provision.

The laws define relevant terms:

- Personal data is data on facts, events and particulars of citizen's life, allowing his identification

- Data protection is limited to natural persons

- There are special restrictions on the processing of confidential information about individuals' social, racial or national origin, language or political affiliation

**For additional analytical, business and investment opportunities information,
please contact Global Investment & Business Center, USA
at (202) 546-2103. Fax: (202) 546-3275. E-mail: rusric@erols.com**

- Personal data may not be collected, retained, used or disseminated without the data subject's consent or a court decision.

- The laws protect the rights of data subjects to:

- access, correct and update personal information,

- be informed about who is using the information and for what purpose.

The data controller is obliged to:

• provide data subjects, upon request, with information related to the processing of their personal data free of charge.

The laws include only vague and ambiguous restrictions on transborder data flows.

The primary legislation affecting information technologies including the Internet is the 1995 federal "Law on Information, Informatisation and the Protection of Information", that provides general protection for personal data (articles 11 and 21) and regulates access to information. The law on mass media (adopted in 1991 with numerous additions since then) covers freedom of speech and the media, and bans censorship. Many issues concerning online censorship, freedom of speech, freedom of information and privacy/data protection are not stipulated in current laws and regulations, and Russia lacks legislation specifically about the Internet. Cases of websites being shut down are rare.

The draft law on Personal Data ("the Act") is highly influenced by the Council of Europe Convention 108 and the European Union Data Protection Directive.

1. General Provisions

The right to privacy is set out in the preamble of the Act. The Act covers both public and private sectors as well as computerized and manual data.

Most definitions are very close to those in the EU Directive. A notable difference can be found in the definition of data holder, which combines the features of data controller and data processors into one single entity.

The Act establishes a commissioner on data protection who is to be appointed by the President for a 5-year term. The Commissioner is responsible for:

- investigation of alleged instances of non-compliance,

- • overseeing national registers on personal data bases and data holders,

- informing the government as to public sector data processing,

- publishing annual listings of all licensed data holders, and

- auditing data processing activities.

The commissioner may also initiate court proceedings on behalf of the data subject.

The Act includes principles of fair information handling that are identical to those in the EU Directive. In addition, it includes a principle that explicitly prohibits unification of different databases.

1. Rights of Data Subjects

For additional analytical, business and investment opportunities information, please contact Global Investment & Business Center, USA at (202) 546-2103. Fax: (202) 546-3275. E-mail: rusric@erols.com

2. The Act includes the data subject's rights to access, correct and block personal data. The main difference from the EU Directive is the absence of special protections for data subjects regarding automated processing and decision making.

2. Obligations of Data Holders

Similar to the EU Directive, the Act requires data holders to provide data subjects with information about themselves and the purpose(s) of data processing.

The Act includes specific licensing and registration requirements. Data holders must:

• obtain a license for data processing,

- register with the data protection commissioner,

- register themselves and the personal data bases under their control, and

• obtain certification of information systems and technologies applied to data processing.

4. Transborder Data Flows

The Act does not provide clear guidance on this point. It seems to leave open the question of restrictions on data transfers to countries and regions that lack adequate protection.][2]

Specifically:

a. Is there a law on data protection or privacy that covers information in the hands of the government (i.e. how personally identifiable information on citizens can be collected and or used by the government)?

According to the federal 1995 "Law on Information, Informatization and the Protection of Information", governmental data resources are open for general use except for documented information of limited access (data

[2] I was unable to find out if this law has been already passed.

relevant to state secrets and confidential information). Personal data is considered confidential information. The Law states, in particular, that collection, storage, use and distribution (processing) of information pertaining to the private life of a natural person without his or her permission, shall be prohibited, except for processing implemented on the basis of judicial warrant. The term "personal data" and some guarantees for personal data protection appear in new laws, in particular, the Tax Code, the Labor Code and the federal Law on Statements of Civil Status. Also, confidentiality of information has been mentioned in various laws relevant to professional secrets. Russian federal laws establish over 30 types of classified data while other governmental regulations add about 10 types of data to the list. Approximately 45 laws of the Russian Federation have provisions concerning various classified data.

The federal 1995 "Law on Information, Informatization and the Protection of Information" addresses data protection with respect to information in electronic records system. However, the provisions of the law are very general. For example, Article 21(2) merely states that "government bodies and organizations which are responsible for the structuring and use of the information resources which require protection, and similarly bodies and organizations which produce and use information systems and information technologies for processing restricted access information, are subject to the legislation of the Russian Federation in their activity"; and Article 21(3) provides that "the government bodies exercise control of information protection, of the corresponding software and hardware resources and also of the organizational rules by which the restricted access information is processed in the information systems. This control is executed according to the rules determined by the government of the Russian Federation."

c. Does the law require designation of a government-wide or agency-level privacy officer or commissioner with responsibility for government information systems?

Russian legislation does not establish a central regulatory body for data protection and the Office of the Federal Ombudsman pays little attention to data protection cases. Some efforts are being carried out by regional ombudsmen, e.g., the Ombudsman of the region of Perm that initiated an investigation on the practices of a local communications company that used clients' phone numbers for commercial purposes. The Chamber of Appeals on Informational Conflicts, a quasi-judicial body which scope includes the protection of privacy, was also active. This "structure" operated with the support of the mass media, and although its decisions were not binding, they were usually complied with. The Chamber of Appeals was closed during President Putin's presidency.

Article 23(3) of the federal 1995 "Law on Information, Informatization and the Protection of Information" merely states that "responsibility for violations of law which can arise in dealing with the documented information is borne by the government bodies, organizations and responsible persons according to the legislation of the Russian Federation and the legislation of its subjects."

The federal 1995 "Law on Information, Informatization and the Protection of Information" is very general. For example, Articles 21 provides that "3. The government bodies exercise control of information protection, of the corresponding software and hardware resources and also of the organizational rules by which the restricted access information is processed in the information systems. This control is executed according to the rules determined by the government of the Russian Federation.

1. Organizations which process government-owned restricted access information are also obliged to set up special information protection services.

2. The holders of information resources, or the persons authorised by them, can check the observance of the information protection measures, and forbid or suspend information processing if the protection rules are not observed.

3. The owner or possessor of the documented information may approach the government bodies to discover whether his information is processed in observance of the information protection rules. Appropriate monitoring bodies are named by the government of the Russian Federation. These bodies are obliged themselves to observe the conditions of information confidentiality, and regard monitoring results as confidential."

The federal 1995 "Law on Information, Informatization and the Protection of Information" does not address this issue. I was unable to find any other information.

Until 1993, the Russian telecommunication network was fully controlled by the Russian Ministry of Communications. That year, local network operators were privatized so that each of the 85 regions had one provider. Rostelecom became the single national network operator. (32)

In 1995 the Russian government consolidated its stakes in the regional companies into a national holding company, Svyazinvest. The government tried to start the privatization process in 1997 through the sale of 25% interest in Svyazinvest to a Cyprus-based consortium, Mustcom. They had planned to sell a second interest of 25% but it was delayed because of the 1998 economic crisis. (32)

For additional analytical, business and investment opportunities information, please contact Global Investment & Business Center, USA at (202) 546-2103. Fax: (202) 546-3275. E-mail: rusric@erols.com

In 2002, the industry was reorganized and seven new interregional companies were formed, but their market capitalization is small by international standards. The proclaimed goal of the reorganization is to centralize cash flows and increase operations efficiency in the industry. (33)

Until 2010, the Russian government insists on retaining the monopoly of Rostelecom for long distance services. WTO specialists have criticized this plan, stating that "delays in the liberalization of service provision may slow the development of the commercial data transmission infrastructure, casuing problems for the development of the Russian economy as a whole."

The general legal climate is increasingly improving with Putin's commitment to accession to the WTO. But he is putting off most major decisions until after the election this year (2004). For the IT legal environment there has been steady progress towards a legal environment comparable to other Western nations. This has a huge impact on the ICT market.

Russia's Copyright Protection laws provide protection for images, music, software programs, and video. It also clearly extends to protect copyrighted material once such material has been digitized. This is comparable with most Western nation's laws on the subject.

New leaps in Patent Protection were announced in February of 2004 when a government decree will permit state scientific institutions to grant patents and other intellectual property rights to actual inventors. Russia has traditionally had problems turning their inventions into viable business products.

As for Trademark Protection there are several key factors that must be considered in Russia:

- Russia is a "first to register" jurisdiction, which means that cases occur where a party is able to register a trademark only because it was the first to do so

- They still do not have formal rules to recognize famous or well-known trademarks from international companies

- RosPAtent has taken a formalistic approach – possible registration of the same rademark in different classes of goods

As a follow up to the trademark protection, there are specific Domain Name Issues. RosNIIRos (administers the .ru zone) sees no obligation to verify whether an applicant's proposed domain name might already be a registered trademark. This has played an important role in several cases:

- Case of Eastman Kodak vs. Grundul

    o   Grundel registered the domain name Kodak.ru

    o   Decision for Grundel

- Quelle Aktiengesellschaft vs OOO "TF Tandem-Yu"

    o   Russian company OOO "TF Tandem-Yu" registered the domain name 'quelle.ru'

    o   Decision for German company Quelle

- OOO "Kodak" vs. Grundel

    o   Eastman Kodak Russian subsidiary ‚OOO "Kodak," also brought suit against Grundel o   Decision for OOO "Kodak"

o   Note: the court's decision did not include an order to RosNIIRos to cancel the registration of the domain name or re-assign it to anyone else.

Software Piracy in Russia continues to be a major inhibitor to the ICT market. In the early to mid 90s, it was common for most of Russian businesses to be using pirated copies of the Windows Operating System. The piracy rate has steadily dropped over the past ten years according to the Business Software Alliance, reporting an 87% rate in 2002. As of January 2004, piracy is down to 79%.

Competition Law in Russia can apply to asset transactions or outsourcing deals and is limited to commercial transactions. Its main application is IP infringement as an unfair trade practice.

In Russia, any company selling goods over the Internet needs to be aware that the ultimate consumer will have enforceable rights under the Law on Protection of Consumers' Rights. This is applicable to both companies internal and external to the country.

There is a basic constitutional right to privacy (section 24.1) which reads "The collection, keeping, use and dissemination of information about the private life of a person shall not be allowed without his or her consent." This right is further supplemented by the Law "On Information, Informatisation and Protection of Information." This law provides expressly that the collection, storage, use and dissemination of personal data is allowed only with the consent of the person who the data belongs, or by court decision.

Russian's attitudes towards privacy are most likely influenced by their long-term Soviet rule. They are probably more likely to share information because it was so ingrained in Soviet culture for everyone to know what everyone else was doing.

There are possible censorship issues with Putin as he makes another play for the presidential position.

STRATEGY FOR DEVELOPING AN INFORMATION SOCIETY IN RUSSIA

Strategy of the Information Society in Russia on February 7, 2008 N Pr-212

I. GENERAL

The information society is characterized by a high level of development of information and telecommunication technologies and their intensive use by citizens, businesses and public authorities.

Increased value added in the economy is today largely at the expense of intellectual activity, improving the technological level of production and dissemination of modern information and telecommunication technologies.

Current economic systems are integrated in the knowledge economy. The transition from an industrial to a postindustrial society significantly enhances the role of intellectual factors of production.

International experience shows that high technology, including information and telecommunications, have become the locomotive of economic and social development in many countries around the world, and guaranteed free access to information for citizens - a major concern of the States.

The evolution of the development of information and telecommunications infrastructure and high technologies in Russia can not expect significant changes in the near future without a concerted joint effort of public authorities, business and civil society. Necessary in the medium term to implement the existing cultural, educational, scientific and technological potential of the country and to Russia a worthy place among the leaders of the global information society.

In this Strategy are fixed purpose, objectives, principles and main directions of state policy regarding the use and development of information and communications technology, science, education and culture to move the country towards the formation and development of information society.

II. PURPOSE AND POLITICO-LEGAL FRAMEWORK OF THIS STRATEGY

This strategy is the basis for the preparation and refinement of doctrinal, conceptual, policy and other documents that define the objectives and activities of public authorities, as well as the principles and mechanisms of their interactions with organizations and individuals in the field of information society development in Russia.

This strategy has been prepared in accordance with international obligations of Russia, the Doctrine of Information Security of the Federation, federal laws and normative legal acts of the RF Government, determine the direction of socio-economic development, improve governance and collaboration of public authorities and civil society in Russia .

This Strategy takes into account the basic provisions of the Okinawa Charter on Global Information Society Declaration of Principles for the Information Society Plan of Action, the Tunis Commitment and other international instruments adopted at the World Summit on the Information Society.

III. THE AIM, OBJECTIVES AND PRINCIPLES OF THE INFORMATION SOCIETY IN RUSSIA

The purpose of the formation and development of information society in Russia is to improve the quality of life of citizens, ensuring the competitiveness of Russia, the development of economic, social, political, cultural and spiritual spheres of life, improvement of public administration through the use of information and telecommunication technologies.

The main tasks to be tackled to achieve this goal include:

formation of modern information and telecommunications infrastructure, providing its customers quality services and ensuring high availability to the public information and technologies;

the quality of education, health care, social welfare through the development and use of information and telecommunications technologies;

improving the system of state guarantees of constitutional human and civil rights in the information sphere;

economic development of Russia through the use of information and telecommunications technologies;

Improved public administration and local self-interaction of civil society and business with public authorities, the quality and timeliness of delivery of public services;

development of science, technology and engineering, skills training in information and telecommunications technologies;

preservation of the culture of multinational people of Russia, the strengthening of moral and patriotic principles in the public consciousness, the development of cultural and humanitarian education;

For additional analytical, business and investment opportunities information,
please contact Global Investment & Business Center, USA
at (202) 546-2103. Fax: (202) 546-3275. E-mail: rusric@erols.com

opposition to use of the potential of information and telecommunications technologies to the threat of Russia's national interests.

Development of information society in Russia is based on the following principles:

partnership between the state, business and civil society;

freedom and equality of access to information and knowledge;

support domestic producers of goods and services in the field of information and telecommunications technologies;

promoting international cooperation in information and telecommunications technologies;

national security in the information sphere.

To achieve the objectives state:

developing key measures for the development of information society, creating conditions for their implementation, in collaboration with business and civil society;

defines the control values of information society development in Russia;

ensures the development of legislation and improving law enforcement practices in the use of information and telecommunications technologies;

creates favorable conditions for intensive development of science, education and culture, development and introduction of high-tech information and communications technologies;

enhances the quality and timeliness of delivery of public services to organizations and individuals through the use of information and telecommunications technologies;

creates the conditions for equal access of citizens to information;

takes advantage of information and telecommunication technologies to strengthen the country's defense and national security.

IV. Guidelines for implementing this Strategy

1. In the area of modern information and telecommunications infrastructure, providing its customers quality services in the field of information and telecommunication technologies and high availability to the public information and technology:

creation of broadband infrastructure throughout the territory of Russia, including through the mechanisms of public-private partnership;

improving accessibility for people and organizations of modern services in the field of information and telecommunications technologies;

formation of a common information space, including to meet the challenges of national security;

modernization of broadcasting, expanding the coverage zone Russian TV and radio programs;

For additional analytical, business and investment opportunities information, please contact Global Investment & Business Center, USA at (202) 546-2103. Fax: (202) 546-3275. E-mail: rusric@erols.com

a system of public centers of public access to government information resources, including the state system of legal information.

2. In the area of improving the quality of education, health care, social welfare through the development and use of information and telecommunication technologies:

increased use of information and communication technologies for development of new forms and methods of instruction, including distance education;

introduction of new methods of medical care, as well as remote patient care;

provide citizens with social services throughout the Federation with the use of information and telecommunication technologies.

3. In the area of improving the system of state guarantees of constitutional rights and freedoms of man and citizen in the area of information the main focus is the development of legislative mechanisms.

4. In the field of economic development in Russia through the use of information and telecommunication technologies:

promotion of organizations and citizens of information and telecommunications technologies;

creating conditions for the development of competitive domestic industry of information and telecommunication technologies, computer technology, radio electronics, telecommunications equipment and software;

attracting investments for the development of Russia's industry information and telecommunication technologies, as well as the domestic electronic industry;

creating the conditions for the development of companies operating in the field of electronic commerce;

development of high-tech venture capital financing of innovative projects in the field of information and telecommunications technologies;

stimulating the creation of new companies engaged in the production of high-tech equipment and products in the field of information and telecommunications technologies;

increase in exports of goods and services in information and telecommunications technologies;

economic efficiency used by Russia's holders of intellectual property;

development of regional informatization.

5. In the area of improving public administration and local self-interaction of civil society and business with public authorities, the quality and timeliness of delivery of public services:

effective inter-agency and inter-regional exchange of information;

integration of government information systems and resources;

increasing the quantity and quality of public services provided by organizations and citizens in electronic form;

For additional analytical, business and investment opportunities information, please contact Global Investment & Business Center, USA at (202) 546-2103. Fax: (202) 546-3275. E-mail: rusric@erols.com

improving regulatory standards for administration and public services;

improving the delivery of public and municipal services to citizens and organizations.

6. In the field of science, technology, equipment and training of qualified personnel in the field of information and telecommunication technologies:

development priorities of science, technology and engineering on the basis of long-term forecasts generated by technological development (Forsyth);

creating the conditions for commercialization and implementation of scientific research and experimental development, as well as increased exchange of scientific information;

creation of legal, organizational and other conditions to strengthen the research sector of higher education, state academies of science and industry, equipping universities, research organizations and research centers with modern scientific research, technological and educational equipment;

improving the quality of training and a system of continuous training of public servants in the field of information and telecommunication technologies.

7. In the field of preservation of the culture of multinational people of Russia Federation, the strengthening of moral and patriotic principles in the public consciousness, the development of cultural and humanitarian education:

development of library collections, including the Presidential Library behalf BN Yeltsin, on the basis of information and telecommunications technologies;

support the implementation of socially significant projects in the media;

formation of state order for the creation and distribution of film and print, TV and radio programs and Internet resources in the field of culture;

support the activities of governmental and nongovernmental organizations to preserve the cultural and moral values, traditions of patriotism and humanism in the society;

promotion of cultural and moral values of Russia's people;

preservation of cultural heritage of Russia, ensuring its accessibility to citizens.

8. In the field of countering the potential of information and telecommunications technologies to the threat of Russia's national interests:

safe operation of information and telecommunications infrastructure;

safe operation of information and telecommunication systems of key infrastructure, Russia, including critical facilities and major hazard installations;

increase the security level of corporate and individual information systems;

creation of a unified system of information and telecommunications security needs of public administration, national defense, national security and law enforcement;

improving law enforcement in countering the threats of the use of information and telecommunication

For additional analytical, business and investment opportunities information,
please contact Global Investment & Business Center, USA
at (202) 546-2103. Fax: (202) 546-3275. E-mail: rusric@erols.com

technologies for hostile purposes;

ensuring the inviolability of private life, personal and family secrets, compliance with the security of restricted information;

countering the spread of the ideology of terrorism and extremism, advocating violence.

V. International cooperation in the development of information society

The main directions of implementation of this Strategy in the framework of international cooperation in the field of information society development are:

participate in the development of international law and mechanisms, regulating relations in the field of global information infrastructure, including the internationalization of control of the Internet;

participate in international exchange of information;

participate in the formation of an international information security, improved cooperation between law enforcement bodies of Russia and foreign countries to prevent, detect, deter and eliminate the consequences of using information and communication technology in terrorist and other criminal purposes;

Russia's participation in international research projects in priority fields of science, technology and engineering;

participate in the development of international standards in information and telecommunication technologies, harmonization of the national system of standards and certification in this field with the international system.

VI. THE IMPLEMENTATION OF THIS STRATEGY

In order to implement this Strategy was adopted plan, the drafting of which involved the federal executive bodies, executive authorities of RF subjects, representatives of business, academia and civil society.

Implementation of the plan of activities carried out within the framework of the implementation of relevant programs at the expense of the budgets of all levels of budget system of Russia, as well as extra-budgetary sources.

In order to ensure the implementation of this Strategy are monitored and statistical monitoring of development indicators of information society in Russia.

According to the results of monitoring for the President is an annual national report on the status of information society development in Russia.

Application

Control values of information society development in Russia for the period up to 2015

As a result of the main directions and activities of the Strategy of the Information Society in Russia (hereinafter - the Strategy) by 2015 to be achieved following reference values of indicators:

place Russia in the international rankings in the development of information society - including twenty leading countries of the world;

For additional analytical, business and investment opportunities information, please contact Global Investment & Business Center, USA at (202) 546-2103. Fax: (202) 546-3275. E-mail: rusric@erols.com

place Russia in the international rankings in terms of availability of national information and telecommunications infrastructure for the subjects of the information sphere - not less than nine;

level of accessibility for the population of basic services in the field of information and telecommunication technologies - 100%;

share of domestic goods and services in the domestic market of information and telecommunication technologies - more than 50%;

post volume of investments in information and telecommunication technologies in the national economy compared with the year 2007 - not less than 2,5 times;

the differences between the subjects of Russia by a combined indicator of Information Development - up to 2 times;

level of use of broadband lines per 100 inhabitants at the expense of all technologies: 2010 - 15 lines and by 2015 - 35 lines;

availability of personal computers, including those connected to the Internet - not less than 75% of households;

share research and development in information and telecommunication technologies in the total research and development work undertaken at the expense of all sources of funding: 2010 - At least 15% by 2015 - 30%;

increase in the proportion of patents granted in the field of information and telecommunication technologies, the total number of patents: in 2010 - not less than 1,5 times and by 2015 - in 2 times;

proportion of public services that people can get by using information and telecommunication technologies, in the total amount of public services in Russia - 100%;

proportion of electronic documents between public authorities in the total volume of documents - 70%;

proportion of orders placed for the supply of goods, works and services for state and municipal needs of self-government through electronic trading platforms in the total amount of orders placed - 100%;

proportion of archival holdings, including funds of audio and visual archives, translated into electronic form - not less than 20%;

percentage of library funds transferred into electronic form, of the total funds public libraries - at least 50%, including library catalogs - 100%;

proportion of electronic catalogs in the total catalog of the Museum Fund of the RF - 100%.

Approved
President of Russia Vladimir Putin

For additional analytical, business and investment opportunities information,
please contact Global Investment & Business Center, USA
at (202) 546-2103. Fax: (202) 546-3275. E-mail: rusric@erols.com

STRATEGY PARTNERSHIP FOR INFORMATION SOCIETY DEVELOPMENT IN RUSSIA - PRIOR (2003-2010)

1. INTRODUCTION

The e-Development Partnership in Russia (hereafter Partnership or PRIOR) was established on November 30, 2001 on the basis of consortium of the Russia Development Gateway Project, the latter being initiated in March 2001 with the support of the *info* Dev Program of the World Bank.

The Partnership has been developing dynamically: since it was founded the number of the participants has increased more than five times. The member organizations of PRIOR represent all major development communities: the government, business, civil society, research and educational community, donors and investors [1].

The Partnership members represent different organizations - from individual entrepreneur companies to the major Russian universities and research institutes, renowned public organizations, and leaders of the Russian ICT market, including RosBusinessConsulting, IT, Borlas IBC, Cyril and Methodius, Compulink, Moscow Telecommunications Corporation COMCOR, NIKoil Financial Group, Rambler Internet Holding, Research Institute "Voskhod", ASVT Public Corporation, Institute of the Information Society, ROCIT, as well as local representative offices of Verysell, Golden Telecom, Sybase, Microsoft, UnitSpace, and others. Starting in February 2003, individual participants and online media started joining PRIOR. The Partnership membership includes different organizations - from one-man companies to the major Russian universities and research institutes, renowned social organizations, leaders of the Russian ICT market, including RosBusinessConsulting, IT, Borlas IBC, Cyril and Methodius, Compulink, Moscow Telecommunications Corporation COMCOR, NIKoil Financial Group, Rambler Internet Holding, Research Institute "Voskhod", ASVT Public Corporation, Institute of the Information Society, ROCIT, as well as local representative offices of Verysell, Golden Telecom, Sybase, Microsoft, UnitSpace and others. Starting from February 2003, individual participants (private persons, online media) started joining PRIOR.

PRIOR's principles and philosophy are shared by 29 Russian regions. Independent regional segments of PRIOR were created in the North-Western Federal District, in Stavropol Territory, as well as in Kaliningrad, Novgorod, Tula and Perm regions, in South Ural region (in Chelyabinsk region as well as municipal segment in the City of Magnitogorsk), in the Republic of Tatarstan, and in Khanty-Mansi autonomous region (Yugra) with its municipal segment in Nizhnevartovsk.

PRIOR is a voluntary association of organizations interested in assisting Russia to gain a prominent position among the leading developed countries within the emerging Information Society by way of implementing the modern technologies and utilizing its strong intellectual potential and rich scientific and cultural resources.

This large-scale problem can be resolved only through synergetic collaboration and systematic long-term efforts of all stakeholders in the process of developing and implementing Russia's national development strategy for the emerging global Information Society [2] and the Knowledge Economy [3]. Such approach corresponds to the recommendations provided by the competent international associations.

In particular, the Digital Opportunities Task Force (DOT Force), created upon signing of the Okinawa Charter of the Global Information Society in July 2000, emphasized in its recommendations to the G8 leaders at the July 2001 Summit in Genoa that the strategy for the Information Society development should become the main and unalienable part of the national development strategy of any state in present conditions. In addition, in the process of preparing for the World Summit on Information Society (WSIS) much attention is paid to the development of clear expression of political will and of

For additional analytical, business and investment opportunities information,
please contact Global Investment & Business Center, USA
at (202) 546-2103. Fax: (202) 546-3275. E-mail: rusric@erols.com

concrete action plan aimed at achieving the goals of the Information Society reflecting multiple interests of all stakeholders.

The Millennium Development Goals (MDGs) reflect the necessity to undertake the measures to enable everyone to benefit from the new technologies, particularly information and communication technologies.

United Nations Information and Communication Technologies Task Force (UN ICT Task Force) created a special working group on national and regional e-Strategies. The purpose of this working group is to expand the international cooperation and experience sharing in the area of e-Strategy development.

Acting as an independent public-private initiative, PRIOR studies thoroughly all global development [4] tendencies, but is largely guided by the practical experience of its numerous participants and takes into account Russia's specificity.

The objective of the present document is creation of a "guidebook" for the Partnership's further development, which implies development of strategic vision and presenting mission, goals and objectives, main directions and implementation stages as well as methods of evaluation of the PRIOR Strategy implementation and correcting its activity. The first version of the PRIOR Strategy was adopted at the Organizational Conference of the Partnership, which took place in November 2001. The present edition of the Strategy is summing up almost three years of activity of the Partnership taking into account the accumulated experience and new circumstances.

PRIOR Strategy contains the most important conditions for planning further activity and represents the basis for dynamic development of the PRIOR Action Plan.

2. CONTEXT

INCREASING ROLE OF KNOWLEDGE FOR DEVELOPMENT

The present time can be called a period of knowledge revolution, when the ability to produce, receive, and apply knowledge becomes the key factor of the socio-economic development and international competitiveness. The role of knowledge is significantly increasing; the information and communication technologies (ICT) and life-long learning play an important role in its acquisition and use. A good reflection of this fact is the developed countries' "investments into knowledge" (R&D, education, ICT), which are catching up to the investments in the fixed capital.

Processes related to the knowledge revolution are of importance both for the developing countries and countries in transition. Since the world economy grows ever more dynamic and competitive, each country faces the necessity to develop its own strategy for knowledge utilization to increase efficiency of traditional industries, develop new industries, and support such pace of development that would allow to gradually reach the leaders.

The experience of the countries developing most successfully and dynamically shows that the following conditions determine favorable economic development:

- Competitive economy stimulating the growth of production efficiency;

- Financial system stimulating optimization of financial investment flows;

- Flexible labor market stimulating the improvement of personnel qualification;

- Efficient and transparent government system;

- Regulatory and legal environment favorable for business activity; and

- Active system of social protection facilitating citizens' adaptation to continuing structural shifts.

In addition to the above, the successful development of the Knowledge Economy, which forms the basis for the Information Society, requires the following elements:

- Creation of economic and institutional system promoting efficient use of the present information resources and creation of new ones;

- Increase of the educational level, developing a system of training the qualified personnel;

- Development of dynamic infrastructure of information processing and transfer; and

- Efficient national innovation system.

The effective use of knowledge in all sectors of the economy and social life becomes the priority task. Its achievement demands improved coordination between the governmental policy and societal institutions and civil society forces, between developing technologies and people's mentality. The ultimate goal is improving the standard of living by providing access to knowledge for all social groups from governmental officials to housewives.

RUSSIAN SITUATION REGARDING INFORMATION SOCIETY AND KNOWLEDGE ECONOMY DEVELOPMENT

SPECIFICS OF THE ECONOMIC SITUATION [5]

The review of the past four years demonstrates that the tendency of growth of the Russian economy (the domestic economy grew 5.8 percent annually on the average or over 25 percent during this whole period) is weakening. Further exploitation of the growth mechanism based on the flow of "cheap" petroleum money and post-crisis ruble devaluation will not provide the sustainability of the economic growth.

The reforms of the past four years allowed the government to resolve a number of problems, which were the focus of previous program documents of the Russian government:

- Important legislative acts were adopted (package of tax laws, Labor Code, Land Code, etc.);

- Several reforms were initiated, including the pension reform, railway transport reform and electrical energy industry reform;

- Some progress has been achieved in the sphere of eliminating excess administrative pressure on business; and

- There has been progress in negotiations on Russia's participation in the World Trade Organization (WTO).

The effectiveness of the Russian reforms as well as the macroeconomic stability are proven by the gradual increase of Russia's credit rating and acknowledgement by both the European Union and the USA of Russia's status as the country with market economy.

For additional analytical, business and investment opportunities information,
please contact Global Investment & Business Center, USA
at (202) 546-2103. Fax: (202) 546-3275. E-mail: rusric@erols.com

At the same time, Russia continues to face serious socio-economic problems, which signifies of the instability of economic growth and results achieved recently. Russia's level of economic development remains unacceptably low. The GDP per capita is slightly over seven thousand USD at purchasing power parity and less than 2.5 thousand USD according to the current exchange rate. These numbers are several times lower than the indicators not only for the leading but also for the considerable part of the developing countries. This results in the low quality of life with high rate of differentiation of the citizens' income and unacceptably high share of people below poverty line.

Several major problems limiting the country's economic growth can be identified:

1. The present state of market institutions and infrastructure sets high level of expenditures on the domestic economy;

2. Governmental interference into the economic activity remains excessive and disruptive;

3. In terms of implementing efficient foreign trade policy, the Russian economy remains essentially closed due to excess customs and currency regulation and control as well as lack of harmonization of the Russian standards and international foreign trade standards;

4. Level of taxation of entrepreneurial activity remains very high, which significantly slows down the increase of investments and general economic growth;

5. There is no effective law enforcement system in the country; and

6. Inefficient system of social services combined with low salary levels impedes normal reproduction of human capital.

The economic structure remains deformed with the raw energy materials and transport sectors representing the dominant areas. Given the absence of adequate inter-sectoral flow of capital, such imbalance preserves the lagging position of processing and service sectors and complicates the task of modernizing the economy. There are major deficiencies in the regulatory environment, including the sphere of export policy, competition stimulation, resistance to corruption, and protection of people's personal contribution to the global knowledge.

If the current pace and structure of growth remain the same, Russia will not be able to reach an adequate standard of living in the next decade. The sustainable economic growth is only possible in the conditions of diversification and increase of investment activity.

ICT INFRASTRUCTURE AND USE IN KEY SPHERES OF ACTIVITY [6]

Over the last two years Russia witnessed high pace of growth in the ICT sector: this segment of the Russian market is among the fastest-growing in the world. At the same time, Russia still spends less than the developed countries on the ICT. The country takes one of the last places in Europe in terms of ICT investments surpassing only Ukraine and Romania. Such strategy does not create favorable economic conditions for the development of ICT infrastructure and application of ICT. Some estimates state that Russia is at least five years behind the leading Western countries in the level of ICT development.

Russia also takes one of the last places in Europe in terms of *telephone density*, but this gap is gradually narrowing. The following problems remain urgent: unequal distribution of phone penetration throughout the country, substandard technical level of the Russian fixed-line telephone communication networks, and monopolized markets of local, intercity and international communications.

For additional analytical, business and investment opportunities information, please contact Global Investment & Business Center, USA at (202) 546-2103. Fax: (202) 546-3275. E-mail: rusric@erols.com

There has been an intensive growth in the number of *mobile communications* subscribers recently, especially in the Russian regions. The Volga, Ural and Siberian federal districts are among the fastest growing regions in this regard. The disproportionate distribution of cellular communications in Russia is even more obvious than in the case of fixed-line telephony. Cellular communications market is characterized by high competitiveness which results in lower prices and extended the range of services. The period of 2001-2002 clearly showed the tendency of consolidation of cellular communication companies; several of them turned to national or regional operators as a result of mergers and developing of their own networks. The mobile Internet access has not been sufficiently developed in Russia so far.

The *cable television* networks providing possibilities of high-speed Internet access, interactive television and a number of other services are less common in Russia than in Western European countries and considerably less than in North America.

The number of *Internet* users in Russia in 2003, according to the data obtained by the Public Opinion Foundation, amounted to nine percent of adult population of 18 years and older, which corresponds to the indicators of the leading Latin American countries but is much less than in the developed countries. There are also considerable interregional differences. The number of people accessing the Net from home is growing faster than the number of corporate users; at the same time, the corporate customers do and will continue to shape the income from access services in the following five years.

The broadband access was adopted in Russia at a later time; therefore, the majority of individual users still access the Internet via fixed telephone landlines. Among the major tendencies of Internet development are sustainable growth of subscribers base, introduction of new access technologies by providers, expansion of the range of operators' services, development of the system of community access (for instance, as part of the Kiberpocht@ program.)

The monthly fee for local telephone in the Russian cities is rather low, and it does not impede using dial-up Internet access unless the countrywide system of time-scale payment will be established. At the same time, the prices of Internet service providers remain rather high relative to the income level, which naturally limits Internet access from home.

The digital divide, which can be clearly observed in the sphere of Internet use, represents a serious and urgent problem for Russia. According to the data of sociological polls, the Internet audience in Russia is represented mostly by young, male, educated, rich, urban users, which diverges substantially from the general population structure. The average income per family member using Internet in Russia is twice as high as the same number for those not using the Internet. The widest digital gap is reflected in education and age parameters. For instance, the share of people with higher and unfinished higher education among Russian Internet users is three times higher than the corresponding share in the general population.

As for the ICT application in the key areas of the Information Society and Knowledge Economy development, the situation can be summarized by the sector as follows.

Education sector . The level of ICT infrastructure development in the Russian institutions of higher education is in general in line with the average European indicators. Government and private business helped to create a large-scale system of teacher training and ICT application in the educational process. Informatization of education became a priority for the governmental policy since 2001; the governmental programs aiming to create basic prerequisites for introducing modern technologies in education were adopted at the federal and regional levels.

Nonetheless, the current state of the ICT use by the Russian educational institutions is characterized by a set of problems, which require coordinated efforts of public authorities and the society in general. These problems include unacceptably low levels of computerization and Internet access in schools (especially in distant and rural areas) and introduction of broadband Internet access on all

For additional analytical, business and investment opportunities information, please contact Global Investment & Business Center, USA at (202) 546-2103. Fax: (202) 546-3275. E-mail: rusric@erols.com

educational levels; inefficient use of existing educational ICT infrastructure; deficit of educational software tools, specialized Internet resources, educational courses on the basis of ICT; teachers' reluctance to use ICT in the educational process, lack of corresponding methodological materials.

Bridging the digital divide among the higher and secondary education levels, development of network infrastructure in educational institutions, creation of educational e-resources and tools, methodological training for ICT use by teachers in educational processes – all these issues are included in the agenda of the next stage of ICT use in the education process.

e-Government . The issues of creating ICT infrastructure for the government authorities have been chiefly resolved. The federal and regional information systems have been implemented and function successfully. However, several key problems should be taken into account: there remains a weak system of data exchange between different state offices; the overwhelming majority of governmental information systems and databases are closed for external access and are used for departmental needs only; the interaction of public authorities with the citizens and economic agents is a one-way communication channel of general information present on the web sites and departmental gateways; the pilot projects of electronic two-way interaction are very rare.

e-Business. Different forms of e-Commerce are actively developing in Russia today. Retail e-Business turnover ("business for customer" model) shows the tendency towards fast growth. Intercorporate e-Business turnover in the Internet ("business to business" model) doubles annually. The environment in the country favors further development of different forms of e-Commerce: the Internet audience is growing fast; the adoption of the Federal law "On Electronic Digital Signature" forms the basis for legal regulation of electronic transactions; federal program "eRussia" covers a number of events aimed at promoting e-Business; there is human potential for ICT use for developing different models of e-Commerce; changes in the Russian taxation system stipulate transition to transparent forms of transactions, wage payment, etc.; the share of monetary forms of payment between enterprises is growing, which is an important factor of intercorporate e-Business development.

It should be noted, however, that e-Commerce development in Russia is still at its early stages and its role in the economy is very low. There are also a number of factors impeding its development: low level of Internet penetration in Russia, insufficient development of telecommunications infrastructure of the Russian market, lack of adequate legislative basis in the sphere of e-Commerce, low level of credit card penetration, few convenient and secure systems for Internet purchases payment, low mutual trust among market players. In addition, the entrepreneurial and managerial culture of the Russian business is not very high as well as the levels of business processes automation in Russian enterprises.

STATE REGULATION AND BUSINESS CLIMATE

Over the last several years, Russia has been actively shaping an information policy including such tools as legislative environment, governmental programs for ICT use and development, and adoption of strategic documents. At the same time, there are many problems impeding further development of the information environment:

- There is no comprehensive governmental policy ("national strategy") of the Russian Federation in the sphere of Information Society development, although there were attempts to draft the concept of national strategy " Russia in the Information Age." Separate elements of the policy (strategy) in the sphere of information technologies use and development are present in the documents of the federal level bearing non-normative nature (adopted in 2000-2002) [7];

For additional analytical, business and investment opportunities information,
please contact Global Investment & Business Center, USA
at (202) 546-2103. Fax: (202) 546-3275. E-mail: rusric@erols.com

- Although present, the normative base of the "information legislation" of the Russian Federation is rather fragmentary; there are substantial gaps, and the majority of normative acts are obsolete; special normative acts of the federal level were adopted in mid-90s, they need to be updated; the adaptation of "general" Russian legislation to the reality of the Information Society is very slow;

- Legal status of the information as a separate object of normative regulation is not finalized in Russia; the notion of 'information' is not defined, the specificity of regulation of the corresponding legal object is not fixed; although the notion of 'information resources' is introduced legally [8], the description of their legal status makes them resemble the items of property (tangible objects) of the right of ownership, however, according to the meaning of the law only documentary information can be attributed to such resources, while the absolute majority of information circulated in the information and telecommunications information systems does not have documentary form;

- Although intellectual property protection mode in the Russian Federation formally corresponds to the foreign regulation practice, its weak component is an imperfection (in some instances - total lack of development) of procedural and law enforcement mechanisms that can be legally fixed only in the criminal, administrative and procedural law - that is outside the limits of "information" legislation;

- Although e-Business ("e-Trade" or "e-Commerce") has existed in the Russian Federation in the embryo state for a long time, there is no special legislation regarding this area; as a result, the possibilities of conducting business in the electronic form are strictly limited due to the absence of any normative guarantees that the transactions be legally accepted - contrariwise, federal law on electronic digital signature (EDS) is actually discriminating electronic forms of business by introducing highly complicated and financially heavy procedures of EDS application for identifying the participants of electronic (network) economic turnover;

- The issues concerning electronic interaction between government and society, governmental bodies and citizens ("e-Government") have surfaced recently and have not been legally resolved so far; currently being developed are a number of legislative documents on "e-Openness" of the public authorities, on the order of citizens access to the information on governmental activity and adopted legislative acts, etc. This work was initiated as a result of adoption and implementation of "eRussia" Federal Program, although the activities still cover only an initial (informational) aspect of electronic interaction with the government - providing access to the governmental information resources, while interactive cooperation between citizens and organizations and public authorities via information technologies is still a matter of distant future;

- During the last few years the Russian Federation adopted a considerable number of legislative documents aimed at liberalizing the telecommunications market (in particular, due to the anticipated entrance of the RF into the World Trade Organization). At the same time, antimonopoly policy in the sphere of communications has not been formulated, and the regulatory measures are randomly applied by antimonopoly institutions. There is no agreed upon practice of their implementation; moreover, there is a contrary tendency towards strengthening, at least temporarily, of the monopoly of "traditional" operators (with considerable governmental share) in the key segments of the market. Same tendencies can be observed in the new version of the Federal law "On telecommunications" adopted in 2003;

- The situation with licensing communications services is very complicated and ambiguous; the list of licensed types of activity in the sphere of telecommunications is not legally fixed; the

For additional analytical, business and investment opportunities information, please contact Global Investment & Business Center, USA at (202) 546-2103. Fax: (202) 546-3275. E-mail: rusric@erols.com

existing (often contradictory) normative acts do not provide straightforward answers to the questions of which services are licensed and in which order; process of issuing licenses and permissions for exploitation of telecommunications objects is highly non-transparent and ineffective from the financial and organizational standpoint. There are no normative rules for the majority of services, the corresponding acts are adopted in arbitrary order and bear individual influence ("supplements to licenses" can be unilaterally changed by the licensing authority at any time.) A number of activities (for example, the use of radio-frequency spectrum) need obtaining at least two licenses, which includes dealing with other governmental authorities (for example, for the TV and radio broadcasting activity).

In terms of the business climate, there are a number of positive changes in the Russian economy, favorable for the country's development:

- The economic growth continues and tax levies are growing, which increases consumer demand of commercial enterprises and public sector on information products and services;

- Real cash income of the population is growing [9],

- which favors citizens' expenditures on ICT and information.

At the same time, a number of business climate parameters bear negative influence both upon the development of goods and services production in the sphere of ICT and their consumption in different spheres of activity:

- Russia remains a country with high administrative barriers [10];

- Russian legal system does not provide sufficient protection of property rights - illegal seizure of property is widespread [11];

- Notwithstanding attempts to cut taxes, tax load is still very high, which is extremely unfavorable for the development of high-technology enterprises, including the ICT sector;

- Access to financial resources necessary for the innovative activity of enterprises both in ICT introduction and development of competitive ICT production is insufficient due to the underdeveloped banking system, stock market and venture financing.

HUMAN CAPITAL

A country's ability to participate in the development of the global Information Society is largely determined by the presence of necessary human potential - high educational level, people's ability to collect, process, and efficiently use digital information, etc. Russia is very rich in human resources and has a high potential. In this regard, it has advantages for the Information Society and Knowledge Economy development:

- Traditional accessibility of education at all levels, high quality of education materials and of the process itself, containing base technical and general knowledge and skills, current situation, and orientation towards development of creativity;

- Major indicators of educational level position Russia among the economically developed countries. These include the share of people with higher and unfinished education and scientists in the economically active population (20% and 1.37% respectively), the number of students per 1,000 population (56), etc.;

For additional analytical, business and investment opportunities information,
please contact Global Investment & Business Center, USA
at (202) 546-2103. Fax: (202) 546-3275. E-mail: rusric@erols.com

- Growing number of students in the sphere of ICT, their share per 1,000 population is at the level of such countries as France, Sweden and Germany (although considerably lower than in Finland and Ireland - countries with export-oriented developed ICT sector);

- According to the poll conducted by the Institute of the Information Society together with the Higher School of Economics in 2002, over 35 percent of economically active population in Russia have (28.5%), acquire or are going to acquire computer skills in the nearest future;

- Considerable share of economically active population use personal computer for work (25% according to the above poll), which is lower than average European value (45% in 2000), but, taking into account the level of economic development and country's computerization, is a rather high index.

At the same time, there are a number of problems of human potential development as a factor of information development:

- Notwithstanding the remaining high average education level with considerable share of technical students, there is no optimum balance of different educational levels;

- There are a relatively small number of people with PC skills in Russia - 5.6 percent of economically active population (in contrast to the EU, where their share was 22.8 percent in 2000). Russian employers spending less time on PC training for personnel than those in the developed countries;

- Weak links between education system and labor market cause the so-called 'brain drain.' According to international organizations, the flight of specialists in ICT is estimated at 3.6 points (according to seven-point scale), at the same time the maximum estimate for the affluent countries - like USA and the Netherlands - is 6.7 and the minimum of 2.2 points is in Romania;

- Specialists and scientists are leaving science and higher educational institutions for other spheres of activity and to emigrate abroad as well as the overload of the remaining specialists with additional work have negative influence on the educational level and scientific research in the areas crucial for the Information Society development;

- The system of education and personnel training in Russia is not flexible enough to adequately and promptly react to changing conditions: there are issues concerning people's readiness to adapt to the new conditions after the change of qualification - there are difficulties due to the set mentality and objective lack of possibility of further and life-long education.

NATIONAL INNOVATION SYSTEM

An important prerequisite for the creation of promising national innovation system is the access to the global stock of knowledge, creation and adaptation of knowledge for domestic needs. Russian situation is characterized by the following features:

- Russia has big potential in the innovation sphere: it is one of the world leaders, but there is an imbalance of innovative high technologies being present in each sector but not widespread in the overall economy. The innovation activity of the Russian enterprises remains very low [12];

- Science and technology have great potential in Russia, the share of specialists and scientists is high: Russia takes one of the leading positions in this area, but research intensity of the Russian economy lowered drastically in the recent decade; this can be partly explained by insufficient governmental and private investments in R&D [13],

- fundamental and applied research, breaking ties between research institutes and production. This also impedes widespread dissemination of knowledge accumulated by advanced enterprises via supplies of new equipment, technical and information services;

- Level of access to the knowledge accumulated worldwide [14] and efficiency of its utilization in Russia remain rather low, which can lead not only to information poverty but also to poverty in general;

There is a threat that Russia will fall hopelessly behind the developed countries if it does not strive to improve access to the global information wealth while wasting its own scientific and technical potential. In order to prevent this, a reform of scientific and educational sector should be carried out in accordance with the economic needs, in particular, new programs of professional retraining and adult education should be developed and implemented overcoming inertia of old organizational structures. The problem of brain drain should be resolved on the national level. The problem of fulfilling the ICT potential and introducing new infrastructures can be resolved only on the national level.

STRATEGIC VISION AND OBJECTIVES

The context shaping the PRIOR activity, which was described in the previous section, differs from the conditions in both the developed countries and the developing countries. The specific Russian situation requires developing it own vision of development directions.

PRIOR APPROACHES TO FORMING THE NATIONAL E-DEVELOPMENT STRATEGY

The official strategic documents, mid-term governmental program of socio-economic development for the next few years and statements of the Russian government officials identify two major objectives that are to be achieved for sustainable socio-economic development of Russia:

1. Diverging from the de-facto national development scenario of Russia serving as a supplier of raw materials to the world market and shifting the focus of the economic and export structures towards industries with high added value; and

2. Increasing the competitiveness of the national economy and ensuring rapid and sound economic growth.

Russia faces the necessity to mobilize such an important and renewable resource as information and knowledge for its sustainable economic growth.

A strategic document entitled *The Main Aspects of the Russia's Long-Term Social and Economic Development* was approved by the government in 2001. It contains some items dealing with the strategy for Russia's development in the Information Age. However, they are integrated into a very broad context of problems for Russia's development and are not clearly formulated or systematized. The *Program of Russia's Medium-Term Socio-Economic Development* (2003-2005) was adopted by the Russian Federal Government in August 2003. It clearly states that the level of country's level of development, well-being of the community, potential economic dynamics will be largely determined by the level of knowledge rather than by mere presence of natural resources.

As part of the national strategy of Russia's socio-economic development it is necessary to clearly identify the priorities concerning the development of the Information Society and the Knowledge

For additional analytical, business and investment opportunities information, please contact Global Investment & Business Center, USA at (202) 546-2103. Fax: (202) 546-3275. E-mail: rusric@erols.com

Economy. It is also important that the main directions for reforms stated in the aforementioned strategic document (educational, business environment reforms, development of the financial system and others) be supplemented by such items as development of efficient national innovation system and building the national information infrastructure.

Development of the Information Society in Russia requires a proactive government policy and reallocation of "natural rent" (income from the use of natural resources) from the mining industries to science, education, information and communication technologies, and support for innovations. At the same time, a simple redistribution of funds is not sufficient. It is necessary to accomplish a number of tasks, including the reform of science and education, the creation of infrastructure and legal framework that would support commercial use of applied scientific research and design work, development of the information and communication infrastructure, etc. The accomplishment of these large-scale tasks is only feasible within the framework of a coordinated and efficient policy based on a thoroughly designed strategy and a program of the development of the Information Society.

Such a document could become an important supplement and an extension of the adopted strategy of Russia's long-term socio-economic development; it would clearly reflect Russia's political will to follow a clear development scenario in the context of emerging Information Society.

Taking into account the specifics of the Russian situation and drawing from the international experience in this area, it is possible to identify several basic conditions that should be created through the national strategy of transition to the Information Society and developing the Knowledge Economy. It is necessary to ensure the presence of the following aspects:

1. Favorable regulatory and business environment facilitating the use of the existing knowledge and producing new knowledge and supporting entrepreneurship [15];

2. Modern ICT infrastructure; widespread use of ICT; competitive industries of information services and knowledge production;

3. Human capital including the critical mass of people possessing knowledge, skills and ability to participate in the development of the Information Society and Knowledge Economy; and

4. Efficient national innovation system representing a network of structures utilizing the growing wealth of global knowledge, assimilating and adapting it to local needs as well as creating new knowledge and technologies.

The strategy of transitioning to the Information Society should determine "horizontal" and "vertical" directions of the economic policy (or the combination of these directions), identify the measures of functional interference into the market processes, and explore other possibilities of influencing the developmental process.

An important factor determining the success of this strategy is active participation and close collaboration in its development and implementation of all forces of the Russian community interested in postindustrial development. Hence, it is plausible to talk about the *national strategy* and to invite all driving forces of the society to participate in its development and implementation - the business, government, research and education community, institutes of the civil society, sponsoring organizations. This corresponds to the modern approaches and international practice.

The realization of the national strategy will require development and effective implementation of one or several of the interrelated programs, which would supplement the existing federal programs, such as "eRussia (2002-2010)" and "Creation of an Integrated Educational Information Environment." The next step would entail the development and implementation of regional strategies and programs of development concurrent with the new national strategy.

For additional analytical, business and investment opportunities information, please contact Global Investment & Business Center, USA at (202) 546-2103. Fax: (202) 546-3275. E-mail: rusric@erols.com

PRIOR POSITIONING

On the one hand, PRIOR is an integral part of the World Bank initiative on creating national development gateways [16], on the other hand, it is a national community initiative aimed at supplementing the present governmental and non-governmental programs and projects directed at developing different components of the Russian Information Society. PRIOR recognizes the importance of participating in the most crucial programs of development communities, including governmental programs. These initiatives include the federal target program "eRussia (2002-2010)", city target program "e-Moscow", program "e-St.Petersburg" and others.

The key project of PRIOR is creating the Russia Development Gateway (RuDG) as an environment for partner interaction aimed at achieving common goals and a tool for integrating expert knowledge in the sphere of development.

Essentially, PRIOR is an organized space for resolving problems related to Russia's transition to the Information Society, and the RuDG is an informational basis and a platform for exchanging ideas and practical experience of the participants.

For the first time an alliance in Russia offered to consider all the development communities to be equal partners attempting to achieve common social goals. At the same time, the traditional Russian perception remains of seeing government as the sole 'decision maker' and, consequently, being singly responsible for the results of these decisions. PRIOR views the government as one of several key development communities playing its role together with business, civil society, research and education community, and sharing responsibility for the accomplishment of coordinated decisions. At the same time, PRIOR completes its activities in accordance with the policy developed and adopted by the Russian government and renders assistance to the government.

The Partnership is oriented towards the international practice of partnership and partnership networks construction as an important tool of transition to the Information Society and Knowledge Economy. PRIOR participates in the following international network initiatives:

- Development Gateway Program (DG);

- UN Information and Communication Technologies Task Force (UN ICT Task Force) and its regional networks, in particular, UN ICT Task Force European and Central Asia Network (UN ICT TF EuCAs);

- Global Knowledge Partnership (GKP).

Taking into account the size of the country and substantial differences in the levels of the socio-economic and demographic development of its regions, special attention will be paid to the regional aspects of the Partnership activity.

Within the system of various initiatives aimed at the development of the Information Society in Russia, PRIOR's role is positioned as follows:

- A platform for cooperation between different participants of the development process;

- The creator of the Russia Development Gateway - a distributed, easily accessible knowledge warehouse accumulating the most important information regarding development and providing efficient navigation over the existing resources related to development issues;

- A forum for a national dialogue on development issues;

- A leading expert and analytical center on the development issues;

- A center supporting innovative projects related to using ICT for development;

- A center supporting efforts to bridge the digital divide in Russia, in particular in remote and rural areas; and

- An instrument of developing a positive image of modern Russia for the international community.

The Partnership is open to everybody interested in contributing to the process of Russia's transition to the Information Society and Knowledge Economy; it provides independent and politically neutral platform for cooperation, expressing ideas and putting forth the proposals, and offering constructive criticism.

MAIN LINES OF PRIOR ACTIVITIES

PRIOR Strategy is based on combining several lines of activity, both online and offline.

ONLINE ACTIVITY

This kind of activity is related to the use and expansion of the functional capacity of the Russia Development Gateway Portal. The RuDG Portal is viewed as a multidimensional and multifunctional information system, which allows to:

- Accumulate and efficiently use the international expert knowledge and practical information dealing with development in general and with the use of ICT in all spheres of human activity;

- Support an environment for collaboration between the participants of the Partnership and provide platform for discussion, exchange of opinions, and conflict resolution; and

- Establish various online services for users and clients of the Russia Development Gateway, such as forums, consulting centers, market places, virtual educational environment, digital libraries, etc.

OFFLINE ACTIVITY

This direction of activity implies development and expansion of online functions and services of the RuDG in the form of specific offline activities. At the same time, various kinds of offline activities corresponding to the PRIOR mission will be taken into account or used by the RuDG. These functions include the following key activities:

- *Informational, analytical and consultative activity* aimed at providing high-quality expert knowledge and services related to the ICT and knowledge application for development using the potential of the Partnership;

- *Developing recommendations* on improving the policy and legislative basis for the development of the Information Society, taking into account the opinions of the key players in the sphere of development;

- *Innovative activity* of supporting promising projects in the sphere of ICT and knowledge use for development in the priority areas;

For additional analytical, business and investment opportunities information, please contact Global Investment & Business Center, USA at (202) 546-2103. Fax: (202) 546-3275. E-mail: rusric@erols.com

- ***Publishing and awareness raising activity*** intended to promote the potential of ICT for development and explanation of the advantages of living and working in the Information Society; and

- ***Public activity*** intended to form a nation-wide partnership and an open forum on development.

Based upon the aforementioned strategic directions of activity, PRIOR goals and objectives are formulated next, and a strategy for the Partnership's activity in the main spheres is defined as well.

PRIOR GOALS AND OBJECTIVES

PRIOR is a voluntary association of organizations and individuals joining their efforts and resources, providing mutual information, technological, advisory, organizational, and other types of support to achieve common goals and objectives.

PRIOR strives to ensure the dynamic and full-fledge Russia's development in the context of the global Information Society and creation of the Knowledge Economy in Russia.

PRIOR activity is directed at supporting:

- Development of an *economic and legal regime* that will enable Russia to obtain a prominent position among the developed countries as a result of the effective use of new technologies, utilizing its intellectual potential and scientific and cultural resources;

- Creation of a *new public culture* including citizens' participation in the development and implementation of the most important decisions influencing social life;

- *Bridging the socio-economic gap* by providing the access to socially valuable sources of information and services to all citizens;

- *Raising the standard of life* by expanding production and consuming more quality products and services created on the basis of modern technologies.

The above aims should be achieved by:

The above goals should be achieved with the help of:

1. Creation of equitable partnership of the major development communities for elaborating and implementing the national strategy of the Russia's transition to the Information Society and corresponding strategies and programs on regional and local levels;

2. Supporting the development of:

   o Legislative base of the Information Society;

   o Infrastructure of information processing and transfer;

   o Efficient national innovation system;

   o System of training the "knowledge workers" [17];

   o Socially important information resources and services;

3. Promotion and practical realization of the concepts and technologies of the Information Society, such as:

  o Governance [18];

  o e-Government [19];

  o Networked Society [20];

  o e-Business [21];

  o Distant Learning [22];

  o Digital Library [23] and others;

4. Active dissemination of innovations, knowledge, and practical experience in the sphere of development on the international, national, regional, and local levels;

5. Attracting international organizations, sponsors and investors to assist in resolving the developmental problems of Russia and its regions;

6. Contributing to the mutual strengthening of the international, national, and local initiatives through the active dissemination of experience and knowledge related to the sphere of development.

In order to achieve these goals, the following tasks should be accomplished:

- Organization of a national and international dialogue on the Information Society and Knowledge Economy development issues through the use of the traditional and electronic media, online forums, conferences and seminars, etc.;

- Initiation and assistance in implementation of partnership-based programs and projects aimed at the Information Society and Knowledge Economy development;

- Assistance in self-organization of development communities, integration of knowledge and exchange of practical experience in the sphere development;

- Organization of public activity to foster the development of the Information Society;

- Formation of a single methodological and terminological base related to the Information Society development;

- Implementation of projects and events directed at engaging socially disadvantaged population groups in active use of knowledge and information for development, including the establishment of public access centers and providing basic training for users;

- Implementation of a system of measures to increase public awareness of the advantages of ICT and knowledge use for development (conducting awareness-raising campaigns and carrying out demo-projects);

- Organization of consulting services dealing with development opportunities through ICT for various groups of users (decision makers, managers and specialists of different organizations; representatives of small and medium-size enterprises; individuals, etc.);

For additional analytical, business and investment opportunities information,
please contact Global Investment & Business Center, USA
at (202) 546-2103. Fax: (202) 546-3275. E-mail: rusric@erols.com

- Promoting development and use of the Russian information resources accessible via the Internet;

- Accumulation and dissemination of expert knowledge on development;

- Provision of access to high-quality solutions and know-how in the field of development for Russian users;

- Assistance to the Russian companies in entering the markets of the information products and services;

- Providing expert knowledge and assistance in developing effective and efficient business models with the use of ICT; organization of experimental facilities for their testing and implementation;

- Provision of concentrated and coordinated information on the existing programs, projects and initiatives in the development area for potential investors and sponsors as well as for potential applicants.

In addition to the aforementioned tasks, PRIOR aims to achieve the following *systemic objectives*:

- Creating an efficient system of coordinating PRIOR activities, supporting active involvement of participants representing government, business, civil society, research and education community, and sponsoring organizations;

- Supporting the Russia Development Gateway as an efficient environment for cooperation of all driving forces of the development community that facilitate development and an efficient instrument for integration of the expert knowledge in the development area;

- Creating a system of project financing in the civil sphere, including fundraising and search for investments for the implementation of PRIOR projects and events;

- Creation of a system of public support for PRIOR activities.

Realization of PRIOR aims and objectives will allow for expanding the existing initiatives on the Information Society and Knowledge Economy development and supporting new types of activity demanded by the society.

PRIOR MISSION

Partnership is an independent, politically neutral community initiative which aims to promote the Information Society and Knowledge Economy development in Russia as well as assist in the implementation of the relevant programs and projects.

CREATION OF THE PARTNERSHIP OF DEVELOPMENT COMMUNITIES

The key distinctive characteristic of PRIOR is formation of a nationwide consortium of public, private, and nonprofit organizations on a voluntary basis in order to unify the efforts of partners representing various development communities to achieve mutual goals and objectives.

BASIC PRINCIPLES OF THE PARTNERSHIP

The activity of PRIOR is based on the following main principles:

- *Openness* - the opportunity to freely join PRIOR or withdraw from it; the transparency of decision making and implementation;

- *Holistic approach* - the reliance on a general strategy, reflecting the global development trends, the philosophy of the Development Gateway Program, and the priorities of the Russian national government policy;

- *Sustainability* - the ability to generate and implement ideas that appeal to sponsors and investors; integration and redistribution of the partners' own resources; providing products and services demanded by the society; and

- *Ownership* - the right of every participant making contribution to PRIOR activities to openly declare their input, to use the common brand, to participate in strategic and organizational decision-making, including decisions related to administrative and resource allocation issues.

The combination of the aforementioned principles forms an effective synergetic environment favorable for cooperation between various participants of the e-Development process. This interaction process aims to facilitate the emergence of a critical mass of ICT users and developers of new informational resources and services, thus contributing to the sustainable development of an Information Society in Russia.

COOPERATION WITH SYSTEMIC PARTNERS

PRIOR strives to facilitate and promote equitable collaboration between all the societal participants supporting e-Development. The initial stage prioritizes the cooperation between the **key partners**, such as the Development Gateway Program, government, business, civil society, research and education community, sponsors and investors. Over time the strengthened relationships among the participants of the Partnership will result in the greater number of communities and the elimination of the existing borders between them.

THE DEVELOPMENT GATEWAY PROGRAM

The Development Gateway Program, initiated by the World Bank, is one of the philosophical grounds for PRIOR activity, particularly in forming and developing the RuDG. As an independent national partner of the Development Gateway, PRIOR will become one of the sources of its content and innovative ideas. PRIOR activity will be conducted in close coordination and cooperation with the Development Gateway Team. This will be particularly relevant for content creation for the Russian and international gateways as well as development and implementation of technical solutions and online services.

For additional analytical, business and investment opportunities information,
please contact Global Investment & Business Center, USA
at (202) 546-2103. Fax: (202) 546-3275. E-mail: rusric@erols.com

GOVERNMENT

Given the national scale of the PRIOR mission, cooperation with government agencies is crucially important for the Partnership. PRIOR functions within the framework of the Russian governmental policy and provides relevant assistance to the state, such as:

- Participating in preparation of the conceptual and strategic governmental documents concerning the Information Society development;

- Providing expertise and drafting recommendations on improving laws and regulations to facilitate Information Society development and Russia's full-fledged participation in the global Knowledge Economy;

- Providing access to the most important sources of information, best technological solutions and know-how, advanced practical experience in the sphere of development;

- Participation in preparation and implementation of joint pilot projects intended to bridge the digital divide;

- Efficient and timely dissemination of current information through all channels of the Partnership and promotion of the governmental policy related to the Informational Society development; and

- Rendering consulting services and assistance in Russia's participation in the international initiatives that are crucial to its positioning as a world information power.

The government can use PRIOR as a public platform, expressing the consolidated position of institutes of the civil society, private sector, research and education community and sponsoring organizations regarding the development problems; as an experimental site for interaction between the government and society with the use of ICT. PRIOR can assist the government in providing financial and human resources for the development and implementation of initiatives corresponding with the common goals of Russia's development in the Information Age.

In its turn, PRIOR counts on the governmental support, which may include incorporating a number of PRIOR initiatives into the state programs and projects related to the Information Society and Knowledge Economy development.

CIVIL SOCIETY

Collaboration with the civil society organizations (civil society organizations) is rather important for PRIOR, because they help to resolve social problems, have a developed network of contacts with representatives of various communities, and are well aware of their needs. Representing interests of various social groups, civil society organizations can help the Partnership, on the one hand, to work out a broader view of the development problems and, on the other hand, to articulate concrete PRIOR aims and objectives taking into account the needs of specific user groups.

C ivil society organizations may act both as users of various PRIOR information resources and services and as experts and consultants, topic guides of the Russian Development Gateway, moderators of forums, leaders of initiative projects, etc.

PRIOR plans to facilitate the development of the Russian civil society by engaging in the following activities:

- Promoting the achievements and experience gained by civil society organizations in Russia and abroad;

- Supporting the key initiatives and projects of the civil society organizations aimed at facilitating development and bridging the digital divide;

- Providing a platform for an open national dialogue on development issues, exchange of experience as well as instruments for self-organization of different communities;

- Facilitating cross-sector exchange of information and increasing the potential of networking;

- Expanding the access to the information on the sources of funds for the implementation of development projects, potential sponsors and investors, etc.;

- Supporting the institutional competency of the civil society organizations through the use of ICT.

PRIOR activity will be chiefly geared towards coordinating and consolidating the existing initiatives of the civil society organizations rather than replacing them with the new ones. At the same time, the civil society is viewed as one of the major sources of new participants of the Partnership's activities.

BUSINESS

The private sector is one of the key driving forces of e-Development; therefore, collaboration with business is vitally important for the Partnership. PRIOR looks forward to finding loyal consumers for its products and services among private companies, which will provide the sustainability of the Partnership.

The most likely partners of PRIOR are hi-tech companies, interested in the development of the ICT industry; companies offering solutions and products related to e-Business, construction of corporate information systems, electronic systems for document processing, etc.; telecommunications companies; small and medium enterprises interested in e-Development.

The business community can use PRIOR as:

- A platform for displaying their goods and services, rapid dissemination of up-to-date information about their operations on the national and international markets;

- An instrument of obtaining investments and financing promising projects based on the use of ICT;

- An instrument for promotion of their brands, products and services;

- A source of information concerning trade, legislation and regulations as well as specific methods of e-Business;

- A source of information and expert knowledge on the state and development trends of various segments of the ICT market, as well as on tenders and contests within the framework of the most important national and international development programs and projects;

- A consulting center for ICT use in various spheres, e-Business, preparation of bids and grant applications, etc.;

For additional analytical, business and investment opportunities information, please contact Global Investment & Business Center, USA at (202) 546-2103. Fax: (202) 546-3275. E-mail: rusric@erols.com

- An instrument for feedback from the public in the course of implementation of their own innovative projects; and

- An instrument for establishing new contacts in Russia and abroad.

One of the first business proposals made by PRIOR will be to establish a pilot e-Procurement platform on the basis of the RuDG, including purchases for projects financed by international financial institutions and multilateral sponsoring organizations.

One of the most important tasks in terms of interaction between PRIOR and its partners from the private sector is to work out a system of coordinated measures to foster the development of the information and communication industry and creation of the market for information and communication products and services.

RESEARCH AND EDUCATION COMMUNITY

Russia is distinguished by its powerful and well-structured research and education communities, which are integrated in various professional and public organizations. Despite the difficult financial situation, they continue to actively generate new knowledge and disseminate it in the society. Given the high potential of this community for the Knowledge Economy development, PRIOR views it as one of the driving forces of the emerging Information Society.

In Russia, as well as in the rest of the world, research and education community has always been among the pioneer groups generating and utilizing the ICT. Most new technologies are applied by this community and are handed over to others afterwards. That is why PRIOR considers interaction with research and educational institutions extremely important.

PRIOR will provide assistance to the research and education community in the following areas:

- Access to distributed databases concerning the development problems;

- Promotion of the results of the community's work, popularization of its achievements in Russia and worldwide;

- Assistance in obtaining funds for scientific and educational projects that are in line with PRIOR goals and objectives;

- Provision of up-to-date information on sponsor organizations, contests, tenders, innovative programs;

- Organization of access to the latest teaching techniques based on ICT;

- Informational support for scientific and educational work (creation of digital libraries and specialized subject-oriented information systems, provision of access to national and foreign distributed sources of scientific and educational information, etc.);

- Assistance in organizing joint research activity based on ICT, in establishing and developing professional contacts.

Representatives of this community may act as users of various information resources and services provided by PRIOR as well as experts and consultants, topic guides for the Russian Development Gateway, moderators of forums, leaders of initiative projects, etc.

For additional analytical, business and investment opportunities information,
please contact Global Investment & Business Center, USA
at (202) 546-2103. Fax: (202) 546-3275. E-mail: rusric@erols.com

Attracting students of the higher educational institutions to work in the RuDG and other PRIOR institutions is regarded as one of the priority tasks.

DONORS AND INVESTORS

PRIOR views public and private donor organizations and investment institutions providing financial support for projects and initiatives related to e-Development as its key systemic partners. Although they have different goals, these organizations need comprehensive and accurate up-to-date information on financial aid and investments provided for various sectors.

The major problems that donors and investors encounter include the lack of information and insufficient coordination of efforts, which sometimes result in duplication and inefficiency of the support provided.

PRIOR emphasizes cooperation with donors and investors in the following directions:

- Presentation of PRIOR project portfolio to get financial support, matching funding or investments;

- Joint development of the development project database supported by sponsors and investors;

- Provision of information on the country and its social and economic development, as well as on the sectors that can be attractive to investors and those in need of the sponsor assistance;

- Organization of discussions of the results of implementation of projects supported by sponsors and investors, exchange of experience and ideas through the RuDG online forums and jointly organized offline events;

- Promotion of the activities undertaken by sponsors and investors, dissemination of information on the results of development projects implementation in Russia;

- Strengthening cooperation between sponsors and coordination of their aid policies; and

- Provision of a platform for announcing contests and tenders conducted by sponsors and investors, as well as for e-Procurement.

In its turn, PRIOR counts on establishing long-term partner relations with various sponsoring organizations and investment institutions, which will facilitate implementation of the Partnership's projects and initiatives.

COOPERATION WITH PARTNERS IN SPECIFIC AREAS

PRIOR recognizes the importance of building not only vertical partnership relationships with representatives of the key communities, but also horizontal ones, dealing with partners in specific areas. In order to achieve PRIOR's goals, it is crucial to engage experts and consultants from various fields, suppliers of various products and services, partners for public relations and marketing, distributors.

CONTENT PARTNERS

Using the national and regional portals, PRIOR will provide its partners with instruments and a platform for establishing and maintaining knowledge networks in the sectors related to development as well as for exchanging experience in different kinds of operations.

The content partners can do the following:

- Manage a thematic section in one of the subject areas (e.g., healthcare, education, etc.) and build up a respective development community;

- Cooperate with the respective sectional groups of the Development Gateway, Russia and regional development gateways by means of information and knowledge exchange;

- Recommend experts and consultants on certain topics;

- Participate in discussion forums, provide consulting services and materials, assist in the promotion of the Partnership; and

- Promote their products under a mutual brand with PRIOR and RuDG; the method of such promotion will correspond to the contribution made to PRIOR.

Cooperation with the Russia Development Gateway and the international Development Gateway in the area of content creation will allow organizations to expand their audience in various segments of professional activity, in the regions of Russia, and in other countries. It will also facilitate implementation of joint projects with other PRIOR participants.

TECHNOLOGY PARTNERS

PRIOR technology partners can include the companies that provide the Partnership with assistance in specific technological spheres, such as IT, telecommunications, hardware, etc.

Cooperation with technology partners is important for PRIOR in terms of supplying the Partnership with computers, software, network services, as well as solutions for databases, e-Business, design for RuDG and regional portals, etc.

It is important to first establish cooperation with the leading national and regional Internet service providers and technology companies, which could support sustainable operation of RuDG and regional portals.

CONSULTING PARTNERS

In order to gain competitive advantage, all participants of the economic relations have to use ICT nowadays; however, the technological generations replace one another very rapidly. Given the fact that activities of PRIOR involve various organizations that need qualified consulting services related to the use of ICT, it is important to establish sustainable partner relationships with the leading domestic and foreign consulting companies. In addition, many enterprises and companies participating in PRIOR need investments to organize or reorganize their business processes on the basis of ICT. Hence, they need advice on obtaining investment funds.

Cooperation with PRIOR can give consulting companies the following benefits:

For additional analytical, business and investment opportunities information,
please contact Global Investment & Business Center, USA
at (202) 546-2103. Fax: (202) 546-3275. E-mail: rusric@erols.com

- Broadening their client base by providing consulting services for the participants of the Partnership;

- Opportunity of accessing the accumulated experience in ICT use in various spheres of human activity;

- Discovering the needs emerging during the development process among participants of the Partnership - representatives of civil society, private sector, research and education community, etc.;

- Access to information on PRIOR projects, which could be of interest for the investors;

- Contracts for expertise, preparation and management of programs and projects, business models and business plans related to development; and

- Promotion of companies' activity, especially in terms of development projects they implement.

MASS MEDIA AND PUBLIC RELATIONS PARTNERS

Taking into account the need of public support for Russia's transition to the Information Society and the novelty of the initiative to establish a national development partnership, PRIOR recognizes the importance of interaction with the media and professional Public Relations (PR) companies.

Establishing partner relations with the leading media and the leaders of the PR services market in Russia, PRIOR hopes to get a broad coverage of its activities, assistance in gaining positive attitude from various social groups, and to draw public attention to the opportunities offered by the Information Society.

The leading traditional and electronic media, such as newspapers, magazines, TV channels, radio stations, news agencies, online news services, as well as professional PR companies can become PRIOR partners.

Cooperation with PRIOR may allow this group of partners to attract new clients and subscribers, to create new ideas and media events, and to become aware of their own involvement in Russia's transition to the Information Society.

MARKETING AND DISTRIBUTION PARTNERS

Companies interested in promoting the Partnership's activities and services via their market niches and cooperation networks can become PRIOR partners.

Cooperation with the Partnership can enable the marketing and distributor companies to:

- Broaden their clientele by including PRIOR participants;

- Increase their influence on the market through advertising their services under a mutual trademark with PRIOR and RuDG;

- Promote the companies' activities, especially in terms of development projects they implement;

For additional analytical, business and investment opportunities information,
please contact Global Investment & Business Center, USA
at (202) 546-2103. Fax: (202) 546-3275. E-mail: rusric@erols.com

- Discover the needs for marketing and distribution services emerging among the Partnership participants; and

- Access the accumulated experience in ICT use for marketing and distribution purposes.

PRIOR counts on professional distribution of its products and services as well as on promotion of the trademarks of the Partnership and Russia Development Gateway in cooperation with marketing and distribution partners.

REGIONAL OUTREACH

PILOT REGIONS

A number of regions expressed the highest activity in the course of establishing regional partnerships for the Information Society development, drafting regional strategies for the Information Society development and creation of the regional development gateways at the initial stage of PRIOR activity. These regions include the North-Western District (federal district level); Republic of Tatarstan, Stavropol Territory, Kaliningrad, Novgorod, Perm, Tula and Chelyabinsk regions, Khanty-Mansi Autonomous Area, St. Petersburg (subject of the federation level); the City of Magnitogorsk (municipal level). The Partnership will continue to put forth its best efforts to develop its activities in other regions ("subjects of the federation") and federal districts.

Based upon the analysis of project implementation in the pilot regions, PRIOR will expand its work to other regions of the country. Such an approach will allow to:

- Take into account specific conditions in different Russian regions while organizing informational and investment services within PRIOR;

- Correct the model for the creation of country gateways within the Development Gateway Program; and

Create an extensive network of branch offices within the PRIOR organizational structure.

APPROACHES TO THE REGIONAL OUTREACH POLICY

One of PRIOR's primary tasks is providing assistance to regions in developing and implementing development programs in close cooperation with local authorities, private sector, civil society organizations, research and education community, sponsors and investors.

The main provisions of the regional outreach policy shall correspond to PRIOR goals and objectives while also taking into account the specific conditions for their realization in each region. PRIOR will assist regions in identifying the main factors hindering their dynamic development in the Information Society as well as recommend the basic ideology and methodology for the preparation of regional development concepts and programs.

Accumulating the experience of the international Development Gateway and information on development activities in various countries, PRIOR can provide regions with know-how, technologies and knowledge banks on specific issues. PRIOR has its own substantial expertise and consultative and methodological resources to develop documents and solutions meeting international standards. With the international Development Gateway brand and the special status of a non-commercial initiative, it can request consultations from the leading experts and companies of the world.

On the one hand, PRIOR will provide assistance in attracting sponsor aid and investments to the regions and, on the other hand, it will represent regional interests in terms of their participation in federal or international programs.

The Partnership shall facilitate the monitoring of the Information Society development in the regions and providing public access to the results of this process. PRIOR can also assist in the organization of awareness-raising campaigns in the regions, which could be addressed to decision makers and citizens.

ORGANIZATION OF **PRIOR** REGIONAL ACTIVITY

PRIOR regional activity will be headed by a partner organization holding the status of the Regional Coordinating Organization (RCO) and possessing the following qualities:

- Knowledge of the key problems of the region;

- Strategic vision of the ways for the region's development in the emerging Information Society;

- Ability to hold a dialog, receive new ideas and recommendations;

- Capacity building approach and readiness to invest in the future; and

- Leadership qualities combined with a manifest ability to cooperate with partners.

The Regional Coordinators shall complete the following tasks:

- Form a coalition of partners consisting of representatives of regional administrations, businesses, civil society organizations, research and education institutions, sponsor and investment organizations;

- Assist in working out a common vision and "rules of the game" that would suit all partners;

- Take into account the specific conditions in a region, identifying areas of growth and "gaps in development;"

- Create a regional development gateway on the basis of consolidation and generation of regional information resources as part of the Russia Development Gateway and provision of services that are in demand;

- Facilitate preparation and/or implementation of a development program for the region, using domestic and international experience;

- Foster "horizontal" initiatives brought up by non-governmental organizations, private enterprises, and individuals;

- Hold consultations with representatives of all societal forces interested in the region's e-Development;

- Support establishment and operation of such services as e-Government, e-Learning, e-Procurement, Digital Library, etc. on the basis of regional development gateway portal;

- Facilitate search for partners and clients, as well as online consultations, e-Transfers, creating online communities, etc. on the basis of the regional development portal;

- Provide incentives for the regional partners to make their contribution in the form of content, technologies, ideas, or financial support; and

For additional analytical, business and investment opportunities information,
please contact Global Investment & Business Center, USA
at (202) 546-2103. Fax: (202) 546-3275. E-mail: rusric@erols.com

- Initiate regional projects aimed at bridging the Digital Divide and developing through the ICT, coordinate and/or manage these projects.

It is important for an RCO to gain the trust of local authorities and bring the activities that are part of the Partnership's work in line with the provisions of the regional policies. Participation of officially delegated representatives of the governmental authorities in PRIOR regional governing bodies can become an important factor contributing to the overall success.

An organization can obtain the RCO status either by the recommendation of local authorities or by its own initiative supported by local partners and approved by the PRIOR Coordinating Board.

An RCO recommends candidates for the positions of the Regional Coordinator and the Regional Representative, which can become PRIOR full-time staff members.

CREATION OF THE RUSSIA DEVELOPMENT GATEWAY

THE PURPOSE OF THE GATEWAY

The creation of the Russia Development Gateway (hereafter Gateway, or RuDG) commenced on March 1, 2001 and is conducted with the financial support of the World Bank info Dev Program as well as the Russian Federal Program "eRussia (2002-2010)" and the municipal program "e-Moscow".

Russia Development Gateway is:

- A key project of PRIOR and

- A participant of an international network including development gateways of over 50 countries of Europe, Asia, Africa and Latin America created within the Development Gateway Program.

A team of RuDG developers initiated its creation and is a part of the professional community of developers of the technological platform "Gateway in the box" (Development gateway Collaborative network, DgCn).

THE GOALS OF THE GATEWAY

The goals of the Gateway correlate with the goals of PRIOR: the Portal serves the dynamic and full-fledged Russia's development in the course of transition to the Information Society and Knowledge Economy.

RuDG content and services are directed to provide the following:

- Development of the legal base for the Information Society, information processing and transfer infrastructure, effective national innovative system, the education and training system for the "knowledge workers," socially relevant information resources and services;

- Promotion and practical implementation of concepts and technologies of the Information Society, such as Governance, e-Government, Networked Society, e-Business, Distant Learning, Digital Libraries, etc.

- Active dissemination of innovations, knowledge and practical experience in the sphere of development on the international, national, regional and local levels;

For additional analytical, business and investment opportunities information,
please contact Global Investment & Business Center, USA
at (202) 546-2103. Fax: (202) 546-3275. E-mail: rusric@erols.com

- Involvement of international organizations, sponsors and investors in the process of resolving Russia's national and regional development problems; and

- Contribution to mutual strengthening of international, national and local initiatives through active distribution of development knowledge and experience.

THE MISSION OF THE GATEWAY

The mission of the Gateway is serving as a collaborative environment for the key development communities and as a tool for integrating expert knowledge in the development sphere.

The gateway strives to become:

- A platform for collaboration and interaction among the key development communities;

- A platform for discussing and developing the national strategy and the program of transition to the Information Society using international experience as well as providing the necessary publicity and support for its implementation;

- Knowledge warehouse accumulating the most important information on the development issues and providing efficient use of this information;

- Forum for a national dialog on the Information Society and Knowledge Economy development;

- Site for self-organization of the development communities;

- A tool for promoting Russia's positive image as a mature participant of the global Information Society.

RuDG TARGET AUDIENCE

The target audience of the Gateway includes the key development communities, which form the most active part of the Russian society, as well as foreign and international organizations and experts interested in the realization of the above mission. These include the representatives from:

- Governmental offices of all levels;

- Business, including members of the investment companies;

- Civil society and sponsor organizations;

- Educational, scientific, and cultural domains;

- Sphere of information production, processing and dissemination and other hi-tech industries and the service sector;

- Mass media.

UNIQUE FEATURE OF THE RuDG

The Gateway's primary objective is becoming the tool for discussing and developing the national strategy and the program of transition to the Information Society using international experience as well as providing the necessary publicity and support for its implementation. Evolving as a unique expert resource on the Information Society and Knowledge Economy development in Russia, the RuDG offers its users the following tools and possibilities:

- Direct access to quality information necessary for better understanding of the issues and opportunities of the Information Society and specifics of the Knowledge Economy;

- Access to reliable information regarding the problems and level of development of the Information Society and Knowledge Economy elements in Russia;

- Access to advanced domestic and foreign experience on developing and implementing strategies and programs of the Information Society development on the national and regional levels;

- A platform where PRIOR integrates representatives of the key development communities to develop and disseminate its vision of the future for Russia and proposals regarding obtaining it;

- Tools for discussing the national strategy and the program of Russia's sustainable development in the course of transition to the global Information Society and Knowledge Economy;

- Mechanisms for resolving the most important issues for specific communities, knowledge and practical experience exchange;

- Information, consultative and other services needed by the target audience and contributing to the realization of the RuDG mission;

- Dissemination of information on the activity of development communities in Russia and abroad.

CONTENT

RuDG CONTENT

The core content of the Russia Development Gateway is comprised of the information and knowledge on the Information Society and Knowledge Economy development.

Creating of the Gateway Portal was geared towards professionally selecting and providing user access to various information and viewpoints and, as the result, ensuring constant access to new understanding and real possibilities (resources and tools) for development in the priority directions of Russia's transition to the Information Society.

RuDG ARCHITECTURE

The RuDG Portal architecture is multidimensional, i.e. its content is organized by topic, type, region, user category and functional platform. This means that at the stage of publication of an information resource, it is assigned to a specific topic, a forecast for the audience (target communities) is given, the geographic relevance is defined, and the resource type (news, article, link, etc.) is recorded. Such a system allows for subsequent efficient filtering through the information during the search process.

In the course of content creation of the different level gateways, the key general principle is publishing the most valuable information of common interest on a higher-level portal in order to make sure that the users are well informed about local development processes.

Description of information resources shall be supplemented by coordinated sets of metadata; all the metadata of the network of regional and municipal gateways shall be also placed in the centralized stock of the RuDG metadata in order to provide efficient search mechanisms through the whole gateway network.

RuDG TAXONOMY

RuDG content structure is determined by *thematic rubricators (taxonomies)*, which represent an evolving system of rubrics and sub-rubrics coordinated with the international, national and regional development gateways.

The evolution of the taxonomy implies the following:

- Research and practical work on developing a balanced list and hierarchy of topics sections covering all the areas of the Information Society and Knowledge Economy development and

- Technological support for a distributed system of taxonomies, including the possibility of maintaining them at the global, national and regional levels.

MAIN PROVISIONS OF THE RuDG CONTENT POLICY

The main provisions of the RuDG content policy are listed below:

1. *Expert competency and quality of resources.* Selection of information resources, topics, news, discussion issues and offered technologies is based on thorough professional analysis, factual information and forecasts of the target audience needs. RuDG creators seek the most valid and accurate information related to authoritative and verified sources, cooperation with highly qualified experts, and regular control of the information quality.

2. *Openness and objectivity.* RuDG aims to create a high-quality resource representing different information sources and constructive points of view regarding the development problems. The Gateway creators establish contacts among different groups of experts and users to ensure free and fruitful exchange of ideas. The opinions contained in the materials published by the Gateway, represent only the opinions of the authors of texts or statements and are not always consistent with the position of the Partnership of RuDG editorial staff.

3. *Rejection of unacceptable information.* Although RuDG creators strictly abide by the policy of neutrality in terms of political, scientific and expert views of all participants, the generally accepted norms of interaction should nonetheless be followed. RuDG editorial staff reserves the right of final decision on accepting materials for publication on the Gateway. If the information is viewed as propagating violence, containing offensive language, representing provocation, conflicting with the theme of the portal sections, or is objectionable for other reasons, then the material may not be approved for publication.

4. *Proper references to the origins of the information and citation of the sources.* The RuDG Portal publishes both the original research and the references to the already published online

resources. In all cases the brief summary is prepared. The original works include their author. The use of the hyperlinks in the Portal documents does not represent the support of a company, product or opinion not does it reflect the RuDG Portal's subscription to the corresponding materials containing the link. The RuDG Portal does not have an obligation to include the link to a website; this is done for convenience of access to relevant and useful information.

5. *Correction of errors.* The editors of the RuDG Portal take an obligation to correct as quickly as possible any factual errors and misinterpretations. If a dispute occurs regarding an interpretation, the RuDG Portal staff should undertake active steps toward resolving the issue through negotiations and diplomatic coordination.

6. *Responsibility for the information.* The Portal draws the information from carefully selected Russian and foreign sources. The initial selection process is based on the expert opinion of the RuDG Portal editorial board and external consultants. The sources and links are constantly checked for consistency with the Editorial Policy and information quality standards. However, the RuDG Portal cannot guarantee the absolute reliability and accuracy of the information received from other sources and, thus, does not take the responsibility for the dependability of the secondary information.

CONTENT ORGANIZATION

Creators of the RuDG Content

RuDG is a controlled system of public presentation of the most important information on the Information Society and Knowledge Economy development. The system is based on coordinated efforts by individual experts and organizations that are acknowledged specialists in a specific area from the standpoints of objectivity and openness. The experts are attracted through the process of interaction with various partners representing the key development communities.

RuDG encourages active cooperation in the sphere of content creation (publishing) between organizations and individuals with expert knowledge and practical experience in different aspects of development.

The RuDG content is regulated by a specific document - Editorial Policy of the Russia Development Gateway.

RuDG content is provided by the Russian Corps of Development Experts (RCDE) - association of experts on a number of issues concerning the Information Society and Knowledge Economy development. An RCDE expert can fulfill one or several functions from the following list:

- Member of the RuDG Editorial Board;

- Chief Editor of the RuDG;

- Head of one or several thematic pages;

- Member of the editorial team of one or several themes;

- External expert attracted to provide consultations on a temporary basis.

RuDG Editorial Board is the highest governing body regulating the process of publishing content on the Gateway and created within the PRIOR Expert Council.

Chief Editor is a person facilitating content publishing on particular thematic page(s) including all subsections and responsible for the quality of the content and controlling maintenance of publication standards.

Head of a thematic page is responsible for content creation for specific topic/topics, including all the relevant subtopics and responsible for the quality of the content and controlling maintenance of publication standards.

Editorial team of themes are groups of experts issuing recommendations regarding the general editorial policy, regarding a particular thematic page including recommendations on setting publication standards and materials selection criteria; assisting in determining information providers and strengthening cooperation with them.

The content for thematic pages can be obtained from the following sources:

- Contributions by topic guides and heads of editorial boards;

- Contributions by communities when any user registered for the respective thematic page of the RuDG Portal shall be able to add information, which will later be reviewed by the topic guide, and, upon meeting the acceptance standards, published on this page;

- Discussions and debates on key problems, initiated by topic guides on the basis of recommendations given by editorial boards and suggestions made by users;

- Commentaries by topic guides and users;

- Requests from users for specific information and answers to these requests given by other members of the topic community;

- News bulletins prepared by topic guides and authorized partners;

- Statistical data and information from databases on development projects, provided by the international Development Gateway.

CONTENT ORGANIZATION

Decentralization. The RuDG provides an opportunity to publish content via the Internet, using:

- Forums available for all users;

- Administrative interface available only for the editorial staff.

Users and RCDE can publish content from any computer having the Internet access.

Access division. One of the main peculiarities of the RuDG content publishing is access division. Depending on the function he or she fulfills, an RCDE member can perform the following activities:

- Add or delete content on any thematic page of the Gateway both through the forum and administrative interface - *first category of access* (RuDG Chief Editor);

- Add or delete content on any thematic page within the section of the first level both through the forum and administrative interface - *second category of access* (head of a thematic page);

For additional analytical, business and investment opportunities information,
please contact Global Investment & Business Center, USA
at (202) 546-2103. Fax: (202) 546-3275. E-mail: rusric@erols.com

- Add or delete content on one or several particular thematic pages within the section of the second level both through the forum and administrative interface - *third category of access* (topic subsection guide);

- Any registered user can add content through the discussion forums on any thematic page of the Gateway - fourth category of access.

RELATIONS WITH SPONSORS, PARTNERS AND ADVERTISERS

RuDG can attract additional support in the form of various grants, equipment and services provided by development agencies, foundations, individuals and companies. RuDG publishes the list of all organizations and persons providing gratis contribution; however, such contribution is only accepted if the editorial independency is preserved. The logos of those who provide uncompensated contribution are marked as "partner" or "sponsor."

The staff involved in selecting information content should reject offers that can be misinterpreted by those who provide them in case of their acceptance, or that can give an impression to the users that RuDG is in any way obliged to particular sponsors or companies.

RuDG can place paid advertisements in the form of banners and special advertising sections. The relations with advertisers should be transparent and clear to the Gateway users; therefore, the informational and commercial content should be clearly separated. A necessary condition of financial support is prior agreement by the provider to the RuDG's full freedom to select the information provided to the users. Advertising materials should be clearly marked on the Gateway Portal.

CONTENT TRANSLATION

In order to cover the largest audience possible, the RuDG Portal shall publish information in Russian and English. The Russian and English versions shall de identical in those parts that are of interest to both domestic and foreign users. In addition to Russian and English, regional gateways within RuDG can also publish information in local languages. The selection of materials to be translated is the responsibility of the topic guides, editorial boards of the RuDG Portal, and editorial councils of the regional development gateways.

There shall be two translation methods, depending on the type of information resource:

- Translation made by people (for the most important documents requiring qualified translation and editing by the experts) and

- Machine translations (for documents that can be adequately translated automatically).

Specially selected experts shall conduct scientific editing of translations related to their respective fields.

Taking into account high cost of translation and editing work, the RuDG shall provide instruments for machine translation of the documents published on the Portal as one of its services.

RUDG SERVICES

A distinctive feature of the RuDG is high concentration of various modern services and functional elements provided by various Internet portals.

For additional analytical, business and investment opportunities information, please contact Global Investment & Business Center, USA at (202) 546-2103. Fax: (202) 546-3275. E-mail: rusric@erols.com

The attractiveness of the RuDG will depend primarily upon the set of services offered to users and developers. In providing these services, the RuDG shall try to implement the "one-stop-shop" principle so that a user could receive the maximum number of services without leaving the Gateway. At the same time, the RuDG should provide not only for its users and clients but also for the participants of the Partnership who make substantial contribution to its development. Therefore, the services to be offered by the Portal are tentatively divided into two groups: a user group and an administrative group.

The RuDG Portal offers the following kinds of services to its users and clients:

- Personalization;

- Information about development problems;

- Instruments for cooperation;

- Sub-portals;

- Database of development projects;

- Consulting center;

- Virtual university;

- Digital library;

- E-commerce market place;

- Navigation instruments;

- Automatic translation;

- Help.

The following key services will be provided to support PRIOR and RuDG Portal operation:

- Instruments for content management;

- Instruments for informational support of PRIOR and RuDG activities;

- Instruments for the monitoring of RuDG Portal users.

The set of RuDG administrative services is not limited to the above list since their composition will evolve as the Portal develops.

In order to ensure effective interaction between partners within the organizational structure of PRIOR, the common access to corporate data will be provided. This will help to solve the following tasks:

- Developing a common interface for individual information systems of PRIOR participants;

- Creating a digital library with a convenient internal structure, an efficient search system, and a reliable scheme of delineation of users' rights;

- Establishing a starting point for retrieving the Partnership's internal information; and

- Providing application developers with an architecture integrating the newly-created components into the overall system.

As interaction with users and clients evolves, the range of RuDG Portal services will enlarge and adjust to the new needs emerging in the process of the Information Society development.

RUDG TECHNOLOGY

RuDG shall represent a single distributed system of the national and regional portals, which have a common information infrastructure and technological architecture.

The national and regional portals should be technologically compatible with the international Development Gateway and other countries' national portals; therefore, the technological strategy for the RuDG Portal development is based on the following principles:

- Use of technologies based on open system standards and using open software [25];

- Scalable and modular architecture of the technological platforms used;

- Decentralization and distributed nature of content management and the portals system administration;

- Use of metadata to standardize data representation and exchange;

- Organization of information classification and retrieval on the basis of thesauri and metadata;

- Use of the XML/RDF standards to ensure interaction between development gateway portals and outside portals, regardless of their technological platforms;

- Support for personal adjustments and the high level of personal information security;

- Support for multilingualism based on the Unicode.

The technological platforms and designing tools offered by the international Development Gateway correspond to the aforementioned principles. The components of the Development Gateway technological platform are open software, which allows for transferring technologies and inviting partners for collaborative design work.

In order to support further interaction between development gateway portals on all levels, the corporate metadata standard for the description of information resources should be developed and adopted. Implementation of such a standard will allow for efficient search throughout the whole network, because the regional portal metadata will be transferred to the centralized RuDG metadata bank.

For the purposes of coordinated development of technological platforms of national development gateway portals, including RuDG, a collaborative effort should be organized between the Development Gateway and country technology teams; this will allow for coordination of plans for the introduction of new functional modules and standards, transfer to new versions, etc.

For additional analytical, business and investment opportunities information, please contact Global Investment & Business Center, USA at (202) 546-2103. Fax: (202) 546-3275. E-mail: rusric@erols.com

ORGANIZATIONAL STRUCTURE DEVELOPMENT

The Partnership for Information Society Development in Russia is established on the basis of a partnership coalition formed during the Planning Phase of the Russia Development Gateway Project supported by the info Dev Program of the World Bank.

PRIOR is a voluntary association of legal entities and individuals sharing common goals and objectives, which were listed in a previous section. The Partnership's activity is regulated by a Memorandum on PRIOR Creation approved at the PRIOR Organizational Conference and modified by the decision of the PRIOR Coordinating Board.

COLLEGIATE GOVERNING BODIES

In order to implement the above stated partnership principles - openness, holistic approach, sustainability and ownership, the **collegiate governing bodies** of PRIOR are to be established. At present the governing bodies include: the Supervisory Board, the Coordinating Board and the Expert Council, their activity is regulated by the following provisions.

The Supervisory Board is created to guarantee public support for the Partnership's activity as well as for general control and supervision of the Partnership's work.

The Coordinating Board is established to define the development strategy and priority goals of the Partnership activity.

The Expert Council is created to provide expert advice and consultations for the PRIOR Supervisory and Coordinating Boards.

On the regional level, **PRIOR regional governing bodies** are formed; their responsibilities and membership are defined with respect to the specific conditions and needs of a particular region. The organizers' assumption is that the necessary balance of opinions for making decisions will be achieved with the assistance of a supervisory (advisory) council, consisting of representatives of the government and influential people of the region, and an expert (consultative) council, which will include specialists from various sectors of ICT development and use.

COMPONENTS OF PRIOR ORGANIZATIONAL STRUCTURE

PRIOR aims and objectives are to be achieved within the framework of the organizational structure, which is comprised of several main components:

1. Coordinating Organization

2. Regional Coordinating Organizations (RCOs)

3. PRIOR Foundation

4. Information & Analytical Center

5. Technical Support Center

6. Information & Publishing Center

7. Ad Hoc Groups

8. New Organizations founded during the implementation of specific projects.

For additional analytical, business and investment opportunities information, please contact Global Investment & Business Center, USA at (202) 546-2103. Fax: (202) 546-3275. E-mail: rusric@erols.com

In the future, the Coordinating Board can make decisions regarding changes in PRIOR's organizational structure.

At the initial stages, one of PRIOR members is charged with managing its administrative and business operations. Upon expiration of the agreement period, the Coordinating Board can make a decision to transfer this responsibility to another member of the Partnership or to found a new legal entity as a **Coordinating Organization** . The Coordinating Organization creates PRIOR Directorate within its structure.

PRIOR Foundation is intended to facilitate the e-Development process in Russia and to stimulate the innovative activity in the sphere of ICT use for comprehensive development. The Foundation's chief goal is supporting promising projects aimed at attaining the aforementioned PRIOR goals.

PRIOR Information and Analytical Center (hereinafter - IAC), as well as the Foundation, has been established to facilitate Russia's e-Development and to stimulate innovative activity in the sphere of ICT use for comprehensive development. The main goals of the IAC is conducting a wide range of research, informational, analytical, consultative, and organizational work intended to achieve the aforementioned PRIOR goals as wall as providing Russia's e-Development monitoring.

The Partnership, represented by its Coordinating Board, authorizes one of more of its partners to perform the functions of IAC for a certain period. At the end of this period the Coordinating Board makes a decision either to extend this authority or to transfer the functions of IAC to another member of the Partnership, or to found a separate legal entity to perform IAC functions.

The main purpose of **PRIOR Technical Support Center** (hereinafter - TSC) is to ensure smooth continuous operation of the RuDG and cooperation with the international Development Gateway, to provide technological support for the regional development gateways as well as PRIOR activities in general.

At the same time, TSC can play the role of an online business center, providing services for "renters" to increase PRIOR efficiency and sustainability.

The Partnership, represented by its Coordinating Board, authorizes one or more of its members to carry out the functions of TSC for a specified period. At the end of this period the Coordinating Board makes a decision to either extend this partner's authority or to transfer its functions to another member of the Partnership, or to establish a separate legal entity as TSC.

PRIOR Information and Publishing Center (hereinafter - IPC) is created to prepare, collect, and disseminate original e-Development information, to provide content for the Russia Development Gateway Portal and regional development gateway portals, and to implement PRIOR publishing projects, such as analytical magazine on the Information Society development and PRIOR newsletter both in electronic and print versions.

The Partnership, represented by its Coordinating Board, authorizes one or more of its members to carry out the functions of IPC for a specified period. At the end of this period the Coordinating Board makes a decision to either extend this partner's authority or to transfer its functions to another member of the Partnership, or to establish a separate legal entity as IPC.

As part of PRIOR's work on specific projects and actions, **ad hoc working groups** are formed. Members of these groups can work on the basis of contracts with PRIOR Coordinating Organization or PRIOR Foundation, or be delegated by partner organizations (in which case their salaries can count as contributions to the Partnership), or participate on a voluntary basis.

For additional analytical, business and investment opportunities information,
please contact Global Investment & Business Center, USA
at (202) 546-2103. Fax: (202) 546-3275. E-mail: rusric@erols.com

Some PRIOR projects may require establishing **new organizations** , affiliates of the Coordinating Organization, business entities established by the Foundation, or separate legal entities as a part of PRIOR organizational structure.

ACTION PLAN IMPLEMENTATION

PRIOR activity shall be based on its Action Plan, which includes specific projects and activities. National and international experience in using program methods for the implementation of different-scale projects accumulated by the participants of the Partnership will be taken into account when implementing this Action Plan.

PRIOR ROLE IN PROJECT FINANCING IN THE PUBLIC SECTOR

By this time, a rather comprehensive system of support for various type projects on competitive basis has been formed out in the public and private sectors. Rapid dissemination and adoption of this approach is due to the fact that government and business have recognized the selective investment as one of the key factors in overcoming the economic crisis.

The support of e-development and ICT projects in the non-government sector was carried out mainly by various non-governmental foundations, including international ones (e.g., the Soros Foundation, the Eurasia Foundation and others.) The private capital is not inclined to invest sufficient funds in e-development projects partly due to the high level of inherent financial risks.

Hence, currently there is virtually no mechanism for supporting ICT projects in the non-governmental sector, and PRIOR strives to fill this gap.

MAIN PRINCIPLES OF PROJECT SELECTION

The official procedure of PRIOR competitions is approved by the Coordinating Board following the recommendations provided by the Expert Council. The main principles guiding the selection process procedures are as follows:

- Openness of the concept, goals and objectives of a competition;

- Opportunity and equal participation requirements for all applicants;

- Competent and unbiased expert council interested in the selection of high-quality projects;

- Evaluation and selection criteria set beforehand;

- Properly organized anonymous scientific and technical examination of applications and results of project implementation;

- Immunity of the Expert Council members and independent experts against any outside pressure;

- Guaranteed confidentiality of personal data and commercial information not specified for dissemination;

- Protection of intellectual property and copyright of researchers and developers.

For additional analytical, business and investment opportunities information,
please contact Global Investment & Business Center, USA
at (202) 546-2103. Fax: (202) 546-3275. E-mail: rusric@erols.com

MAKING DECISIONS REGARDING PROJECT FINANCING

The suggested procedure provides for the following:

- Self-registration of an application in a special PRIOR information system;

- Initial assessment of an application by at least two anonymous experts working independently from each other;

- Reviewing the results of the initial review by appropriate sections of the PRIOR Expert Council;

- Reviewing the results of the assessment by the PRIOR Expert Council;

- Approving the project budget by the PRIOR Coordinating Board.

The main criteria for the selection of application are the following:

- Innovativeness;

- Focus on user needs;

- Sustainability;

- Transferability: possibility to transfer the results, methods and ideas of the given project in Russia and abroad;

- Co-funding available (30-50% of the total project budget).

Evaluation and other procedures shall be financed by the PRIOR Foundation.

SUPPORT FOR PROJECTS AND ACTIONS

PRIOR projects, activities and events are financed from the funds of PRIOR Foundation, partners' resources, and other co-funding sources.

Further support for the selected projects requires constant cooperation with organizations and ad hoc groups. This is a specific, rather complex and laborious managerial procedure, requiring constant efforts by the PRIOR Directorate and Foundation.

Methodological support in organization of competitions and project management can be provided by the Russian Foundation for Basic Research (RFBR), Russia's leading expert organization in this sphere.

PRIOR MARKETING STRATEGY AND PUBLIC RELATIONS

PRIOR marketing strategy is aimed at positioning the Partnership as a prominent nationwide organization, which has a unique instrument for supporting its activity - the Russia Development Gateway. The latter represents an extensive network of partners in Russia and a powerful expert resource, which allows for substantial influence upon the Information Society development in the country.

PRIOR positioning as an independent public-private initiative serves as a basis for consolidation and coordination of efforts aimed at fostering development. In addition, Partnership's positioning as the leader of project support in the public sector allows it to occupy unique social and market niches. Accordingly, a "different" or unique approach shall be used as the central marketing strategy, which focuses primarily on promoting distinct and unique characteristics of the PRIOR and RuDG brands.

GOALS AND OBJECTIVES OF THE MARKETING STRATEGY

The Partnership's marketing strategy follows three main aims:

- Establishing PRIOR brand and subsequent promoting of the RuDG brand to the target audience;

- Attracting new partners and clients, including users of the RuDG and regional development gateways;

- Tuning PRIOR activities according to the needs of the society.

These aims are to be achieved through monitoring, advertising and PR activities conducted with assistance of the mass media.

The key tasks of PRIOR marketing strategy include the following:

- Reaching and maintaining high level of awareness of the brands, logos and missions of PRIOR and RuDG among the target audiences;

- Forming an adequate idea of PRIOR and RuDG aims and objectives, PRIOR Action Plan, products and services, advantages of participation in the Partnership and using the RuDG;

- Promoting PRIOR and RuDG as stable formations;

- Providing an incentive to the target audience to collect and analyze additional information on PRIOR activity so as to make a decision on cooperation with or purchasing products and/ or services from PRIOR and RuDG; and

- Ensuring flexibility in providing products and services on the basis of regular monitoring of domestic and foreign users' needs.

MAIN TARGET GROUPS OF PRIOR AND RUDG

PRIOR marketing strategy shall be aimed at the following target groups:

- The World Bank and other multilateral international organizations;

- Sponsors and investors (international and domestic);

- Government of the Russian Federation of all levels;

- Civil society organizations;

- Large businesses and industry;

For additional analytical, business and investment opportunities information, please contact Global Investment & Business Center, USA at (202) 546-2103. Fax: (202) 546-3275. E-mail: rusric@erols.com

- Small and medium enterprises;

- Research and educational institutions and organizations;

- Russian contestants for investments.

Given the heterogeneous target audience of PRIOR, the marketing activity shall be adapted to specific characteristics of the members of each group listed above taking into account regional specifics and PRIOR priorities.

The socio-demographic profile of the target audience is characterized mainly by active men and women aged 25-60 years old, holding university degrees, earning incomes above the average level, and leading active lifestyle.

IMPLEMENTATION OF THE MARKETING STRATEGY

One of the main directions of PRIOR marketing strategy will be the monitoring of Russia's readiness for the Information Society and the Knowledge Economy and analyzing related needs through sociological surveys and questionnaires, expert evaluations, focus groups, user feedback via the RuDG and regional development gateways.

In order to form the user demand for PRIOR products and services, various kinds of advertising channels will be used, which shall depend upon PRIOR's tactical goals: the Internet, PR actions, the media (newspapers, magazines, radio and TV), presentations, forums, and exhibitions.

RuDG and the network of regional development gateways shall become the main carriers of information about PRIOR; therefore, the attention should be focused on the corporate design and style of PRIOR / RuDG.

The main channels of PRIOR and RuDG promotion include the following:

- Publishing PRIOR bulletin and newsletter;

- Publishing presentation, informational and advertising materials;

- Placing advertisements in well-known catalogues and reference books with wide circulation and broad geographical distribution;

- Making presentations;

- Disseminating press releases among the leading mass media;

- Publishing challenging, research, and popular articles in well-known journals and newspapers highlighting PRIOR and RuDG;

- Supporting public events organized by other parties but attended by representatives of PRIOR target groups;

- Creating activities and events that can be attractive for the press, radio and TV.

To create PRIOR brand and to further promote the RuDG one a number of targeted actions will be implemented, such as:

For additional analytical, business and investment opportunities information, please contact Global Investment & Business Center, USA at (202) 546-2103. Fax: (202) 546-3275. E-mail: rusric@erols.com

- Attracting the most recognizable brands and trademarks to join the Partnership;

- Active participation in public events (forums, exhibitions, competitions, etc.);

- Establishing regular working contacts with mass media;

- Conducting press conferences and meetings with journalists;

- Conducting regular PRIOR events (conferences and seminars);

- Issuing and distributing periodicals, books and video recordings of PRIOR activities; and

- Issuing and distributing CD-ROMs providing free time-limited access to RuDG commercial services.

The franchising mechanism can be used as a method of raising awareness of the PRIOR and RDG trademarks, as well as for increasing the influence of PRIOR and RuDG on the regional level. Franchising opens broad opportunities for reaching regions and building a partnership network at a low cost, since the cost of its creation is much less than that of building a network of regional branches and offices.

An additional method of attracting public attention to PRIOR and RuDG will be establishing a national Information Society award under their aegis. It would be feasible to position this award as a national initiative within the framework of international awards and contests, such as Stockholm Challenge Award, European IT Award, World Summit Award, Global Junior Challenge and others.

A special department of public relations, whose responsibility will be to implement and tune the marketing program, will be established within the PRIOR Directorate.

PRIOR FINANCIAL STRATEGY

KEY PRINCIPLES OF PRIOR FINANCIAL STRATEGY

PRIOR is a non-commercial initiative focusing its efforts on achieving socially relevant goals. Such a mission implies certain obligations regarding the implementation of the financial strategy, which is guided by the following main principles:

- Use of the entire spectrum of accessible financial sources for sustainable operation of the RuDG and regional development gateways, implementation of PRIOR projects and actions;

- Attracting material, informational, organizational, technological and other support from the partners, which can be considered a financial contribution;

- Gaining revenues from entrepreneurial activities exclusively for achievement of PRIOR's socially relevant goals.

MAIN SOURCES OF FINANCING

The following sources are viewed as the main sources of financing for PRIOR:

- **Grants** from foundations and other financial institutions, international organizations and programs to support non-commercial socially important projects and actions;

- **Federal budget funds** of the Russian Federation as part of special federal programs;

- **Regional and municipal budget funds** as co-financing of partnership projects supported by the local authorities as priorities for e-Development;

- **Voluntary financial and property contributions** made by participants and founders of the Partnership and PRIOR Foundation;

- **Partners' contributions** in the form of consulting, informational resources, hardware and software, network services, research results, organizational support, office space, and other values facilitating PRIOR development;

- **Revenues from business operations** conducted by PRIOR structural components - Directorate, Foundation, IAC, TSC, IPC and newly established ventures;

- **Venture investments** , provided by investment companies and groups for the implementation of hi-tech projects with long-term payoff periods;

- **Loans** granted on preferential terms by the World Bank and other financial institutions for the implementation of large projects, guaranteed by the Government of the Russian Federation and regional governments.

Most of the funds shall be accumulated in the PRIOR Foundation and allocated in accordance with decisions of the Coordinating Board, based on recommendations made by the Expert Council. In accordance with the legislation of the Russian Federation, the Foundation must publish annual reports on its operations, including on the allocation of its financial resources.

FUNDRAISING POLICY

Fundraising is regarded as a business priority, which supports the functioning of PRIOR and RuDG.

The main provisions of the fundraising policy include the following:

- Implementation of the principle of participation in the Partnership on the basis of a specific contribution in the form of financial, technological, organizational, intellectual, and other necessary support;

- Organization of co-financing for PRIOR projects and actions from various sources, using the potential of the Partnership;

- Implementation of the principle of equal stakes in the investment development projects by PRIOR Foundation and other foundations and/or investment funds;

- Analysis of PRIOR participants' needs to support development projects and initiatives;

- Conducting regular investment forums within the PRIOR Action Plan.

PRIOR fundraising program includes the following main aspects:

- Active interaction with government agencies at the federal, regional and municipal levels, including exchange of information on planned or active initiatives, analysis of opportunities to include PRIOR's actions in special development programs and projects, and joint implementation of specific projects and activities;

- Regular contacts with representatives of government agencies of all levels, sponsor organizations, investment companies and large businesses to persuade them to participate in PRIOR's actions, to place information about their operations on the RuDG and regional development gateways, participation in these organizations' actions and initiatives;

- Participation in competitions announced by foundations and programs that support development initiatives as well as federal and regional authorities as part of the specific corresponding programs;

- Proposals on financing PRIOR project portfolios and actions for national and international investment companies and venture funds;

- Involvement of organizations interested in promoting their services;

- Search for organizations interested in lobbying laws and standards facilitating the Information Society and Knowledge Economy development; implementation of joint programs;

- Involvement of organizations that actively use or intend to use ICT in their work in order to increase their attractiveness to investors and build the image of an innovative hi-tech company;

- Identification of organizations interested in attracting resources of international sponsor organizations and financial institutions, consulting these organizations on optimum financial plans, assistance in attracting grants, loans and credits;

- Selection of promising services for potential investors, preparation of a cooperation program, elaboration of profit sharing principles.

MAJOR INVESTMENT NEEDS

PRIOR activity inevitably requires investments in its expenditure components, which include the following activities:

- Creation and maintenance of the RuDG and regional development gateways;

- Implementation of projects and events focused exclusively on social needs, for example, establishing facilities of public access to the ICT, including the Internet; organizing awareness-raising campaigns; providing ICT-based services for disadvantaged social groups, etc.;

- Organization of a marketing campaign;

- Payment of salaries for PRIOR permanent staff;

- Expenditures on purchasing books, analytical materials, consulting services, etc.;

- Maintaining equipment and technical support for PRIOR organizational structures: office rental, payment for communication channels, purchasing and maintaining software and hardware, purchasing office equipment and supplies, furniture, payment for Internet access.

For additional analytical, business and investment opportunities information,
please contact Global Investment & Business Center, USA
at (202) 546-2103. Fax: (202) 546-3275. E-mail: rusric@erols.com

Any organization or individual interested in cooperation with PRIOR can act as an investor. Advantages of such cooperation for various organizations are described in detail in Paragraphs 4.1.2.1 - 4.1.2.6, 4.1.3.1 - 4.1.3.5. of the present document.

MAJOR REVENUE SOURCES

During the Planning Phase of the Russia Development Gateway Project an e-Needs assessment was conducted, based upon:

- Review of open public sources used during the preparation of reports on the Russia's e-Readiness;

- Analysis of the information obtained from workshops and negotiations with different organizations and companies;

- Polling of numerous participants of events organized by the PRIOR Team or with its active assistance;

- Vast practical experience of the RuDG partners.

In terms of meeting the potential users' needs, the following services to be implemented on the basis of the PRIOR Foundation, IPC, IAC, and TSC appear to have the most promise and use:

- Provision access to materials of sociological, socio-psychological and marketing surveys and reviews of ICT impact on the development of the Russian economy, society and state;

- Development and expert analysis of laws, bills and standards related to the Information Society development;

- Providing consultations on e-Development issues and opportunities for growth for various groups of users;

- Provision of services dealing with preparation of e-Development concepts, business models, business plans, grant applications, feasibility studies, system projects, etc.

- Conducting applied research and design work related to the Information Society and Knowledge Economy for development;

- Examination and management of projects aimed at ICT and knowledge use for development;

- Publication of periodicals: a popular magazine, a specialized analytical bulletin on the Information Society development, PRIOR newsletter, etc.;

- Organization of conferences and seminars on various aspects of the Information Society and Knowledge Economy development;

- Provision of services dealing with recruitment of qualified personnel in the sphere of ICT for development;

- Provision of analytical information and news, results of monitoring of the Information Society development in Russia;

For additional analytical, business and investment opportunities information,
please contact Global Investment & Business Center, USA
at (202) 546-2103. Fax: (202) 546-3275. E-mail: rusric@erols.com

- Preparation and implementation of modern solutions and know-how in the sphere of development;

- Examination and preparation of efficient business models implying ICT use, organization of experimental production facilities for their testing and implementation;

- Receiving interest from servicing the investments;

- Revenues from paid services provided on the basis of RuDG and regional gateways, including revenues from displaying other organizations' ads, fees for transactions as part of implementing e-Procurement function, rent for the Market Place, fees for electronic document delivery, etc.;

- Hosting for servers (placed at the TSC facilities) and sites (placing partners' information resources and applications at the TSC servers);

- Provision of individual and collective communication services (e-mail, mailing lists, forum, forum archive, chat, video conferencing, Internet telephony, network broadcasting);

- Application service providing (ASP);

- Provision of DNS services (registration of domain names and support at primary and auxiliary servers); and

- Provision of call-center services and others.

RIOR Directorate and PRIOR Foundation are authorized to develop, implement, and modify PRIOR fundraising and revenue generating programs.

STAGES OF DEVELOPMENT

The present strategy covers the period of formation and gaining sustainability of the Partnership. This period comprises four stages planned to be carried out within 10 years:

PLANNING PHASE

The Planning Phase of 2001 achieved the following tasks:

- Establishing a preliminary partner consortium, including representatives of government, business, civil society, research and education community and sponsor organizations;

- Forming a working group and collegiate governing bodies (Steering Committee and Advisory Committee) of the Russia Development Gateway Project, which included representatives of the partner organizations;

- Analyzing Russia's e-Readiness and e-Needs, preparing an analytical report based on the methodology offered by the Center for International Development of Harvard University;

- Creating an active prototype of the RuDG Portal in Russian and English;

- Conducting a broad awareness campaign on the RuDG goals and objectives;

For additional analytical, business and investment opportunities information, please contact Global Investment & Business Center, USA at (202) 546-2103. Fax: (202) 546-3275. E-mail: rusric@erols.com

- Holding a series of workshops with partners in Moscow, Saint Petersburg, Kazan, Yaroslavl, and Chelyabinsk in order to work out approaches to further development of the RuDG Project at the national level;

- Discussing and deciding upon the institutional and legal status of the Russia Development Gateway organization [26],

- outlining its organizational structure and coordinating it with RuDG governing bodies;

- Developing the strategy and the business plan for PRIOR's sustainable development in the intermediate term based on consultations with partners and the results of workshops and the e-Needs assessment;

- Holding negotiations with sponsors and investors, making a decision to register PRIOR Foundation as a separate legal entity, preparing and discussing the draft of the Foundation statute;

- Forming of PRIOR's initial project portfolio and Action Plan; and

- Preparing applications to be submitted to sponsor organizations for PRIOR project funding.

PILOT IMPLEMENTATION PHASE (2002-2003)

T he pilot implementation phase includes the following events and activities:

- Holding PRIOR Organizational Conference, approval of its organizational structure and founding documents, formation of PRIOR collegiate governing bodies, distribution of responsibilities between partner organizations within PRIOR organizational structure;

- Creation and launch of PRIOR key organizational components - Directorate, IAC, TSC, Foundation, and IPC;

- Extension of PRIOR membership, balancing participation of the key development communities in PRIOR;

- Formation of Information Society development partnerships in 7-9 regions of Russia;

- e-Readiness assessment in several pilot regions of the Russian Federation, including estimation of the level of information infrastructure development and ICT use in the key spheres of activity (government, education, healthcare, business, etc.), analysis of zones lagging behind and barriers to the efficient use of ICT for the development of each region;

- Further development of draft plans of development strategies for the selected regions in the emerging Information Society with participation of the key development communities;

- Marketing analysis of RuDG and regional portals operations, study of needs for new services, bugs fixing, improvement of the taxonomy, content development;

- Broadening functions and services of the RuDG Portal (forums, Consulting Center, Virtual University, subscriptions, search, etc.);

For additional analytical, business and investment opportunities information, please contact Global Investment & Business Center, USA at (202) 546-2103. Fax: (202) 546-3275. E-mail: rusric@erols.com

- Conducting a series of workshops and conferences to specify PRIOR objectives and forms of activities and to develop partnerships;

- Conducting local, national or international events aimed at the realization of PRIOR aims and objectives;

- Cooperation with sponsor organizations and investment companies to obtain new funds for the implementation of PRIOR projects and actions;

- Implementation of the most urgent socially important pilot projects and initiatives, including the publishing ones;

- Preparation and pilot implementation of an awareness campaign intended to propagate ICT potential for improvement of the quality of life and work;

- Provision of services for partners and clients on the basis of RuDG, IAC, TSC and IPC;

- Conducting a PR campaign intended to popularize PRIOR activities in cooperation with the leading media and their professional associations;

- Study of needs for loans for the implementation of the programs for the Information Society development, assistance to partner organizations in holding negotiations and preparing applications;

- Analysis of the planning and pilot implementation phases of PRIOR activities, correction of PRIOR structure, preparation of an updated version of the business plan and other basic documents; and

- Search for additional investment resources and strategic partners to achieve goals of the third stage of the PRIOR activities.

IMPLEMENTATION PHASE (2004-2005)

The plan for the Implementation Stage includes the following tasks:

- Further improvement of PRIOR organizational structure, modifying the founding documents of the Partnership;

- Further extension of PRIOR membership, balancing participation of the key development communities in PRIOR;

- Creating independent partnerships for the Information Society development in another 8-10 Russian regions;

- Assessing e-Readiness in a number of Russian regions; development and realization of development strategies of the Russian regions in the emerging Information Society with participation of the main developing communities;

- Extending and supporting efficient functioning of a distributed network of regional development gateways within the RuDG;

For additional analytical, business and investment opportunities information,
please contact Global Investment & Business Center, USA
at (202) 546-2103. Fax: (202) 546-3275. E-mail: rusric@erols.com

- Conducting further marketing analysis of the use of the RuDG and regional portals, study of needs for new services, content development;

- Organizing workshops and conferences to define PRIOR tasks and forms of activity and further broadening of PRIOR partnerships;

- Holding local, regional, national and international events directed at implementing PRIOR aims and objectives;

- Cooperation with sponsoring organizations and investment companies aimed to obtain new funds for the implementation of PRIOR projects and actions;

- Realization of socially relevant PRIOR projects and initiatives;

- Conducting an awareness-raising campaign to propagate the possibilities of the Information Society aimed at increasing the quality of life and work;

- Providing services to partners and clients on the basis of RuDG, IAC, TSC and IPC;

- Organization of a PR campaign to popularize PRIOR activities in cooperation with the leading media and their professional associations;

- Determining needs for loans on the realization of the Information Society development programs, support to organizations in conducting negotiations and drafting corresponding documents;

- Analysis of the first three stages of PRIOR activity, drafting updated versions of the business plan for the next stages; and

- Search for additional investment resources, strategic partners to achieve the goals of the fourth stage of PRIOR activities.

SUSTAINABLE GROWTH PHASE (2006-2010)

During long-term sustainable growth phase, further development and expansion of PRIOR activities will be completed almost in all subjects of the Russian Federation . At the same time, the revenues from services and commercial use of the systems and projects created during the first three stages will support PRIOR's continued sustainable development.

More exact timeframe and specific tasks of the stages, the composition of specific projects and actions will be defined in the course of consultations with partners interested in the PRIOR successful operation.

EVALUATION OF PRIOR STRATEGY

Evaluation of PRIOR Strategy implementation will be conducted in accordance with the following basic criteria:

- Concurrence of current activities of PRIOR and the declared mission, goals and objectives;

- Scale and effectiveness of the partnership's activity;

For additional analytical, business and investment opportunities information,
please contact Global Investment & Business Center, USA
at (202) 546-2103. Fax: (202) 546-3275. E-mail: rusric@erols.com

- Scope and quality of content and services, the demand for the RuDG and regional development gateways, and the number of regional gateways;

- Adequacy of PRIOR managerial and organizational structure to its goals and objectives;

- Quality, degree of support, and efficiency of PRIOR projects and events implementation;

- Effectiveness of PRIOR marketing and financial programs.

Relevance and alignment with PRIOR mission, aims and objectives will be assessed by the PRIOR Supervisory and Coordinating Boards at their regular meetings. The activity will be adjusted on the basis of feedback and recommendations received.

The criteria for evaluating the scale and effectiveness of *the partnership program* shall include the following:

- The degree of support for PRIOR activity by government at the federal, regional and local levels;

- The number of signed declarations on joining PRIOR and the extent of participation (provision of financial, equipment, informational, technical, organizational and other necessary support);

- The balanced structure of the partnership program (the extent of participation of all development communities: government, business, civil society, research and education community, sponsors and investors);

- The quantity and effectiveness of activities completed: extent of participation, focused audience, quality of reports and presentations made, publication of results, preparation and submission of recommendations, response to the recommendations);

- The intensity of practical experience exchange between the participants of the Partnership with recorded results, which contributed to the development community in Russia and worldwide;

- The diversity and extent of use of various means of dissemination of information on the most important issues of the Information Society development: digital divide, governance transparency and active governance, e-Government, e-Business, creation of local information resources accessible via the Internet, "knowledge workers" training, developing the innovative system, etc.

The criteria for assessing the efforts to create *the RuDG and regional development gateways* shall include the following:

- The degree and intensity of use of the RuDG online interaction instruments (forums, mailing lists, etc.), and correspondence between these instruments and the RuDG goals and objectives;

- Stages of development reached: the informative stage, provision of instruments for exchange of information, additional services, correspondence to the stage of development of the global Development Gateway;

- Volume of content and efficiency of content management: adequacy of the taxonomy for the needs of the country (region) and standards of the global Development Gateway, percentage of covering topics and sub-topics; the ratio between external content and PRIOR's own content; the extent of participation of various development communities in the creation of content and important discussions; availability and the quality of search and navigation mechanisms (guides, portal maps, instructions for content providers and users);

- Quality, accessibility and practical value of the content: correspondence of the content with PRIOR and RuDG mission, goals and objectives, the intensity of exchange of knowledge and practical experience between users, the popularity of topics, creation of new thematic rubrics, the permanence of topic guides;

- Availability, quality, and use of personalization tools: e-mail subscription, security management, privacy management;

- Level of technical support: correspondence between the technological platform and the goals and objectives of the gateways (design, functionality, effectiveness of search engine, etc.); turnaround time for troubleshooting;

- The quality of the architecture: availability of contact information; visibility of logos of the organizations that contributed to the creation of the portals; accessibility of navigation tools and links to the regulations on confidentiality policy and personal information security from any page of the portal; the availability of help mechanisms and FAQs; possibility to submit a question/feedback; availability of forums and online registration, common design on every page of the portal;

- Availability of special services: customization tools ("My portal"), access for people with disabilities, tools for online translation;

- Statistics of site visits: the number of visitors per month; average time spent at the portal during a specified period; dynamics of page downloads per month;

- The speed of downloading: downloading time for various types of channels (dedicated line, modem, etc.);

- Degree of consumer satisfaction: on the basis of analysis of the "feedback" tool, online and offline polls related to the quality of services and user expectations.

The adequacy of PRIOR **administrative and organizational structure** to its aims and objectives will be assessed by the PRIOR Supervisory and Coordination Boards at their regular meetings. The structure could be modified on the basis of their feedback and recommendations, and the changes will be reflected in the annual reports.

PRIOR Expert Council will regularly monitor the quality, degree of support and efficiency of implementation of **PRIOR projects and activities** . The policy for PRIOR project portfolio and Action Plan formation as well as the procedure of project selection could also be altered on the basis of the recommendations provided by the Expert Council.

The assessment of the effectiveness and efficiency of PRIOR **marketing and financial programs** will be based on the following criteria:

- The number of projects in PRIOR portfolio supported by sponsors and investors;

For additional analytical, business and investment opportunities information,
please contact Global Investment & Business Center, USA
at (202) 546-2103. Fax: (202) 546-3275. E-mail: rusric@erols.com

- The amount of funds accumulated for the implementation of PRIOR projects, primarily those conducted by the RuDG and regional gateways;

- The quantity and quality of coverage of PRIOR activities in the media;

- The amount of investments attracted to different regions of Russia as part of PRIOR activities and the number of investors;

- The number of agreements completed at the RuDG market places and e-Procurement sites; the volume of interest for these transactions paid for the support of PRIOR activities.

General results of PRIOR work accomplished in the main lines of its activities will be discussed at its annual conferences.

The present document serves as a starting point for a whole system of targeted efforts undertaken by all development forces in Russia for the development of the Information Society and Knowledge Economy. The core of this Strategy is forming an equitable partnership of the key forces driving the e-development: government, business, civil society, sponsors and investors. This partnership is based on the idea of a widespread use of ICT for life and work, which is expected to ensure the following socio-economic effect:

- Reducing the digital gap as a result of broadening public access to the major sources of information and social services;

- Forming new public social culture, where people are actively involved in adopting and implementing decisions influencing life of a society as a whole;

- Increasing government transparency and reducing budget expenditures due to the implementation of e-Government methods; and

- Improving standard of living due to the production and consumption of high-quality products and services created with the use of modern ICT.

The planned PRIOR activity deals with all of the above issues and is rather sensitive of responding to the modern development trends and Russia's vital needs.

In order to ensure a more dynamic transition to the Information Society, it is important to achieve mutual understanding between all the development forces, to study and disseminate most successful experiences and lessons learned, to organize exchange of best practices and innovations at the international and national levels, to organize programs and projects for the Information Society and Knowledge Economy development on the national, regional and local levels. PRIOR will complete these tasks through the use of the Russian Development Gateway and regional development gateways integrated in an effective network, through conducting regular conferences and workshops, informational, analytical and awareness raising activities.

PRIOR defines its role as a politically and economically neutral voluntary association of organizations and individuals willing to make a feasible contribution to the Russia's development. Each member of the Partnership has the right to participate in making key decisions via PRIOR collegial governing bodies – the Supervisory Board, the Coordinating Board, and the Expert Council.

PRIOR activity is not aimed at competing with any initiatives, projects and programs of public, private and non-commercial sectors; on the contrary, it strives to rationalize and complement efforts undertaken in the country through modern interaction and information exchange technologies.

PRIOR specific feature is an active promotion of the Information Society principles and technologies to the Russian regions through the creation of regional partnership networks, selection and support of the most prospective e-Development projects dealing primarily with:

- Implementation of the national strategy of Russia's transition to the Information Society and respective strategies and programs on the regional and local levels;

- Promoting development of the legal basis for the Information Society, information processing and transfer infrastructure; efficient national innovative system, system of "knowledge workers" training, and creating socially relevant information resources and services;

- Practical realization of concepts and technologies of the Information Society, such as participatory governance, e-Government, Networked Society, e-Business, Distant Learning, Digital Library, etc.; and

- Intensive dissemination of innovations, knowledge and practical experience in the sphere of development on the international, national, regional, and local levels.

This Strategy represents a framework, which shall be further improved and developed with the active involvement of partners in the course of PRIOR activities development.

1. The present document defines the **major development communities** as government, business, civil society, research and education community, donors and investors.

2. The **Information Society** is understood as a stage of development of the modern civilization that is characterized by the increasing role of information and knowledge in life of a society, growing share of telecommunications, information products and services in gross domestic product (GDP), creating global information infrastructure to provide effective information interaction for the people, widespread access to the world information resources and satisfying people's social and personal need in information products and services. The notion of e-development or Information Society development refers to:

- Intensified and expanded use of knowledge and information in the economic and social spheres;

- Shift in the relative balance of the public production sectors towards the increased share of the service sector in terms of the number of those employed and its GDP share;

- Evolving to the human-oriented and politically unbiased social state wherein the type of resources used is changed, the influence of professionals is increased, and the traditional social structures are modified.

3. There are many definitions of **Knowledge-Based Economy**, or **Knowledge Economy**, or **k-Economy**. The definition used in these documents is one offered by one of the leading specialists in the field - Karl Dahlman, Program Director of Knowledge Products and Outreach division of the World Bank: "A type of economy where innovation - the creation, acquisition and dissemination of knowledge - is the major driving force of economic and social development."

4. The classical interpretation views **development** as a non-reversible, directed, plausible change of the material and ideal objects. Only the simultaneous presence of the aforementioned qualities separates the development processes from all other changes. As a result of development process, the qualitative shift takes place, which signifies of a modification of structure or composition of an

For additional analytical, business and investment opportunities information, please contact Global Investment & Business Center, USA at (202) 546-2103. Fax: (202) 546-3275. E-mail: rusric@erols.com

object (i.e., appearance, transformation or loss of its elements and relationships.) In the context of this document, the concept of "development" is used to mean "information society development."

5. The present section utilizes the analytic materials included in the Program of Medium-Term Socio-Economic Development of the Russian Federation (2003-2005).

6. More detailed data on Russia's readiness for the Information Society and Knowledge economy development are presented in the analytic report "ICT Infrastructure and e-Readiness Assessment for Russian Federation", prepared by the Institute of the Information Society with financial support of *info*Dev program of the World Bank (grant # ICT 018) in 2003.

7. The Federal Program "e-Russia" and the Doctrine on Information Security of the Russian Federation.

8. Federal law "About Information, Informatization and Information Protection" and other laws.

9. Growth in 2002 by 10.3% as compared to the 2001 index.

10. According to the available estimates, the potential growth of the Russian economy blocked by excess administrative barriers amounts to 5-7% of GDP; excess initial inspection (activity licensing) contribute to that considerably - for example, in the European Union 4% of the product range is subject to obligatory certification, in Russia this share reaches 80%, the number of licensed types of activity varies in the EU countries from 30 to 90, in Russia it exceeds 200.

11.For example, the level of software, audio and video piracy in Russia reached 88% in 2000, according to the data achieved by BSA; in 2002 this level decreased only by 1%.

12. The share of innovation-active enterprises in the Russian economy reached in 2000 only 8.8%, whereas average EU value reached 50% (in Germany, for example, over 60%).

13. The share of expenditures on R&D in GNP varies about 1% (in developed countries - from 2 to 4%, in USSR in 1990 it slightly exceeded 2%), in constant prices expenditures on research and development dropped three times as compared to 1990, the number of workers in the scientific sector decreased more than twice and continues to fall.

14. In terms of the volume of knowledge received from the outside, in China this indicator is 70 times higher.

15. Important components of **business environment** should include the system of venture financing, efficient system of intellectual property protection, developed infrastructure of innovations support and others.

16. In 2000, the World Bank put forward an initiative of creating an international Development Gateway and announced as part of the *info*Dev program the competition for creating country gateways (CGs), the independent partners of the Development Gateway with over 70 participants in two years. National partnerships with representatives of the main driving forces of the Information Society development - government, business, civil society - are being created for the gateways formation. Today it is a network of over 50 national partnerships integrating representatives from public, nonprofit, and private sectors. Their mission is contributing to the innovative and effective use of the Internet and other ICT to reduce poverty in their countries and gaining sustainable development. CGs are viewed internationally as tools for creating development communities, their efficient cooperation, and realization of their community and business interests corresponding with the stated mission.

17. **Knowledge worker** of the 21st century is any worker operating in the networked, fully integrated world. They are not simply carrying out repetitive operations but formulating and implementing their

For additional analytical, business and investment opportunities information,
please contact Global Investment & Business Center, USA
at (202) 546-2103. Fax: (202) 546-3275. E-mail: rusric@erols.com

understanding of the task at hand. This can be reflected in the form of critical data analysis, decision making (including key decisions), innovative actions or giving their interpretation of the data available for other people. They can use data developed by integrated systems, analyze these data, and apply them for the benefit of both a particular enterprise and society on the whole (Shawn Lake, Content and Technologies Director, Global Trade Training, Republic of South Africa).

18. **Governance** - the process when organizations, enterprises and groups shape their interests and needs, enjoy their rights and opportunities and complete their obligations, and resolve emerging disputes. This leads to the search of methods helping knowledge societies to use more effective, transparent and active forms of governance on the local, regional, national and global levels.

19. **e-Government** - metaphor describing interaction of public authorities and society with the use of ICT.

20. **Networked Society**- society, wherein a considerable part of information interaction is carried out via information and communication networks.

21. **e-Business** - conducting business with the help of electronic documentation processing in the Internet. It includes presence of the company's Internet site, virtual shop, company management system, use of e-Advertising, marketing, "business to business" or "business to customer" model.

22. **Distant learning** - new type of completing the learning process based on the use of modern ICT allowing distance learning without direct, personal contact between the teacher and the student.

23. **Digital library**- distributed information system allowing safe and efficient use of dissimilar collections of e-documents (text, graphics, audio, video, etc) via global data transfer network in the form that is convenient for the end user.

24. Creation of the pilot network of regional development gateways is planned to be commenced in 2003 as part of the Federal Program "eRussia (2002-2010)", Program Event #11.

25. More exact formulation of this provision in terms of a possibility and, in some cases, necessity to use in-house products, which are not open software, is assigned to the PRIOR Expert Council. Until such a formulation is available, the current one is used.

26. It was decided to establish PRIOR as a voluntary public-private association without founding a separate legal entity.

STRATEGIC OFFICIAL MATERIALS AND BUSINESS OPPORTUNITIES IN INTERNET AND ICT DEVELOPMENT

"ON AMENDMENTS TO THE FEDERAL TARGET PROGRAM" ELECTRONIC RUSSIA RF GOVERNMENT RESOLUTION

dated 10 September 2009 N 721

THE PASSPORT OF THE FEDERAL TARGET PROGRAM "ELECTRONIC RUSSIA (2002 - 2010 YEARS)"

Name - the federal target program "Electronic Russia Program (2002 - 2010 years) "

Date of decision - the disposal of the Government of Russia the development of the Federation of February 12, 2001 N 207-p; Program, the date of its Government resolution approval of the Federation of January 28, 2002 N 65

State - Ministry of Communications and Mass Media Employer - Coordinator Russia Programs

Government - Ministry of Communications and Mass Media

Customers Program Russia, Ministry Economic Development, Federal Agency for Information Technology, Federal Education Agency, the Federal Service of Russia

Major developers - Ministry of Communications and Mass Media
Program of Russia, Ministry of Economic Development

The purpose of the Program - the formation in Russia e-government infrastructure necessary for: improve the quality of relationships state and society by increasing citizens access to information about
activities of public authorities, expediting of state and municipal services, introduction of uniform service standards population;

improve inter interaction and the internal organization of public authorities through the organization of inter - information exchange and ensure effective use of authority information and telecommunication technology, efficiency management and implementation of information telecommunication technologies
activities of public authorities;

improve systems information and analytical support good governance, timeliness and completeness of control activities of public authorities

Challenges Program - designing the infrastructure for electronic Governments a technology platform e-government infrastructure in the basis of a single national operator e-government infrastructure; creation of functional elements e-government infrastructure;

development of inter-and Interdepartmental Information interaction, providing integration government information systems
based technology platform e-government infrastructure;

creation of a unified state system control effectiveness of public authorities for ensure socio-economic development of RF-based technological platform infrastructure electronic government;

For additional analytical, business and investment opportunities information, please contact Global Investment & Business Center, USA at (202) 546-2103. Fax: (202) 546-3275. E-mail: rusric@erols.com

organizational and methodological support building infrastructure of electronic Government

Key targets - the number of projects developed by the introduction indicators and information and telecommunication indicators of technology in the activity of State power in accordance with common standards;

number of federal agencies public authorities, with subscriber access points to information system interagency electronic workflow;

of state information resources to which access is provided at inter-agency level;

number of software and hardware solutions, provide an automated exchange
between individual government information systems;

The number of established software and hardware complex information management system consolidated register of public services;

number of public authorities, equipped with workbenches places, providing access to the consolidated
roster of public services;

number of commissioned software and hardware solutions ensuring provision public services to citizens and organizations using electronic Communications;

The number of established centers in the situational higher bodies of state authority;

The number of established regional clearing houses;

The number of established automated jobs, providing access to electronic document management system in Presidential Administration Federation and the Staff of the Government
Russia;

number of standard software developed solutions support the execution of their functions
public authorities and bodies local government;

number of standard software solutions, implemented under co-financing regions of Russia and municipalities;

number of state and municipal services, automated based on a single portal for government and municipal Internet services, as a percentage of their
total;

number of centers of public access to information about the activities of public authorities and their services, provided in electronic form;

number of embedded information systems a multi-center support state and municipal services;

number of certifying centers within in the unified network of certifying centers;

number of interagency information systems that use the infrastructure electronic government;
number of public authorities,
connected to a single state control system performance activities of public authorities;

readiness system and technical projects for the creation and operation of territory of Russia e-government infrastructure; number of organized channels of communication for connectivity infrastructure e-government and bodies state power to a single telecommunications network

For additional analytical, business and investment opportunities information,
please contact Global Investment & Business Center, USA
at (202) 546-2103. Fax: (202) 546-3275. E-mail: rusric@erols.com

The number of established centers data in a distributed infrastructure All-Russia State information center;

The number of established call-center Service (departmental and regional);

number connected to the information systems, the official site of the state purchases on the Internet and public municipal customers, ensuring its content;

number of developed functional subsystems, and (or) related automated systems for the official site procurement on the Internet;
proportion of the official websites of the information in which fully meets the requirements legislation on Russia disclosure of information about activities of state authority;

proportion of public authorities, fulfilling requirements for access of citizens and organizations through official sites of the Internet to the law of Russia Federation of information;
number connected to the automated
information processing system information
bankruptcy of state and municipal
information systems, providing its
content;

number of developed functional subsystems, and (or) related automated systems for automated information information processing system of bankruptcy;
number of developed functional subsystems, and (or) related automated systems for automated information of public services in the area estate;
number of regions in which introduced typical automated information system that ensures the maintenance of the Register small business;
number of state and municipal civil servants have improved qualifications in the use of Information Technology

Dates and milestones - 2009 - 2010 years

Program implementation
The amount and sources - the total amount of financing programs for
funding 2002 - 2010 years will be Program 21,237.902 million rubles (in prices respective years), including:

the expense of the federal budget --   19,952.441 million rubles;

at the expense of budgets of Russia -   1,285.462 million rubles.

Total funding programs 2002 - 2008 years was 15,299.56 million rubles (in prices respective years), including:

at the expense of federal budget -   14104.56 Million rubles, of which:
research and development work --   1,559.81 million;
other needs -   5,863.18 million;
state investments --   6,681.57 million;
at the expense of budgets of Russia -   1195 million rubles.
Total funding for the Program 2009 - 2010 years will be 5,938.342 million rubles (in prices respective years), including:
the expense of the federal budget --   5,847.881 million, of which:
research and development work --   437.15 million;
other needs -   2,888.645 million;

**For additional analytical, business and investment opportunities information,
please contact Global Investment & Business Center, USA
at (202) 546-2103. Fax: (202) 546-3275. E-mail: rusric@erols.com**

state investments --	2,522.086 million;
at the expense of budgets of Russia -	90.462 mln rubles

Expected final - the infrastructure of electronic results of the government, providing access to Program and performance information on the activities and services of socio-economic state authorities in electronic form, effective interagency electronic interaction and unified state control effectiveness of the bodies State, which will reduce level of administrative burden on organizations and citizens, and give an annual Save up to 10 billion rubles;

improving budget the introduction of information and telecommunication technologies activities of public authorities 10 per cent;

reduce the cost of public authorities to organize the exchange of information on inter-ministerial level to 25 per cent;

reduce the administrative burden on citizens and organizations associated with submitted to state authorities the necessary information, reducing number of forced recourse to the public authorities to obtain public services and reducing the time expectations for services by 10 percent;

guaranteed level openness of information government, raising trust and collaboration, reduce costs time to implement the citizens of Russia Federation of his constitutional rights and responsibilities;

improving efficiency and quality decisions, reduce costs organization of administrative and managerial
processes in government;
development of the project long program "Information Society (2011 - 2018 years) "events aimed at continuing the formation of Russia e government in 2011 - 2018 respectively, that ensure the safety of public investment and long-term economic effectiveness of the implementation obtained from Program implementation results;

increasing demand for information and telecommunication technologies by public authorities and, as Consequently, the growth of their proposals with Russian manufacturers by up to 10 percent per year through increased preparedness and motivation organs public authorities for use in its activities today information and telecommunication technologies, as well as by promoting development of programs and projects, departmental informatization; provide a single information space of the country through the development National Information and telecommunications infrastructure state needs and connect to it public authorities throughout territory of Russia

I. CHARACTERISTICS OF THE PROBLEMS ADDRESSED BY THE PROGRAM, THE RATIONALE FOR ITS DECISION PROGRAMMING METHODS

With the development and penetration of information and communication technologies in all spheres of public life public authorities are increasingly using them to effectively manage its activities and improve the quality of services provided to the public. The use of such technology in the modern information society is essential to ensure compliance with government expectations and needs of the population.

Today, Russia has all the necessary prerequisites for improving the performance of the state apparatus in the widespread use of information and telecommunication technologies. In general, solved problems related to the formation of organs of state power base of modern information technology infrastructure. Basically meet the needs of public authorities in computer engineering, are formed geographically distributed departmental computer network. Many government agencies set up workstations, providing access to the Internet. Some of the federal bodies of state power and bodies of state power of RF subjects successfully implemented programs and projects of public sector information systems that provide automated data collection, processing and storing data necessary for proper and effective discharge of their duties. There is experience of the successful exchange of data electronically between departments and between government agencies, communities and organizations. Many public authorities set up Internet sites that host the normative legal, news and background information related to the activities of these bodies. In the framework of administrative reform is working systematically to describe the functions and processes of public administration, analysis of opportunities for their optimization and improvement through the application of modern technologies. At the federal level, prepared regulations governing access to information of public authorities and local authorities.

However, despite rapid growth in demand of public authorities for information and telecommunication technologies, their implementation do not always lead to improving the quality of the functioning of the state apparatus, and often reinforces the negative impact of ineffective management and administrative processes.

There remain significant differences between the public authorities on the use of information and communication technologies in their activities, the results of such technology are mainly local departmental nature. There is a serious backlog of bodies of state power of RF subjects of federal authorities in terms of information technology for administrative and management processes, as well as the level of development of information technology infrastructure and government information systems. Many federal authorities do not have comprehensive programs the introduction of information and telecommunications technologies and improve on their basis of their activity, which leads to wasteful spending. The bulk of budgetary spending in the acquisition and installation of computer and networking equipment, which indicates an insufficient level of development and use of applied information systems, as well as the dominance of the technological approach to problem solving information. At the same time public authorities in most cases overlap with the development of standard software solutions. Purchase and implementation of software products without the use of open standards, which leads to the incompatibility of software and hardware solutions, the impossibility of communication between different government information systems.

At the initial stage of development are the main public information systems that contain account information about key sites of public administration. Only in some government agencies are deployed and used by the integrated electronic document management systems. In a few cases introduced information-analytical systems for planning and monitoring the activities of public authorities. There are automated procedures for collecting and processing information necessary for planning and performance targets of government bodies, as well as a unified information system of monitoring their achievement. There is no unified system of planning and monitoring effectiveness of government programs and projects.

New on the Web sites of government practically implemented promptly update the information and does not contain the necessary information about the procedure and conditions for obtaining public services, which also complicates the interaction of citizens with authorities. In this rapidly evolving inadequate public infrastructure (public) access to sites of public authorities and other means of reference and support services.

Getting people and institutions of public services, as well as information related to the activities of public authorities, in most cases requires their personal appeal to state authorities, the submission of queries and other information in paper form. This leads to time-consuming and creates a significant inconvenience to the public.

There is no necessary legal and regulatory framework, as well as standards and regulations of public authorities to the population, organizations and other public authorities required information. Not established infrastructure, ensuring information security of electronic forms of interaction between the public authorities themselves, with the people and organizations. There are no mechanisms available

For additional analytical, business and investment opportunities information, please contact Global Investment & Business Center, USA at (202) 546-2103. Fax: (202) 546-3275. E-mail: rusric@erols.com

to ensure the "digital trust" in a system of certifying centers that use the technology of electronic digital signature. Created certifying centers are not integrated in the domains of mutual trust, their services are actually available to the public and organizations. In electronic form does not provide services in the field of Notaries, placement of regulatory legal acts on the Internet is not an official publication, etc.

Used public information systems were formed by individual state authorities in the absence of a unified regulatory framework governing these processes, and overall coordination. Information within them are often not available to other authorities for operational use, which in practice leads to considerable time delays in information sharing at the interagency level, its multiple and overlapping collection of individual systems. As a result, these information systems contain information varying degrees of relevance and reliability. In this part of the information is not updated promptly, which also leads to inconsistencies and contradictions contained in these data. Different formats of data storage limit the ability to use automated tools to search and analytical processing of the information contained in various systems. All this reduces the efficiency of the preparation of management decisions and the quality of public services to the public.

Uncontrolled growth of information about citizens, organizations and sites of economic exchange, contained in public information systems, in the absence of effective mechanisms to control its use also poses a threat to civil rights violations.

The lack of a unified infrastructure, standard solutions and standards for data exchange in electronic form at the interagency level, as well as with people and organizations has become particularly relevant as further penetration of information and telecommunication technologies in the socio-economic development and public information systems.

Lack of uniform requirements for the improvement of administrative processes through the use of information and telecommunication technologies, a common approach to the formation of departmental programs in this area, as well as systems for monitoring and controlling the quality of their implementation leads to a lack of effect of the introduction of such technologies and significantly reduces the effectiveness of budget spending this purpose. The situation now in the planning and monitoring the effectiveness of budget expenditures for the introduction of information and telecommunication technologies leading to further differentiation of organs of state power and the inability to ensure the coordinated development of public information systems in accordance with the priorities of the modernization of public administration.

The absence of common requirements in the management of individual programs and projects to introduce information and communication technologies at the level of public authorities reduces the effectiveness and quality of their performance, resulting in a significant number of unsuccessfully completed projects or projects completed in violation of the terms or excess costs. Lack of a common classification used in government information systems, as well as basic standards and recommendations for their implementation in practice leads to the use of inefficient technologies. The overall level of training of public authorities for the ownership of modern information and communication technologies also remains low, which is particularly critical in connection with the implementation of the activities of public authorities increasingly complex integrated solutions.
In order to improve the efficiency of the federal target program "Electronic Russia (2002-2010)" (hereinafter - the Program) in 2008, the Ministry of Communications and Mass Communications of Russia was an analysis of its implementation in 2002 - 2007. The results showed that a significant portion of the activities carried out until 2008, wore overly departmental in nature and was aimed at addressing mainly specialized tasks that do not improve the quality of the relationship between the state and society. Implementation of information systems has led to duplication of the traditional paper-based, making it uneconomical automation, rather than fundamentally changing the concept of information based on freedom of access to information, improve efficiency of service processes and the transfer of the majority of transactions between the state, regional, municipal government, citizens and business in electronic form.

For additional analytical, business and investment opportunities information, please contact Global Investment & Business Center, USA at (202) 546-2103. Fax: (202) 546-3275. E-mail: rusric@erols.com

In this connection directions of state policy in the development and dissemination of information and communication technologies must be determined in accordance with current priorities and objectives of the country.

In 2008, approved a number of normative documents, which determined the direction of Russia in the medium and long term, including the dissemination of information and telecommunication technologies:

Strategy of the Information Society in Russia, approved the request of the President of Russia on February 7, 2008 N Pr-212;

The concept of long-term socio-economic development of Russia for the period up to 2020, approved by the Federal Government on 17 November 2008 N 1662-p;

The main activities of the Government of Russia for the period until 2012, approved by the Federal Government on 17 November 2008 N 1663-p.

Formation in Russia e-government is one of the priorities set out in the Concept of establishing in Russia e-government until 2010, approved by the Federal Government on May 6, 2008 N 632-p. In 2009, the plan was adopted for the implementation of this Concept. However, there are problems, without which the formation of e-government in Russia is impossible:
no systematic e-government projects, providing a complete and effective interaction of all subsystems of electronic government;

you must change the model of information interaction of state and society for the removal of citizens and organizations to address the public authorities, the responsibility for confirmation of the primary rights of applicants and transfer this responsibility to the public authorities;
not carried out optimization of departmental and interdepartmental administrative procedures for the transfer of public services in electronic form;

no corresponding problems of optimization of administrative procedures, uniform standards for establishment and operation of departmental and inter-departmental information systems, standardized technologies and protocols of departmental and inter-electron interactions;
there is no necessary laws providing for the provision of public services in electronic form (laws on electronic document, a single ID and civil registry, etc.);
There is no unified infrastructure for a legally significant electronic interaction through the use of electronic digital signature;

no single technology platform and, most importantly, management systems and e-government infrastructure;

have not developed mechanisms for managing the departmental and regional programs of informatization of public authorities, taking into account the problems of optimization of administrative procedures and the need for funding by the federal executive bodies, bodies of state power of RF subjects, local self-government;
number of targets is an artificial one, weakly associated with the requirements of government customers of the Program and objective results of the implementation of the program.
To solve these problems requires the creation of a single center of decision-making responsibility for:
elaboration of a common ideology and system of the project of introducing electronic government;
developing a regulatory framework necessary for the formation of e-government;

implementation of departmental and regional programs of information, taking into account the need for optimization of administrative procedures based on the introduction of information technologies in the activities of public authorities in the provision of services electronically.

For additional analytical, business and investment opportunities information, please contact Global Investment & Business Center, USA at (202) 546-2103. Fax: (202) 546-3275. E-mail: rusric@erols.com

This situation does not allow for new levels of quality of governance and the provision of public services to citizens and organizations on the basis of information and telecommunication technologies, and significantly reduces the effectiveness of budget spending on the creation and development of public information systems.

Obstacles to more effective use of information and telecommunication technologies in the activities of public authorities, are complex inter-agency in nature and can not be solved at the level of individual public authorities. Their elimination will require significant resources, a coordinated organizational changes and ensure coherence of action of public authorities.

This can be realized only within the program-target approach, aimed as a priority for development and interoperability of government information systems, development of standards and technologies for their interaction, as well as the formation of inter-agency infrastructure for information exchange. The use of program-target method will ensure a focused implementation of state policy in the sphere of information and communication technologies in public administration.

The existing level of conceptual and technical study of these issues can count on the successful implementation of the Program, provided an adequate institutional and resource support. As a result of the Program will be greatly enhanced efficiency of budget funds allocated to the introduction of information and telecommunication technologies in the activities of public authorities.

A possible alternative to using the software method to solve these problems involves the implementation of individual measures at the level of specific bodies of state power. However, such an approach would require establishment of a permanent agreement-making at the interagency level, the adoption of RF Government decisions related to the coordinated development and organization of the interaction of government information systems, as well as funding the development of software solutions that are interagency in nature, and technology adoption in each case.
Implementation of this approach in practice will lead to considerable time delays, excessive load on the participating agencies and will not provide the required intensity, efficiency and complexity of addressing these problems.

The use of program-target method will minimize the risks associated with the implementation of the Program, through the establishment of adequate mechanisms to control the execution of activities. Can distinguish the following most significant risks associated with the implementation of the Program:

risk of lack of quality of public administration from the introduction of information and telecommunication technologies. To minimize the risk of the programs include the formation requirements for information and telecommunication technologies used in government and aimed at achieving the targets of government bodies;
the risk of passive resistance to the spread and use of organs of state power outputs of the Program's activities and lack of motivation. In order to minimize this risk is expected in the performance of individual activities of the Program to form a joint working group with participation of concerned agencies to plan expenditure on information and telecommunication technology and operational coordination of programs and projects. Should also be consolidating the results of the implementation activities of the Program acts of the RF Government and the acts of individual federal government agencies;

risk of low efficiency of program activities, and failure to reach the planned results of its implementation. This risk is minimized by the introduction of a system of program management principles and techniques of project management, mechanisms for independent review of programs (projects, design decisions), full disclosure to the public the results of the Program and the organization of their broad public discussion, as well as strengthening the personal responsibility of employees of public authorities for achieving the planned results of their implementation;

For additional analytical, business and investment opportunities information,
please contact Global Investment & Business Center, USA
at (202) 546-2103. Fax: (202) 546-3275. E-mail: rusric@erols.com

risk of lack of flexibility and adaptability of the Program to changes in the organization and activities of public authorities. In order to minimize the risk of the activities of the Program is expected to include the establishment of a monitoring system using information and communication technologies in public administration and control to achieve the anticipated results of its implementation, to organize a feedback system that provides data on the works performed under the basic needs of public authorities in the field improve the efficiency and quality of their work;

risk of duplication and inconsistency of the work under the Program and other government programs and projects, implementation of information and telecommunication technologies in the activities of public authorities. In order to minimize this risk is planned to implement only the activities of a comprehensive interdepartmental nature. Projects aimed at meeting the needs of individual public authorities in information and telecommunication technologies will be implemented in the implementation of departmental and regional programs such technology;

the risk of passive resistance of individual citizens and public organizations to the activities of the Program for the creation of information databases, registers, classifications, a single identifier citizens on the ethical, moral, cultural or religious reasons. In order to minimize this risk, the working group of experts on harmonization of the regulatory framework is expected to include religious leaders, intellectuals, experts on public morality and ethics. To assist state and local government services to citizens and organizations, for whatever reasons, consider obtaining services in electronic form for themselves unacceptable, is expected to maintain availability of services in the traditional way.

II. THE MAIN PURPOSE AND OBJECTIVES OF THE PROGRAM, DEADLINES, MILESTONES, TARGETS AND PERFORMANCE INDICATORS FOR ITS IMPLEMENTATION

The main objective of the Program in 2009 - 2010 years is the formation in Russia e-government infrastructure needed for:

improve the quality of relations between the state and society through the empowerment of citizens' access to information about the activities of public authorities, expediting the delivery of public and municipal services, the introduction of uniform standards for services;

enhance interagency cooperation and the internal organization of public authorities through the provision of interagency information sharing and effective use of public authorities of information and telecommunication technologies, improving the management of the introduction of information and telecommunication technologies in the activities of public authorities;
enhance the effectiveness of information and analytical support to good governance, efficiency and completeness of control over the activities of public authorities.
To achieve the objectives of the Program to ensure the following tasks:
Designing e-government infrastructure;
creation of technological infrastructure of e-government platform based on a single national operator of e-government infrastructure;
creation of functional elements of e-government infrastructure;
development of intra-and inter-agency information exchange, ensuring the integration of government information systems based on technology platform e-government infrastructure;
creation of a unified state system of monitoring performance of government bodies to ensure the socio-economic development of RF-based technology platform e-government infrastructure;
organizational and methodical support of the formation of e-government infrastructure.
Planned in 2009 - 2010 years of analysis of information processes in public administration and public service delivery and provide a systematic and technical projects for the creation and exploitation in Russia e-government infrastructure.

Also to be established in accordance with the technical project of the technology platform e-government infrastructure (telecommunications network, specialized server platform and network of

For additional analytical, business and investment opportunities information, please contact Global Investment & Business Center, USA at (202) 546-2103. Fax: (202) 546-3275. E-mail: rusric@erols.com

trusted certifying centers of digital signature) on the basis of a single national operator.
By the end of 2010 will be created and put into operation a number of functional elements of e-government infrastructure, in particular multi-functional centers of state and municipal services, a unified portal and a consolidated register of state and municipal services, the centers of public access to information, public authorities and public electronic services, call centers of citizens and organizations, to develop separate functional elements of the program of departmental and inter-agency information.

The Program will be working to ensure open access to information about the activities of public authorities, in particular, modernization and development of official sites of public authorities.
In the direction of the management of program activities will be undertaken work to improve the methodology for determining the target indicators and indicators of its effectiveness. Provided government customers of the Program method for measuring the target indicators:
should be based on the principles of objectivity, independence, measurable target indicators;
have the property comparable results at different periods of the Program.
The ratio of the current targets for the basic targets will be used in the system of quality management system and evaluate the effectiveness of the implementation of both individual events and programs in general.

Main target indicators and performance indicators for the implementation of Program activities in 2009 - 2010 are set out in Annex N 1.

III. SYSTEM OF PROGRAM ACTIVITIES

Provision of program activities from 6 major areas.

1. Designing e-government infrastructure

The objectives of the direction "Designing e-government infrastructure" are the analysis of the development of information and telecommunication technologies, the analysis of information processes of public administration and public service delivery, development of a system project, the technical project on creation of technology platforms and e-government infrastructure, defining the list of necessary laws and regulations to ensure effective establishment and operation of e-government infrastructure.
Within these lines are carried out:
analysis of the development of information and telecommunication technologies and their use by citizens, organizations and public authorities;
analysis of information processes, interagency cooperation, and training systems and technical projects for the establishment and operation on the territory of Russia e-government infrastructure.

Analysis of the level of development of information and telecommunication technologies and their use by citizens, organizations and public authorities

The Concept formation in Russia of e-government until 2010, argues the case for the provision of public services to citizens using modern information and communication technologies. Section II of this concept describes the difficulty of establishing e-government infrastructure in the old architecture of the state, departmental and municipal information systems.
In 2002 - 2008 years the results of the implementation of information computer systems in government were mainly in-house character that does not allow to significantly improve interagency cooperation and improve the quality of public services to citizens.
Using undocumented data formats, protocols, and other private information technology and lack of common classifications, guides and schemes of data limit the ability to use automated tools to search and analytical processing of information in different systems and make it difficult for organizations and citizens to public information systems. This reduces the efficiency of the preparation of management

For additional analytical, business and investment opportunities information,
please contact Global Investment & Business Center, USA
at (202) 546-2103. Fax: (202) 546-3275. E-mail: rusric@erols.com

decisions and compatibility of information systems, which negatively affects the quality of public services provided by organizations and citizens.

The tasks outlined in the Concept of establishing in Russia eGovernment 2010, calls for research and policy analysis, which then will be trained and the system of technical projects to develop e-government infrastructure, further development of e-government infrastructure and a long-term program "Information Society (2011 - 2018 years).

Completed analysis will identify the key requirements of the state and society in the field of high technologies and develop a common vision and strategy for implementation of activities, including in part:

provide citizens with information on the safety and quality of life, including quality standards, the current environmental monitoring, natural resources, domestic animals, as food and industrial products, medicines and their manufacturers, consumer rights, etc.;
creating an enabling environment for open and doing business, including enhancing the competitiveness of Russian enterprises through the establishment of e-commerce systems, public databases, manufacturers, products and intellectual property, offers investors information on the acquisition and the rules of doing business, promotion in foreign markets, marketing automation research, exchange of pirated and counterfeit goods;
increasing use of information and communication technologies in traditional learning, distance learning, training programs, certification and recognition of qualifications, conducting teleconferences, forums, expert meetings, meetings;

creating thematic federal portals devoted to the law, freedoms, rights and responsibilities of citizens in their use of information and communication technologies;

of the federal telecommunications infrastructure that provides broadband Internet access, including those based on wireless technologies, for the majority of citizens and organizations of Russia.
As part of this event will be set up sub regional and departmental information.

The aim of the development of sub regional informatization bodies of the government entities and local governments for the period 2011 - 2018 period is the development of concepts and programs of the regional automation. Under the regional informatization is the process by creating the necessary conditions for the realization of the rights and freedoms of citizens, ensuring social and economic development and efficiency of public administration subject of the RF and local self-government through the use of information technology.

Within the development of the subprogramme will be established types of infrastructure subject of the RF, including:
information and analysis subsystem of electronic government in the region;
functional subsystems of electronic government in the region;

subsystem and subsystem integration of information communication e-government in the region;

subsystem to ensure people's access to socially important information and the formation of open information resources of the region;
subsystem of housekeeping;
subsystem information security of e-government in the region;
integration of information technology infrastructure of the region with the overall information technology infrastructure of e-government at the federal level;

legal and regulatory basis of regional informatization;
organizational, personnel and methodological support for regional informatization.

For additional analytical, business and investment opportunities information,
please contact Global Investment & Business Center, USA
at (202) 546-2103. Fax: (202) 546-3275. E-mail: rusric@erols.com

The development objective of the subprogramme departmental information for the period 2011 - 2018 period is to prepare policy documents to ensure transparency and streamlining of departmental information, as well as improving the implementation and use of information and communication technologies in the activities of federal government agencies for the period 2011 - 2018 period. Under the departmental computerization means the introduction and use of information and communication technologies to improve administrative and management processes in the federal state authorities concerning the provision of public services and performance of public functions.

Within the development of the subprogramme is expected to create conditions for the following tasks: improving the management of departmental information systems; examination of programs and projects, departmental and inter-agency information; formation of a single departmental information technology policy; a system of coordination of budgetary expenditure on departmental information systems; information-analytical and expert support of the Council of Chief Designers of departmental information federal authorities;

methodological support and a system of advice to public bodies on issues related to the improvement of departmental management information systems;

improvement of public procurement for the purposes of information federal authorities; establishing a system of evaluating the effectiveness of departmental information systems; preparation of statistical data on current information and telecommunications technologies; evaluating indicators of sensitivity of information technology to control action, the construction of models depending on the quantitative and structural changes;

definition of the structure and characteristics of information security technology challenges; formation of functional requirements.

Analysis of information processes, interagency cooperation, and training systems and technical project for the establishment and operation on the territory of Russia e-government infrastructure

By 2009, the following was achieved: developed a concept formation in Russia of e-government until 2010, containing the main provisions of the implementation of standard functions of e-government that provide public services to citizens and organizations;

developed requirements for technology, software, linguistic, legal and institutional means to ensure the use of official sites of state bodies and local self-government; developed normative, organizational, methodological and software to the formation and registration schemes for the data used in inter-agency information exchange for the provision of public services in the formation of the system requirements for the use of information and communication technologies in public administration.

In connection with the approval of this concept requires a shift activities of the Program on a systematic approach to designing and implementing the elements of e-government infrastructure. The systems approach provides a unified formulation of technology policy, system of standards and uniform requirements for the effective use and implementation of information and telecommunication technologies in the activities of public authorities.

The purpose carried out in 2009 - 2010 years of activity is the analysis of existing information processes in public administration and public service delivery, interagency and interdepartmental interaction for their support in order to obtain relevant information schemes, descriptions of flow data, the parameters of their functioning, modeling of the light expected quantitative and structural changes.

For additional analytical, business and investment opportunities information, please contact Global Investment & Business Center, USA at (202) 546-2103. Fax: (202) 546-3275. E-mail: rusric@erols.com

In the implementation of these activities are expected to:
a study of existing information processes of public administration and public service delivery as a complex socio-economic systems;

diagnostic analysis of information processes to their subsequent multi-criteria optimization;
preparation of descriptions of optimal processes, provision of public services, interagency and interdepartmental interaction for their support;

determination of the composition, structure and performance of functional tasks in the framework of e-government;

determination of the composition and structure of software for the automation of information processes of state services, technology problem solving;
formation of functional requirements, common classifications and guides the process of providing public services;

development of technical solutions for creating information management, logical database structures; detailed design of the technological platform and e-government infrastructure, including the structure and interface elements and subsystems.

2. Creating the technological infrastructure of e-government platform based on a single national operator of e-government infrastructure

The most effective way of solving the problem of the formation of e-government is the creation of the state of the operator of the technological platform of electronic government (perhaps with the use of public-private partnership) for the functioning of e-government infrastructure, built on the basis of this technology platform.
Within the specified direction is carried out:
telecommunications infrastructure of e-government on the basis of a single operator;
creation of a distributed infrastructure of all-Russia public information center on the basis of a single operator;
a network identity centers on the basis of a single operator;
establishment of management systems and e-government infrastructure on the basis of a single operator.

Telecommunications infrastructure of e-government on the basis of a single operator

Concept formation in Russia of e-government until 2010, provides public services to citizens using modern information and communication technologies. Section II of this concept describes the key elements of e-government infrastructure.

One of the key elements in building a technology platform is the creation of a specialized telecommunications infrastructure based on a single operator.
To fulfill the goals of this concept requires the inclusion in the Program for 2009 - 2010 years, a number of activities.

As part of activities in 2002 - 2008 years of telecommunications infrastructure design and construct for each departmental public information system separately, which leads to duplication of investments, the cost of commissioning, as well as operating costs, the inability to compare the financial performance of the project.

When you create a single telecommunications infrastructure will be a full outline of the project, which will provide necessary for nation-wide scale reliability, safety and quality of data transmission.

For additional analytical, business and investment opportunities information,
please contact Global Investment & Business Center, USA
at (202) 546-2103. Fax: (202) 546-3275. E-mail: rusric@erols.com

As a single operator's telecommunications infrastructure is expected to identify an organization with an extensive network of branches in the territory of the RF subjects, a license to perform work programs, the necessary competence, positive experience of implementing large-scale public projects and successful financial performance in the capital structure and management of a leading part take citizens and resident organizations Russia.

The purpose of this activity is to create a secure telecommunications network, providing automatic information interaction between the functional components of e-government infrastructure. Telecommunications infrastructure should ensure equal and safe access to the functions of e-government for geographically distributed user locations in all regions and municipalities in Russia. As part of the activities envisaged:

organization of a unified telecommunications center for the connection of distributed subscribers; Organization of the required number of telecommunications links to connect geographically distributed user locations;

providing terminal equipment of telecommunication channels;
Installation requires a computer and peripheral equipment;
installation of the necessary system and application software;
operation of telecommunication network systems management and security.

Creating a distributed infrastructure of all-Russia public information center on the basis of a single operator

RF Government Decree of 25 December 2007 N 931 "On some measures to ensure the information interaction of state bodies and local authorities in providing public services to citizens and organizations was set up all-Russia State Information Center.

By 2009, based on the federal government created prototypes of software and hardware systems, and identifying federal information centers and perfected the technology of their interactions within the center, purchased and installed the necessary computer and network hardware and licensed software. On the platform of all-Russia public information center established and operated in a mode of experimental operation of internet-portal of public services, implementing the model provision of public services in electronic form.

In 2009 - 2010 years to ensure the development of infrastructure of all-Russia public information center in the direction of a geographically distributed network of data centers in accordance with the requirements of the technological infrastructure of e-government, which will be posted certifying centers and sites of inter-electron interactions, as well as software and hardware complex information systems of electronic government.

The Ministry of Communications and Mass Communications of Russia, which is government contracting - program coordinator, responsible for ensuring that activities on the creation, development and operation of all-Russia public information center. Simultaneously, according to the Concept formation in Russia of e-government until 2010 to ensure the provision of federal executive bodies of government services to citizens and organizations through the portal of public services, located in the infrastructure of all-Russia public information center.
As part of the activities envisaged:
prepare building a distributed network of all-Russia public information center and the necessary engineering systems in buildings (electricity, air conditioning, fire alarm and protection, access control and video surveillance, structured cabling system, etc.);

organize a local area network;

For additional analytical, business and investment opportunities information,
please contact Global Investment & Business Center, USA
at (202) 546-2103. Fax: (202) 546-3275. E-mail: rusric@erols.com

organize a storage area network for information systems infrastructure of e-government;
establish the necessary computer equipment system-wide use (servers, workstations, etc.);
establish the necessary system and application software;
place and establish an ongoing access to computerized information systems, developed under the Program and in need of guaranteeing the operation in the long term;
ensure the functioning of management systems infrastructure and security.

Creating a network identity centers on the basis of a single operator

In 2002 - 2008 years of the works on the design and creation of a federal identity center the first level through the use of digital signature, which is now a basic element of infrastructure for electronic commerce, created on the basis of full implementation of the Federal Law "On Information, Information Technologies and Information Protection .

However, the concept of formation in Russia of e-government until 2010, has expanded the use of certifying centers, including them in the essential elements of e-government infrastructure.
To support e-government creates a system of trusted certifying centers to ensure a legally significant electronic interaction through the use of electronic digital signature.

The system of certifying centers must provide the information communication actors (public authorities, communities, and organizations) physical and affordability of services certifying centers, as well as the confidence of participants to the interaction of system reliability.

Creating such a system would provide reliable electronic identification of subjects information interaction, security, reliable delineation of their rights of access to information resources.

As part of this event will provide:

modernization of the Federal certifying center the first level;
a network of regional centers of the trusted identity of the second level.

Establishment of management systems and e-government infrastructure on the basis of a single operator

Given the national importance of electronic government, the scope and territorial remoteness from each other RF subjects, the highest standards of reliability and quality infrastructure for e-government, we need a technology platform consisting of a specialized subsystem that allows for monitoring the health of nodes and elements of the infrastructure in real time and perform actions to restore the efficiency of nodes and elements in case of errors and failures.
The functions of a single operator of e-government infrastructure problems include the operation and management of infrastructure and technological platform for e-government infrastructure.
As part of this event is expected to provide:

determine the level of service to the infrastructure of e-government;
preparing a detailed description of information services;
determination of levels of privacy for users of information systems;
definition of service availability;
Identifying opportunities for scaling;
defining the list of quality parameters of operation, methods and means of control;
Rules for creating backup and data recovery;
Rules for the establishment of customer support, query processing, escalation procedures, the definition of acceptable response time to requests, time troubleshooting, etc.;
establishment of regulations made adjustments to your existing automated information systems.

For additional analytical, business and investment opportunities information,
please contact Global Investment & Business Center, USA
at (202) 546-2103. Fax: (202) 546-3275. E-mail: rusric@erols.com

3. Creating functional elements of e-government infrastructure

The purpose of direction "Creating functional elements of e-government infrastructure is the creation of the functional elements of e-government infrastructure in accordance with the developed system and technical projects.

Within the specified direction, the following activities:
creation and development of information systems for the delivery of public and municipal services on the basis of multi-centers;

establishment and development of regional registries and portals of government and municipal services;

creation of public access to information about the activities of public authorities and their services available via the Internet;

providing regulated access of public authorities, citizens and organizations to information contained in public information systems;

development of call-center services for citizens and organizations;
ensure openness of information on the activities of public authorities and the availability of public information resources for citizens and organizations;
the creation of Russia official site on the Internet to post information on placing orders for goods, works and services for federal needs, the needs of federal entities and municipal needs.

Creation and development of information systems for the provision of public and municipal services on the basis of multi-center

The Concept formation in Russia of e-government until 2010, argues the case for the provision of public services to citizens using modern information and communication technologies. For this purpose, is expected to create special objects in the infrastructure of e-government - multi-functional centers of government and municipal services (hereinafter - the multifunctional centers).
Multi-purpose centers are established to ensure the provision of public and municipal services to the federal executive bodies, executive authorities of RF subjects and local authorities on the principle of "one window". This interagency cooperation necessary for the provision of public services (including necessary approvals, obtaining statements, certificates, etc.) occurs without the participation of the applicant.

As part of the Program for the period to 2009, developed a model of software and technical solution for 2 technology platform that implements the necessary basic functionality and is designed for implementation in multi-centers and networks of multipurpose centers set up in regions across Russia. In addition to the information system model developed software and hardware solution includes user documentation on the system specifications for the information and telecommunications infrastructure, a sample package of normative legal acts necessary for the commissioning and operation of the system, training materials for the preparation and implementation of introduction. Provedeno testing of an automated information system, multi center, as well as prepare for the introduction of an automated information system, multi center in the RF subjects.
Create an information system to provide public and municipal services on the basis of multifunctional centers aimed at improving the efficiency of services, including in part:
provide timely information about the procedure and conditions for providing state and municipal services, as well as the status of their delivery via the Internet, call center people, information kiosks located in the multipurpose center;

For additional analytical, business and investment opportunities information,
please contact Global Investment & Business Center, USA
at (202) 546-2103. Fax: (202) 546-3275. E-mail: rusric@erols.com

reduce the amount of time applicants in the case of state and municipal services in an electronic form;

reduce the number of errors in treatment of applicants to state authorities and local governments in the provision of state or municipal services;

reduce the complexity of gathering the applicant a set of documents required for reservation services, through the use of electronic interaction between the various state authorities, providing government and municipal services based on multifunctional centers.

The main objectives of an information system for the provision of public and municipal services on the basis of multifunctional centers are:

automation of procedures of filing, processing, review applications for state and municipal services, as well as the issuance of the results of state and municipal services;
management of archival data accumulated in the information resources of multifunctional centers during the interaction with the citizens in the provision of public and municipal services;
accounting and monitoring of the actions of the multifunctional centers and executing government agencies involved in the provision of public and municipal services;
provide citizens and organizations with information on events and facts related to the progress of state and municipal services;

control flow of applicants through the organization of electronic pre-appointment;
ensuring the exchange of information with the information systems of public authorities involved in the provision of public and municipal services;
providing information interaction with the regional portal of public services.
As part of this event in 2009 - 2010 years is expected to provide:
development of a model information system that provides for the automation of multi-functional center and its interaction with both the applicants and with the public authorities engaged in the provision of public and municipal services based on multi-center, using information and telecommunications technologies;

replicating the model of information systems for the provision of public and municipal services on the basis of multi-centers;

integration of information systems, multifunctional centers with state and municipal information systems that provide state and municipal services, including information systems for the conduct of a consolidated register of public services, portals, government and municipal services, other information systems.

CREATION AND DEVELOPMENT OF REGIONAL REGISTRIES AND PORTALS OF GOVERNMENT AND MUNICIPAL SERVICES

As part of this event in 2009 developed the concept of portals public authorities on the Internet, has developed a range of methodological, legal documents to ensure the establishment of government services portals and model the software necessary for the functioning of the federal portal and regional portals of public services and maintain registers public services. Typical solutions, including a sample package of normative legal acts could be adapted to each region individually and incorporated into the overall system. The approbation of standard software and hardware solutions to regional portals, and registries of public services in 4 pilot regions of Russia, as well as preparation for the introduction of the 13 regions of Russia.

Develop model solutions can provide:

For additional analytical, business and investment opportunities information,
please contact Global Investment & Business Center, USA
at (202) 546-2103. Fax: (202) 546-3275. E-mail: rusric@erols.com

gathering information on how to assist state and municipal services in electronic form, address, and contact information on state and municipal agencies providing these services;
gathering information on the provision of public and municipal services in electronic form and automated control of the conformity of the performance of regulatory services outlined regulations provide services at the regional or municipal level;

automatic publication of free access to Internet information on the order of state and municipal services, address and contact information about state and local government agencies providing these services on typical municipal, regional and federal government service portals;
recipients of services to access information on the provision of public and municipal services through the Internet;

collect and analyze information on the order of the federal, regional and municipal services in a single information center.

The level of information and telecommunication technologies can begin to make greater use of electronic forms of interaction between state authorities, local governments, citizens and organizations in the provision of public and municipal services. However, the condition of specific sites of public authorities on the Internet does not allow them to use for public services to citizens and organizations.

The aim of this exercise is to provide free access of citizens and organizations to complete, relevant and reliable information on public and municipal services provided by various state authorities and local authorities, as well as the establishment of information systems that provide individuals and organizations to provide data services in the electronic form.
The Concept formation in Russia of electronic government up to 2010 anticipated change in the technological infrastructure for the provision of public services. Instead of individual departmental and regional portals in the Internet has created a technological infrastructure of e-government on the basis of a single national operator and its platform creates a single portal providing government services and other functional elements.
To provide comprehensive information and support to help individuals and organizations on the interaction with the authorities at all levels, including in parts of the state and municipal services, as well as to provide access to state and municipal services provided in electronic form, are public information systems of a consolidated roster of public and municipal services and a single portal of public and municipal services.

To achieve this goal will create a system of regional registries and portals of government and municipal services. To do this, planned to introduce a model of information system of a consolidated roster of government and municipal services, the conduct of federal, regional and municipal registries of services and types of information system operation of regional portals of government and municipal services. In carrying out these works must:

ensure technological ability to gather, store and analyze complete and accurate information on state and municipal services, including services provided by the federal executive bodies, executive authorities of RF subjects and local authorities, its actualization. To solve this problem should be designed and implemented at the federal, regional and municipal levels, the model replicated the software to maintain the registry of public and municipal services. Furthermore, there should be an information system to collect and analyze information sent from the set of registers in the consolidated register of public and municipal services;
implement techniques of the presentation, classification, search and access to information about the procedure and conditions for providing state and municipal services for citizens and organizations on the Internet, as well as provide the ability to control citizens and organizations of the actual performance of the state and municipal authorities, state and municipal services and targets set by

For additional analytical, business and investment opportunities information,
please contact Global Investment & Business Center, USA
at (202) 546-2103. Fax: (202) 546-3275. E-mail: rusric@erols.com

administrative regulations and other laws and regulations. In addition, it is necessary to provide support for feedback from citizens and organizations in terms of addressing the functioning of public services portals, as well as issues of state and municipal authorities, state and municipal services. To solve this problem should be designed and implemented at different levels, types of software for the portal for government and municipal services, as well as ensure its integration with the Judicial authority;

provide unique identification of citizens and organizations for the personalized delivery of public and municipal services in an electronic form and introduce the technology into account citizens' organizations and state authorities, local self-government through the portals of government and municipal services. To solve this problem should be an integration of portals of government and municipal services infrastructure certifying centers;

create and implement technology in the electronic filing of applications and accompanying documents of citizens and organizations in the state authorities and local governments that provide public and municipal services. To solve this problem should be designed and implemented a standard server software based electronic forms that allows configuration, deployment and filling of the electronic versions of documents, as well as ensure its integration with the portal of public services;

ensure the exchange of legally relevant information using inter-electronic exchange between public authorities in the provision of these organs of government and municipal services, based on the use of standardized technologies, protocols, data formats, as well as standard software and hardware tools. To solve this problem should be designed and implemented a standard software for accounting system that integrates all the legal acts, as well as providing information communication between the portal of public services and public authorities and to take account of information both in the presence or absence of a body public authorities own automated information system;
ensure the necessary level of information security for personal data posted or processed in the information system of the portal of public services. To solve this problem it is necessary to develop a model methodology for organizational and technological measures to protect personal data and to implement these activities.

BUILDING THE INFRASTRUCTURE OF PUBLIC ACCESS TO INFORMATION ABOUT THE ACTIVITIES OF PUBLIC AUTHORITIES AND THEIR SERVICES AVAILABLE VIA THE INTERNET

As part of the Program in 2009 established an experienced infrastructure of public access via the Internet to government information resources on the basis of municipal libraries and post offices, community access points are installed in individual subjects of the Federation. This infrastructure of public access is essentially the problem of informing citizens about the activities of public authorities, but by 2009 the public services to citizens and organizations are not provided.
To ensure public access to information about the activities of public authorities and public services provided by them to provide for the establishment of model elements in the infrastructure of public access centers.

During the event, expected to provide:
multiple-use public access centers based in the offices of the federal postal service, regional and municipal libraries, based on access points, set up to provide universal services;
centers of public access or information terminals in the premises occupied by public authorities providing public services to organizations and citizens;
organization of access points of public access to information about the activities of public authorities and public services provided by them placed in the departmental information network or the Internet, including those placed in accordance with federal law on access to information about activities of state bodies and local government;

For additional analytical, business and investment opportunities information,
please contact Global Investment & Business Center, USA
at (202) 546-2103. Fax: (202) 546-3275. E-mail: rusric@erols.com

organization of access points of public access to government services provided in electronic form.

PROVIDING REGULATED ACCESS OF PUBLIC AUTHORITIES, CITIZENS AND ORGANIZATIONS TO INFORMATION CONTAINED IN PUBLIC INFORMATION SYSTEMS

The said action enables deployment of departmental databases and the establishment of a regulated access to the federal executive bodies, executive authorities of RF subjects, other public bodies and local self-government software and hardware of all-Russia public information center.
In 2006 - 2008 years in the framework of this event:

has been developed and the RF Government portal on the Internet;
created a prototype of the portal of the Maritime Collegium of the RF Government on the Internet;
Created and developed parliamentary portal of Russia on the Internet;

established software and hardware solution for monitoring the media for the Administration of President of Russia and the RF Government Staff;

purchased and installed hardware, licensed software for website support priority national projects on the Internet;

implemented design system for monitoring the spread of extremist material on the Internet.
Sites and portals, government agencies on the Internet in accordance with the provisions of the Concept of establishing in Russia e-government by 2010 should provide:
speedy deployment of information related to the activities of a public authority, its organizational structure, address and reference information, regulatory and legal acts regulating the activities of a public authority, information on their ongoing programs and projects, as well as information about the target and actual impact of its activities ;

Publication of a public service providers and the conditions of their production, including the rules of supply, forms of forms and applications, references and guidelines for their completion and delivery of, explanations for non-citizens categories;

organization of interactive communication with citizens through the provision of public services; feedback and processing of applications of citizens.

At the federal level and at the level of each RF subject to post information on the activities of government provides for a single Internet-based portal (the portal of public services), which brings together within a common navigation system sites of government on the Internet.
As part of this event in 2009 - 2010 years would include:

provide sites of government in accordance with legislation Russia, in particular with the requirements for listing of the published information, as defined by the Federal Law "On ensuring access to information about the activities of state bodies and local self-government, as well as in accordance with the technological, policy and linguistic requirements and means of ensuring the use of official government website;

resources to modernize the RF President in the Internet;

develop a new version of the portal of the Government of Russia on the Internet;
modernize portal on the Internet for the Federal Security Service of Russia;
create an information system for the analysis of information on state and local government auctions held for the sale of state property;

For additional analytical, business and investment opportunities information,
please contact Global Investment & Business Center, USA
at (202) 546-2103. Fax: (202) 546-3275. E-mail: rusric@erols.com

a portal of all-Russia public procurement for state needs in the All-Russia State Information Center; create a portal of state, regional and municipal services in the Internet;

DEVELOPMENT OF CALL-CENTER SERVICES FOR CITIZENS AND ORGANIZATIONS

In order to ensure the comfort of citizens and organizations in the public authorities and obtaining the necessary background information to be set up in the event departmental and regional call centers, providing:

reception and processing of telephone calls of organizations and citizens; providing background information on the time and place of reception of citizens by public authorities, phones are responsible for interaction with the citizens of staff, the conditions and procedure for the provision of public services;

routing calls if you need advice staff multifunctional centers of state and municipal services, or consulting staff of a public authority or local government; providing applicants information on the status of requests and the results were of public service.

Ensuring transparency of information about the activities of public authorities and the availability of public information resources for citizens and organizations

The purpose of this activity is to increase the transparency of information on the activities of public authorities (to ensure access by all categories of citizens, organizations and institutions of civil society) and the quality of administrative and management processes by ensuring the transparency of public authorities.

In 2002 - 2008 years in an event concept has been developed and implemented practical measures to ensure the accessibility of government information resources in the context of measures to ensure their integrity and reliability, as well as: conducted annual monitoring of openness of official sites of the federal bodies of executive power in the Internet;

An information system for monitoring the quality of public and municipal services; A method of monitoring the openness and accessibility of information on the official websites of federal bodies of executive power in the Internet;

developed an automated information system registry of official sites of the federal bodies of executive power in the Internet;

developed requirements for technology, software and linguistic tools for use official websites of federal bodies of executive power in the Internet;

Normative legal acts and administrative regulations of the state authorities do not contain rules that fix the requirements for the tools to ensure the availability of information on the activities of public authorities. Against the background of the absence of traditions of openness of government information that leads to the fact that access to information about the activities of public authorities, including the socially significant information (for example, information about expenditure of budgetary funds on the order of public service delivery, data on government information systems), is extremely difficult. In turn, the limited public inquiry to public information and the availability of informal mechanisms to obtain information from stakeholders (government officials, experts, journalists) to promote conservation of the situation.

The described situation, which itself has a negative impact on the quality of life of citizens and the

For additional analytical, business and investment opportunities information, please contact Global Investment & Business Center, USA at (202) 546-2103. Fax: (202) 546-3275. E-mail: rusric@erols.com

state's image in the eyes of citizens and the international community, entails a reduction in the quality of administrative and management processes, and their lack of transparency encourages corruption and other abuses.

As part of this activity is necessary to solve the following tasks:
access of citizens and organizations to relevant and reliable information on the activities of the RF Government and the federal bodies of executive power, placed on the official websites on the Internet;

access via the official Internet sites of relevant and reliable information on how to assist the federal executive bodies of government services to citizens and organizations, as well as templates, forms and forms required to obtain government services;
access of citizens and organizations, through official websites on the Internet for relevant and reliable information contained in public information databases (registers, registers, accounting systems), which are public authorities;

organization of monitoring and verification processes to ensure the effectiveness of public authorities access of citizens and organizations through the official websites on the Internet to the law of information and data.

ESTABLISHMENT OF RUSSIA OFFICIAL SITE ON THE INTERNET TO POST INFORMATION ON PLACING ORDERS FOR GOODS, WORKS AND SERVICES FOR FEDERAL NEEDS, THE NEEDS OF FEDERAL ENTITIES AND MUNICIPAL NEEDS

Since January 1, 2010 shall come into force amendments to the Federal Law "On Procurement of goods, works and services for state and municipal needs," involving placement of information on state and municipal orders for a single portal all-Russia public procurement in Internet.
Public portal of public procurement on the Internet is an information system of national significance and should be established on the basis of highly reliable and high-performance industrial technologies.

In accordance with the Federal Government Oder on 20 February 2006 N 229-P to maintain and administer a public portal for government and municipal purchases on the Internet by the Ministry of Economic Development.

By 2009, have been developed conceptual design and prototype the official site of Russia on the Internet to post information on placing orders for goods, works and services for federal needs, the needs of federal entities and municipal needs, the technical design of all-Russia portal for government and municipal purchases on the Internet, the technical design of software and system platforms, methods of acceptance activities of hardware-software complex, technical project on the subsystem information security, technical regulations of the portal operation of all-Russia public procurement on the Internet, as well as testing conducted and carried the load testing of the prototype of the portal of all-Russia public procurement on the Internet.

As part of this event in 2009 - 2010 years would include:

creation of a pilot technology platform to verify that software and technical solutions proposed to use the portal for all-Russia public procurement on the Internet;

develop a prototype of the portal of all-Russia public procurement on the Internet, which includes such information subsystem of all-Russia official site on the Internet, as a subsystem of analysis and processing, forecasting, roster management subsystem unscrupulous suppliers, subsystem roster of complaints, the subsystem order placement, and others;

For additional analytical, business and investment opportunities information, please contact Global Investment & Business Center, USA at (202) 546-2103. Fax: (202) 546-3275. E-mail: rusric@erols.com

refinement and the introduction of commercial operation of the portal of all-Russia public procurement on the Internet and its subsystems.

DEVELOPMENT OF INTRA-AND INTER-AGENCY INFORMATION EXCHANGE, ENSURING THE INTEGRATION OF PUBLIC INFORMATION SYSTEMS-BASED TECHNOLOGY PLATFORM E-GOVERNMENT INFRASTRUCTURE

In order to improve the quality and efficiency of public administration is required to carry out work to ensure prompt interdepartmental interaction of public authorities in electronic form as part of their duties.

Under the direction "The development of intra-and inter-agency information exchange, ensuring the integration of public information systems-based platform technology infrastructure of e-government", the following activities:

creation of a secure system of interdepartmental electronic document;
ensuring the provision of public services in electronic form, including using the Internet;
integration of public information systems within the specific tasks of government;
a system of information and analytical support for special purposes;
development of information technology support of the Administration of the RF President, RF Government Staff, the Federal Assembly;
creation of a unified federal information system information about bankruptcy;
creating a single portal of state real estate cadastre and a single state register of real estate rights and transactions;

translated into electronic form the provision of public services in the area of notification for the registration of small and medium-sized enterprises, licensing, declaration and certification of goods, issuing permits to business entities.

CREATING A SECURE SYSTEM OF ELECTRONIC DOCUMENTS

The purpose of this arrangement is to provide information technology infrastructure for information exchange between the Administration of RF President, RF Government Staff and federal legislative and executive branches, as well as for their effective documentation support.
As part of this event is expected to provide:

creation of site-isolated computer networks and secure access nodes in Moscow in accordance with the structure of federal bodies of executive power;

connect segments to the site-nodes of the head of interdepartmental electronic document in the Administration of President of Russia and the RF Government Staff;

creation of regional assemblies secure electronic document management systems;
connect regional nodes protected electronic document management systems to the lead inter-node system of electronic document in the Administration of President of Russia;

expanding and complex configuration headend system of interdepartmental electronic document in the Administration of President of Russia and the RF Government Staff;

introduction of program-technical means to guarantee authenticity and integrity of information transmitted.

For additional analytical, business and investment opportunities information,
please contact Global Investment & Business Center, USA
at (202) 546-2103. Fax: (202) 546-3275. E-mail: rusric@erols.com

ENSURING THE PROVISION OF PUBLIC SERVICES ELECTRONICALLY, INCLUDING ON THE INTERNET

The use of electronic forms of communications for the delivery of public services can significantly expedite and streamline its procurement, to increase access by citizens and organizations, as well as reduce the costs of public authorities to perform those functions.

However, depending on public services and level of development to ensure its provision of departmental information systems, electronic forms of communication may be used at one or all stages of obtaining public services.

Obtaining government services using electronic communications means a complete automation of all associated with their provision of administrative and management procedures.

The greatest effect on the provision of public services in electronic form can be obtained by integrating support appropriate processes of departmental information systems and automation of information exchange between them, if they require the provision of treatment in various organs of state power or interdepartmental cooperation.

The purpose of this activity is to introduce information and communication technologies in the activities of public authorities in order to increase the availability of public services to citizens, including those offered on the Internet.

Due to increased relevance of the tasks carried out in support of 2002 - 2008 years of social reform and public administration settled a number of tasks aimed at improving information transparency of state power of the RF. In particular, projects have been implemented, significantly improved the quality of information resources on the Internet for the President of Russia and the RF Government.

As part of this event in 2002 - 2008, in line with the concept of a system for calling emergency services through a single number "112" on the basis of single dispatch services, municipalities have developed a system for calling emergency services through a single number "112" (Further - the system-112).

System-112 delivers efficient solutions to problems related to security, and disaster situations. Appointment System-112 is to implement the following major tasks:

Organization convenient call emergency services on a "single window" lets you call a person in the event of accident were not thinking about what kind of service he needs and what number you want to use to access it;

improving the response and improve the interaction of emergency services that are accessed the population;

reduce the possible socio-economic damage due to accidents and emergencies (a reduction of deaths and property losses);

providing a single standard of care in emergency situations, regardless of region, Russia or the location in need of assistance;

implement ways to invoke the emergency services in accordance with the European Union rules.

System-112 is expected to deploy in all regions of Russia, its framework the call centers. System-112, created on the basis of single dispatch services, municipalities, will be integrated with the dispatch service emergency services.

In 2006 - 2008 years was carried out development of a unified state automated system for legislative activities of the Federal Assembly and the legislative authorities of RF subjects in the following areas: completion of the prototype software and hardware complex of this automated system;

carrying out work on the integration of the automated system operated in the State Duma of information retrieval system on the Law "The Law for Access members of the legislative process to-date legal information;

informed by the principle of "one window" of citizens on the legislative activities of the Chambers of the Federal Assembly and the legislative authorities of RF subjects, as well as providing them with free access to relevant legal information through parliamentary portal on the Internet.

As part of this event in 2009 - 2010 years would include:

automation of data exchange processes between the various public information systems in the provision of public services electronically, the processing and routing of inter-agency information flows to meet the requirements on information security through the development of a unified

For additional analytical, business and investment opportunities information, please contact Global Investment & Business Center, USA at (202) 546-2103. Fax: (202) 546-3275. E-mail: rusric@erols.com

information technology infrastructure of all-Russia public information center;
develop and test solutions that support the provision of public services electronically, integrate them with government information systems;
modernization and development of departmental information systems to enable the provision of public services electronically, including on the Internet, which financing is carried out with funds allocated by public authorities on the introduction of information and telecommunications technologies;
A nationwide search system for e-government infrastructure;
continued work on the development of functional and spatial deployment of the system-112;
infrastructure to ensure uninterrupted operation of information resources on the Internet for the President of Russia and the RF Government;
completion of the first stage of a unified state automated system of legislative activities of the Federal Assembly and the legislative authorities of RF subjects.

Integration of state information systems within the specific tasks of public administration

The purpose of this activity is to increase the effectiveness of the implementation of public authorities for their assigned functions, requiring rapid interagency cooperation, through the integration of departmental information systems.
To solve this problem would include:
identification of the main challenges and ways of increasing the efficiency of public administration, requiring prompt interagency cooperation, as well as the priorities for their implementation;
Analyzing the needs of public authorities to obtain information on the integrated state information systems;
formation requirements for modernization and development of government information systems based on the analysis prepared by state authorities for feasibility studies;
software design, development and testing of technology-aided information systems of public interaction among themselves;
ensure the establishment and exercise of model design decisions necessary for automated information exchange;
software at the end of the modernization of state information systems, introduction of appropriate technology and software solutions.
In 2006 - 2008 years in the framework of this event:
development of project documents for the creation of the interagency integrated automated information system of federal bodies of executive power, exercising the powers of the state border Russia;
development of project documents for the creation of a unified national information system to ensure transport safety, created in accordance with the Federal Law "On transport security";
created an experimental site based on the data center of state information-analytical system for control of audit bodies Russia, taking into account the infrastructure of the Federal Information Center;
an automated information system support the work of officials of the Administration of the President of Russia;
prepared software and hardware solution for the deployment of an automated information system of the Federal Antimonopoly Service;
prepared software and hardware solution for the deployment of an automated information system of state cadastral services in an electronic form;
A pilot version of the portal system of information disclosure to the municipal register and the Federal Register of the Ministry of Justice of Russia;
prepared software and hardware complex information system of the organization of employment and inform Russian and foreign citizens on the situation on the labor market in Russia;
purchased and installed the necessary computer equipment to create a test area of automated system of interdepartmental cooperation for monitoring potentially dangerous objects Russia for the RF Ministry for Civil Defense, Emergencies and Elimination of Consequences of Natural Disasters.

For additional analytical, business and investment opportunities information,
please contact Global Investment & Business Center, USA
at (202) 546-2103. Fax: (202) 546-3275. E-mail: rusric@erols.com

As part of this event in 2009 - 2010 years would include:
modernization and development of departmental information systems to enable their automated interaction;
creation of an interdepartmental integrated automated information system of federal bodies of executive power, exercising the powers of the state border Russia;
refinement and development of applied systems of public information and analytical system of control and audit bodies of Russia;
development of federal data bank containing information in the field of transport security;
create intranet portal a unified system of information-analytical support of the President of Russia to implement the constitutional powers and the provision of information interaction with government information systems of federal bodies of executive power;
development using the services of All-Russia State Information Center full-featured software-hardware complex federal portal management personnel.

Creating a system of information and analytical support for special

The purpose of the implementation of this exercise is to provide effective information and analytical support to the activities of public authorities in the special period and during an emergency by creating a comprehensive system of monitoring, analysis, forecasting and simulation of socio-economic development, threats to public safety and national security.
As part of this event in 2009 - 2010 years would include:
establishment and development at the federal and regional levels of information-analytical centers for collecting and processing information necessary for effective monitoring of socio-economic environment;
the establishment of the Presidential Administration of Russia, as well as the plenipotentiary representatives of the RF President in the federal districts of the Situation Center, integrated with information and analytical centers to analyze the collected information, preparation of management decisions, forecasting and modeling of the situation in some areas.
The result of the implementation of this activity will enhance the quality, completeness and timeliness of information and analytical support to management decision-making at the leadership level of the country.

The development of information technology support of the Administration of the RF President, RF Government Staff, the Federal Assembly

The main purpose of this event is to create conditions for improved efficiency in public administration through the establishment of protected information and telecommunications environment and the introduction of modern technology in the Administration of RF President, RF Government Staff and the Federal Assembly.
As part of this event in 2009 - 2010 years would include:
creation and development of site-transport and communication systems, including subsystem of dynamic monitoring of their condition;
modernization program-technical means of telecommunications to improve the electronic document;
establishment of central computing systems of automated information systems;
improving information and communication centers for information exchange with the federal bodies of executive power;
creation of complex software and hardware tools for mass processing of documents, including the production and reproduction regulations;
modernization and development of complex software / hardware computer system for the archive documents;
creation of applications of information technology systems, including secure electronic document management system;
creation of certifying centers and the introduction of electronic digital signature;
creation of a technology network access to information and reference, information and analytical and

For additional analytical, business and investment opportunities information,
please contact Global Investment & Business Center, USA
at (202) 546-2103. Fax: (202) 546-3275. E-mail: rusric@erols.com

legal information collections and systems;
establishing systems to ensure information security.

Creating a unified federal information system information on bankruptcy

Entered into force on the Federal Law "On Insolvency (Bankruptcy) establishes mandatory disclosure in the public network information provided by arbitral managers and self-regulating organizations of arbitration managers, as well as other information provided by public authorities.
Bodies of executive power to regulate bankruptcy, receive and store a significant amount of information about organizations in respect of which proceedings have been initiated on bankruptcy and on passage of bankruptcy procedures. However, the bulk provided by the state authorities to official information, including for public disclosure, creditors, debtors and other interested parties is often unavailable.
An account of the arbitration courts of bankruptcy cases are published haphazardly and mostly in print. Information resources that exist in the judicial system in electronic form, maintained regularly and do not contain the full and timely information on the subject.
Thus, a need for a unified federal information system information on bankruptcy in order to ensure the availability of information to be disclosed in the bankruptcy process (including prior periods) for interested persons. Online access to information about the bankruptcy of the entity, in many cases allow for measures to restore the solvency of the debtor and thereby prevent its liquidation by reason of the existing temporary financial difficulties.
Automated information system for information about bankruptcy will promptly disclose information regarding the cases of bankruptcy procedures in cases of bankruptcy, as well as help in ensuring information transparency in the sale of the property of the debtor bankrupt. Information system of information about bankruptcy will provide this information in full, will simplify access to information about bankruptcy for all stakeholders and will contribute to the efficiency of execution by authorized state bodies functions to regulate procedures in cases of bankruptcy and the power to monitor implementation of legislation in this area.
In 2007 - 2008 years of the Program were developed first and the second stage of the automated information system, information about bankruptcy, and prepared drafts of the legal, organizational and administrative documents necessary for implementation of this automated system. Implemented pilot operation of an information system on the entire array of data with a full load.
As part of this event in 2009 - 2010 years is planned to develop an automated information system, information about bankruptcy in the following order:
preventing the use of procedures in cases of bankruptcy, for the unlawful seizure of property of the debtor;
increase openness and transparency of bankruptcy procedures for creditors, the owners of businesses and all stakeholders;
improving information exchange and cooperation between the participants of the process associated with the bankruptcy proceedings;
increasing information transparency institute self-regulation in the field of arbitration managers;
improving the implementation of bankruptcy procedures (shortening of the procedures, improving the level of creditors' claims, reducing the costs of carrying out procedures).
To achieve the objectives of this exercise is necessary to solve the following tasks:
establishment of "single window" for the publication of information about bankruptcy in the automated information system, information about bankruptcy in the printed edition;
refinement of the security arrangements of input, storage and use of information;
introduction of a system for monitoring the implementation of electronic trading in the debtor's property in order to create anti-corruption legal framework in the field of insolvency (bankruptcy);
ensuring the integration of automated information system, information about bankruptcy with the information systems of public authorities carrying out enforcement functions in the field of insolvency (bankruptcy).

Creating a single portal of state real estate cadastre and a single state register of real estate rights

For additional analytical, business and investment opportunities information,
please contact Global Investment & Business Center, USA
at (202) 546-2103. Fax: (202) 546-3275. E-mail: rusric@erols.com

and transactions

As part of the activities in the period before 2009:
an automated information system of state cadastral services in an electronic form;
establish a legislative and organizational support in the provision of electronic public services in the field of cadastre and registration of rights;
created a set of software tools, including portal and support tools for electronic document delivery of public services to provide the State Land Cadastre of the registered land plots (at the federal level and the level of RF subjects), including the direction of the persons concerned with the use of Internet applications for data contained in the State Land Cadastre (for example, the Kirov and the Kemerovo cadastral districts);
The approbation translated into electronic form of administrative regulations the state duty for state registration of rights to immovable property and transactions, including issuing information and communicate with remote instruments.
To provide in electronic form documentary (documentary) background, analytical and other services to citizens and organizations, as well as state authorities and local authorities on the basis of information contained in the State Real Estate Cadastre and the General State Register of rights to immovable property and transactions with it is necessary to establish a single portal of state real estate cadastre and the single state register of real estate rights and transactions with them.
Web-Portal of the State Real Estate Cadastre and the General state register rights to immovable property and transactions with them to ensure that an electronically using the Internet for information about real estate, such as accounting and registration data, reflecting the legal aspect, including the aggregate background and analytical information necessary for the execution of transactions with real estate development and management of territories at the level of federal entities and municipalities.
The purpose of creating a single portal of state real estate cadastre and state register rights to immovable property and transactions with it is the efficiency of delivery to citizens and organizations of public services electronically, as well as providing information to public authorities and local authorities in the implementation of activities related to immovable property.
To achieve this goal within the specified activities would include:
elaboration of regulatory, organizational, methodological, technological and systemic issues in the establishment and operation of a single portal of state real estate cadastre and state register rights to immovable property and transactions with it;
organization of the security of information systems and different levels of access to information of a confidential nature;
security for citizens and organizations, as well as government bodies and local authorities are interested in accessing information relating to immovable property and rights to it, access to accounting and registration information obtaining more specific identification parameters requested information;
training and provide citizens and organizations, as well as state authorities and local authorities access to records and registration information, consolidated at the federal and regional levels to quickly obtain current detailed and aggregated data on real property;
training and provide citizens and organizations, as well as public authorities and local authorities and statistical information and analytical materials generated on consolidated data in a data warehouse appropriate level of accounting and registration information;
design, develop and implement a single portal of state real estate cadastre and a single state register of real estate rights and transactions for the provision of electronic information, reference and analytical services to the public authorities, local authorities, businesses and individuals.

Translated into electronic form the provision of public services in the area of notification for the registration of small and medium-sized enterprises, licensing, declaration and certification of goods, permitting businesses to

As part of the activities in the period before 2009 were created on the Internet specialized information

For additional analytical, business and investment opportunities information,
please contact Global Investment & Business Center, USA
at (202) 546-2103. Fax: (202) 546-3275. E-mail: rusric@erols.com

system "Information portal of small business and a regionally-distributed structure portals supporting small business in the subjects of the Federation as part of a standard software and hardware solutions support the activities of public authorities in RF subjects. Also developed a package of methodological, organizational and normative documents for the transition of federal executive authorities, working in the field of business regulation, the provision of public services electronically. In accordance with Federal law "On protection of rights of legal persons and individual entrepreneurs in the exercise of state control (supervision), and municipal control" and Presidential Decree dated May 15, 2008 N 797 "On urgent measures on elimination of administrative restrictions on doing business "in order to eliminate administrative restrictions on doing business primarily in small and medium-sized businesses need to take steps to predominantly notification procedure start a business, reducing the number of permits required for its implementation, the replacement of (mostly) a compulsory certification of the quality of producer goods declaration.

Currently in business interaction of economic agents with state authorities in the provision of public services, including part of business registration, licensing, declaration and certification of goods, issuing permits to business entities is done using paper documents, significantly reducing the effectiveness of public authorities and entails additional time and financial costs to businesses.

In this case there are problems of the normative, methodological, organizational and technical measures that impede the implementation and transition to the provision of public services electronically.

The main problem is that:

lack of accessible, complete and current information about the procedure and conditions for obtaining public services in the area of admission to business, as well as information about the procedure and how to obtain the subjects of entrepreneurial activities of the various forms of state support;

virtually no overall regulatory framework of public authorities in the field services business in electronic form;

information systems of public authorities, their technological and telecommunication infrastructure is not fully prepared to provide such services throughout Russia.

To solve these problems within the specified events will develop information systems to inform citizens and organizations that receive government services electronically in the field of entrepreneurship, as well as to improve the performance of authorized bodies in this area, including:

Federal portal to the Internet for business support and model information system for management of regional portal of business support to ensure a free and convenient access to the full and timely information about the procedure and conditions for granting state and municipal services, procedures and how to get the subjects of entrepreneurial activities of the various forms of State support to ensure the principle of "one-stop shop for government services in the field of entrepreneurship;

typical information system roster of small businesses - the recipients of state support;

management information system of state support of small businesses and monitoring the effectiveness of government support measures;

information systems which collect, process and review of notices of commencement of the business, including the possibility of realizing their submission in electronic form, beginning in 2011;

model information systems that provide public authorities of public services and public functions, including the licensing of certain types of activities.

5. Creating a unified state system of monitoring performance of government bodies to ensure the socio-economic development of RF-based technology platform e-government infrastructure

The purpose of the direction "Creating a unified state system for monitoring the impact of government bodies to ensure the socio-economic development of RF-based technology platform e-government infrastructure is improving coordination among public authorities to promote socio-economic development of Russia on the basis of unification and automation collection and harmonization of sectoral plans and reporting on their performance, determination of target values of the impact of public authorities and monitoring their achievement.

In 2007, approved the Concept of the state automated information system for management of priority national projects (Government Decree of 24 April 2007 N 516-p), defined the task of automating the

**For additional analytical, business and investment opportunities information,
please contact Global Investment & Business Center, USA
at (202) 546-2103. Fax: (202) 546-3275. E-mail: rusric@erols.com**

collection, processing and reporting on progress in implementing priority national projects .
In this direction are taking steps to develop a single vertically integrated automated information system for monitoring the effectiveness of the federal bodies of state power, bodies of state power of RF subjects and local authorities to meet their key performance indicators for socio-economic development of RF, industrial development, implementation of priority national projects and state programs (State Automated System "Control").
The need to automate the process of information security management implementation of priority national projects and to monitor the impact of the activities of state and municipal authorities is due to:
significant budget allocation;
limited periods of implementation of priority national projects;
organizational and geographical dispersion of executive authorities and organizations involved in the implementation of priority national projects.
The concept of the state automated information system for management of priority national projects means for placing individual program-technical complexes of the use of infrastructure interagency information-technology center of the Ministry of Communications and Mass Communications of Russia.
On this platform by 2009 had developed the following information and analysis subsystem of the state automated system of control:
information system for monitoring the socio-economic development of RF subjects - in the interest of the Government of Russia. The system is designed for monitoring, analysis and socio-economic development and fiscal status of the RF subjects, evaluate the effectiveness of executive authorities of the regions;
monitoring system of industries - in the interest of the Ministry of Industry and Trade of Russia. The system is designed for monitoring and analysis of indicators of the development of industry Russia and individual enterprises of the military-industrial complex on an industry basis, activity, subject of the RF;
information-analytical system for monitoring and analysis of information and communication technologies in public administration - in the interest of the Ministry of Communications and Mass Communications of Russia. The system provides monitoring and analysis of the use of technologies in socio-economic and governance, monitoring programs and projects in the field of communication;
unified inter-agency information-statistical system of state statistics - within the federal target program "Development of State Statistics of Russia in 2007 - 2011 years. The system is aimed at providing users of reliable statistical data, according to international statistical standards;
information-analytical system for monitoring and comprehensive analysis of the implementation of priority national projects - in the interest of the Administration of President of Russia and the RF Government Staff, on the basis of which the preparation of information-analytical materials;
first and foremost an information portal on the preparations for the XXII Winter Olympic Games and XI Winter Paralympic Games 2014 in Sochi.
As part of this event in 2009 - 2010 years would include:
further development of functional elements in the state automated system management, including information systems, project management and monitoring of the implementation of priority public projects and programs - national priority projects, management training for the XXII Winter Olympic Games and XI Winter Paralympic Games 2014 in Sochi, XXVII Summer Universiade 2013 in Kazan, the summit of the Asia-Pacific Economic Cooperation in 2012 in Vladivostok;
development regulations submission of information by public authorities for the purposes of government, their subsequent processing and analysis;
design and development of Federal Information Center program-technical complex, providing an opportunity to collect and analyze the performance of public authorities, including the implementation of priority national projects;
integration of software and hardware complex with the public information system containing data on socio-economic development of Russia;
creation of special jobs to work with management information system for all federal executive bodies and executive authorities of RF subjects, as well as the organization of its content.

For additional analytical, business and investment opportunities information,
please contact Global Investment & Business Center, USA
at (202) 546-2103. Fax: (202) 546-3275. E-mail: rusric@erols.com

6. Organizational and methodological support of the formation of e-government infrastructure

Under the direction "Organizational and methodological support of the formation of e-government infrastructure" would include:
examination established under the Program of the infrastructure of e-government;
a system of management of program activities, departmental and regional informatization;
development of a unified system of planning and monitoring the use of information and communication technologies in the activities of public authorities;
creation of a uniform system of professional development for civil servants applying in their work information and communication technologies to assist state and municipal services.

Conducting examination established under the Program of the infrastructure of e-government

The most important factor in the success and effectiveness of programs and projects in information and telecommunication technologies is to provide a full assessment created under the program design decisions, as well as examination of proposals for government bodies and local authorities to establish a funded from the federal budget program-technical complexes .
The purpose of this activity is to improve the planning of program activities, and quality control results of their performance at the expense of an external independent expertise on all the major stages of projects - from planning and preparation of projects to the stage of making the results of operations.
Carried out earlier work on the assessment of projects implemented under the Program's activities, have shown good results of expertise, its importance and relevance.
The results of the examination in the preceding period (through 2008) were prepared by expert opinion on the technical requirements to perform work, contest entry form and the results of work performed.
Based on comments and suggestions contained in these expert opinions, fine-tuned as the competition and reporting documents, and actual results of projects that will improve their quality.
As part of the activities carried out formation of requirements to fulfill the Program's activities, carrying out an assessment of the results of their conformity with initial requirements, ensures quality control of proposed design solutions.
To avoid conflict of interest as an external independent expert in the implementation of this activity may not act as companies that are suppliers to the market of information and communication technologies (software vendors, hardware or communication facilities, systems integrators and other companies engaged in implementing their own decisions or decisions of third companies in the field of information and communication technologies), as well as their partners, subsidiaries and affiliated with the company.
To avoid conflict of interest as an external independent expert in the implementation of this activity may not act as companies that are implementing (accomplices) to other activities of the Program, as well as with other forms of conflict, their interests and the interests of the customer.
Every year on the formation of requirements to implement the activities of the Program and conducted a complete examination of the results for their adherence to these requirements, provides quality control of proposed design solutions.

Creating a management system of program activities, departmental and regional informatization

Management and coordination of efforts to establish e-government guarantees the achievement of the objectives, the effectiveness of the formation of e-government, as well as long-term sustainability of the results.
In the period before 2009, the Ministry of Economic Development of Russia was created and implemented an automated information system of regulation of the project activity, developed the project and technical documentation on the system. Using the information system is the publication of the results of work performed under government contracts, Ministry of Economic Development of Russia in the Program. Using the system enhances the quality and effectiveness of program

**For additional analytical, business and investment opportunities information,
please contact Global Investment & Business Center, USA
at (202) 546-2103. Fax: (202) 546-3275. E-mail: rusric@erols.com**

management.
In order to improve project implementation of information and telecommunication technologies and analyzing their performance is necessary to form a unified system of management of program activities, departmental and regional informatization.
As part of this activity:
development of project management methodology, which provides uniform guidelines for all activities and procedures for managing their implementation and regulatory procedures for their implementation;
planning of program activities, including monitoring compliance with departmental, interdepartmental and regional projects, the formal requirements of the methodology and content of activities of the Program;
development and improvement of methods of determining target indicators and indicators of program outcomes to meet the requirements of objectivity, independence and measurability, comparability of results of different periods of the program, the inclusion of targets for quality management and assessment system for the effective implementation of the Program's activities in general;
planning and program management through the organization of Council of Chief Designers on departmental and regional information and organizational support to the work of those councils;
prioritizing programs and projects, implementation of information and communication technologies in public administration in the medium term;
creation and implementation of an information system that supports procedures calendar resource planning programs, management of project documents and the interactions between project participants, as well as the preparation and presentation in various formats for reporting on project implementation;
reducing price and technological dependence of public authorities from providers of design solutions in information and telecommunication technologies, the promotion of free software;
organization of technical service and support for users of government information systems, including through the transfer of functions to implement these tasks to third parties.

Develop a unified system of planning and monitoring the use of information and communication technologies in the activities of public authorities

To ensure the effectiveness of interagency planning and coordination of programs and projects to introduce information and communication technologies in the activities of public authorities should develop procedures for:
review of departmental and inter-targeted programs and projects, implementation of information and telecommunication technologies in the activities of public authorities;
monitoring expenditure of the federal budget for the implementation of these projects and make appropriate conclusions.
In 2006 - 2008 years of a unified system of information and statistical support for the Ministry of Communications and Mass Communications of Russia was established concept of a monitoring system using information technology activities of state power of RF subjects and local authorities, including a system of indicators characterizing the state of this work, documents on the organization and monitoring, electronic files of data on the status of work on the use of information technology activities of state power of RF subjects and local authorities.
In order to improve program and project implementation information and telecommunication technologies in the work of state bodies and analysis of such performance is necessary to establish a unified system of planning and monitoring the use of information and communication technologies in public administration.
To solve this problem it is necessary to ensure:
development of techniques for monitoring and analysis of the level and effectiveness of information and telecommunication technologies in the work of public authorities, implementation and use of government information systems, development of information technology infrastructure of public authorities, the impact of projects in this area;
description of the experience of the successful application of information and communication

For additional analytical, business and investment opportunities information,
please contact Global Investment & Business Center, USA
at (202) 546-2103. Fax: (202) 546-3275. E-mail: rusric@erols.com

technologies in public administration and its subsequent replication techniques;
establishment of an information system that provides automated procedures for collecting, processing, storage and presentation in a convenient form for analysis of information, registry and registries of public information systems and projects working on the creation and development;
the organization collecting the relevant data and content information system;
establishing a system of rating the effectiveness of the use of information and communication technologies in government;
Archiving of the most successful examples and solutions applied in information systems of public authorities.

Creating a uniform system of professional development for civil servants applying in their work information and communication technologies to assist state and municipal services

The purpose of this activity is to create conditions to ensure the necessary level of knowledge and skills of state and municipal employees in the use of information technology.
In 2002 - 2008 years have produced the following results:
developed training programs for public authorities use modern information technologies;
methods have been developed and program-technical means of appraisal and assessment of skills of employees of public authorities in the use of modern information technologies;
Approaches to improve the quality of public servants in the use of information technology;
recommendations for the effective application of modern communication technologies in the management of managers at the example of video conferencing;
conducted training and testing of employees of several ministries and under the orders of federal services and agencies in using information and telecommunication technologies.
As part of this event in 2009 - 2010 years provides:
conducting research in the field of special, higher professional and postgraduate education of adults with specific requirements and state and municipal services;
Narrow the development of training courses on software used in government and municipal service;
holding short-term training of state and municipal employees;
dissemination of research carried out in the framework of the event, including by holding all-Russia conferences;
prepare proposals for inclusion in the draft long-term program "Information Society (2011 - 2018 years), the programs of regional informatization bodies of state power of RF subjects and local authorities, departmental information on the program 2011 - 2018 years.

IV. Rationale resourcing Program

Resource support programs are based on analysis of costs and duration of the execution of each program's activities. Cost of person-days was adopted based on an average salary of the specialist (expert) in the state organization of the Executive with the necessary overhead. This takes into account the nature of work and identifies the relevant articles of the budget.
Financing Program for 2002 - 2010 is given in Annex N 2.
The amount and sources of funding for the Program for 2009 - 2010 years, the directions given in Appendix N 3.
The distribution between the state customers of the Program of the federal budget to finance its implementation in 2009 - 2010 are set out in Annex N 4.
One of the Program is to implement projects at the regional level. Funding for such projects are funded from the federal budget in the framework of the Program, as well as the budgets of RF subjects under co-financing.
Active development of standard solutions in the field of information technology for federal entities and municipalities. Testing standard solutions in the field of information technology at the expense of the federal budget in the framework of the Program, as well as the budgets of RF subjects under co-financing. Refinement of standard solutions in the field of information technology at the expense of the federal budget as part of the Program.

For additional analytical, business and investment opportunities information,
please contact Global Investment & Business Center, USA
at (202) 546-2103. Fax: (202) 546-3275. E-mail: rusric@erols.com

Activities Program for 2009 - 2010 are set out in Annex N 5.
Distribution of the federal budget for activities of the Program for 2009 - 2010 are set out in Annex N 6.
Planned indicators of program activities, funded through public capital investments in 2009 - 2010, respectively, are given in Appendix N 7.
Methods of assessing the effectiveness of the Program is given in annex N 8.
Terms of delivery and distribution of subsidies from the federal budget the budgets of RF subjects are given in Appendix N 9.

V. The mechanism of the Program

The program is implemented in accordance with the development and implementation of federal target programs and inter-state target programs, which participates in the implementation of Russia, approved by RF Government Resolution of 26 June 1995 N 594 "About realization of the Federal Law" On the supply of products for federal state needs .
State customer - coordinator of the Program is the Ministry of Communications and Mass Communications of Russia.
Government customers on certain activities of the Program are the Ministry of Communications and Mass Communications of Russia, Ministry of Economic Development of Russia, Federal Agency for Information Technologies, the Federal Agency on Education and the Federal Guard Service of Russia.
System Office, programs designed to achieve goals in a timely manner within the allocated resources. In order to ensure effective implementation of the Program management implementation of its activities are carried out in accordance with the project approach, which involves the implementation of activities under the plan, defining goals, objectives, indicators and stages of its execution, the requirements for composition and expected results of these studies at each stage, as well as the amount of necessary resource support.
Ministry of Communications and Mass Communications of Russia as a state customer - Program Coordinator shall:
planning the implementation of the Program, including monitoring compliance with the plan of projects included in the formal requirements of the methodology and content of the Program's activities, ensuring a coherent sequence and priorities for their implementation, analysis and coordination provided by government customers for feasibility studies, preparation and submission in due course a summary of budget requests for financial ensure the Program's activities through the federal budget for next fiscal year;
regular information from government customers of the Program on the implementation of the Program in order to improve the effectiveness of implementation for their assigned areas and activities;
monitor the effectiveness of program activities and spending of government customers on budget funding, analysis and synthesis results of the implementation activities of the Program, provided by government customers, reports on the implementation of programs and present them in the prescribed manner to interested public authorities.
State customers into the program are:
planning the implementation for their assigned areas and activities of the Program within allocated resource supply, including the definition of the composition, timing and expected results of operations, as well as the requirements for the content of reporting forms based on performance at each stage, the development of the feasibility of their implementation, preparation and provision of state customer - the coordinator of the Program budget requests for budget funding;
management of specific projects, the choice in the legislation of Russia order of artists works (projects), monitoring the timeliness of receipt, quality and consistency of the results of their implementation of the original performance specifications, reporting the results of the harmonization of state customer - Program Coordinator;
analysis and synthesis of execution of work, assess the effectiveness of the achievement of a state customer trends and activities of the Program, prepare and submit to the state customer - Program

For additional analytical, business and investment opportunities information,
please contact Global Investment & Business Center, USA
at (202) 546-2103. Fax: (202) 546-3275. E-mail: rusric@erols.com

Coordinator reports to produce reports on the implementation of the Program.
To implement an effective program management and monitoring of the implementation of state customer - Program Coordinator and government customers of the program are officers and relevant units, which will be responsible for implementing the program. Heads of state of the customer - the coordinator of the Program and government customers of the Program shall designate a person responsible for implementing programs, usually at the level of Assistant Federal Minister (Deputy Head (Director), FSB, or Federal agency) shall establish internal rules laid down for managing the implementation of government contracting trends and Program activities.
To ensure effective coordination of the implementation of activities carried out by the state customer of the Program on behalf of other government bodies, among the relevant public authorities may have a cooperation agreement to form joint working groups comprising representatives of the state customer of the Program, the state of the customer - the Program Coordinator and concerned public authority (functional customer). Joint order of the state authorities approved the working group and plan its activities. In this case, implementation plan, the composition of works and their requirements, as well as intermediate and final results of their implementation should be considered at a meeting of the working group and agreed by all concerned government bodies - the functional customers.
In order to effectively coordinate projects in the sphere of regional informatization within the framework of a council of regional informatization, as well as the Council of Chief Designers of information programs of the federal bodies of executive power under the Ministry of Communications and Mass Communications of Russia.
Quality control of standard solutions in the sphere of information technologies and their relevance to the state authorities of RF subjects carried out within the framework of a regional council information, including through independent examination.
Typical solutions in the field of information technologies, developed under the program, distributed free of charge for use by public authorities of RF subjects and local authorities.
Termination of the Program is reached in the case of the completion of its implementation, and early termination - in the case of recognition of the ineffectiveness of its implementation on the basis of the decision of the Government of Russia, received in the prescribed manner.

VI. ASSESSMENT OF THE SOCIO-ECONOMIC IMPACT OF THE PROGRAM

The program is comprehensive in nature, aimed at improving efficiency in the use of information and telecommunication technologies in the activities of public authorities and the impact of budget funds allocated for this purpose. A new quality of governance is an important factor in socio-economic development and improve the quality of life.
Given the stated objectives of the Program and its main directions is possible to evaluate the effect of program activities in 2009 - 2010 years in the following areas:
creation of e-government infrastructure that provides access to information about activities and services of public authorities in electronic form, electronic interagency collaboration and unified state control performance of the public authorities, which will reduce the administrative burden on organizations and citizens, and give an annual saving of up to 10 billion . rubles;
efficiency of budget expenditures for the introduction of information and communication technologies in the activities of public authorities at 10 per cent;
reduce the cost of public authorities to organize the exchange of information on the interdepartmental level to 25 percent;
reduce the administrative burden on citizens and organizations related to the submission to state authorities the necessary information, reducing the number of internally displaced appeals to the government authorities to obtain government services and reducing waiting times for services by 10 percent;
a guaranteed level of information openness of public authorities, raising the level of trust and collaboration, reducing time spent on the implementation of RF citizens of their constitutional rights and responsibilities;
improving efficiency and quality of decisions, reducing costs for the organization of administrative and management processes in government;
development of the project long-term program "Information Society (2011 - 2018 years) activities

For additional analytical, business and investment opportunities information, please contact Global Investment & Business Center, USA at (202) 546-2103. Fax: (202) 546-3275. E-mail: rusric@erols.com

designed to keep forming in Russia e-government in 2011 - 2018 years, which will ensure the safety of public investment and long-term economic viability of the introduction derived from the Program results ;

increased demand for information and communication technologies by public authorities and, consequently, increase their offer from the Russian manufacturers to 10 percent per year through increased commitment and motivation of public authorities to use in their work of modern information and telecommunication technologies as well as by promoting the development of programs and projects, departmental information systems;

provide a single information space of the country through the development of national information and telecommunications infrastructure for public use and connect it to state authorities throughout Russia.

TERMS OF DELIVERY AND DISTRIBUTION OF SUBSIDIES FROM THE FEDERAL BUDGET THE BUDGETS OF RF SUBJECTS

These Regulations establish the procedures and conditions of the federal budget regional budgets in the form of grants within the funds provided for specific activities of the Program, subject to inclusion in the appropriate long-term program, implemented through the regional budgets, and if approved by the established basis of design estimates.

Financing of the activities of the Program, implemented by the RF subjects, carried out through a selection of RF subjects and opinions as established by RF legislation way government customers of the Program with the state authorities of RF subjects grant agreements from the federal budget regional budgets for co-financing facility.

The level of co-financing expenditure commitments of the RF subject may not be set above 95 per cent and below 5 per cent of expenditure commitments.

The balance of unused subsidies in establishing the chief manager of the federal budget no need for them subjects of Russia shall be returned to the federal budget.

Balance is not used in the current fiscal year, subsidies, demand for which is preserved, to be used in the next fiscal year for the same purpose.

Released funds can be reallocated among the other subjects of Russia, are eligible to receive them..
"

For additional analytical, business and investment opportunities information,
please contact Global Investment & Business Center, USA
at (202) 546-2103. Fax: (202) 546-3275. E-mail: rusric@erols.com

SUPPLEMENTS

RUSSIA AREA CODES AND SPECIAL NUMBERS

Region	Area code	Old code (inactive)
Republic of Adygea	877	
Altai Krai	385	
Altai Republic	388	
Amur Oblast	416	
Arkhangelsk Oblast and Nenets Autonomous Okrug	818	
Astrakhan Oblast	851	
Belgorod Oblast	472	072
Bryansk Oblast	483	083
Republic of Buryatia	301	
Vladimir Oblast	492	092
Volgograd Oblast	844	
Vologda Oblast	817, 820	
Voronezh Oblast	473	073
Republic of Dagestan	872	
Jewish Autonomous Oblast	426	
Sverdlovsk Oblast	343	
Ivanovo Oblast	493	093
Republic of Ingushetia	873	
Irkutsk Oblast	395	
Republic of Kabardino-Balkaria	866	
Kaliningrad Oblast	401	011
Republic of Kalmykia	847	
Kaluga Oblast	484	084
Kamchatka Krai	415	
Republic of Karachay–Cherkessia	878	
Republic of Karelia	814	
Kemerovo Oblast	384	

For additional analytical, business and investment opportunities information, please contact Global Investment & Business Center, USA at (202) 546-2103. Fax: (202) 546-3275. E-mail: rusric@erols.com

Region	Area code	Old code (inactive)
Kirov Oblast	833	
Komi Republic	821	
Kostroma Oblast	494	094
Krasnodar Krai	861, 862	
Krasnoyarsk Krai	391	
Kurgan Oblast	352	
Kursk Oblast	471	071
Leningrad Oblast	813	
Lipetsk Oblast	474	074
Magadan Oblast	413	
Republic of Mari El	836	
Republic of Mordovia	834	
Moscow City	495, 499	095
Moscow Oblast	496, 498	096
Murmansk Oblast	815	
Nizhny Novgorod Oblast	831	
Novgorod Oblast	816	
Novosibirsk Oblast	383	
Omsk Oblast	381	
Orenburg Oblast	353	
Oryol Oblast	486	086
Penza Oblast	841	
Perm Krai	342	
Primorsky Krai	423	
Pskov Oblast	811	
Rostov Oblast	863	
Ryazan Oblast	491	091
Samara Oblast	846, 848	
Saint Petersburg	812	
Saratov Oblast	845	

For additional analytical, business and investment opportunities information, please contact Global Investment & Business Center, USA at (202) 546-2103. Fax: (202) 546-3275. E-mail: rusric@erols.com

Region	Area code	Old code (inactive)
Sakhalin Oblast	424	
Republic of North Ossetia–Alania	867	
Smolensk Oblast	481	081
Stavropol Krai	865, 879	
Tambov Oblast	475	075
Republic of Tatarstan	843, 855	
Tver Oblast	482	082
Tomsk Oblast	382	
Tula Oblast	487	087
Republic of Tyva (Tuva)	394	
Tyumen Oblast	345	
Republic of Udmurtia	341	
Ulyanovsk Oblast	842	
Republic of Bashkortostan	347	
Khabarovsk Krai	421	
Republic of Khakassia	390	
Khanty–Mansi Autonomous Okrug	346	
Chelyabinsk Oblast	351	
Republic of Chechnya	871	
Zabaykalsky Krai	302	
Republic of Chuvashia	835	
Chukotka Autonomous Okrug	427	
Sakha Republic (Yakutia)	411	
Yamalo-Nenets Autonomous Okrug	349	
Yaroslavl Oblast	485	085

TOLL-FREE & PAY-LINE CODES

Code	Service
800	FPH- Freephone
801	AAB – Automatic alternative billing
802	CCC – Credit card calling
803	VOT – Televoting

For additional analytical, business and investment opportunities information, please contact Global Investment & Business Center, USA at (202) 546-2103. Fax: (202) 546-3275. E-mail: rusric@erols.com

804	UAN - Universal access number
805	PCC – Prepaid card calling
806	ACC – Account card calling
807	VPN - Virtual private network
808	UPT – Universal personal Telecommunication
809	PRM- Premium rate
881-899	Reserved
970	Data transfer services
971	Telematic services

SPECIAL NUMBERS (EMERGENCIES)

Number	Service
01	Fire service
02	Police
03	Ambulance
04	Gas service
07	Directory assistance, Rostelecom
09	Directory assistance (free, limited info)
009	Directory assistance (pay service, 35 rub./min.) in Moscow
100	Talking clock in Moscow

SELECTED U.S. AND RUSSIAN CONTACTS

RUSSIAN GOVERNMENT AGENCIES:

*Ministry of Trade and Industry:
Yuri Dmitrievich Maslyukov, Minister-Designate
18/1, Ovchinnikovskaya Nab., Moscow
Tel: (095) 220-1064; Fax: (095) 220-1684, 231-9220
*Note: The Russian Government announced that in August 1998, the
Ministry for Foreign Economic Relations and Trade would be abolished,
and that some of its functions would be assumed by a new Ministry of
Trade and Industry. Mr. Maslyukov was appointed by President Yeltsin
in July 1998.

Ministry of Finance:
Mikhail Mikhailovich Zadornov, Minister of Finance
Ulitsa Ilyinka 9, Entrance 1, Moscow
Tel: (095) 298-9130; Fax: (095) 925-0889

Ministry of Fuel and Energy:
Sergei Vladimirovich Generalov, Minister of Fuels and Energy
7, Kitaigorodskiy Proyezd, Moscow 103074
Tel: (095) 220-4659; Fax: (095) 975-2045 (International Dept.)

Ministry of Agriculture and Food:
Viktor A. Semyonov, Minister of Agriculture and Food
Orlikov Pereulok, 1/11, Moscow
Tel: (095) 207-4243; Fax: (095) 207-8362

For additional analytical, business and investment opportunities information,
please contact Global Investment & Business Center, USA
at (202) 546-2103. Fax: (202) 546-3275. E-mail: rusric@erols.com

State Customs Committee:
Vitaly G. Draganov, Chairman, State Customs Committee
1a, Komsomolskaya Ploshchad, Moscow 107842
Phone: (095) 975-1918; Fax: (095) 975-4823

State Committee for Standardization, Metrology and Certification
(GOSSTANDART
Gennady Petrovich Voronin, Chairman
9, Leninskiy Prospekt, Moscow 117049
Phone: (095) 236-6208, -4044; Fax: (095) 236-6231, 237-6032

Russian Copyright Agency:
Georgiy Artashessovich Ter-Gazariyants, Chairman of the Board;
Vadim Serafimovich Dunin, Head of Foreign Relations Department
6a, Bolshaya Bronnaya Ul., Moscow 103670
Phone: (095) 203-2996, -4599; Fax: (095) 200-1263

Committee for Patents and Trademarks (Rospatent
Alexander Dmitrievich Korchagin, General Director
2/6 Cherkasskiy Pereulok, Moscow
Tel: (095) 206-6203; Fax: (095) 923-4093

State Investment Corporation:
Yuriy Vladimirovich Petrov, Chairman
35, Myasnitskaya Ul., Moscow 103685
Phone: (095) 925-6796; Fax: (095) 207-6936
Regional Governments:

Moscow City Administration:
Iosif N. Ordzhonikidze,
Deputy Mayor and Minister for External Relations
13 Tverskaya Ulitsa, 103032, Moscow
Tel: 095-229-6360; Fax: (095) 883-6208

Moscow Registration Chamber:
Vladimir Ivanovich Sobolyev, Chairman
Mokhovaya Ul., 11, Bld. 8-E, Moscow 103009
Tel/Fax: (095) 202-2787;

Roald Nestorovich Lebedinskiy,
Dir., Registration/Accreditation (information in English)
Tel: (095) 132-0500

Tatyana Kuzminichna Nikanorkina, Expert
for Registration of Companies with Foreign Capital
(information in Russian)
Tel: (095) 202-4042

St. Petersburg City Administration:
Gennady I. Tkachev, Chairman, External Relations Committee
1, Smolniy, St. Petersburg 193060
Phone: (812) 276-1204; Fax: (812) 276-1633

For additional analytical, business and investment opportunities information,
please contact Global Investment & Business Center, USA
at (202) 546-2103. Fax: (202) 546-3275. E-mail: rusric@erols.com

Ilya I. Klebanov, First Vice Governor
Chairman, Cmte. on Economy and Industrial Policy
16 Voznesensky Prospect, St. Petersburg, Russia 190000
Phone: (812) 315-5152; Fax: (812) 319-9292.

Igor Yu. Artemiev, First Vice Governor
Chairman, Committee on Finance
16 Voznesensky Prospect, St. Petersburg, Russia 190000
Phone: (812) 319-9308; Fax: (812) 319-9967.

Leninrad Oblast Administration:
Inna L. Bigotskaya, Chief of Protocol Department
External Relations Committee,
67, Suvorovskiy Prospekt, St. Petersburg 193311
Phone: (812) 274-4859; Fax: (812) 274-2463.

Mark A. Vybornov, Chairman,
Committee on Foreign Economic Relations and Investments
67, Suvorovskiy Prospekt, St. Petersburg 193311
Phone: (812) 278-5587 or 274-4742; Fax: (812) 274-5986.

Yekaterinburg Oblast Administration:
Igor Ivanovich Arzyakov, Dir., Foreign Relations Department
1, Oktyabrskaya Ploshchad, Yekaterinburg 620031
Phone: (3432) 51-54-97, 58-96-56; Fax: (3432) 51-98-70

Yekaterinburg City Administration:
Vladimir I. Lomovtzev, Dir., Foreign Relations Department
1, Oktyabrskaya Ploshchad, Yekaterinburg 620031
Phone: (3432) 51-13-07, 51-43-83; Fax: (3432) 51-90-05

Primorskiy Territorial Administration:
Andrey Gennadyevich Zagumyonnov, Chairman
Committee for Foreign Economic Relations and Regional Trade
 of the Dept. for Foreign Economic Relations and Tourism
22 Svetlanskaya ulitsa, 690110, Vladivostok
Phone: (4232) 22-08-52
Fax: (4232) 22-10-19

Khabarovsk Territorial Administration:
Sergey I. Lopatin, Chief, Foreign Economic Relations Dept.
56 ul.K.Marksa, Khabarovsk
Phone/fax: (4212) 32-41-21

Sakhalin Regional Administration:
Vitaly Nikolaevich Elizariev, Director
Department of Foreign Economic Relations
32 Kommunisticheskiy prospect, "Sakhincenter", office 236
693000 Yuzhno-Sakhalinsk 693000
Phone: (4242) 72-74-94
Fax: (4242) 72-74-93; International fax: 7 509-95-1236

State Duma (Lower chamber of Parliament

For additional analytical, business and investment opportunities information,
please contact Global Investment & Business Center, USA
at (202) 546-2103. Fax: (202) 546-3275. E-mail: rusric@erols.com

--Cmte. on Budget, Taxes, Banking and Finance:
Alexander Zhukov, Chairman
2, Georgiyevskiy Pereulok, Moscow
Tel: (095) 292-3618; Fax: (095) 292-5601

--Cmte. on Property, Privatization and Economic Activity:
Pavel Grigoryevich Bunich, Chairman
2, Georgiyevskiy Pereulok, Moscow
Tel: (095) 229-9559; Fax: (095) 229-6996

--Cmte. on Industry, Construction, Transport and Energy:
Vladimir Kuzmich Gusev, Chairman
2, Georgiyevskiy Pereulok, Moscow
Tel: (095) 292-0365; Fax: (095) 292-3763

TRADE ASSOCIATIONS/CHAMBERS OF COMMERCE IN RUSSIA:

American Chamber of Commerce in Russia (Amcham)
Scott M. Blacklin, President
Kosmodamianskaya Nab. 52, Building 1, 8th floor, Moscow
Phone: (095) 961-2141; Fax: (095) 961-2142

American Chmbr. of Commerce in Russia, St. Petersburg Chapter:
Slava Bytchkov, Executive Director
25, Nevsky pr., St. Petersburg, 191186
Tel: (812) 326-2590; Fax: (812) 326-2591

St. Petersburg International Business Association (SPIBA)
Anna Kessner, Executive Administrator
27, Naberezhnaya Moiki, 5th Floor, St. Petersburg, 191186
Tel: (812) 325-9091; Fax: (812) 325-9933

Vladivostok International Business Association (VIBA)
Andrew Wilson, President
c/o U.S. and Foreign Commercial Service, Vladivostok
32 Pushkin Street, Vladivostok, Russia 690000
Phone: (4232) 300-093; Fax: (4232) 300-092
e-mail: csvlad@online.ru

Council for Trade and Economic Cooperation (CIS-USA)
Boris Petrovich Alekseyev, President
3, Naberezhnaya Shevchenko, Moscow 121248
Phone: (095) 243-5514, -5470; Fax: (095) 230-2467

Russian Chamber of Commerce and Industry
Stanislav Alekseyevich Smirnov, President;
Yuriy Nikolayevich Denissenkov, Head,
Sergey B. Kulyba, Expert on Accreditation, Protocol Department
6, Ilyinka Ul., Moscow 103684
Phone: (095) 929-02-86,-60,-61,-62,-63; Fax: (095) 929-0356

Primorskiy Territory Chamber of Commerce
Vladimir Borisovich Brezhnev, Chairman

For additional analytical, business and investment opportunities information,
please contact Global Investment & Business Center, USA
at (202) 546-2103. Fax: (202) 546-3275. E-mail: rusric@erols.com

13a Okeanskiy prospekt, Vladivostok
Phone: (4232) 26-96-30
Fax: (4232) 22-72-26

Khabarovsk Territory Chamber of Commerce and Industry
Mikhail Kruglikov, President
113, Shevronova Ulitsa, Khabarovsk 680000
Phone: (4212) 33-03-11, 33-11-30; Fax: (4212) 33-03-12

U.S. GOVERNMENT PERSONNEL HANDLING BUSINESS ISSUES IN RUSSIA:

U.S. EMBASSY IN MOSCOW:

--John Peters, Minister Counselor for Commercial Affairs
U.S. and Foreign Commercial Service
Bolshaya Molchanovka 23/28, Moscow 121019
Phone: (095) 967-3414; Fax: (095) 967-3416
Satellite phone: 7 (502) 224-1105;
Satellite fax: 7 (502) 224-1106

--Michael Matera, Minister Counselor for Economic Affairs
21, Novinskiy Bulvar, Moscow 121099
Phone: (095) 956-4220; Fax: (095) 956-4146

--Asif Chaudry, Minister Counselor for Agricultural Affairs
21, Novinskiy Bulvar, Moscow 121099
Phone: (095) 956 4103; (502) 221 1245
Fax: (095) 975 2339; (502) 224 1356

--James Waller, Treasury Attache
21, Novinskiy Bulvar, Moscow 121099
Phone: (095) 956-4258; Fax: (095) 956-4146

--U.S. Agency for International Development
Office of Privatization and Economic Restructuring
U.S. Embassy, Moscow
21 Novinskiy Bulvar., Moscow 121099
Phone: (095) 956-4281

U.S. and Foreign Commercial Service, St. Petersburg
James McCarthy, Principal Commercial Officer
25, Nevsky prospekt., St. Petersburg, Russia 191186
Tel: (812) 326-2560; Fax: (812) 326-2561/62

American Business Center, St. Petersburg
Zhanna Agasieva, Assistant Manager
25, Nevsky prospekt, St. Petersburg, Russia 191186
Tel: (812) 326-2570; Fax: (812) 326-2571

U.S. and Foreign Commercial Service, Vladivostok
Richard Steffens, Principal Commercial Officer
32 Pushkin Street, Vladivostok, Russia 690000

For additional analytical, business and investment opportunities information,
please contact Global Investment & Business Center, USA
at (202) 546-2103. Fax: (202) 546-3275. E-mail: rusric@erols.com

Satellite phone/fax: (509) 851-1211
Phone: (4232) 300-093; Fax: (4232) 300-092
e-mail: csvlad@online.ru

American Business Center, Vladivostok
Inna Nazarova, Assistant Manager
2, Batareynaya Ul., Vladivostok
Satellite phone/fax: (509) 851-1212
Phone: (4232) 25-46-25; Fax: (4232) 25-46-61

U.S. Consulate-General in Yekaterinburg
Alexander Deyanov, Commercial Assistant
15A Gogol Street, Third Floor
Yekaterinburg, Russia
Phone: (3432) 564-619; Fax: (3432) 564-515
Phone: (3432) 564-736 (Foreign Commercial Service)

Federal Aviation Administration (FAA)
Dennis B. Cooper, Senior Representative
American Embassy, Brussels
27 Boulevard du Regent, B-1000 Brussels, Belgium
Phone: 322 508-2700; Fax: 322 230-06428
Phone: (095) 956-4036; Fax: (095) 956-4293

WASHINGTON-BASED U.S. GOVERNMENT CONTACTS FOR RUSSIA:

Business Information Service
 for the Newly Independent States (BISNIS)
Anne Grey, Director
U.S. Department of Commerce, Rm.7413, Washington, D.C. 20230
Phone: (202) 482-4655; Fax: (202) 482-2293

U.S. Export-Import Bank
David Fiore, Loan Officer
811 Vermont Avenue, N.W., Washington, D.C. 20571-0999
Phone: (202) 565-3815; Fax: (202) 565-3816

Overseas Private Investment Corporation
Peter Ballinger, Manager, NIS Investment Development
1100 New York Avenue, N.W., Washington, D.C. 20527
Phone: (202) 336-8618; Fax: (202) 408-5145

U.S. Trade and Development Agency
Daniel Stein, Regional Director
U.S. Department of State, SA-16, Rm.301
Washington, D.C. 20523-1602
Phone: (703) 875-4357; Fax: (703) 875-4009

U.S. Department of State, Office of Russian Affairs
Thomas K. Huffaker, Chief Economist
2201 C Street, N.W., Washington, D.C. 20520
Phone: (202) 647-6747; Fax: (202) 736-4710

For additional analytical, business and investment opportunities information,
please contact Global Investment & Business Center, USA
at (202) 546-2103. Fax: (202) 546-3275. E-mail: rusric@erols.com

U.S. Department of Commerce -- Market Access and Compliance
Russia and Independent States Division
Jack Brougher, Director,
U.S. Department of Commerce, Rm.3318, Washington, D.C. 20230
Phone: (202) 482-3952; Fax: (202) 482-3042

U.S. Agency for International Development
Office of Privatization and Economic Restructuring
Washington, D.C. 20523
Phone: (202) 736-4410

U.S. Department of Agriculture
Russian Area Officer
14th St. and Independence Avenue S.W., Washington, D.C. 20250
Phone: (202) 720-3080

U.S. Bureau of Export Administration
Export Counselling Division
U.S. Department of Commerce, Rm.3898, Washington, D.C. 20230
Phone: (202) 482-4811; Fax: (202) 482-3911

Special American Business Internship Training Program (SABIT)
Liesel Duhon, Director
U.S. Department of Commerce, Rm.3006, Washington, D.C. 20230
Phone: (202) 482-0073; Fax: (202) 482-4098

U.S.-Based Multipliers and International Organizations
with Interests in Russia:

U.S.-Russia Business Council
Eugene K. Lawson, President
1701 Pennsylvania Ave., N.W. Suite 650, Washington, D.C. 20046
Phone: (202) 956-7670; Fax: (202) 956-7674

Russian-American Chamber of Commerce
Deborah Palmieri, President
6200 South Quebec St., Suite 210, Englewood, Colorado 80111
Phone: (303) 689-8642; Fax: (303) 689-8762

Foundation for Russian-American Economic Cooperation
Carol Vipperman, President
1932 First Avenue, Suite 803
Seattle, WA 98101
Tel: (206) 443-1935; Fax (206) 443-0954

National Association of State Departments of Agriculture
Richard Kirchhoff, Executive Vice President
1156 15th Street, N.W. Suite 1020, Washington, D.C. 20045
Tel: (202) 296-9680; Fax: (202) 296-9686

The World Bank
Thomas Kelsey, U.S. Department of Commerce liaison
1818 H Street, NW, Washington, DC, 20433
Phone: (202) 458-0118; Fax: (202) 458-0118

For additional analytical, business and investment opportunities information,
please contact Global Investment & Business Center, USA
at (202) 546-2103. Fax: (202) 546-3275. E-mail: rusric@erols.com

International Finance Corporation (IFC)
Mark Constantine
1850 Eye Street, NW, Washington, DC 20433
Phone: (202) 473-9331; Fax: (202) 676-1513
Moscow Office: Roger Gale
6, Neglinnaya St., Moscow
Tel: 7-095-928-5328; Fax: 7-095-927-6832

International Bank for Reconstruction and Development
U.S. Department of Commerce Liaison
 to the U.S. Executive Director's Office
1818 H Street, N.W., Room D-13004
Washington, D.C. 20433
Phone: (202) 458-0118; Fax: (202) 477-2967

Office of Multilateral Development Banks,
 U.S.& Foreign Commercial Service
U.S. Department of Commerce, Room H-1107
Washington, D.C. 20230
Phone: (202) 482-3399; Fax: (202) 273-0927

European Bank for Reconstruction and Development (EBRD)
One Exchange Square, London EC2A 2EH, United Kingdom
Dean Peterson, U.S. Department of Commerce Liaison
Tel: 011-44-171-338-6569; Fax: 011-44-171-338-6487

BUSINESS ACTIVITIES SUBJECT TO SPECIAL AUTHORIZATION BY THE GOVERNMENT (APPLICABLE BOTH TO LOCAL AND FOREIGN ENTREPRENEURS)

1. Activities referring to the construction of complexes in Krays, Regions, Autonomous Regions, and cities. Production of building constructions (local authorities)
2. Activity of specialized privatization investment funds and companies (State Committee for Investments)
3. Activity on servicing population and factories
4. Advertising and designing activity using city territory, buildings surfaces, streets, etc.
5. Banking operations (Central Bank)
6. Banking Operations with foreign currency (Central Bank)
7. Clearing operations (Central Bank)
8. Commodity Exchanges operations (Commodity Exchange Commission)
9. Communication services (except government systems) (Ministry of Communication)
10. Construction activities: designing, researching, investigating, contracting, assembling.
11. Construction and maintenance of nuclear and radioactive installations, technology and products, wastes of their production (Rosatomnadzor)
12. Construction, leasing, re-equipment of fishing-factories, research and fisheries patrol vessels (Roskomrybolovstvo)
13. Customs activities (State Customs Committee)
14. Customs warehouses activities (local customs)
15. Entertainment, sports and show business
16. Gambling and casino business
17. Inspection of State monopoly of alcohol products

For additional analytical, business and investment opportunities information, please contact Global Investment & Business Center, USA at (202) 546-2103. Fax: (202) 546-3275. E-mail: rusric@erols.com

18. Insurance (Rosstrachnadzor)
19. Inter-mediation in securities transactions (for companies with foreign participation) (Ministry of Finance)
20. Investment companies, financial brokers, investment consulting (Ministry of Finance)
21. Investment Funds operations (Ministry of Finance)
22. Investments abroad (not identified)
23. Land designing and surveying (Roscornzem)
24. Maintenance of engineering systems, territory improvement, maintenance of residential and nonresidential accommodations, town roads and bridges (local authorities)
25. Maintenance of refueling stations
26. Medical practice (except treatment of infection and oncology patients) (local authorities)
27. Organization of employment of Russian citizens abroad
28. Organization of local lotteries
29. Pawnshop operations
30. Pharmaceutical activity (License commission of the Ministry of Health, local authorities)
31. Private detective and security services (Ministry of Internal Affairs)
32. Private notary activity (Ministry of Justice)
33. Production and import of securities blanks (Ministry of Finance)
34. Production and sale of homemade products and other goods on public catering factories, including public servicing (local authorities)
35. Production and sale of perfumery and cosmetic products
36. Production and wholesale trade of other alcohol products
37. Production of food
38. Production, storage and wholesale trade of ethyl alcohol (except crude alcohol, produced from the wastes of main production)
39. Public showing of movie and video films
40. Publishing activity
41. Reconstruction and restoration of monuments and buildings of historical and architectural value (local authorities)
42. Reproduction and museum exhibits copy making
43. Sale of goods (services) for foreign currency on the Russian territory (Central Bank)
44. Sale of wine, liquor and vodka products (local authorities); sale of tobacco products; retail trade in temporary shops - including individual trade - except sale of agricultural products
45. Stock Exchange operations (Ministry of Finance)
46. Stocking up and sale of medical herbs
47. Tourist and excursion activity
48. Transportation of goods and passengers by road, freight forwarding activity, loading and unloading operations, storage services
49. Transportation, expedition and other activities connected with transportation process, repair and maintenance of automotive means of transportation (Russian transport inspection)
50. Use of natural resources, mining (Roskomzem)
51. Use of underground space construction and repair of underground communications (local authorities)
52. Veterinary activity (State veterinary department)
53. Veterinary practice (Local authorities)

SUPPLEMENT 2. INTERNATIONAL TREATIES. COUNTRIES WITH MOST FAVORED NATION STATUS

1. Afghanistan   2. Albania

3.	Angola	61.	Jordan
4.	Argentina	62.	Kenya
5.	Australia	63.	Korea(North)
6.	Austria	64.	Korea(South)
7.	Bangladesh	65.	Kuwait
8.	Belgium	66.	Laos
9.	Benin	67.	Lebanon
10.	Bolivia	68.	Liberia
11.	Bosnia-Herzegovina	69.	Libya
12.	Botswana	70.	Luxembourg
13.	Brazil	71.	Macedonia
14.	Bulgaria	72.	Madagascar
15.	Burkina Faso	73.	Malaysia
16.	Burundi	74.	Mali
17.	Cabo Verde	75.	Malta
18.	Cambodia	76.	Mauritania
19.	Cameroon	77.	Mauritius
20.	Canada	78.	Mexico
21.	Chad	79.	Mongolia
22.	Chili	80.	Morocco
23.	China	81.	Mozambique
24.	Colombia	82.	Myamnar
25.	Congo	83.	Nepal
26.	Costa Rica	84.	Netherlands
27.	Croatia	85.	New Zealand
28.	Cuba	86.	Nicaragua
29.	Cyprus	87.	Niger
30.	Czech Republic	88.	Norway
31.	Denmark	89.	Pakistan
32.	Djibouti	90.	Panama
33.	Ecuador	91.	Peru
34.	Egypt	92.	Philippines
35.	Equatorial Guinea	93.	Poland
36.	Ethiopia	94.	Portugal
37.	Finland	95.	Qatar
38.	France	96.	Romania
39.	Gabon	97.	Rwanda
40.	Gambia	98.	Salvador
41.	Germany	99.	San Tome and Principe
42.	Ghana	100.	Sierra Leone
43.	Great Britain	101.	Singapore
44.	Greece	102.	Slovak Republic
45.	Grenada	103.	Slovenia
46.	Guinea	104.	Somalia
47.	Guinea-Bissau	105.	South African Republic
48.	Guyana	106.	Spain
49.	Honduras	107.	Sri Lanka
50.	Hungary	108.	Sudan
51.	Iceland	109.	Sweden
52.	India	110.	Switzerland
53.	Indonesia	111.	Syria
54.	Iran	112.	Tanzania
55.	Iraq	113.	Thailand
56.	Ireland	114.	Tunisia
57.	Israel	115.	Turkey
58.	Italy	116.	Uganda
59.	Jamaica	117.	United States of America
60.	Japan	118.	Uruguay

For additional analytical, business and investment opportunities information,
please contact Global Investment & Business Center, USA
at (202) 546-2103. Fax: (202) 546-3275. E-mail: rusric@erols.com

119. Venezuela	122. Zaire
120. Vietnam	123. Zambia
121. Yemen	124. Zimbabwe

BILATERAL INVESTMENT PROTECTION TREATIES

1. Austria*	17. Korea (South)
2. Belgium*	18. Kuwait
3. Bulgaria	19. Luxembourg*
4. Canada*	20. Netherlands*
5. China*	21. Norway*
6. Cuba	22. Poland
7. Czech Republic	23. Portugal
8. Denmark	24. Romania
9. Finland*	25. Slovenia
10. France*	26. Spain*
11. Germany*	27. Sweden*
12. Great Britain*	28. Switzerland*
13. Greece	29. Turkey*
14. Hungary*	30. United States of America
15. India	31. Vietnam
16. Italy*	

* The treaties were signed by the Soviet Union and are to be resigned by Russia.
** The treaties have been agreed upon and will be signed in the near future.

BILATERAL TRADE TREATIES

1. Albania	29. Cyprus
2. Algeria	30. Dominica
3. Angola	31. Dominican (Rep.)
4. Anguilla	32. Ecuador
5. Antigua and Barbuda	33. Egypt
6. Antilles (Netherlands)	34. Fiji
7. Argentina	35. Gabon
8. Aruba	36. Gambia
9. Bahamas	37. Ghana
10. Bahrain	38. Grenada
11. Barbados	39. Guatemala
12. Belize	40. Guyana
13. Bermuda	41. Honduras
14. Bolivia	42. Hong Kong
15. Bosnia-Herzegovina	43. India
	44. Indonesia
16. Brazil	45. Iran
17. British Virgin Islands	46. Iraq
18. Brunei	47. Jamaica
19. Cote d' Ivoire	48. Jordan
20. Cameroon	49. Kenya
21. Cayman Islands	50. South Korea
22. Chili	51. North Korea
23. China	52. Kuwait
24. Colombia	53. Lebanon
25. Congo	54. Libya
26. Cook Islands	55. Macedonia
27. Costa Rica	56. Malaysia
28. Cuba	

For additional analytical, business and investment opportunities information, please contact Global Investment & Business Center, USA at (202) 546-2103. Fax: (202) 546-3275. E-mail: rusric@erols.com

57. Malta		76. Qatar	
58. Mauritius		77. Saint Heléna	
59. Mexico		78. Saint Kitts and Nevis	
60. Micronesia		79. Saint Lucia	
61. Mongolia		80. Saint Vincent and the Grenadines	
62. Montserrat		81. Salvador	
63. Morocco		82. Saudi Arabia	
64. Namibia		83. Senegal	
65. Nauru		84. Seychelles	
66. Nicaragua		85. Singapore	
67. Nigeria		86. Slovenia	
68. Niue		87. Sri Lanka	
69. Oman		88. Surinam	
70. Pakistan		89. Swaziland	
71. Panama		90. Syria	
72. Papua New Guinea		91. Thailand	
73. Paraguay		92. Tonga	
74. Peru		93. Trinidad and Tobago	
75. Philippines			

COUNTRIES EXEMPT FROM RUSSIAN IMPORT TARIFFS

1. Afghanistan
2. Bangladesh
3. Benin
4. Botswana
5. Burkina Faso
6. Burundi
7. Bhutan
8. Cabo Verde
9. Cambodia
10. Central African Republic
11. Chad
12. Comoros
13. Equatorial Guinea
14. Ethiopia
15. Guinea
16. Guinea-Bissau
17. Haiti
18. Kiribati
19. Laos
20. Lesotho
21. Liberia
22. Madagascar
23. Malawi

24. Maldives
25. Mali
26. Mauritania
27. Mozambique
28. Myanmar
29. Nepal
30. Niger
31. Rwanda
32. Samoa
33. San Tome and Principe
34. Sierra Leone
35. Solomon Islands
36. Somalia
37. Sudan
38. Tanzania
39. Togo
40. Tuvalu
41. Uganda
42. Vanuatu
43. Yemen
44. Zaire
45. Zambia

FREE TRADE AGREEMENTS

1. Armenia
2. Azerbaijan
3. Belarus
4. Moldova
5. Kazakhstan

6. Kirgizstan
7. Tadzhikistan
8. Turkmenistan
9. Ukraine

For additional analytical, business and investment opportunities information, please contact Global Investment & Business Center, USA at (202) 546-2103. Fax: (202) 546-3275. E-mail: rusric@erols.com

GOVERNMENT ORGANIZATIONS RESPONSIBLE FOR FOREIGN INVESTMENT

Ministry of the Economy of the Russian Federation (Minekonomiki of Russia)

- Formulation and implementation of the State Policy for attracting foreign investment.
- Coordination of the activities of the federal bodies regarding cooperation with foreign investors.
- Establishment of free economic zones.
- Arranging for and holding international tenders and bidding.
- Arranging for Concession agreements and deals on production sharing.

Central Bank of the Russian Federation (Bank of Russia)
Administration of Exchange Control over Capital Transactions

- Governing bank transactions with foreign capital.
- Licensing of capital transactions in foreign currencies - including long-term credits.

Ministry of Finance of the Russian Federation
Department of Securities

- Licensing the activities of financial and of the Russian Federation investment companies.
- Governing the participation of foreign investment projects.

Ministry of Finance of the Russian Federation
Department of Tax Reforms

- Drafting taxation laws and regulations.
- Designing procedures for tax laws to be enforced.

State Property Committee (Goskomimushestvo of Russia - GKI)
Administration for Foreign Investment

- Formulation of options for participation of foreign investors in privatization.
- Administration of foreign investors participation in privatization.

Russian Fund for Federal Property (RFFP)

- Arranging for and holding investment and monetary auctions in the privatization process of state property.
- Control over the implementation of investment programs.

State Taxation Service of the Russian Federation (Gosnalogslujba of Russia)
Administration for Foreign Economic Relations and International Taxation

- Explanation of the enforcement of tax laws.
- Control over the implementation of tax laws.

State Customs Committee of the Russian Federation (SCC of Russia)

- Arranging for the customs legalization of foreign economic transactions.
- Customs regulation of foreign economic transactions.
- Control over the use of customs incentives.

For additional analytical, business and investment opportunities information, please contact Global Investment & Business Center, USA at (202) 546-2103. Fax: (202) 546-3275. E-mail: rusric@erols.com

State Registration Chamber of the Ministry of Economy of Russia

- Registration of ventures with foreign investments.
- Accreditation of the missions of foreign companies.
- Support in obtaining visas.

Foreign Investment Promotion Center (FIPC) of the Ministry of Economy of Russia

- Informational and advisory services for foreign investors.
- Dissemination of investment information - including information on investment projects in the Russian Federation.
- Assistance to businessmen in their quest of investment opportunities and particular partners.
- Coordination of the activities of the overseas investment offices.

Investment offices of the FIPC

- Dissemination of investment information, including investment projects in the Russian Federation.
- Promotion of investment projects in and offers of Russian enterprises.
- Advisory services for potential investors.

Federal Center for Project Financing

- Investment consulting.
- drafting of business plans.

INTERNATIONAL AGREEMENTS - BILATERAL INVESTMENT PROTECTION TREATIES AND OTHER INVESTMENT LEGISLATION[3]

As of June 1997, there were 11 bilateral investment protection treaties (BITs) in the Russian Federation. Most of these treaties were concluded by the former Soviet Union but are recognized by Russia as the USSR's legal successor. Additional treaties are under negotiations

The BITs are reciprocal treaties between Russia and individual foreign states that provide legal guarantees to investors from treaty states in Russia as well as to Russian investors in treaty states. Such guarantees normally pertain to the transfer of funds related to foreign investment activities, expropriation and similar measures, losses as a result of armed conflict and civil disturbance as well as the legal succession of investment insurance agencies (subrogation). Under these treaties, foreign investors are assured of either:

1) **"national treatment" - treatment no less favorable than the one accorded to Russian investors;**
2) **"most favored nation treatment" - treatment no less favorable than the one accorded to investors from any third country; and,**
3) **"full protection and security".**

Furthermore, they provide international arbitration for the resolution of disputes arising under the treaties. Such recourse applies to disputes between the contracting states ("state-to-state disputes") and disputes between protected foreign investors and the host state ("investor disputes").

---

[3] For the complete texts of legislation, please contact Russian Info&Business Center, Inc. at (202) 546-2103

For additional analytical, business and investment opportunities information, please contact Global Investment & Business Center, USA at (202) 546-2103. Fax: (202) 546-3275. E-mail: rusric@erols.com

The treatment of "indirect" and "creeping" expropriations are some of the important differences between BITs - even though most of them have similar provisions. In several BITs, transfer guarantees are subject to qualifications.

Under the "umbrella clause", any obligation toward a protected investor that is not fulfilled is considered a violation of the BIT. In this way, investors can obtain treaty protection of their contractual rights against Russian agencies.

In theory, differences among the BITs should not work against the investor. Because of the most favored nation treatment (MFN) provisions, investors from any country that has concluded a BIT with Russia can invoke in their favor the guarantees under any treaty between Russia and any third country. Thus, German investors in Russia are entitled to all the guarantees provided in the BITs of Russia with Austria, Canada, China, etc. The MFN provisions link all the Russian investment related treaties into a comprehensive network establishing the highest level of protection and investor freedoms envisaged under any one of these treaties.

MULTILATERAL CONVENTIONS

Russia is a member of several multilateral conventions which have the potential to affect the legal protection of investors on its territory. They include:

1 the 1988 **Multilateral Investment Guarantee Agency Convention** (the MIGA Convention) that facilitates the insurance against non-commercial risks in all signatory countries of investors from those countries;

2. the **Convention on the Recognition and Enforcement of Foreign Arbitrage Awards** signed in New York on June 10, 1958 (the New York Convention); and

3. the **Cooperation Agreement between Russia and the European Union.**

Other important conventions such as the one governing the settlement of investment disputes between states and nationals of other states - signed in Washington on March 18, 1965; the Convention on the International Center for the Settlements of Investment Disputes (ICSID Convention); and, the Energy Charter Treaty - signed in Lisbon on December 14, 1994 have not yet been ratified. The latter applies only to investments in the energy sector but lays out detailed standards for investment protection that reflect investment principles recognized internationally. Foreign investors may find this a useful reference in their negotiations with Russia.

RUSSIAN DOMESTIC LAWS

As of June 1997, most guarantees concerning foreign investment were embodied in the Foreign Investment Law. Foreign investors are assured of the following in Chapter 2 of this law:

1. Treatment no less favorable than that accorded to domestic investors (Article 6). Such national treatment, however, is subject to exceptions which may be established by domestic law, notably in the area of ownership or leasing of land and acquisition of rights to natural resources (Article 38) and in connection with privatization (Article 37).

2. Protection against nationalization, confiscation and illegal actions of state bodies and officials (Articles 7 and 8). Nationalization and confiscation measures require enacting legislation by Parliament - in case of confiscation by Parliament, the president or the government is responsible. Such procedures can be contested in Russian courts and must be accompanied by prompt, adequate and effective compensation. However, this guarantee does not explicitly extend to cases of so-called "indirect" and "creeping" expropriation, which are the main concern

of investors. Russian authorities compute the amount of compensation after the official announcement of confiscation. However, the value of the affected property may already have been largely discounted in anticipation of the measure.

3. Transfer abroad of investment proceeds in foreign currency (Article 10). One has to keep in mind that 50 percent of the revenues from Russian exports must be converted into rubles at the official exchange rate.

4. Reinvestment or other use inside Russia of investment proceeds in local currency (Article 11). While the conversion of local currency proceeds is not guaranteed by the Foreign Investment Law, investors can buy hard currency for rubles through banks or currency exchanges; and

5. Recourse to Russian courts and, in some instances, arbitration proceedings for the settlement of investment disputes (Article 9). However, according to international treaties, foreign investors are entitled to international arbitration. Investors from countries that have a BIT with Russia have access to international arbitration while investors from other countries do not.

Although the investment protection guarantees of the Foreign Investment Law overlap with those found in the BITs of Russia, the latter are frequently more comprehensive, avoid technical loopholes and can be enforced through recourse to international arbitration and diplomatic protection. Article 5 of the Law is particularly important. It provides that international treaties apply directly to foreign investments in Russia and take precedence over domestic law in cases of conflict. However, the latter rule may be subject to question if a conflict arises between an international treaty's provision and the Constitution of Russia.

ECONOMIC STABILIZATION TOOLS

Russian legislation provides a number of stabilization mechanisms in order to limit the damage a foreign investor may suffer in a deteriorating investment climate. The **Foreign Investment Law** includes a provision that postpone for one year the enforcement of a law or any legal act that deteriorates the conditions of preexisting foreign investments. **Presidential Decree No. 1466** "**On the Improvement of Work with Foreign Investment**", adopted on September 27, 1993 provides that legal acts will not be applied to already existing wholly or partly foreign-owned enterprises for a period of three years if they introduce changes for the worse. The law provides that they will apply immediately if they improve the present conditions. **Presidential Decree No. 2285 "On Issues of Agreements on Production Sharing in the Mineral Resource Sector",** adopted on December 24, 1993, applies the "grandfather" clause to production-sharing agreements between foreign investors and Russian state bodies. The clause calls for the agreement to be modified in order to keep the foreign investors as a whole entity. Thus, the Russian side to the agreement is the one that solely shoulder all the losses.

While "grandfather" schemes may provide some comfort to foreign investors, they afford only limited protection. First, they do not encompass all the types of adverse legislative changes. Second, the one to three years "freezing periods" are frequently too short, especially when investment projects have considerable lead times before they yield returns. Third, and foremost, the grandfather clauses are themselves part of domestic Russian legislation. As with any other piece of legislation, they can, at any moment, be changed or repealed by the Russian legislature.

Under the Russian Constitution, considerable powers have devolved to the Federation's jurisdictions and even to its municipalities. Local legislation can affect federal legislation on the rights of foreign investors. To safeguard investors against this possibility, the two presidential decrees mentioned above have provisions that void sub-federal legislation impairing federal laws or decrees. The validity and scope of these provisions might, however, raise questions about their constitutionality.

DISPUTE RESOLUTION

As mentioned above, Russia is a member of the ICSID Convention - an important international convention for the resolution of disputes with foreign investors. This Convention was opened to signature on March 18, 1965 on behalf of member countries of the International Bank for Reconstruction and Development to provide facilities for the conciliation and arbitration of investment disputes between contracting states and nationals of other contracting states. There are clear indications that Russia might adhere to the Convention in the near future. According to Article 9 of the Foreign Investment Law, "investment disputes" are to be settled by the Supreme Court or by the Supreme Arbitration Court of the Russian Federation - if no other methods of settlement are stipulated by international agreements. Therefore, the Russian Foreign Investment Law leaves a door open for the international settlement of investment disputes.

Furthermore, Russia has subscribed to several bilateral treaties on investment protection - these usually incorporate provisions on the settlement of investment disputes. Foreign investors must keep in mind that the stipulation of international treaties prevail over Russian domestic legislation. As to "other disputes" where a treaties prevail over Russian foreign interest is involved, these would typically be decided by Russian Courts, unless the parties have agreed to have them settled by arbitration.

Disputes involving an enterprise with foreign interest are usually considered, under Russian law, as disputes having an international character. Therefore, upon agreement between the parties, such disputes can be submitted for arbitration in any country. The parties are free to choose either *ad hoc* or "institutional" arbitration, and under certain circumstances they have also the choice of the substantive law.

Several Russian bodies are members of the International Chamber of Commerce - though Russia is not a member of the ICC's International Court of Arbitration. Nevertheless, ICC arbitration is increasingly being adopted involving foreign investment in Russia.

Foreign investors are advised to pay particular attention when choosing the most appropriate provision for arbitration in their contractual relationships with Russian partners or Russian subjects, as well as in the relationships between their fully or partially owned Russian enterprise and other physical and legal persons.

Special courts have been set up in Russia to replace the previous body - State Arbitration or *Gosarbitrazh* - for the settlement of economic disputes. The jurisdiction of these courts (commonly referred to as arbitrage tribunals) should not generally apply to foreign investors and/or enterprises with foreign participation. Their jurisdiction would apply only if the disputing parties agree, or if stipulated by intergovernmental or international agreement. In certain areas - mainly administrative disputes - the competence of these tribunals is considered exclusive and mandatory.

INCENTIVES & PRIVILEGES FOR INVESTORS

Incentives are granted to producers and investors promoting the development of various regions or economic sectors. The system of incentives, however, is subject to frequent changes.

SPECIAL TAX INCENTIVES

The Foreign Investment Law (Article 28) provides that tax incentives may be granted to enterprises with foreign investments operating in priority areas and in certain regions. In practice, however, a two year tax break previously applicable to enterprises with foreign investment (three years in the Far East Region) was repealed. Special tax incentives currently available are extremely limited. At the present time, enterprises registered after January 1, 1994 are the beneficiaries - under

For additional analytical, business and investment opportunities information,
please contact Global Investment & Business Center, USA
at (202) 546-2103. Fax: (202) 546-3275. E-mail: rusric@erols.com

those tax incentives - of a two year tax break (reduced to 25 percent and 50 percent of the base tax rate in years three and four, respectively) if they:

- **are involved in the material production activities, and;**

- **have at least 30 percent paid in foreign equity participation - the sum must be equal to a minimum of $10 million.**

Moreover, tax breaks are only available if the income from production activities during the first two years is greater than 70 percent of the enterprise's total income from all activities (90 percent during years three and four).

CUSTOMS INCENTIVES

Property imported into Russia by foreign investors as a contribution to the charter capital is exempt from customs duties upon importation (also see Chapter 5). Tariff incentives, such as return of earlier paid customs, lower tariff rates or total exemptions, apply to:

- **imported goods that will be contributed to the authorized capital;**
- **certain products and exports;**
- **property imported by foreign employees for their own needs.**

With a special permission of the Russian Government, tariffs are reduced by 50 per- cent on certain goods imported as foreign investments if:

- **the foreign suppliers are, at the same time, the founders of enterprises producing similar goods on the Russian territory;**
- **these enterprises use Russian raw materials and labor;**
- **foreign companies invest into material production;**
- **total investments into the enterprise are no less than US$ 100 million;**
- **foreign contribution to the authorized capital of the enterprise is not less than US$ 10 million.**

EXPORT AND IMPORT ACTIVITY

Foreign affiliates and enterprises with more than a 30 percent equity stake in Russian companies may export their products and import goods for their needs without any import or export license. Since 1994, export licenses have been required only for "strategic natural resources" products.

HARD CURRENCY RECEIPTS

Enterprises operating in Russia are obliged to exchange 50 percent of their hard-currency income into rubles on the domestic currency market. It is, however, possible to buy hard currency for import needs or for transfers abroad.

FINANCING FACILITIES

Presidential Decree No. 1928, "On Private Investments in the Russian Federation", adopted on September 17, 1994 authorizes the Russian Government to allocate 0.5 percent of its gross domestic product to finance highly efficient investment projects that have a commercial participation. The State contribution to such projects is usually 20 percent - it is no greater than 80 percent of the investment. The balance of funds in the project must be made up by private investors.

These are some of the possible forms that State participation can take in a project:

For additional analytical, business and investment opportunities information, please contact Global Investment & Business Center, USA at (202) 546-2103. Fax: (202) 546-3275. E-mail: rusric@erols.com

- **loan by the Russian Central Bank, denominated in foreign currency for a maximum of 24 months;**
- **government purchases of equity in joint-stock companies that can be sold on the market once the project is profitable; and**
- **special incentives for large investments when a foreign contribution exceeds 30 per- cent of share capital.**

FREE ECONOMIC ZONES

Russia is eager to use free economic zones (FEZs) to encourage foreign investment. About 15 FEZs exist in Russia, the most advanced of which are in **Nachodka** - in the Far East - and **Yantar** - in Kaliningrad.

The conditions for investments in FEZs differ from zone to zone and are regulated by each zone's laws and regulations. Federal legislation regulates only the most important issues.

The incentives may be the following:

- **simplified registration of enterprises in the FEZs;**
- **lower rates of taxation - they can, however, not be lower than 50 percent of the rate being applied on the Russian territory;**
- **lower leasing rates for land and leasing terms up to 70 years;**
- **lower tariffs on imports and exports, and expedient border procedures;**
- **simplified procedures for the entry and exit of foreign citizens, including waiver of visa requirements.**

All incentives are to be endorsed by the Russian Council of Ministers and approved by the Parliament.

Free Customs Zones and Bonded Warehouses are the two specific types of FEZs detailed in the Customs Code of the Russian Federation - adopted on June 18, 1993.

INVESTMENT PROMOTION

A system of foreign investment promotion has been established in the Russian Federation (see Appendix E). The Ministry of the Economy assumes the leading role in the promotion of foreign investment and is responsible for: drafting and implementing state policy aimed at attracting foreign investment; coordinating the activities of the federal and regional executive bodies regarding the cooperation with foreign investors; establishing free economic zones; arranging for and holding international tenders; arranging for concession agreements and production sharing deals; and, allocating loans provided by international financial organizations and foreign states. The Department for International Investment Cooperation has been established within the Ministry of the Economy for the purpose of dealing with the specific FDI promotion issues. This Department ensures the interaction with other executive bodies and deals practically with all major issues of state DFI policy.

The State Registration Chamber has been established within the Russian Ministry of the Economy. Registering ventures with foreign investments, keeping a State register of ventures, and accrediting the missions of foreign companies is authorized under the law.

Information and consultative services for foreign investors are rendered by the Foreign Investment Promotion Center (FIPC) - which is affiliated to the Ministry of the Economy.

The Federal Center for Project Financing makes pre-feasibility studies. It also makes expert analysis of international investment cooperation and the use of credits granted under the guarantees of the Russian government.

The Ministry of Finance, the State Property Committee (GKI), the Federal Property Fund, the State Tax Service, the State Customs Committee, and the Russian Central Bank also play an active role in foreign investment promotion.

ADVISORY COUNCIL ON FOREIGN INVESTMENT

In June 1994, the Advisory Council on Foreign Investment was created to promote foreign investment. It was created on the initiative of the Government of the Russian Federation and more than 20 representatives of major international corporations. The Advisory Group is chaired by Prime Minister .

Governmental Decree No. 1108 dated September 29, 1994 officially established the Advisory Group. According to the Decree the three working groups have been formed to draft proposals:

- to upgrade Russia's attractiveness as an investment location, especially for foreign investors - this group is headed by the Minister of the Economy

- to eliminate external barriers for Russian exporters - this group is headed Deputy Prime Minister and Minister of Foreign Economic Relations, and,

- to improve tax legislation and incentive measures for foreign investments - this group is headed by the Minister of Finance

Proposals and recommendations were drafted by these groups and presented to the first meeting of the Advisory Council in November 1994. Many of the recommendations have been taken under consideration by the Government and proposed to the Duma. A special plan on implementing these recommendations has been developed by the different Russian ministries involved and by representatives of the work groups. The plan includes concrete measures which could improve banking and currency regulation, introduce changes in the tax law and clarify some articles concerning tax legislation.

FOREIGN INVESTMENT PROMOTION CENTER

The **Foreign Investment Promotion Center (FIPC)** was created in June 1997 as a standard framework for the long-term attraction of foreign capital. The FIPC, in accordance with Governmental Decree No. 657, adopted on June 30, 1997, is a government body subordinated to the Russian Ministry of the Economy.

The mission of the FIPC is to attract, facilitate and increase foreign investment into the Russian Federation.

The main objectives of the Centers are:

- **to effectively encourage foreign investment into the Russian economy;**
- **to study investment projects and bring together potential partners;**
- **to make it attractive for foreign investors to establish a presence in Russia;**
- **to advocate laws and regulations to improve Russia's investment climate;**
- **to offer pre- and post-investment services to foreign investors;**
- **to give support and guidance to Russian regions and to their investment promotion agencies for local industries;**

For additional analytical, business and investment opportunities information,
please contact Global Investment & Business Center, USA
at (202) 546-2103. Fax: (202) 546-3275. E-mail: rusric@erols.com

In accordance with its objectives the FIPC carries out the following services:

- **promulgates cooperation and ensures the assistance of Russian federal and regional executive government bodies to potential investors;**
- **assists, advises and renders administrative support to foreign companies already present in Russia;**
- **supplies information on new investment opportunities in Russia and its Regions and markets Russian investment projects abroad through FIPC's offices in Western Europe;**
- **provides the foreign investor with all of the basic data he requires in order to structure his project and appraise it in advance;**
- **informs foreign investors on the changes in the Russian foreign investment legislation and consults on the existing laws and regulations concerning foreign companies activities in Russia;**
- **identifies Russian partners for foreign firms and business people looking for partnership in Russia and its different regions;**
- **arranges contacts and prepares the itineraries for the prospective investors visiting business locations of Russian partners;**
- **assists in the negotiation process between foreign investors and Russian partners and holds talks with potential investors on the required conditions to attract and use foreign investment credits in Russia.**

In order to fulfill these objectives, the FIPCs decided to open overseas offices in Frankfurt, Paris, London and Milan during the next two years. The first two offices - Frankfurt and Paris - started their activities in the Fall of 1997.

The European Bank for Reconstruction assists the FIPC in its activities. The FIPC has elaborated its investment promotion methodology based on the practices which have been successfully developed by such prominent investment promotion institutions as the Industrial Development Agency of Ireland and the Foreign Investment Advisory Service and Multilateral investment Guarantee Agency - both divisions of the World Bank.

According to the existing foreign investment promotional techniques, the following forms of activity will be undertaken by FIPC through its Moscow led network of offices:
- **advertising,**
- **direct mailing;**
- **investment seminars;**
- **investment missions;**
- **participation in trade shows and exhibitions;**
- **distribution of literature;**
- **one-to-one direct mailing efforts;**
- **preparation for the visits of prospective investors;**
- **matching prospective investors with local partners;**
- **acquiring permits and approvals from various governmental departments;**
- **preparing project proposals;**
- **conducting feasibility studies;**
- **providing services to investors after the projects have become operational.**

Russian Foreign Investment Promotion Center:
Smolensky Bulvar, 3/5, Moscow, Russia,.
Tel: 7 095 245 21 71 or 7 095 246 94 39, Fax: 7 095 246 94 39.

For additional analytical, business and investment opportunities information,
please contact Global Investment & Business Center, USA
at (202) 546-2103. Fax: (202) 546-3275. E-mail: rusric@erols.com

OTHER ORGANIZATIONS

Several "joint ventures" associations and clubs are currently in existence in Russia. Two of the most prominent ones - the Association of joint Ventures and the International Associations and Organizations - unite joint ventures and 100% foreign owned enterprises from all over the country. Similar organizations exist in Moscow and St. Petersburg. The aim of these organizations is to bring together managers with similar purposes and problems, to exchange information, to support business conferences, to help in the search of partners, to provide legal support, etc.

Recently, several State and privately-owned insurance companies have begun to operate with
        foreign investors covering non-commercial risks. One of them is the International Agency for
        Insurance of Non-Commercial Risks. This Agency is supported by the Russian Government.

Foreign investors can also apply to the Russian Finance Corporation - created in April 1993. It primarily works as an agent of the Russian Government and finances investment projects with centralized finance and credit resources. The Corporation has preferential treatment when it comes to finance and foreign trade operations.

Foreign firms can also get the support from the Russian Chamber of Commerce and Industry, the Ministry of Foreign Economic Relations, various Russian-foreign associations, and others - all of them well-known in the Russian Federation Foreign Economic Relations.

For additional analytical, business and investment opportunities information,
please contact Global Investment & Business Center, USA
at (202) 546-2103. Fax: (202) 546-3275. E-mail: rusric@erols.com

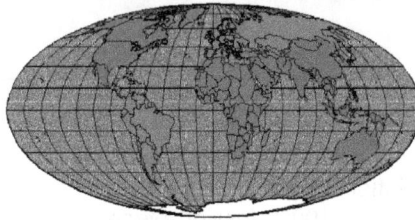

WORLD BUSINESS AND INVESTMENT OPPORTUNITIES YEARBOOK LIBRARY

World Business Information Catalog, USA: http://www.ibpus.com
Email: ibpusa3@gmail.com

Price: $99.95 Each

TITLE
Abkhazia (Republic of Abkhazia) Business and Investment Opportunities Yearbook Volume 1 Strategic, Practical Information and Opportunities
Afghanistan Business and Investment Opportunities Yearbook Volume 1 Strategic, Practical Information and Opportunities
Aland Business and Investment Opportunities Yearbook Volume 1 Strategic, Practical Information and Opportunities
Albania Business and Investment Opportunities Yearbook Volume 1 Strategic, Practical Information and Opportunities
Algeria Business and Investment Opportunities Yearbook Volume 1 Strategic, Practical Information and Opportunities
Andorra Business and Investment Opportunities Yearbook Volume 1 Strategic, Practical Information and Opportunities
Angola Business and Investment Opportunities Yearbook Volume 1 Strategic, Practical Information and Opportunities
Anguilla Business and Investment Opportunities Yearbook Volume 1 Strategic, Practical Information and Opportunities
Antigua and Barbuda Business and Investment Opportunities Yearbook Volume 1 Strategic, Practical Information and Opportunities
Antilles (Netherlands) Business and Investment Opportunities Yearbook Volume 1 Strategic, Practical Information and Opportunities
Argentina Business and Investment Opportunities Yearbook Volume 1 Strategic, Practical Information and Opportunities
Armenia Business and Investment Opportunities Yearbook Volume 1 Strategic, Practical Information and Opportunities
Aruba Business and Investment Opportunities Yearbook Volume 1 Strategic, Practical Information and Opportunities
Australia Business and Investment Opportunities Yearbook Volume 1 Strategic, Practical Information and Opportunities
Austria Business and Investment Opportunities Yearbook Volume 1 Strategic, Practical Information and Opportunities
Azerbaijan Business and Investment Opportunities Yearbook Volume 1 Strategic, Practical Information and Opportunities
Bahamas Business and Investment Opportunities Yearbook Volume 1 Strategic, Practical Information and Opportunities
Bahrain Business and Investment Opportunities Yearbook Volume 1 Strategic, Practical Information and Opportunities
Bangladesh Business and Investment Opportunities Yearbook Volume 1 Strategic, Practical Information and Opportunities
Barbados Business and Investment Opportunities Yearbook Volume 1 Strategic, Practical Information and Opportunities
Belarus Business and Investment Opportunities Yearbook Volume 1 Strategic, Practical Information and Opportunities

For additional analytical, business and investment opportunities information,
Please contact Global Investment & Business Center, USA
at (202) 546-2103. Fax: (202) 546-3275. E-mail: ibpusa3@gmail.com

TITLE
Belgium Business and Investment Opportunities Yearbook Volume 1 Strategic, Practical Information and Opportunities
Belize Business and Investment Opportunities Yearbook Volume 1 Strategic, Practical Information and Opportunities
Benin Business and Investment Opportunities Yearbook Volume 1 Strategic, Practical Information and Opportunities
Bermuda Business and Investment Opportunities Yearbook Volume 1 Strategic, Practical Information and Opportunities
Bhutan Business and Investment Opportunities Yearbook Volume 1 Strategic, Practical Information and Opportunities
Bolivia Business and Investment Opportunities Yearbook Volume 1 Strategic, Practical Information and Opportunities
Bosnia and Herzegovina Business and Investment Opportunities Yearbook Volume 1 Strategic, Practical Information and Opportunities
Botswana Business and Investment Opportunities Yearbook Volume 1 Strategic, Practical Information and Opportunities
Brazil Business and Investment Opportunities Yearbook Volume 1 Strategic, Practical Information and Opportunities
Brunei Business and Investment Opportunities Yearbook Volume 1 Strategic, Practical Information and Opportunities
Bulgaria Business and Investment Opportunities Yearbook Volume 1 Strategic, Practical Information and Opportunities
Burkina Faso Business and Investment Opportunities Yearbook Volume 1 Strategic, Practical Information and Opportunities
Burundi Business and Investment Opportunities Yearbook Volume 1 Strategic, Practical Information and Opportunities
Cambodia Business and Investment Opportunities Yearbook Volume 1 Strategic, Practical Information and Opportunities
Cameroon Business and Investment Opportunities Yearbook Volume 1 Strategic, Practical Information and Opportunities
Canada Business and Investment Opportunities Yearbook Volume 1 Strategic, Practical Information and Opportunities
Cape Verde Business and Investment Opportunities Yearbook Volume 1 Strategic, Practical Information and Opportunities
Cayman Islands Business and Investment Opportunities Yearbook Volume 1 Strategic, Practical Information and Opportunities
Central African Republic Business and Investment Opportunities Yearbook Volume 1 Strategic, Practical Information and Opportunities
Chad Business and Investment Opportunities Yearbook Volume 1 Strategic, Practical Information and Opportunities
Chile Business and Investment Opportunities Yearbook Volume 1 Strategic, Practical Information and Opportunities
China Business and Investment Opportunities Yearbook Volume 1 Strategic, Practical Information and Opportunities
Colombia Business and Investment Opportunities Yearbook Volume 1 Strategic, Practical Information and Opportunities
Comoros Business and Investment Opportunities Yearbook Volume 1 Strategic, Practical Information and Opportunities
Congo Business and Investment Opportunities Yearbook Volume 1 Strategic, Practical Information and Opportunities
Congo, Democratic Republic Business and Investment Opportunities Yearbook Volume 1 Strategic, Practical Information and Opportunities
Cook Islands Business and Investment Opportunities Yearbook Volume 1 Strategic, Practical Information and Opportunities
Costa Rica Business and Investment Opportunities Yearbook Volume 1 Strategic, Practical Information and Opportunities

For additional analytical, business and investment opportunities information,
Please contact Global Investment & Business Center, USA
at (202) 546-2103. Fax: (202) 546-3275. E-mail: ibpusa3@gmail.com

TITLE
Cote d'Ivoire Business and Investment Opportunities Yearbook Volume 1 Strategic, Practical Information and Opportunities
Croatia Business and Investment Opportunities Yearbook Volume 1 Strategic, Practical Information and Opportunities
Cuba Business and Investment Opportunities Yearbook Volume 1 Strategic, Practical Information and Opportunities
Cyprus Business and Investment Opportunities Yearbook Volume 1 Strategic, Practical Information and Opportunities
Czech Republic Business and Investment Opportunities Yearbook Volume 1 Strategic, Practical Information and Opportunities
Denmark Business and Investment Opportunities Yearbook Volume 1 Strategic, Practical Information and Opportunities
Djibouti Business and Investment Opportunities Yearbook Volume 1 Strategic, Practical Information and Opportunities
Dominica Business and Investment Opportunities Yearbook Volume 1 Strategic, Practical Information and Opportunities
Dominican Republic Business and Investment Opportunities Yearbook Volume 1 Strategic, Practical Information and Opportunities
Ecuador Business and Investment Opportunities Yearbook Volume 1 Strategic, Practical Information and Opportunities
Egypt Business and Investment Opportunities Yearbook Volume 1 Strategic, Practical Information and Opportunities
El Salvador Business and Investment Opportunities Yearbook Volume 1 Strategic, Practical Information and Opportunities
Equatorial Guinea Business and Investment Opportunities Yearbook Volume 1 Strategic, Practical Information and Opportunities
Eritrea Business and Investment Opportunities Yearbook Volume 1 Strategic, Practical Information and Opportunities
Estonia Business and Investment Opportunities Yearbook Volume 1 Strategic, Practical Information and Opportunities
Ethiopia Business and Investment Opportunities Yearbook Volume 1 Strategic, Practical Information and Opportunities
Falkland Islands Business and Investment Opportunities Yearbook Volume 1 Strategic, Practical Information and Opportunities
Faroes Islands Business and Investment Opportunities Yearbook Volume 1 Strategic, Practical Information and Opportunities
Fiji Business and Investment Opportunities Yearbook Volume 1 Strategic, Practical Information and Opportunities
Finland Business and Investment Opportunities Yearbook Volume 1 Strategic, Practical Information and Opportunities
France Business and Investment Opportunities Yearbook Volume 1 Strategic, Practical Information and Opportunities
Gabon Business and Investment Opportunities Yearbook Volume 1 Strategic, Practical Information and Opportunities
Gambia Business and Investment Opportunities Yearbook Volume 1 Strategic, Practical Information and Opportunities
Georgia Business and Investment Opportunities Yearbook Volume 1 Strategic, Practical Information and Opportunities
Germany Business and Investment Opportunities Yearbook Volume 1 Strategic, Practical Information and Opportunities
Ghana Business and Investment Opportunities Yearbook Volume 1 Strategic, Practical Information and Opportunities
Gibraltar Business and Investment Opportunities Yearbook Volume 1 Strategic, Practical Information and Opportunities
Greece Business and Investment Opportunities Yearbook Volume 1 Strategic, Practical Information and Opportunities

For additional analytical, business and investment opportunities information,
Please contact Global Investment & Business Center, USA
at (202) 546-2103. Fax: (202) 546-3275. E-mail: ibpusa3@gmail.com

TITLE
Greenland Business and Investment Opportunities Yearbook Volume 1 Strategic, Practical Information and Opportunities
Grenada Business and Investment Opportunities Yearbook Volume 1 Strategic, Practical Information and Opportunities
Guam Business and Investment Opportunities Yearbook Volume 1 Strategic, Practical Information and Opportunities
Guatemala Business and Investment Opportunities Yearbook Volume 1 Strategic, Practical Information and Opportunities
Guernsey Business and Investment Opportunities Yearbook Volume 1 Strategic, Practical Information and Opportunities
Guinea Business and Investment Opportunities Yearbook Volume 1 Strategic, Practical Information and Opportunities
Guinea-Bissau Business and Investment Opportunities Yearbook Volume 1 Strategic, Practical Information and Opportunities
Guyana Business and Investment Opportunities Yearbook Volume 1 Strategic, Practical Information and Opportunities
Haiti Business and Investment Opportunities Yearbook Volume 1 Strategic, Practical Information and Opportunities
Honduras Business and Investment Opportunities Yearbook Volume 1 Strategic, Practical Information and Opportunities
Hungary Business and Investment Opportunities Yearbook Volume 1 Strategic, Practical Information and Opportunities
Iceland Business and Investment Opportunities Yearbook Volume 1 Strategic, Practical Information and Opportunities
India Business and Investment Opportunities Yearbook Volume 1 Strategic, Practical Information and Opportunities
Indonesia Business and Investment Opportunities Yearbook Volume 1 Strategic, Practical Information and Opportunities
Iran Business and Investment Opportunities Yearbook Volume 1 Strategic, Practical Information and Opportunities
Iraq Business and Investment Opportunities Yearbook Volume 1 Strategic, Practical Information and Opportunities
Ireland Business and Investment Opportunities Yearbook Volume 1 Strategic, Practical Information and Opportunities
Israel Business and Investment Opportunities Yearbook Volume 1 Strategic, Practical Information and Opportunities
Italy Business and Investment Opportunities Yearbook Volume 1 Strategic, Practical Information and Opportunities
Jamaica Business and Investment Opportunities Yearbook Volume 1 Strategic, Practical Information and Opportunities
Japan Business and Investment Opportunities Yearbook Volume 1 Strategic, Practical Information and Opportunities
Jersey Business and Investment Opportunities Yearbook Volume 1 Strategic, Practical Information and Opportunities
Jordan Business and Investment Opportunities Yearbook Volume 1 Strategic, Practical Information and Opportunities
Kazakhstan Business and Investment Opportunities Yearbook Volume 1 Strategic, Practical Information and Opportunities
Kenya Business and Investment Opportunities Yearbook Volume 1 Strategic, Practical Information and Opportunities
Kiribati Business and Investment Opportunities Yearbook Volume 1 Strategic, Practical Information and Opportunities
Korea, North Business and Investment Opportunities Yearbook Volume 1 Strategic, Practical Information and Opportunities
Korea, South Business and Investment Opportunities Yearbook Volume 1 Strategic, Practical Information and Opportunities

For additional analytical, business and investment opportunities information,
Please contact Global Investment & Business Center, USA
at (202) 546-2103. Fax: (202) 546-3275. E-mail: ibpusa3@gmail.com

TITLE
Kosovo Business and Investment Opportunities Yearbook Volume 1 Strategic, Practical Information and Opportunities
Kurdistan Business and Investment Opportunities Yearbook Volume 1 Strategic, Practical Information and Opportunities
Kuwait Business and Investment Opportunities Yearbook Volume 1 Strategic, Practical Information and Opportunities
Kyrgyzstan Business and Investment Opportunities Yearbook Volume 1 Strategic, Practical Information and Opportunities
Laos Business and Investment Opportunities Yearbook Volume 1 Strategic, Practical Information and Opportunities
Latvia Business and Investment Opportunities Yearbook Volume 1 Strategic, Practical Information and Opportunities
Lebanon Business and Investment Opportunities Yearbook Volume 1 Strategic, Practical Information and Opportunities
Lesotho Business and Investment Opportunities Yearbook Volume 1 Strategic, Practical Information and Opportunities
Liberia Business and Investment Opportunities Yearbook Volume 1 Strategic, Practical Information and Opportunities
Libya Business and Investment Opportunities Yearbook Volume 1 Strategic, Practical Information and Opportunities
Liechtenstein Business and Investment Opportunities Yearbook Volume 1 Strategic, Practical Information and Opportunities
Lithuania Business and Investment Opportunities Yearbook Volume 1 Strategic, Practical Information and Opportunities
Luxembourg Business and Investment Opportunities Yearbook Volume 1 Strategic, Practical Information and Opportunities
Macao Business and Investment Opportunities Yearbook Volume 1 Strategic, Practical Information and Opportunities
Macedonia Business and Investment Opportunities Yearbook Volume 1 Strategic, Practical Information and Opportunities
Madagascar Business and Investment Opportunities Yearbook Volume 1 Strategic, Practical Information and Opportunities
Madeira Business and Investment Opportunities Yearbook Volume 1 Strategic, Practical Information and Opportunities
Malawi Business and Investment Opportunities Yearbook Volume 1 Strategic, Practical Information and Opportunities
Malaysia Business and Investment Opportunities Yearbook Volume 1 Strategic, Practical Information and Opportunities
Maldives Business and Investment Opportunities Yearbook Volume 1 Strategic, Practical Information and Opportunities
Mali Business and Investment Opportunities Yearbook Volume 1 Strategic, Practical Information and Opportunities
Malta Business and Investment Opportunities Yearbook Volume 1 Strategic, Practical Information and Opportunities
Man Business and Investment Opportunities Yearbook Volume 1 Strategic, Practical Information and Opportunities
Marshall Islands Business and Investment Opportunities Yearbook Volume 1 Strategic, Practical Information and Opportunities
Mauritania Business and Investment Opportunities Yearbook Volume 1 Strategic, Practical Information and Opportunities
Mauritius Business and Investment Opportunities Yearbook Volume 1 Strategic, Practical Information and Opportunities
Mayotte Business and Investment Opportunities Yearbook Volume 1 Strategic, Practical Information and Opportunities
Mexico Business and Investment Opportunities Yearbook Volume 1 Strategic, Practical Information and Opportunities

For additional analytical, business and investment opportunities information,
Please contact Global Investment & Business Center, USA
at (202) 546-2103. Fax: (202) 546-3275. E-mail: ibpusa3@gmail.com

TITLE
Micronesia Business and Investment Opportunities Yearbook Volume 1 Strategic, Practical Information and Opportunities
Moldova Business and Investment Opportunities Yearbook Volume 1 Strategic, Practical Information and Opportunities
Monaco Business and Investment Opportunities Yearbook Volume 1 Strategic, Practical Information and Opportunities
Mongolia Business and Investment Opportunities Yearbook Volume 1 Strategic, Practical Information and Opportunities
Montserrat Business and Investment Opportunities Yearbook Volume 1 Strategic, Practical Information and Opportunities
Montenegro Business and Investment Opportunities Yearbook Volume 1 Strategic, Practical Information and Opportunities
Morocco Business and Investment Opportunities Yearbook Volume 1 Strategic, Practical Information and Opportunities
Mozambique Business and Investment Opportunities Yearbook Volume 1 Strategic, Practical Information and Opportunities
Myanmar Business and Investment Opportunities Yearbook Volume 1 Strategic, Practical Information and Opportunities
Nagorno-Karabakh Republic Business and Investment Opportunities Yearbook Volume 1 Strategic, Practical Information and Opportunities
Namibia Business and Investment Opportunities Yearbook Volume 1 Strategic, Practical Information and Opportunities
Nauru Business and Investment Opportunities Yearbook Volume 1 Strategic, Practical Information and Opportunities
Nepal Business and Investment Opportunities Yearbook Volume 1 Strategic, Practical Information and Opportunities
Netherlands Business and Investment Opportunities Yearbook Volume 1 Strategic, Practical Information and Opportunities
New Caledonia Business and Investment Opportunities Yearbook Volume 1 Strategic, Practical Information and Opportunities
New Zealand Business and Investment Opportunities Yearbook Volume 1 Strategic, Practical Information and Opportunities
Nicaragua Business and Investment Opportunities Yearbook Volume 1 Strategic, Practical Information and Opportunities
Niger Business and Investment Opportunities Yearbook Volume 1 Strategic, Practical Information and Opportunities
Nigeria Business and Investment Opportunities Yearbook Volume 1 Strategic, Practical Information and Opportunities
Niue Business and Investment Opportunities Yearbook Volume 1 Strategic, Practical Information and Opportunities
Northern Cyprus (Turkish Republic of Northern Cyprus) Business and Investment Opportunities Yearbook Volume 1 Strategic, Practical Information and Opportunities
Northern Mariana Islands Business and Investment Opportunities Yearbook Volume 1 Strategic, Practical Information and Opportunities
Norway Business and Investment Opportunities Yearbook Volume 1 Strategic, Practical Information and Opportunities
Oman Business and Investment Opportunities Yearbook Volume 1 Strategic, Practical Information and Opportunities
Pakistan Business and Investment Opportunities Yearbook Volume 1 Strategic, Practical Information and Opportunities
Palau Business and Investment Opportunities Yearbook Volume 1 Strategic, Practical Information and Opportunities
Palestine (West Bank & Gaza) Business and Investment Opportunities Yearbook Volume 1 Strategic, Practical Information and Opportunities
Panama Business and Investment Opportunities Yearbook Volume 1 Strategic, Practical Information and Opportunities

For additional analytical, business and investment opportunities information,
Please contact Global Investment & Business Center, USA
at (202) 546-2103. Fax: (202) 546-3275. E-mail: ibpusa3@gmail.com

TITLE
Papua New Guinea Business and Investment Opportunities Yearbook Volume 1 Strategic, Practical Information and Opportunities
Paraguay Business and Investment Opportunities Yearbook Volume 1 Strategic, Practical Information and Opportunities
Peru Business and Investment Opportunities Yearbook Volume 1 Strategic, Practical Information and Opportunities
Philippines Business and Investment Opportunities Yearbook Volume 1 Strategic, Practical Information and Opportunities
Pitcairn Islands Business and Investment Opportunities Yearbook Volume 1 Strategic, Practical Information and Opportunities
Poland Business and Investment Opportunities Yearbook Volume 1 Strategic, Practical Information and Opportunities
Polynesia French Business and Investment Opportunities Yearbook Volume 1 Strategic, Practical Information and Opportunities
Portugal Business and Investment Opportunities Yearbook Volume 1 Strategic, Practical Information and Opportunities
Qatar Business and Investment Opportunities Yearbook Volume 1 Strategic, Practical Information and Opportunities
Romania Business and Investment Opportunities Yearbook Volume 1 Strategic, Practical Information and Opportunities
Russia Business and Investment Opportunities Yearbook Volume 1 Strategic, Practical Information and Opportunities
Rwanda Business and Investment Opportunities Yearbook Volume 1 Strategic, Practical Information and Opportunities
Sahrawi Arab Democratic Republic Volume 1 Strategic Information and Developments
Saint Kitts and Nevis Business and Investment Opportunities Yearbook Volume 1 Strategic, Practical Information and Opportunities
Saint Lucia Business and Investment Opportunities Yearbook Volume 1 Strategic, Practical Information and Opportunities
Saint Vincent and The Grenadines Business and Investment Opportunities Yearbook Volume 1 Strategic, Practical Information and Opportunities
Samoa (American) A Business and Investment Opportunities Yearbook Volume 1 Strategic, Practical Information and Opportunities
Samoa (Western) Business and Investment Opportunities Yearbook Volume 1 Strategic, Practical Information and Opportunities
San Marino Business and Investment Opportunities Yearbook Volume 1 Strategic, Practical Information and Opportunities
Sao Tome and Principe Business and Investment Opportunities Yearbook Volume 1 Strategic, Practical Information and Opportunities
Saudi Arabia Business and Investment Opportunities Yearbook Volume 1 Strategic, Practical Information and Opportunities
Scotland Business and Investment Opportunities Yearbook Volume 1 Strategic, Practical Information and Opportunities
Senegal Business and Investment Opportunities Yearbook Volume 1 Strategic, Practical Information and Opportunities
Serbia Business and Investment Opportunities Yearbook Volume 1 Strategic, Practical Information and Opportunities
Seychelles Business and Investment Opportunities Yearbook Volume 1 Strategic, Practical Information and Opportunities
Sierra Leone Business and Investment Opportunities Yearbook Volume 1 Strategic, Practical Information and Opportunities
Singapore Business and Investment Opportunities Yearbook Volume 1 Strategic, Practical Information and Opportunities
Slovakia Business and Investment Opportunities Yearbook Volume 1 Strategic, Practical Information and Opportunities

For additional analytical, business and investment opportunities information,
Please contact Global Investment & Business Center, USA
at (202) 546-2103. Fax: (202) 546-3275. E-mail: ibpusa3@gmail.com

TITLE
Slovenia Business and Investment Opportunities Yearbook Volume 1 Strategic, Practical Information and Opportunities
Solomon Islands Business and Investment Opportunities Yearbook Volume 1 Strategic, Practical Information and Opportunities
Somalia Business and Investment Opportunities Yearbook Volume 1 Strategic, Practical Information and Opportunities
South Africa Business and Investment Opportunities Yearbook Volume 1 Strategic, Practical Information and Opportunities
Spain Business and Investment Opportunities Yearbook Volume 1 Strategic, Practical Information and Opportunities
Sri Lanka Business and Investment Opportunities Yearbook Volume 1 Strategic, Practical Information and Opportunities
St. Helena Business and Investment Opportunities Yearbook Volume 1 Strategic, Practical Information and Opportunities
St. Pierre & Miquelon Business and Investment Opportunities Yearbook Volume 1 Strategic, Practical Information and Opportunities
Sudan (Republic of the Sudan) Business and Investment Opportunities Yearbook Volume 1 Strategic, Practical Information and Opportunities
Sudan South Business and Investment Opportunities Yearbook Volume 1 Strategic, Practical Information and Opportunities
Suriname Business and Investment Opportunities Yearbook Volume 1 Strategic, Practical Information and Opportunities
Swaziland Business and Investment Opportunities Yearbook Volume 1 Strategic, Practical Information and Opportunities
Sweden Business and Investment Opportunities Yearbook Volume 1 Strategic, Practical Information and Opportunities
Switzerland Business and Investment Opportunities Yearbook Volume 1 Strategic, Practical Information and Opportunities
Syria Business and Investment Opportunities Yearbook Volume 1 Strategic, Practical Information and Opportunities
Taiwan Business and Investment Opportunities Yearbook Volume 1 Strategic, Practical Information and Opportunities
Tajikistan Business and Investment Opportunities Yearbook Volume 1 Strategic, Practical Information and Opportunities
Tanzania Business and Investment Opportunities Yearbook Volume 1 Strategic, Practical Information and Opportunities
Thailand Business and Investment Opportunities Yearbook Volume 1 Strategic, Practical Information and Opportunities
Timor Leste (Democratic Republic of Timor-Leste) Business and Investment Opportunities Yearbook Volume 1 Strategic, Practical Information and Opportunities
Togo Business and Investment Opportunities Yearbook Volume 1 Strategic, Practical Information and Opportunities
Tonga Business and Investment Opportunities Yearbook Volume 1 Strategic, Practical Information and Opportunities
Trinidad and Tobago Business and Investment Opportunities Yearbook Volume 1 Strategic, Practical Information and Opportunities
Tunisia Business and Investment Opportunities Yearbook Volume 1 Strategic, Practical Information and Opportunities
Turkey Business and Investment Opportunities Yearbook Volume 1 Strategic, Practical Information and Opportunities
Turkmenistan Business and Investment Opportunities Yearbook Volume 1 Strategic, Practical Information and Opportunities
Turks & Caicos Business and Investment Opportunities Yearbook Volume 1 Strategic, Practical Information and Opportunities
Tuvalu Business and Investment Opportunities Yearbook Volume 1 Strategic, Practical Information and Opportunities

For additional analytical, business and investment opportunities information,
Please contact Global Investment & Business Center, USA
at (202) 546-2103. Fax: (202) 546-3275. E-mail: ibpusa3@gmail.com

TITLE
Uganda Business and Investment Opportunities Yearbook Volume 1 Strategic, Practical Information and Opportunities
Ukraine Business and Investment Opportunities Yearbook Volume 1 Strategic, Practical Information and Opportunities
United Arab Emirates Business and Investment Opportunities Yearbook Volume 1 Strategic, Practical Information and Opportunities
United Kingdom Business and Investment Opportunities Yearbook Volume 1 Strategic, Practical Information and Opportunities
United States Business and Investment Opportunities Yearbook Volume 1 Strategic, Practical Information and Opportunities
Uruguay Business and Investment Opportunities Yearbook Volume 1 Strategic, Practical Information and Opportunities
Uzbekistan Business and Investment Opportunities Yearbook Volume 1 Strategic, Practical Information and Opportunities
Vanuatu Business and Investment Opportunities Yearbook Volume 1 Strategic, Practical Information and Opportunities
Vatican City (Holy See) Business and Investment Opportunities Yearbook Volume 1 Strategic, Practical Information and Opportunities
Venezuela Business and Investment Opportunities Yearbook Volume 1 Strategic, Practical Information and Opportunities
Vietnam Business and Investment Opportunities Yearbook Volume 1 Strategic, Practical Information and Opportunities
Virgin Islands, British Business and Investment Opportunities Yearbook Volume 1 Strategic, Practical Information and Opportunities
Wake Atoll Business and Investment Opportunities Yearbook Volume 1 Strategic, Practical Information and Opportunities
Wallis & Futuna Business and Investment Opportunities Yearbook Volume 1 Strategic, Practical Information and Opportunities
Western Sahara Business and Investment Opportunities Yearbook Volume 1 Strategic, Practical Information and Opportunities
Yemen Business and Investment Opportunities Yearbook Volume 1 Strategic, Practical Information and Opportunities
Zambia Business and Investment Opportunities Yearbook Volume 1 Strategic, Practical Information and Opportunities
Zimbabwe Business and Investment Opportunities Yearbook Volume 1 Strategic, Practical Information and Opportunities

For additional analytical, business and investment opportunities information,
Please contact Global Investment & Business Center, USA
at (202) 546-2103. Fax: (202) 546-3275. E-mail: ibpusa3@gmail.com

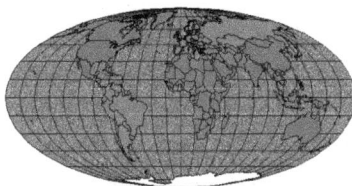

WORLD TELECOM INVESTMENT AND BUSINESS LIBRARY

Price: $199.95 Each

1.	Albania Telecom Industry Business and Investment Opportunities Handbook
2.	Algeria Telecom Industry Business and Investment Opportunities Handbook
3.	Angola Telecom Industry Business and Investment Opportunities Handbook
4.	Argentina Telecom Industry Business and Investment Opportunities Handbook
5.	Armenia Telecom Industry Business and Investment Opportunities Handbook
6.	Australia Telecom Industry Business and Investment Opportunities Handbook
7.	Austria Telecom Industry Business and Investment Opportunities Handbook
8.	Azerbaijan Telecom Industry Business and Investment Opportunities Handbook
9.	Bangladesh Telecom Industry Business and Investment Opportunities Handbook
10.	Belarus Telecom Industry Business and Investment Opportunities Handbook
11.	Belgium Telecom Industry Business and Investment Opportunities Handbook
12.	Bermuda Telecom Industry Business and Investment Opportunities Handbook
13.	Bolivia Telecom Industry Business and Investment Opportunities Handbook
14.	Bosnia and Herzegovina Telecom Industry Business and Investment Opportunities Handbook
15.	Botswana Telecom Industry Business and Investment Opportunities Handbook
16.	Brazil Telecom Industry Business and Investment Opportunities Handbook
17.	Bulgaria Telecom Industry Business and Investment Opportunities Handbook
18.	Cambodia Telecom Industry Business and Investment Opportunities Handbook
19.	Cameroon Telecom Industry Business and Investment Opportunities Handbook
20.	Canada Telecom Industry Business and Investment Opportunities Handbook
21.	Chile Telecom Industry Business and Investment Opportunities Handbook
22.	China Telecom Industry Business and Investment Opportunities Handbook
23.	Colombia Telecom Industry Business and Investment Opportunities Handbook
24.	Cook Islands Telecom Industry Business and Investment Opportunities Handbook
25.	Costa Rica Telecom Industry Business and Investment Opportunities Handbook
26.	Croatia Telecom Industry Business and Investment Opportunities Handbook
27.	Cuba Telecom Industry Business and Investment Opportunities Handbook
28.	Cyprus Telecom Industry Business and Investment Opportunities Handbook
29.	Czech Republic Telecom Industry Business and Investment Opportunities Handbook
30.	Denmark Telecom Industry Business and Investment Opportunities Handbook

For additional analytical, business and investment opportunities information,
please contact Global Investment & Business Center, USA
at (202) 546-2103. Fax: (202) 546-3275. E-mail: rusric@erols.com

31. Dominican Republic Telecom Industry Business and Investment Opportunities Handbook
32. Dubai Telecom Industry Business and Investment Opportunities Handbook
33. Ecuador Telecom Industry Business and Investment Opportunities Handbook
34. Egypt Telecom Industry Business and Investment Opportunities Handbook
35. El Salvador Telecom Industry Business and Investment Opportunities Handbook
36. Equatorial Guinea Telecom Industry Business and Investment Opportunities Handbook
37. Estonia Telecom Industry Business and Investment Opportunities Handbook
38. Fiji Telecom Industry Business and Investment Opportunities Handbook
39. Finland Telecom Industry Business and Investment Opportunities Handbook
40. France Telecom Industry Business and Investment Opportunities Handbook
41. Georgia Republic Telecom Industry Business and Investment Opportunities Handbook
42. Germany Telecom Industry Business and Investment Opportunities Handbook
43. Greece Telecom Industry Business and Investment Opportunities Handbook
44. Guatemala Telecom Industry Business and Investment Opportunities Handbook
45. Guernsey Telecom Industry Business and Investment Opportunities Handbook
46. Guyana Telecom Industry Business and Investment Opportunities Handbook
47. Haiti Telecom Industry Business and Investment Opportunities Handbook
48. Honduras Telecom Industry Business and Investment Opportunities Handbook
49. Hungary Telecom Industry Business and Investment Opportunities Handbook
50. Iceland Telecom Industry Business and Investment Opportunities Handbook
51. India Telecom Industry Business and Investment Opportunities Handbook
52. Indonesia Telecom Industry Business and Investment Opportunities Handbook
53. Iran Telecom Industry Business and Investment Opportunities Handbook
54. Iraq Telecom Industry Business and Investment Opportunities Handbook
55. Ireland Telecom Industry Business and Investment Opportunities Handbook
56. Israel Telecom Industry Business and Investment Opportunities Handbook
57. Italy Telecom Industry Business and Investment Opportunities Handbook
58. Jamaica Telecom Industry Business and Investment Opportunities Handbook
59. Japan Telecom Industry Business and Investment Opportunities Handbook
60. Jordan Telecom Industry Business and Investment Opportunities Handbook
61. Kazakhstan Telecom Industry Business and Investment Opportunities Handbook
62. Kenya Telecom Industry Business and Investment Opportunities Handbook
63. Korea, North Telecom Industry Business and Investment Opportunities Handbook
64. Korea, South Telecom Industry Business and Investment Opportunities Handbook
65. Kuwait Telecom Industry Business and Investment Opportunities Handbook
66. Kyrgyzstan Telecom Industry Business and Investment Opportunities Handbook
67. Laos Telecom Industry Business and Investment Opportunities Handbook
68. Latvia Telecom Industry Business and Investment Opportunities Handbook
69. Lebanon Telecom Industry Business and Investment Opportunities Handbook
70. Libya Telecom Industry Business and Investment Opportunities Handbook
71. Lithuania Telecom Industry Business and Investment Opportunities Handbook

For additional analytical, business and investment opportunities information,
please contact Global Investment & Business Center, USA
at (202) 546-2103. Fax: (202) 546-3275. E-mail: rusric@erols.com

72. Macao Telecom Industry Business and Investment Opportunities Handbook
73. Macedonia, Republic Telecom Industry Business and Investment Opportunities Handbook
74. Madagascar Telecom Industry Business and Investment Opportunities Handbook
75. Malaysia Telecom Industry Business and Investment Opportunities Handbook
76. Malta Telecom Industry Business and Investment Opportunities Handbook
77. Mauritius Telecom Industry Business and Investment Opportunities Handbook
78. Mauritius Telecom Industry Business and Investment Opportunities Handbook
79. Mexico Telecom Industry Business and Investment Opportunities Handbook
80. Micronesia Telecom Industry Business and Investment Opportunities Handbook
81. Moldova Telecom Industry Business and Investment Opportunities Handbook
82. Monaco Telecom Industry Business and Investment Opportunities Handbook
83. Mongolia Telecom Industry Business and Investment Opportunities Handbook
84. Morocco Telecom Industry Business and Investment Opportunities Handbook
85. Myanmar Telecom Industry Business and Investment Opportunities Handbook
86. Namibia Telecom Industry Business and Investment Opportunities Handbook
87. Netherlands Telecom Industry Business and Investment Opportunities Handbook
88. New Zealand Telecom Industry Business and Investment Opportunities Handbook
89. Nicaragua Telecom Industry Business and Investment Opportunities Handbook
90. Nigeria Telecom Industry Business and Investment Opportunities Handbook
91. Norway Telecom Industry Business and Investment Opportunities Handbook
92. Pakistan Telecom Industry Business and Investment Opportunities Handbook
93. Panama Telecom Industry Business and Investment Opportunities Handbook
94. Peru Telecom Industry Business and Investment Opportunities Handbook
95. Philippines Telecom Industry Business and Investment Opportunities Handbook
96. Poland Telecom Industry Business and Investment Opportunities Handbook
97. Portugal Telecom Industry Business and Investment Opportunities Handbook
98. Romania Telecom Industry Business and Investment Opportunities Handbook
99. Russia Telecom Industry Business and Investment Opportunities Handbook
100. Saudi Arabia Telecom Industry Business and Investment Opportunities Handbook
101. Scotland Telecom Industry Business and Investment Opportunities Handbook
102. Singapore Telecom Industry Business and Investment Opportunities Handbook
103. Slovakia Telecom Industry Business and Investment Opportunities Handbook
104. Slovenia Telecom Industry Business and Investment Opportunities Handbook
105. South Africa Telecom Industry Business and Investment Opportunities Handbook
106. Spain Telecom Industry Business and Investment Opportunities Handbook
107. Sri Lanka Telecom Industry Business and Investment Opportunities Handbook
108. Sudan Telecom Industry Business and Investment Opportunities Handbook
109. Suriname Telecom Industry Business and Investment Opportunities Handbook
110. Sweden Telecom Industry Business and Investment Opportunities Handbook
111. Switzerland Telecom Industry Business and Investment Opportunities Handbook
112. Syria Export Import & Business Directory

For additional analytical, business and investment opportunities information,
please contact Global Investment & Business Center, USA
at (202) 546-2103. Fax: (202) 546-3275. E-mail: rusric@erols.com

113. Taiwan Telecom Industry Business and Investment Opportunities Handbook
114. Tajikistan Telecom Industry Business and Investment Opportunities Handbook
115. Thailand Telecom Industry Business and Investment Opportunities Handbook
116. Tunisia Telecom Industry Business and Investment Opportunities Handbook
117. Turkey Telecom Industry Business and Investment Opportunities Handbook
118. Turkmenistan Telecom Industry Business and Investment Opportunities Handbook
119. Uganda Telecom Industry Business and Investment Opportunities Handbook
120. Ukraine Telecom Industry Business and Investment Opportunities Handbook
121. United Arab Emirates Telecom Industry Business and Investment Opportunities Handbook
122. United Kingdom Telecom Industry Business and Investment Opportunities Handbook
123. United States Telecom Industry Business and Investment Opportunities Handbook
124. Uruguay Telecom Industry Business and Investment Opportunities Handbook
125. US Telecom Industry Business and Investment Opportunities Handbook
126. Uzbekistan Telecom Industry Business and Investment Opportunities Handbook
127. Venezuela Telecom Industry Business and Investment Opportunities Handbook
128. Vietnam Telecom Industry Business and Investment Opportunities Handbook
129. Yugoslavia Telecom Industry Business and Investment Opportunities Handbook

For additional analytical, business and investment opportunities information,
please contact Global Investment & Business Center, USA
at (202) 546-2103. Fax: (202) 546-3275. E-mail: rusric@erols.com